A practical guide to the teaching of English
as a second or foreign language

A practical guide to the teaching of

ENGLISH

as a second or foreign language

WILGA M. RIVERS
MARY S. TEMPERLEY

OXFORD UNIVERSITY PRESS

Oxford University Press

200 Madison Avenue
New York, NY 10016   USA

Walton Street
Oxford   OX2 6DP   England

OXFORD is a trademark of Oxford University Press.

Library of Congress Cataloging-in-Publication Data
Rivers, Wilga M.
A Practical Guide to the Teaching of English as a
Second or Foreign Language.
Bibliography: p.
Includes index.
1. English language—Study and teaching—
Foreign students. I. Temperley, Mary S.,
1924—   joint author.   II. Title.
PE1128.A2R53 428'.007 77-2704
ISBN 0-19-502210-6 pbk.

Printing (last digit): 20 19 18 17 16 15 14 13 12 11

Printed in the United States of America.

Acknowledgments

Permission to reprint copyright material is hereby gratefully acknowledged:

To Alfred A. Knopf, Inc., for permission to reprint from "The Garden Party", by Katherine Mansfield, from *The Garden Party and Other Stories*, copyright © 1922 Alfred A. Knopf, Inc.

To Doubleday & Company and Clarke, Irwin & Company Limited, for permission to reprint from *I Heard The Owl Call My Name* by Margaret Craven, Copyright © 1967 Clarke, Irwin & Company Limited.

To Harcourt Brace Jovanovich, Inc., for permission to reprint from the selections "At the Supermarket" and "You Can't Miss It" from *Modern English,* 2d ed., Vol. I, by William E. Rutherford, Copyright © 1975 Harcourt Brace Jovanovich, Inc.

To Harper & Row, Publishers, Inc., for permission to reprint as adapted from pp. 121–22 of *The Big Change,* Copyright © 1952 by Frederick Lewis Allen, Courtesy of Harper & Row, Publishers.

To *Holiday Magazine,* for permission to reprint from "Arizona" by J. A. Corle, Copyright © 1947 The Curtis Publishing Company.

To Holt, Rinehart and Winston and Jonathan Cape Ltd, for permission to reprint from *The Poetry of Robert Frost* edited by Edward Connery Lathem. Copyright 1923, © 1969 by Holt, Rinehart and Winston. Copyright 1951 by Robert Frost. Reprinted by permission of Holt, Rinehart and Winston, Publishers.

To Institute of Modern Languages, Inc., for permission to reprint from *Orientation in American English* series by Eugene Hall and Sandra Costinett, Copyright © 1970 and 1971 Institute of Modern Languages, Inc.

To Macmillan Publishing Co., Inc., and M. B. Yeats, Miss Anne Yeats, and The Macmillan Company of London & Basingstoke, for ˌermission to reprint "Brown Penny" from *The Collected Poems of W. B. Yeats,* Copyright © 1912 by Macmillan Publishing Co., Inc. Renewed 1940 by Bertha Georgie Yeats.

To Oxford University Press for permission to reprint from "The Paradise of Thieves" by G. K. Chesterton from *The Gifts and Other Stories* by O. Henry and Others, Oxford Progressive English Readers, General Editor D. H. Howe, Copyright © 1974 Oxford University Press.

To Pantheon Books, a Division of Random House, Inc., and Wm. Collins Sons & Co. Ltd., for permission to reprint from *Born Free* by Joy Adamson, Copyright © 1960.

To Ramparts Magazine, Inc., for permission to reprint a passage from "Why Women's Liberation?" by Marlene Dixon, Copyright © 1969 by Ramparts Magazine, Inc.

To Regents Publishing Company, Inc., for permission to reprint from "Family Talk" from *Family Life in the U.S.A.: An Easy Reader* by G. Alesi and D. Pantell, Copyright © 1962 by Regents Publishing Company, Inc.

To University of California Press for permission to reprint from *Informal Speech: Alphabet and Phonemic Texts With Statistical Analysis and Tables* by Edward Carterette and Margaret Hubbard Jones, Copyright © 1974 by The Regents of the University of California; reprinted by permission of the University of California Press.

To The University Center for International Studies, University of Pittsburgh, for permission to reprint from *MMC: Developing Communicative Competence in English as a Second Language,* by Mary Newton Bruder, Copyright © 1974 University Center for International Studies and the English Language Institute, University of Pittsburgh.

To The Viking Press, Inc., and William Heinemann Ltd, for permission to reprint from *Sons and Lovers* by D. H. Lawrence, Copyright © 1913 by Thomas B. Seltzer, Inc. All rights reserved. Reprinted by permission of The Viking Press. We also gratefully acknowledge Laurence Pollinger Ltd and the Estate of the late Mrs. Frieda Lawrence.

Preface

Teaching a language is an interesting and exciting occupation. Since the nature of language and its complex operations is still a matter of controversy and since the psychologists have still much to learn about how language is acquired—the native language as well as a second or third language—we, as language teachers, have an open field. We are free to experiment and innovate. We can appropriate what has proved successful in other times and other places. We can repeat and refine what we have found to be effective in our own circumstances with our own students. We can share successes and explore failures with our colleagues, learning much from each other.

Learning to use a language freely and fully is a lengthy and effortful process. Teachers cannot learn the language for their students. They can set their students on the road, helping them to develop confidence in their own learning powers. Then they must wait on the sidelines, ready to encourage and assist, while each student struggles and perseveres with autonomous activity. Some students learn the language well, even while the teacher observes. For those who find the task more difficult, we should at least make every effort to ensure that their language-learning is an enjoyable and educational experience.

As teachers of English to students who are already accustomed to using a different language, we must not become discouraged. Our task is certainly not an easy one. We rarely see the fully developed product of our labors—the autonomous, confident speaker of English—although we will often be rewarded by the enthusiasm of those we have started along that path, and they may pleasantly surprise us when we meet them in later years. Students interested in language and uninhibited in using whatever they have assimilated will have a foundation on which to build when further opportunity presents itself. Surely all true education is beginnings. It is the hope of the authors that this book and its companion volumes will play some part in stimulating imaginative and resourceful teaching which will arouse and sustain effective self-motivated learning.

In these books we do not provide final answers. What we have written is intended to provoke lively discussion. This is clearly an age when flexibility is a prime attribute for the young teacher. As teachers, whether prospective or experienced, consider the many techniques we have described and understand the rationale behind them, they will be establishing a solid basis for choice when they are faced, in a local situation, with a wide variety of students of different ages and personal objectives. Ultimately, their selection should accord with their educational ideals, their own personality potential, and the needs and learning preferences of their students. The one all-sufficient answer for the classroom teacher is an alluring panacea but as illusory and unattainable as the philosopher's stone.

Method books for the preparation of teachers of English abound. Some students using this book may have a background in general methodology such as is provided in *Teaching Foreign-Language Skills** and books of a similar nature. The range of material in that book, however, is not considered in detail in this one. Rather, many ideas implicit and explicit in the earlier book have been developed in practical detail in the light of more recent emphases in the various branches of linguistics and the psychology of language. (Teachers are provided with much information without the confusions of overly technical language.) Stress is laid throughout on using language from the earliest stages for the normal purposes of language. Attention is also paid to some contemporary developments in the study of the English language.

For all the volumes in this series of *Practical Guides* the basic theoretical discussion and the elaboration of techniques remain parallel but for every exercise or activity, and for the types of study materials discussed, examples are supplied in the language the student will be teaching. The books are, therefore, appropriate for simultaneous use in a multiple-language methods class as well as for language-specific courses for the training of teachers at the various levels. The material will also be useful for in-service training courses and institutes, enabling teachers of different languages to consider general problems together while penetrating to the heart of the matter through the language with which each is most familiar. The books will also provide a treasury from which practicing

* Wilga M. Rivers, 1968. Chicago: The University of Chicago Press.

teachers can draw many ideas for individualized learning packets and for small-group activity, as well as for stimulating learning in a more conventional classroom.

A few additional explanations may facilitate the use of the book.

First of all, the terminology of the title may need some elucidation. In this book, we use the term *English as a second language* for the teaching of English to speakers of other languages in an English-speaking environment or in an area where English is widely spoken as a *lingua franca*. We retain the term *English as a foreign language* for areas where the student of English will not often hear or have opportunities to use English for communication. The term "foreign language" will sometimes be used for the target language, in this case English, where the distinction between the two situations is immaterial to the methodology.

This book is intended for a very varied readership: teachers of English to groups with a homogeneous language background who may or may not speak the language of their students; teachers of English to groups from diverse language backgrounds, some, or one, of whose languages the teacher knows or none of which the teacher knows. These programs may be in a country where the student's native language is spoken and English never heard, in an English-speaking country, or in a country where English is a second language. We address teachers of English in bilingual programs; teachers of English to beginners whether they be children, adolescents, adult students, or adult immigrants, teachers of English to students with a high school background of English who wish to study in English at undergraduate or graduate levels; and teachers of English to civil servants or service personnel who expect to fill posts abroad. The objectives of the students in these programs may be partial bilingualism or full bilingualism. They may have as their personal objectives a cursory reading knowledge of English, a thorough reading knowledge, a high degree of listening comprehension and reading ability, or a high degree of aural-oral proficiency. Clearly, all the techniques discussed in this book are not applicable to each of these situations; some will obviously be inappropriate. The teacher of English as a second or foreign language is a professional who must diagnose and select according to the particular situation of a specific class of students and adapt materials and techniques accordingly. In the teacher-training class, the appropriateness of the material being studied to particular situations will be one source of fruitful discussion.

Although there is some detailed discussion of points of English syntax and phonology, these are subordinate to the discussion of the preparation of teaching and testing materials and the elaboration of techniques; no attempt has been made to treat them systematically or exhaustively. Other books and other courses are available to meet this need and many of these are listed in the footnotes and the bibliographies. On the other hand, material used in the examples has been selected with a view to opening up discussion of areas of language about which the less experienced teacher of English may not be quite clear, particular emphasis being laid, in a number of places, on the differences between spoken and written language.

The symbols used for phonemic transcription in this book are set out in Appendix A. They follow closely those currently in use in American and British materials for teachers. The vowel symbols we use for General American (GA) are almost identical with those used by C. H. Prator and B. W. Robinett in their *Manual of American English Pronunciation,* 3d ed. (New York: Holt, Rinehart & Winston, 1972), and by J. D. Bowen in *Patterns of English Pronunciation* (Rowley, Mass.: Newbury House, 1975); the consonant symbols are the same as those used in the Lado-Fries materials from the English Language Institute at the University of Michigan. Symbols for transcribing distinctively different General British (GB) pronunciation are also given in Appendix A. The differences among the various transcribing alphabets in current use are not great, as can be seen from the Table of Transcribing Alphabets in Appendix B. Our final choice of symbols was made on pedagogical and practical grounds. We wished to provide for our readers useful guidance with teaching problems, rather than long discussions of differing opinions among linguists. Our choice, then, is not intended to reflect support of any doctrinal or methodological position regarding phonological analysis, beyond indicating our belief that some alphabetic system for representing the sounds of the language is useful in the study of a new language and in considering the problems of teaching it.

Whenever it seemed appropriate, attention has been drawn to differences between General American (GA) and General British (GB) usage. In some examples, American and British usage are juxtaposed. In these cases a slash (a diagonal line) indicates the alternative usage, the order in each case being American/British, e.g., *apartment/flat; gas/petrol.* Where examples have been drawn from British sources, British spelling has been retained. Examples, as given, are not intended to be complete but illustrative of technique. The suggested exercises, indicated by an asterisk ✷ , then draw the application into other areas of possible confusion or difficulty. One cannot teach what one does not fully understand. Teachers in training will thus have a further opportunity to clarify matters which have worried them in the past.

It should be noted, at this point, that it is the intention of the authors that the asterisked activities be assigned, so that students actively participate in creation of new materials and in the adaptation and refinement of those provided in current textbooks. The close examination and judicious adaptation of text, test, and taped materials should be part of every trainee teacher's experience, along with the trying out in actual teaching situations of what has been developed (whether in micro-lessons or in practice teaching with a class). Students should be encouraged during their training period to begin a permanent indexed file of personally culled teaching materials, together with ideas for activities and projects. They should keep on file reading passages, informative cuttings from newspapers and magazines, cultural insights, poems, scenes from plays, songs, and games appropriate for various ages and levels, informal visual aids, interesting and amusing variations of techniques, practical activities in which their students can use the language informally and spontaneously, and sources of information and supplementary assistance. If students share what they gather during this important period of preparation, they will not approach their first year of full-time teaching empty-handed.

We, as authors, have tried to make a further contribution to the continuing growth in professionalism of our readers in the preparation of the two bibliographies. These are not mere listings of references for the various chapters, since the details of the books and articles consulted or recommended in specific contexts can be readily retrieved from the Notes. The bibliographies are intended rather as guides to references of quality in many central and peripheral areas of concern, while providing useful information for those wishing to update or expand a personal or institutional library.

The artificiality of dealing with various aspects of language use in separate chapters is apparent (e.g., the separation of listening and acceptable production of sounds from communicative interaction and both of these from knowledge of the rules of grammar). Students will need to hold certain questions in abeyance until they can see the whole picture. For those who wish to consider questions in a different order from that supplied, numerous cross-references are included in the text, in addition to the comprehensive information in the detailed list of contents and the index. To facilitate the finding of examples dealing with various aspects of language use, initial letter classifications have been used throughout different sections, viz., C: Communicating, both speaking and listening; G: Grammar; S: Sounds; R: Reading; and W: Writing.

Examples go beyond the elementary course. Although it is difficult to establish a level of difficulty in the abstract, E has been used to indicate the elementary level, I for intermediate level, and A for advanced level. This classification is non-scientific and indicative only. It will be for the instructor, the student, or the experienced teacher to adjust the interpretation of levels of difficulty to particular situations.

Many of the ideas developed and discussed in this text clearly imply an English-language program which embodies a sequential and coherent course of study. Teachers in loosely organized programs and institutes may read these descriptions of stages of development and a careful progression of exercises with a certain envy, not to say skepticism, wondering if such well-ordered worlds exist. We recognize that the variety of situations in which English is taught around the world surpasses classification. We are also aware of the myriad cases where a teacher, often unguided, is confronted with a group of students who are heterogeneous in nearly every respect (native language and culture, ability and experience in English, educational level, classroom expectations, and personal goals), united only by the fact that they meet regularly for their English class. They may not even share the motivation: "wanting to learn (more) English," since it is not unknown for students to be in a language class under duress, at the order of some higher authority or seeking only a formal prerequisite for some other course of study. Whatever the circumstances in which they find themselves, realistic teachers (of any subject) will try to assess accurately two aspects of the situation that bear on what they will do: on one hand, the "givens" (the things over which as teachers they have no control) and, on the other, the matters which they themselves can determine. Among the "givens" may be such physical elements as the number and length of class hours and out-of-class study time available to each student, along with textbook or syllabus to be "covered" and psychological realities such as the attention span of individual students and the degree of cooperation which they are willing to offer. Our hope is that once teachers have made a realistic appraisal of the unalterable features of their situation, however anomalous it may be, they will find among the many methods and techniques discussed in this text some useful additions to their resources.

In conclusion, the authors wish to thank most warmly the numerous persons, scholars and teachers in the field, who have contributed to the development of their thinking through discussion, demonstration, or published work, and particularly to their co-authors in the series. Special thanks must, however, go to Tobie Kranitz for her careful and intelligent preparation of the manuscript; to Jean Praninskas for helpful suggestions for improving several sections of the text; to Nicholas Temperley for unfailing support and for help in preparing the sections on British English; to members of the faculty and staff of the Division of English as a Second Language at the University of Illinois, in particular to Wayne and Lonna Dickerson for their generosity in sharing ideas and materials and their critical reading of Chapter 5, to Lubitsa Katz for help of many kinds, to Pearl Goodman for allowing easy and constant access to the DESL Library, to Barbara Casterline for providing ready and pertinent examples; to Willard D. Sheeler for his help in supplying vocabulary lists; and to Wayne Ishikawa for his help with the index.

Cambridge, Mass.
Urbana, Ill.
October, 1977

W.M.R.
M.S.T.

Contents

*A practical guide to the teaching of English
as a second or foreign language*

I
COMMUNICATING

Communication acts

In Part I, speaking and listening are discussed in separate chapters, although in a communication act one clearly complements the other. The reader will bear in mind that being able to speak a language without understanding what is being said by native speakers is of limited use, while being able to understand a language but not speak it can have specialized utility (for the enjoyment of foreign-language films, broadcasts, plays, and songs, or for professional monitoring purposes) but is very frustrating in normal communication situations. Being able to speak comprehensibly does not necessarily ensure ability to comprehend normal native speech; on the other hand many people develop a very high level of aural comprehension without being able to express themselves freely. Both areas require serious attention.

In a well-rounded program, success in each will be recognized as a separate achievement and given equal importance in the eyes of the students. Nevertheless, practice of each should normally be in relation to the other if communicating is the ultimate goal.

Developing skill and confidence in communication

When selecting learning activities, we must always remember that our goal is for the students to be able to interact freely with others: to understand what others wish to communicate in the broadest sense, and to be able to convey to others what they themselves wish to share (whether as a reaction to a communication or as an original contribution to the exchange). To do this effectively, however, the students must understand how the English language works and be able to make the interrelated changes for which the system of the language provides mechanisms.

The following schema will help us tó see the essential processes involved in learning to communicate.

C1 Processes involved in learning to communicate

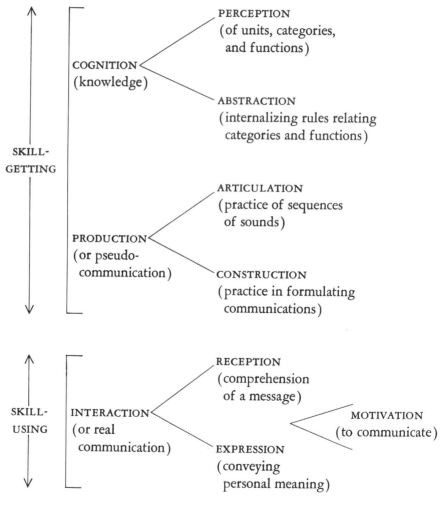

SKILL-
GETTING

COGNITION
(knowledge)

PERCEPTION
(of units, categories,
and functions)

ABSTRACTION
(internalizing rules relating
categories and functions)

PRODUCTION
(or pseudo-
communication)

ARTICULATION
(practice of sequences
of sounds)

CONSTRUCTION
(practice in formulating
communications)

SKILL-
USING

INTERACTION
(or real
communication)

RECEPTION
(comprehension
of a message)

EXPRESSION
(conveying
personal meaning)

MOTIVATION
(to communicate)

Note: 1. This is not a sequential but a parallel schema, in the sense that skill-getting and skill-using[1] are continually proceeding hand in hand. There is genuine *interaction from the beginning*, with students exploring the full scope of what is being learned.

2. *Bridging the gap* between skill-getting and skill-using is not automatic. Skill-getting activities must be so designed as to be already *pseudo-communication*, thus leading naturally into spontaneous communication activities.

3. The terminology of this schema will be used in discussing appropriate activities for skill-getting and skill-using.

Knowledge and intensive practice (skill-getting) are not enough to ensure confident interaction. The latter requires practice in actual, purposeful conversational exchange with others. In Chapter 1 we shall discuss linguistic aspects of the spoken language with which students need to be familiar if their communication is not to be stilted, and various types of bridging activities (e.g., the many uses of dialogues, Cummings devices, and action chains); in Chapter 2, ways of involving students in real interaction.[2] In Chapter 3 the problems of understanding the spoken language are considered in depth. Chapters 4 and 5 give the rationale for techniques and activities for perception, abstraction, articulation, and construction.

1
Structured interaction

Opposing views on the development of speaking skill

According to the *progressive development* view, ability to speak the language derives from the systematic study of grammar, phonology, and lexicon. This is the approach of grammar-translation texts, where it is assumed that accuracy in expressing oneself orally is dependent on prior study of language forms through reading and written exercises; of audio-lingual or aural-oral texts where oral imitation, memorization, and drilling techniques precede attempts to speak spontaneously (although in this case the latter is attempted much sooner than in traditional grammar-translation texts); and of texts which begin with narrative and conversational reading passages.

The *immediate communication* view holds that speaking skill is developed from the first contact with the language. Students may be encouraged to express themselves in simple ways under the guidance of the teacher (What's that? It's a book. Where's the book? The book is on the table). Alternatively, in a simulation of the total immersion experience of the foreigner in another culture, they may be expected to use for the expression of their own messages anything they have acquired of the language from hearing it, supplemented by gestures, pantomime, or the showing of objects, with the teacher suggesting words and expressions only when the students falter.

This chapter takes a *middle position* between these two approaches, advocating that students be encouraged to express themselves freely in the language from the beginning through experiences and games which provide

6

them with a framework for spontaneous communicative creation, while presupposing they will use what they have been learning through an orderly progression of study and practice. The Type B exercises in Chapter 4 prepare students to use the language for expressing their own meanings,[1] and are paralleled from the beginning with extensive opportunities for autonomous interaction of the type discussed in Chapter 2. If students are to develop as uninhibited communicators who seize opportunities to use the language with native speakers, they must overcome early their timidity and the fear of being embarrassed when they express themselves simplistically or awkwardly, as they will often do when their knowledge of the language is at an elementary stage.

Differences between spoken and written English

Much of any foreign language learned at school is acquired from books. Even where conversations and dialogues appear, they are often unrepresentative of authentic speech. Tapes and records attempt to bring the oral language into the classroom but some of these are no more than stilted oral recitations of written forms of the language. If students are to learn to use authentic speech, their teachers must be aware of the features which differentiate the spoken language from the conventional written forms, and particularly from the literary usages to which they have become accustomed in their own advanced studies.

For conciseness and precision of meaning, one usually employs more complicated structures and a wider vocabulary in written English than in spoken English. This is one reason why learning to write English well is an advanced art. In one sense, written English is *less redundant* than the spoken form of the language (that is, it contains fewer signals for the same aspect of meaning) in that repetitions and duplications are avoided and the additional clues provided by such things as intonation contours, stress patterns, junctures (transition and boundary features), and tone of voice are absent. In another sense it is more redundant, in that it contains many signals to meaning which are completely lost when the message is presented orally. Note, for example, how spelling, word boundaries, and punctuation resolve the ambiguity of the following homophonous words and phrases: plain: plane; their books: they're books; you know: UNO; in Oklahoma: in *Oklahoma!*; the sun's rays meet: the sons raise meat.

C2 Analysis of a sample of spoken English (transcribed from a taped conversation among adults) highlights a number of differences between the written and spoken codes in English. The subject of the conversation is the difficulties of being an airline stewardess.

Listen these two girls that I know that fly have been flying exactly three years. And theyve been all over and they Athens Rome Greece Egypt every place. On their passes you know they take two three weeks off and and its just fabulous. And this one girl met this guy in uh in Egypt and she just fell madly in love with him. Well it was so funny and now she cant she had to come home in two weeks. Thats one thing because she cant you know be with him or anything. Egypt. I mean how far away can you get. Kind of a bad problem. Shes supposed to be going back in August. Hes sent her tickets a ticket her and her sister for them to go back.[2]

If this passage were to be put into ordinary written English (such as one finds in feature articles in newspapers, for example), it might appear as follows:

Two stewardesses that I know have been flying exactly three years. They've been to all sorts of places. They can occasionally take two or three weeks off. When they do, they go everywhere—Athens, Rome, Egypt—on their passes. It's a wonderful experience for them. One of the girls met a man in Egypt and fell in love with him. But the difficulty was that she had to come home in two weeks. Now she can't be with him, because Egypt is too far away. This is a real problem for her. She's supposed to go back in August. The man has even sent tickets for her and her sister so that they can go back.

Commentary

1. The *spoken version* would, of course, contain the clues to meaning provided by patterns of stress, intonation, and juncture; it would also be accompanied by the expressive features of tone of voice, gesture, and facial expression. And it would be related in a variety of ways to the extra-linguistic context and the responses of the listeners (e.g., by increasing or decreasing the speed of speech within segments, lengthening pauses, repeating words or adding modifications according to the apparent degree of their comprehension or their momentary inattention).

2. *Pronunciation*. A comparison of items from the phonemic transcription of the passage (made by trained phoneticians from the taped conversation[3]) with citation-form pronunciations shows several characteristics of ordinary spoken English.

a. Loss of initial or final consonants in unstressed words: *and* /æn/; *just* /ǰəs/; *sent her* /sɛntər/.

b. Assimilation of consonants: /ðɛn/ for /ðɛm/ in *for them to go back* /fərðɛntəgowbæk/.

c. Vowel reduction: *that* /ðət/; *you* /yə/; *or* /ər/.

d. Combinations of features a-c produce such forms as /əv/ for *have*, /ən/ for *and*, /hædə/ for *had to*.

e. Close juncture between words in rhythm groups: *how far away can you get* /hawfarəweykɛnyuwgɛt/; *And theyve been all over and they* /ənðeyvbɪnɔlowvərənðey/. The continuous flow of sound produced by the physical linking of one word to the next within phrases is one of the most characteristic (and pedagogically neglected) features of spoken English.

3. *Vocabulary.* The oral version also contains several items of vocabulary peculiar to spoken English. Conversational tags and fillers like *listen, you know, I mean, or anything, kind of*, establish contact with the listener and give the speaker time to organize the succeeding segment for production. Colloquial clichés, normally avoided in written English, abound in the spoken passage: *just fabulous, madly in love, how far away can you get*. The use of the demonstrative pronoun (*this, these*) where the written form would have an indefinite article, or nothing at all, also characterizes the spoken segment (*these two girls*, for *two girls*, *this guy* for *a guy*). (Vocabulary used can give clues as to the sex of the speaker. What words would lead you to guess the sex of the speaker of the above passage?)

4. *Syntax.* The spoken language is said to be marked by a preponderance of simple declarative sentences. While it is not easy to use the notion of "sentence" in dealing with speech, we can observe that the verb phrases in the passage above are almost entirely declarative, and mainly active and affirmative. The sentences that are not simple are often loose, awkward, or vague: *they take two three weeks off and its just fabulous; two girls that I know that fly; thats one thing because she cant.* . . . They may be "mixed" in syntactic form or "stringy": *Hes sent her tickets a ticket her and her sister for them to go back; And this one girl . . . and she just.* . . . Words are often omitted (/wɛʊwəz/ for *well it was*, /tuwθriy/ for *two or three*). Complete utterances in speaking may be phrases which would be regarded as fragmentary in writing: *Egypt. Kind of a bad problem.* Finally, conversational speech is full of hesitations, self-interruptions, and false starts: *. . . this guy in uh Egypt . . . ; and they Athens, Rome, Greece . . . ; and now she cant she had to come home.* . . .

Stress patterns in spoken English

Students whose chief experience in English has been with the written language may not be aware of the functions of stress in the spoken language. To speak and understand English well one needs to be able to use the stress patterns of the language, even if one cannot state the rules. To help others use the language effectively one must have a conscious understanding of the role of stress in conveying meaning.

Growing realization of the fundamental importance of stress patterns in English is reflected by the fact that they are the first subject treated in a recent book on pronunciation. This priority in learning should not be allowed to obscure their complexity. A stressed syllable may be defined as one which is more prominent than the surrounding ones. We must remember, however, that in English the impression of prominence may be due to an increase in loudness or length, a rise in pitch, a particular vowel quality, or a combination of two or more of these features. (Research studies indicate that experienced listeners to English "hear" this prominence where they expect stress, even when no actual difference in length, loudness, or pitch exists in the sound signal emitted.)

It is useful to distinguish two kinds of stress in English: word stress, which is a property of isolated words and constructions such as compounds and two-word verbs and is relatively fixed, and phrase stress, which is a property of an utterance or part of an utterance. The two kinds of stress are related in a hierarchy: phrase stress falls on a particular word in a construction (e.g., I saw him at the ___´__); word stress determines which syllable of that word it falls on (I saw him at the shów; I saw him at the recéption). Together they form a stress system which affects the production of utterances in English in three important ways.

First, the pattern or combination of stressed and unstressed syllables in English forms its characteristic rhythm, stressed-timed rhythm, in which a few stressed syllables are linked by any number of unstressed syllables, and in which the amount of time between the stressed syllables is to a certain extent independent of the number of unstressed syllables in between.

> He fòund the bóok he lòst | at hóme.
> He fòund the edítion he was stùdying | at the muséum.

The two sentences above would be perceived as having the same pattern of phrase stresses, and roughly the same amount of time between stresses, even though one has twice as many syllables as the other. Second, the system of phrase stress is in itself a means for expressing certain kinds of information (for example, compare the difference between *I wonder how much money he éarned* and *I wonder how much móney he earned*).[4] For the student who is more familiar with the written form of the language, however, a third effect of the stress system of spoken English may well be to conceal rather than convey information. In spoken English, the stress system often obscures or obliterates syllables to the extent that they can be identified only by the listener's expectations rather than by actual phonetic representation.

Phrase stress

FOCUS AND EMPHASIS

C3 In the following dialogue, two kinds of phrase stress are marked: normal phrase stress by ´ and contrastive stress by ˝.

A Where are the bóys?
B The boys went to a cóncert
A Went to whát?
B A ˝cóncert—they went to a ˝cóncert.
A With the gírls?
B Nó, the gírls went to *The Cócktail Party.*
A Whát cocktail party?
B No, ˝nó. Yóu know—*The Cócktail Party*—the ˝pláy.

In the normal or neutral way of saying the sentence *The boys went to a concert*, the word *concert* would receive phrase stress: the syllable *con-* (as determined by word stress) would ordinarily be louder than the surrounding syllables, and the word would be marked by an intonation contour, in this case a rise and fall in pitch. This is the way a native speaker of English would probably pronounce the sentence if no further context were supplied. The element under normal phrase stress can be said to be the focus of the phrase or sentence: the stress, combined with the articles in the sentence (*the* boys . . . *a* concert), suggests that *a concert* is the new piece of information being given.

For extra emphasis, as when one is repeating an element that has not been understood or believed by the listener or when one is contrasting two items, a word or syllable may have contrastive stress: A ˝cóncert—they went to a ˝cóncert: The gírls went to *The Cócktail Party.* Any word or syllable may be given the extra prominence of contrastive stress. Contrastive stress may be marked by extra high pitch or extra loudness, particularly if it falls on an element that might have normal phrase stress otherwise.

Neither phrase nor word stress is indicated explicitly in the standard writing system of English. (Contrastive stress is sometimes indicated by special printing devices such as underlining, italicization, or block capital letters.) In reading English native speakers usually know which elements are to receive stress. This knowledge is a part of their (mainly subconscious) mastery of the linguistic and communicative rules of English. Context tells them which will receive contrastive stress. In written English the linguistic context determines the placement of phrase stress in most cases, and effective writers know how to construct their sentences so that their readers will understand the intended focus or emphasis. Often a part of a sentence will be momentarily ambiguous. If some of the determining context follows the item in question, the information the reader needs in order to know the writer's meaning may be delayed, as with the following sentences:

Reading English is easier than speaking it.
Reading English is easier than reading Russian.

Here one cannot determine all of the meaning of the phrase *Reading English* (and hence the appropriate kind of stress for the word English) until one has completed the sentence. (One may, of course, take in the whole sentence at once, in which case the ambiguity would not arise. But readers who 'hear' what they are reading may assign a stress pattern which turns out to be incorrect, in which case they often reread the phrase or sentence with the corrected stress pattern.)

Linguistic context is a determiner of focus or emphasis in speaking and listening just as it is in writing and reading. In spoken English, however, stress is also signalled phonetically. Every utterance, with the exception of a few attention signals or minimal responses, has at least one phonological phrase stress, and native speakers depend on this phrase stress for information in interpreting an oral message. It is one of the devices that permit speech to function with less linguistic context than writing. (The various possible meanings of a simple sentence like *There's a pound of butter in the refrigerator* can be distinguished in writing only by changing the words, that is, the linguistic context—unless one uses the special graphic devices mentioned above.)

In communicating in the spoken language, then, one must be able to use stress patterns correctly. Even at the most elementary stage of learning greetings, for example, students should learn to stress either *are* or *you* in the first instance of *How are you?* and to stress *you* if the question is returned. Later, they must learn to produce and understand the several meanings which can be distinguished by the six possible positions for phrase stress in such a sentence as *I didn't want you to do that.*

* Where would the phrase stress occur in the answers to the three following questions? (There may be more than one possibility.)

How did he find out?	I told him.
Who told him?	I told him.
Did you tell them?	I told him.

WEAKLY STRESSED SYLLABLES

The importance of mastering the stress system of spoken English is increased when we remember that although oral stress patterns convey information which may be only indirectly expressed in the written language, they also obscure linguistic material that the written form displays. With normal English stress patterns, the following sentences might both be spoken in the manner indicated by the transcription on the right:

C4   What does he put it on?   /hwətsiy pútɪtan/
      What has he put it on?

The strong contrast between heavy and weak stresses means that many syllables will be obscure, indeterminate, or even lost. This reduction can result in the loss of grammatical and lexical material.[5]

*   What segments are lost if the following questions are pronounced according to the transcriptions on the right?

      What do you want?   /hwətəyə wánt/
      What are you doing?   /hwətəyə dúwɪŋ/

What other segments of the utterances supply this information?

    Unfortunately, the segments that are lost may be just what the non-native listener to English is looking for in order to understand the message, particularly one who is already more familiar with the written code. When students bring to the task of understanding speech a reliance on their native sound system and on grasping morphemes one by one, it is no wonder that they are bewildered. If they have not learned the phonological system of contrasts that are significant in the new language and the special characteristics of the spoken code, they simply cannot use the data they receive. Many a learner of English who would have no trouble in understanding their written forms has taken one of the following two sentences for the other when dependent entirely on aural material:

        When do you leave?
        Where do you live?

    Language learners sometimes wonder how native speakers understand each other when the signal seems so poor. The answer is in two parts. First, native listeners need very little information. By knowing the various codes which govern social intercourse (codes that determine what may be talked about and what may be said), native listeners know most of what native speakers are going to say before anything is said and hence they require relatively little from the signal. Second, native listeners use many sources of information in the speech event itself which may be unavailable to (or misused by) the non-native: here we are referring not only to the language itself, but to the codes of gesture, facial expression, physical position, proximity, and para-linguistic vocal cues. The signal is poor, but only from the point of view of someone who lacks this linguistic and extra-linguistic knowledge (the foreign learner, for instance). Because native listeners have relatively little uncertainty about the message itself, they do not need much information and they know where to look for what they lack.

The system of stress patterns in English conveys some pieces of information which the written code cannot directly transmit, and obscures or obliterates other material. Students wanting to use English for oral communication should start to learn this system from the beginning of their experience with the language. (For a further discussion of the problems of the listener, see Chapter 3.)

Teachers should be familiar with a current standard analysis of English stress, intonation, and juncture. For American pronunciation, see J. D. Bowen, *Patterns of English Pronunciation* or C. Prator and B. Robinett, *Manual of American English Pronunciation*; for British pronunciation, A. D. MacCarthy, *English Pronunciation* or Appendix II of *A Grammar of Contemporary English* by R. Quirk, S. Greenbaum, G. Leech, and J. Svartik.

Style of language (register or level of discourse)

We use different styles of language in diverse situations—when we are speaking to a person in an official position, to an acquaintance, to a close friend, or within the family circle. Students should be made conscious of this fact and learn to recognize, and eventually use, English in these different styles. They should be able to distinguish platform or careful speech from informal or casual speech. They should be able to understand rather than use *nonstandard English* and current *slang*. These distinctions also help them to recognize the author's intent in conversational material in written English. Most standard dictionaries of English distinguish informal or colloquial and slang expressions from the rest of the lexicon. An American example is *The American Heritage Dictionary of the English Language, AHD,* (New York: The American Heritage Publishing Co. and Houghton-Mifflin, 1969); a British example, *The Pocket Oxford Dictionary of Current English, POD,* (London: Oxford University Press, 1969).

Joos distinguishes for English five styles: intimate, casual, consultative, formal, and frozen. Applying the criteria set out by Joos in *The Five Clocks*[6] we may develop the following sequence at the five levels.

C5 In an *intimate* situation, a parent may say to a child who is embarrassingly present and has shown some reluctance to leave: *Out!* (According to Joos, in intimate style no information is given which is known to the participants.)

In a *casual* style the parent may say: *Run along, now.* (Once again complete information is not supplied and this style involves the use of well-known formulas.)

Consultative style, the style of standard exchange between strangers, would require rather: *Would you mind leaving the room a moment, please?* (Consultative style supplies all necessary background information.)

A *formal* situation, on the other hand, may require: *The audience is requested to kindly leave the room for a few moments.* (In formal style, speakers often do not refer to themselves and do not anticipate any immediate participation on the part of the persons addressed.)

Frozen or printed style may be observed on a notice outside a door: *The management respectfully requests the conferees to vacate the auditorium between sessions in order to facilitate the operations of the custodial staff.*

Compare the following series:

Where's the salt? I'd like some, please. Would you pass me the salt, please? Would you be so kind as to pass me the salt, please? Patrons are respectfully reminded that in view of the unavoidably limited accommodations and the management's sincere desire to honor the wishes of as many diners as possible, some sharing of facilities is desirable.

✱ Try constructing a similar series on the themes: "Please do not talk" and "Write to me about it."

C6 In the light of the above discussion on styles of language, examine the following passage from *House of Stairs* by William Sleator.[7]

... "You still thinking about that? How long does it take you to forget something stupid like that?"

I never forget, thought Blossom.

"I mean, I already told you, I was just worried about the food," Lola went on. .... She shook her head. "You know, we're in a pretty tricky spot as it is. You're just making it worse."

"I ... I guess you're right," said Blossom ... "I never really meant it, really. I just didn't want you to boss me around."

"Mmm," said Lola, her eyes probing. "Sure that's all it was?"

"Yes," Blossom nodded quickly, pursing her lips. "I'm sure."

"Well, let's hope it's all over with now. I won't stand for much more of it."

"I ... I know you wouldn't stand for it," Blossom said softly. "I guess I was just waiting for you to tell me to stop."

"Well, now I'm telling you. And I'll tell you something else. Somebody's got to get bossed around here, you better get used to it, because somebody's got to be the leader. If there's no leader, we'll never get anywhere. I'm not saying the leader's gotta be *me*, necessarily, but there's gotta be one."

✱ Discuss in the above passage: indications of rapid speech; structures commonly used in intimate or casual speech; words and idioms that are particularly indicative of a familiar (intimate or casual) level.

The style of language in dialogues of the sort found in textbooks may not always be used consistently. Consider the following:

C7 Mrs. Smith meets an acquaintance on the street.

MRS. SMITH   Good morning, Mrs. Davis. How are you?
MRS. DAVIS   Very well, thank you.
MRS. SMITH   How's your son?
MRS. DAVIS   He's O.K. now.

Commentary

1. If Mrs. Smith were really a friend of Mrs. Davis's, she would normally say: "Hello, Lucy" or "Hi, Lucy." By the tone of her address, Mrs. Davis is more probably an acquaintance or a neighbor.

2. In response to Mrs. Smith's very polite greeting, Mrs. Davis should add to her reply an inquiry after Mrs. Smith's health: "And how are you?"

3. Mrs. Davis's "He's O.K. now" after Mrs. Smith's polite inquiry is very brusque and out of keeping with the general tone of the exchange. If the son has not been well, one of the following would have been more polite: "He's still not very well, I'm afraid" or "He's much better, thank you."

* Examine dialogues in current textbooks to see if they use different levels of discourse appropriately and consistently.[8]

Bridging activities

All that we can teach students in a foreign language is how to construct the appropriate framework, in all its detail, for the expression of meaning. We cannot teach students to express their own meaning: we can provide opportunities that stimulate motivation for this personal activity and we can help the student to improve the framework so that it can really carry the message intended. We can develop activities where the students construct various types of frameworks and help them try these out to see if they will carry effectively the meanings they intend. Searle calls language "*rule-governed intentional behavior*."[9] We can help the student internalize the rules; we cannot supply the intention, although we can stimulate it by contriving situations and encounters. One way in which we help students try out frameworks of varying degrees of complexity and subtlety, that is, to perform "speech acts,"[10] is by providing practice in *pseudo-communication*. This is communication in which the content is structured by the learning situation, rather than springing autonomously from the mind and emotions of the student. *We bridge the gap to true communication by encouraging the student to use these structured practices for autonomous purposes from the early stages*. In this way, even average students can acquire confidence in their ability to function on their own. (Linguistically gifted students will always develop confidence in their own way, with or without special guidance.)

The concept of *individualization of instruction* has to be very carefully analyzed in relation to the development of communication skills: it can mean small-group practice and interaction, but not independent study, because communication by definition involves more than one person.[11] Students also learn a great deal from listening to the way other people formulate their communications. At the other extreme, communication cannot be efficiently practiced in large groups. For a discussion of suitable groupings of students for communication practice, see Wilga M. Rivers *et al.*, "Techniques for the Development of Proficiency in the Spoken Language" in H. B. Altman and R. L. Politzer, eds., *Individualizing Foreign Language Instruction* (Rowley, Mass.: Newbury House, 1971), pp. 165–74.

RULE-GOVERNED BEHAVIOR

In language use, we fit our meaning into a framework which conforms to many types of rules, or recurring regularities: not only syntactic, morphological, and phonological, but also semantic and cultural. Once we have an intention to express, not only do we have to select the "right words" for our purpose, but the choices we make also entail other lexical selections within the sentence which we must respect, but which function according to rules at present only vaguely understood. Semantics also dictates our choices in syntax[12] and syntactic selection forces certain morphological adjustments. We cannot operate effectively in speech or writing until we have understood the possibilities the rules afford and are able to put into operation the sheer mechanics of the language at the level of verb endings for person and tense, required agreements, conventional word order, and so on.[13] Cultural expectations come into play as well: rules of relationships and obligations in interpersonal communication within a society which are expressed in part through registers or levels of discourse, but also through expected and implied questions and reactions, social taboos, and the mutually understood references of words used in certain associations.

C8 (1)   He wouldn't let me do what I wanted to.
          He interfered with the realization of my plans.

The decision to express this intention at a more formal level in the second sentence motivated the choice of *interfere* instead of *wouldn't let* and this lexical choice entailed other lexical choices and a different syntactic framework from that in the first sentence.

I'm sorry I can't go with you, but I've got to baby-sit for my niece.

Comprehension of this sentence is dependent on comprehension not merely of the individual words and grammatical constructions, but also on knowledge of customs in American and British society.

Supplying the student with a basic corpus

The first problem we face in teaching students to speak a foreign language is how to plunge them into using natural language when they know little or nothing of the new tongue. Proponents of the grammar-translation approach have usually maintained that conversing in the language should not be attempted until students control the essentials of the syntactic and morphological systems intellectually, are able to represent them in graphic form, and have acquired through reading and memorization an extensive vocabulary. At this stage it is felt that they can learn to express themselves orally quite rapidly by drawing on what they have learned. But with the modern emphasis on the importance of oral communication and the present generation's greater familiarity with aural-oral rather than graphic presentations of information, this approach can be discouraging for many students.

A number of approaches have been proposed at different times for plunging the student into active language use. All have proved effective in the early stages when intelligently and imaginatively implemented. We need some way of supplying the student with a basic corpus with which to work.

We can identify four main approaches to this problem: the object centered, the melody and rhythm centered, the verb centered, and the situation centered.

OBJECT CENTERED

In this approach students begin by discussing objects in the classroom in imitation of the teacher. The grammatical structures introduced are demonstrable in relation to these objects, so that students hear and practice them in a realistic setting.

C9 This is a book. That's a window ... What's this? It's a book. It's a window ... Where's the book? The book is on the table ... The book is red ... It's John's book ...

The class then goes on to discuss persons in the classroom in much the same terms:

Jim is a student. He's tall.
Helen is a student. She's short.
She's Jim's sister.

Variant: Teachers sometimes use the contents of a handbag or shopping basket instead of classroom objects. Later, pictures of houses, gardens, airports, farms are used to expand the environment for purposes of description and discussion. Sometimes these pictures are in the textbook. Otherwise, use is made of commercially available wall-pictures, full- or double-page scenes cut from magazines, or projected slides. Students often construct posters, with items labeled in English, to illustrate these environments and these are posted on the bulletin board so that students can assimilate the vocabulary casually through frequent contact. (Unless the teacher is watchful, however, an overemphasis on acquiring names for a multiplicity of objects may develop.)

This approach sometimes limits students to accurate production of very trite sentences which they would not conceivably wish to use in spontaneous conversation: *This is a book. It's red. It's on the teacher's desk. It's the teacher's book.* Modern students find this approach boring and trivial. It is well to remember that in real conversation we rarely comment on things which are visible unless the situation is exceptional: *The chair is on the teacher's desk. Why?* A little whimsy will help to enliven the exchanges and keep the student alert.

MELODY AND RHYTHM CENTERED

In a quite different approach, only one noun is used for quite a long time: *a rod.* This approach, called "the silent way,"[14] concentrates in the beginning on developing sensitivity to the melody and flow of the language. Students listen to tapes of a number of languages trying to recognize which of the speeches they hear is in the language they have been studying.[15] Gattegno considers that

since babies learn to talk their mother tongue first by yielding to its "music," we can . . . trace the first elements of the spirit of a language to the unconscious surrender of our sensitivity to what is conveyed by the background of noise in each language. This background obviously includes the silences, the pauses, the flow, the linkages of words, the duration of each breath required to utter connected chunks of the language, the overtones and undertones, the stresses as well as the special vowels or consonants belonging to that language.[16]

The teacher works with only about thirty words in the initial lessons. Here is Gattegno's list: one noun: *rod*; color adjectives: *red, green, yellow, black, brown, blue*; numeral adjectives: *one, two, three*; articles: *a* and *the*; verbs in the imperative: *take, give,* and, perhaps, *put*; personal pronouns: *me, him, her, it, them*; possessive pronouns: *his, her, my*; the adverbs *here, there*; the preposition *to*; the conjunction *and*.[17] Using a box of colored rods, the teacher induces the student to utter fluent sentences with native-like facility, while the teacher talks as little as possible. There is a minimum of imitation of the teacher and a maximum of concentration by the student on constructing sentences with the help of the rods. The teacher does not explain grammatical features, but encourages the students to think about what they hear and to try to construct utterances that conform to the rules they have discovered for themselves.

C10 Types of sentences practiced with the rods:

Take a blue rod (red, green).
Give it to me.
Take a yellow rod and give it to Rachel.
Take three black rods and give them to me.

The rods continue to be used for learning such things as comparatives, temporal relationships, and tenses.

Later, through the technique of *visual dictation*[18] students are given practice in recognizing the printed equivalents of the words they were using orally as they created situations with the rods, and also in the fluent construction of sentences using these words. Here the teacher points silently and rapidly, but only once, to a succession of words on a chart of scrambled words with phonic color coding, and in a short time students are able to produce with acceptable diction long sentences like: *Take a blue rod and a green rod and give the blue rod to Nancy and give the green rod to me* and to demonstrate through action that they have understood what they were saying.

Gattegno claims to be "rejecting the learning of vocabularies and grammar . . . and replacing it with as thorough a penetration of the spirit of a language as possible."[19]

VERB CENTERED

One of the best-known devices under this head is the *Gouin series*.[20] Gouin had observed the way his child commented on his own actions and he developed from this the idea of an *action series* or *action chain*. He divided common events into five general series: the home, man in society, life in nature, science, and occupations. These were subdivided and resubdivided into shorter series centering on the verb, which, according to Gouin, is "the generating element of the sentence."[21] The language was then taught through a series of commonly performed actions, first orally, then in writing. A different verb was used in each statement and students were expected to acquire the situational vocabulary along with the verb through performing or miming the actions while they described what they were doing. The teacher first demonstrated the series in the native language and then, when the students had understood it clearly, in the foreign language. The students next repeated the actions under the guidance of the teacher or of other students, describing what they were doing in the foreign language as they were doing it. (Gouin advocated peer teaching, saying that "in Nature, one child can and does teach another child to talk."[22] While the students were trying to reproduce the series the teacher would make encouraging remarks in the language. After this aural-oral phase, the series would be read and then written out by the students.

C11 The example Gouin himself gives[23] is the following (the verb is emphasized orally in the initial demonstration) :

walk	I walk towards the door.
draw near	I draw near to the door.
get to	I get to the door.
stop	I stop at the door.
stretch out	I stretch out my arm.
take hold	I take hold of the handle.
turn	I turn the handle.
pull	I pull the door.
moves	The door moves.
turns	The door turns on its hinges.
let go	I let go of the door handle.

We may be surprised at the amount of specialized vocabulary this method entailed. Gouin considered that general terms were infrequently used in comparison with specific vocabulary. His emphasis was, of course, on the verb, but the verb in complete sentences.

This approach can be extended to provide practice in all persons and for different time frames.

C12

STUDENT A   What am I doing?
STUDENT B   You're opening the door.

STUDENTS A & B   We're writing on the blackboard.
TEACHER   What are they doing?
STUDENT C   They're writing on the blackboard.

STUDENTS A & B   What are we doing?
STUDENT C   You're writing on the blackboard.

> TEACHER   What were they doing?
> STUDENT C   They were writing on the blackboard.
>
> STUDENT A   Guess what I'm going to do next week. (Miming action).
> STUDENT B   You're going to pack your suitcase.
> STUDENT C   She's going to pack her suitcase.

Through mime the variety of the actions can be expanded considerably and the activity becomes a competitive game with students describing each movement and then guessing what is being mimed. This may be a completely student-to-student activity in an individualized or group work program.

C13 (I)   In another variation, students are given orders or series of orders (of increasing complexity) by the teacher or other students:

Go to the door; open the door; put the book in the desk drawer; take the book out of the desk drawer; open the book to page twenty and read the first sentence aloud.

The students obey the orders saying what they are doing, or, if they are learning the past tense, what they did. If they make mistakes other students can describe what they actually did and what they should have done. (*He took the book on the desk. He should have taken the book out of the desk drawer*). This provides a useful situational context for learning the difficult expression *should have done (something)* or the useful *instead of doing (something)*.

Recent revivals of this type of activity learning have been called the *strategy of the total physical response*[24] (in which students respond physically to commands in the foreign language of increasing morphological and syntactical complexity) and *Situational Reinforcement*[25] (which uses the techniques of C12).

The Gouin approach can be developed in considerable detail, beyond these simple examples, and can be the basis for factual learning about the geography of the United States, the monuments of London, activities involving holidays, matters of etiquette, and so on.

C14 (I)   A map of the United States is drawn, as a cooperative project, on the floor of the classroom and students are asked to undertake journeys. (A posted map and pointer may be substituted, but this reduces the physical response to a symbolic one.)

TEACHER OR ANOTHER STUDENT   Leave New York City by crosssing the Hudson. Go toward Philadelphia. Don't stop there but go on to Washington, D.C.

The student addressed then describes the journey in the *simple past tense* with personal embellishments.

STUDENT   When I left New York City it was very hot. I crossed the Hudson at 9 a.m.. I went to Philadelphia, but I didn't stop there because it was raining. I went on to Washington, where I had lunch.

The *verbal-active approach*, which has also been called "a rationalist direct method," recognizes its debt to Gouin and to the subsequent work of Emile de Sauzé of Cleveland, whose influence can still be perceived in many a modern textbook.[26] Yvone Lenard says, "The sentence arranges itself around the verb" and "it is, therefore, imperative that the student learn to listen for the verb in the sentence, recognize its form, and answer immediately with the appropriate form."[27] In essence, this echoes Gouin, although Lenard's method adds a question-answer sequence to the action series. Since Lenard's is a direct method, it differs from the Gouin approach in that it excludes the native language from the classroom and the textbook.

In this approach, grammar is learned inductively and through action rather than through deductive grammar rules. Diller says, "Knowing a rule and being able to act on it is quite independent of being able to formulate the rule adequately. The rule can be psychologically real without any formulation of it. . . . Rules for action are best learned in conjunction with demonstration and practice of the action.[28] Both Diller and Lenard emphasize the necessity for the learning stage to develop into opportunities for innovative sentence creation on the part of the student. Quoting de Sauzé's viewpoint, Lenard says, " 'Language is invention.' It has no existence apart from the speaker or the writer who recreates, reinvents the language for his own needs each time he uses it."[29] She lays great stress on a daily oral composition as "the most important exercise of the verbal-active method in building the elements of which fluency is composed."[30] In these oral compositions, prepared in advance in writing but delivered orally in front of their fellows, students try to use only what everyone else is learning, thus cultivating "originality, free invention, and personal expression within a strictly controlled structural framework."[31] (Note that the verbal-active method moves from listening and speaking to writing before reading, another deviation from Gouin which is traceable to de Sauzé.)

C15 *Verbal-active action series.*[32]

Statement and Question	Answer
I wake up at seven in the morning. When *do you wake up?*	*I wake up* at eight.
I get up at once. *Do you get up* at once?	No, *I don't get up* at once. *I don't like to get up* at once.

Then *I wash myself* (with soap and water),
brush my teeth (with a toothbrush), *brush
my hair* (with a hairbrush), and *comb my
hair. Do you comb your hair?*   Yes, *I comb my hair.*

A man *shaves* in the morning (probably   Yes, *I shave*, but *I'm grow-*
with an electric razor). *Do you shave?*   *ing* sideburns and a mus-
                                                                   tache.

SITUATION CENTERED

For many centuries, situationally based dialogues have been in and out of
fashion for providing students with a corpus of foreign-language words and
expressions with which to work.[33] They are very frequently found in
present-day textbooks. The situations chosen may be experiences common
to the native and the foreign culture, or may introduce the student to
typically American or British ways of interacting and reacting. Sometimes
they are printed with a parallel idiomatic translation; at other times students are expected to comprehend the meaning through action or through
simple English explanations.

Dialogue construction can be indicative of diverse philosophies. Some
dialogues are designed to *demonstrate grammatical rules*, and examples of
rules in use and the variations of paradigms are introduced systematically
in the exchanges.

C16   BILL   Where are you going this evening?
       JANE   I'm going out with my family. We're going to the movies/cinema.
       BILL   What are you going to see?
       JANE   *Butch Cassidy and the Sundance Kid*. My cousin's going with us.
              He and his wife are going to meet us there.

Note that *movies/cinema* in this dialogue means that *movies* is the American term and *cinema* the British term. Hereafter in this book a slash (/)
will indicate a distinction between American and British usage, with the
American expression being given first.

The aim of grammar-demonstration dialogues is to lead students to
inductive recognition of the rule or the paradigm. These dialogues need
not be memorized: they can be studied and discussed in English, dramatized, and used as a basis for recombinations. They lead naturally to grammatical explanations and intensive practice exercises through which the
operation of the rule or paradigm becomes clear to the students, enters their
active repertoire, and is then used by them in a genuinely communicative
interchange.

Other dialogues, which we shall call *conversation-facilitation dialogues*, are intended primarily to provide students with a stock of useful expressions (clichés of conversation, frequently used expressions, conventional greetings, expletives, and rejoinders) with which to practice conversing, while the teaching of the grammar proceeds as a parallel but distinct activity.

C17   (American)   (British)

DAN Hi, George. How are you?	Hello, George. How are you?
GEORGE Fine. How about you?	Fine. What about you?
DAN O.K. You going downtown?	All right. Going to town?
GEORGE Yeah. How about coming along?	Yes. Like to come with me?
DAN Fine. Let's go.	Fine. Let's go.

Students memorize the segments, which have been selected because of their potential usefulness, and then practice using them in recombinations to form new dialogues involving different personalities.

Many dialogues combine both of these functions: grammar-demonstration and conversation-facilitation. It is important to decide the type of dialogue with which you are dealing so that it may be used for the purpose for which it was constructed.

A third type of dialogue we may call *recreational*. This is the familiar skit. This activity has always been popular with students and teachers in an orally-oriented approach. It is a true bridging activity which provides for spontaneous creation within the limits of what is being learned. It is discussed under *Dialogue Exploitation,* p. 33.

Dialogue construction and adaptation

You should be able to recognize the good and bad features of dialogues for several reasons:

—so that you can select well-written materials for use in classroom teaching or in individualized learning packets;

—so that you can rewrite poorly constructed dialogues when you are forced to use materials selected by others;

—so that you can write dialogues yourself, if you wish to supplement available materials (e.g., you may decide to prepare a dialogue based on a story which has been read).

GRAMMAR-DEMONSTRATION DIALOGUES

C18   1. BILL   Will you go away this weekend?
      2. TOM   Yes, we shall go to Chicago.

3. BILL   With whom will you go?

4. TOM   John will accompany me. He has some friends there with whom
we can stay.

5. BILL   What will you do there? Have you made any plans?

6. TOM   Yes, we have made some. We should like to visit a museum and
some skyscrapers.

7. BILL   Do you prefer big cities or small towns?

8. TOM   I prefer big cities. I should like to live in one.

9. BILL   Will you stay one night or two?

10. TOM   I shall stay one night, but John may stay two nights. Would you
like to come with us?

11. BILL   I am sorry but I cannot, because I must prepare for an examination in mathematics.

12. TOM   Perhaps you could study on the train. The trip lasts three hours.

13. BILL   I had better not go. I might not have a good time. Anyway, I
prefer small towns.

Commentary

1. As a sustained exchange between two friends, this dialogue is very
artificial and stilted. It has been laboriously constructed to include the
future *shall/will* distinction, various other modal auxiliaries, forms of the
indefinite article, including *some* with plurals and its contrast with *any*.

2. *Contemporary usage.* Certain features of authentic modern speech
have been completely ignored.

a. The ordinary way of expressing future intention is with *be going to*
(main verb). This is carefully avoided in C18. In 5 and 9, Bill would say,
What are you going to do there? and *Are you going to stay one night or
two?* When the main verb is *go*, this form of the future is often omitted,
and the present progressive is used instead. Thus 1 and 2 would probably be
Are you going away this weekend? Yes, we're going to Chicago. The distinction between *shall*, for first person, and *will*, for second and third
persons (when the auxiliary is used for future time, e.g., in conditional
sentences or to express volition) is rare in statements except in the most
formal American English. Quirk et al. (1972), p. 87, points out that
"*shall* in the sense of future is restricted to the 1st person in Standard BrE,
whereas *will* can be used in the same sense in all persons throughout the
English-speaking world."

b. Other forms of questions are common in informal speech. In yes-no
questions, the auxiliary and pronoun subject are often omitted, so that in 1
we might have simply *Going away this weekend?* and in 5, *Made any plans?*

Informal invitations or suggestions often begin with *How'd you like to . . .* or *How about . . . /What about . . .* or *Why don't you . . . /Why not . . .* In 10, Tom might say *How about coming along?/Why not come with us?*

c. Contracted forms of the auxiliaries would be used throughout after nouns and pronouns. In 2, *We're going . . .* ; in 3, *Who're you going with?* or *Who's going with you?*; in 6, *We'd like . . .* or *We're going . . .* ; in 11, *I'm sorry but I can't*; in 13, *I'd better . . .* or *I better. . . .*

3. *Weaknesses in the construction of the dialogue.*

a. Several of the sentences sound old-fashioned or unnaturally formal in structure and vocabulary. In 4, for example, in the first sentence, Tom would say *go with* rather than *accompany*; in the second sentence, the relative *whom* would be omitted and the preposition left at the end of the sentence (*. . . some friends we can stay with*). In 11, Bill should say *I'm sorry but I can't* or *I just can't. I've got a math/maths exam on Monday.*

b. In 12, *takes* would be more idiomatic and easier to pronounce than *lasts*.

c. Certain questions which seem clearly to have been introduced into the dialogue because of their usefulness for an unimaginative question-answer period in class add to the artificiality of the dialogue: 7: *Do you prefer big cities or small towns?* 9: *Will you stay one night or two?*

C19 *Rewritten,* with sentences shortened and language and usage modernized, this dialogue might read as follows:

BILL   Going away this weekend?

TOM   Yes, we're going to Chicago.

BILL   Who're you going with?

TOM   John. He has some friends there we can stay with.

BILL   What're you going to do? Made any plans?

TOM   We want to see a museum and go up a couple of skyscrapers. Why don't you come along?/Why not come with us?

BILL   I can't. I've got a math/maths exam on Monday.

Commentary

This shorter dialogue demonstrates the use of informal question patterns in the matrix of a possible conversation which could be exploited in various ways apart from its grammatical purpose. Clearly not all forms of questions can be appropriately taught through an informal dialogue. But this short version includes two yes-no questions with auxiliary and subject omitted, two question-word questions, and one "suggestion" question. The questions with *going to* can lead to a discussion of the *going to* future and its frequent omission when the main verb is *go*. In C18 questions and future time are expressed in very unrealistic dialogue, with no instances of the *going to* future or of contractions and deletions. Not only is there no clear demonstration of appropriate use, but the student is given a very false view of conversational possibilities.

* Find some grammar-demonstration dialogues, comment on their good and bad features, and practice rewriting the least effective of them.

CONVERSATION-FACILITATION DIALOGUES

Many textbooks include dialogues purely for the purpose of providing students in the early stages with *useful utterances and exclamations* which, with variations of vocabulary, can be recombined in all kinds of personal ways to make possible active classroom conversation and creative skits. Well written and presented, such dialogues can provide students with a fund of very authentic expressions for use at a stage when their overall knowledge of the language is still quite minimal. This ability to put together something meaningful encourages them with a sense of progress.

C20   1. PETE   Hello, Jack.
      2. JACK   Hi/Hello, Pete. Where're you going? The movies/cinema?
      3. PETE   No. I'm hungry. I haven't had lunch yet.
      4. JACK   Neither have I.
      5. PETE   Come on then! Let's go and get something to eat.
      6. JACK   Fine! Where do you want to go?
      7. PETE   There's a good place near the station.
      8. JACK   Look out! There's Helen. I don't want to see her.
      9. PETE   Neither do I. Let's hurry.

Commentary

1. With this type of dialogue, students are expected to memorize the sentences (through active role-playing) so that they can produce them quickly in new situations. This provides practice in the rhythm of the phrase and in specific intonation patterns.

2. The dialogue would be learned and practiced in sections (1–3, 1–7, 1–9). In other words, the dialogue is open-ended.

3. Utterances are short or are easily divided into short, meaningful segments (I'm hungry, near the station, let's hurry). The aim of the memorizing is for the students to be able to use these segments freely in new

combinations, and to learn to vary segments semantically, rather than to know the eighteen utterances by heart so that they can produce them parrot-fashion in the original sequence.

4. Students will learn short utterances like these easily by acting out the dialogue in small groups. The memorization and recall process are aided by visuals: flashcards, stick figures, flannel board, puppets, vanishing techniques (where the dialogue is written on the chalkboard with major elements of the phrase being obliterated one by one until students know the complete utterance thoroughly).

5. Small groups will perform their version of the dialogue for the others. Meaningful deviations from the original wording and paraphrases will be welcomed as indications that the students have indeed assimilated the material in a more than superficial way. The students will be encouraged to develop new situations including as often as possible material learned in other dialogues or in other classwork. (See *Dialogue Exploitation*, below.)

6. Conversation-facilitation dialogues do not follow a question-answer, question-answer sequence. This is not the natural mode of ordinary conversation. C20 consists of greeting, greeting returned, question, question, answer, statement, statement, statement, exclamation, suggestion, acceptance, question, oblique answer, exclamation, statement, statement, statement, suggestion.

7. Items are not exploited grammatically or paradigmatically as they would tend to be in a grammar-demonstration dialogue. Here students are familiarized, in a meaningful context, with constructions which they may not study systematically for some time (e.g., *I don't want to see her*) but which are immediately useable in their present form and in semantic variants (*I don't want to see it, I don't want to read it*).

8. Many modern textbook writers would consider C20 too long for an early dialogue. The material in it can easily be rewritten as a spiral series.

SPIRAL SERIES OF DIALOGUES

Short dialogues are usually more useful than longer dialogues. The interrelated content of two response pairs is more easily remembered than the development of thought in six response pairs. One response pair (A to B) allows little scope for an interesting mini-situation although it is used as the basic unit in the Cummings device illustrated in C29.

Sometimes several short dialogues develop a continuing theme, each in succession using some of the linguistic material from the one preceding. Such a succession of dialogues is called a spiral series. As students exploit each section, they are consolidating material already learned and the now-familiar material makes the learning of the new material more meaningful. Dialogue C19 could be developed spirally as follows:

C21 1. BILL   Are you going away this weekend?
        TOM   Yes, I'm going to Chicago.
        BILL   Who are you going with?
        TOM   John. He has some friends there, and we're going to stay with them.

      2. BILL   What are you and John going to do in Chicago?
        TOM   We're going to visit a museum, and go up a couple of sky-scrapers.
        BILL   How long are you going to stay?
        TOM   I'm going to stay one night, but John's staying two.

      3. BILL   What are you going to do this weekend?
        TOM   John and I are going to Chicago. Why don't you come along?/ What about coming with us?
        BILL   I can't. I've got to study. I have an exam on Monday.

      4. BILL   Where are you and John going?
        TOM   We're going to Chicago. Why don't you/Why not come with us?
        BILL   I've got to study. I have a math/maths exam on Monday.
        TOM   Why don't you study on the train? The trip takes three hours.

Commentary

Practice with expanding dialogues gives students the confidence for making up their own recombinations and original skits and provides a useful link with writing. The spiral sequence above gives experience with expressions for future time, different types of questions, and the varied possibilities of use of simple adverbial phrases.

✳ Rewrite C20 as a spiral series.

INTRODUCING CULTURAL CONTRASTS INTO DIALOGUES

Many textbook writers are criticized for writing dialogues which are culturally neutral, that is, which deal with situations like the one in C20 which could take place in any culture.

Some critics would argue that C20 would convey a feeling for American or British everyday culture if its content were more like one of the following:

C22 (In the United States)

SUSAN   Hi, Maria. Where're you going?

MARIA   I'm going to the post-office. I want to send a telegram.

SUSAN   A telegram? But you don't go to the post-office to send a telegram. You do it by telephone. You call Western Union.

MARIA   How do I pay for it then?

SUSAN   On a pay phone, you pay for it right there, like a long-distance call. On your own phone, you have it put on your phone bill.

(In Britain)

HELEN   Hullo, Jean. Where are you going?

JEAN   I'm going to get a magazine and some chocolate.

HELEN   Let's go to that newsagent on the corner. I want some cigarettes.

JEAN   I want to go to the one down the road. I've got to send off this parcel and there's a post office in that one.

Commentary

The first of these dialogues conveys the useful piece of information that in the United States one sends telegrams by telephone through Western Union, not from a post-office. The second dialogue tells us that in Britain not only does a newsagent's shop often sell sweets and tobacco, but sometimes it has a branch post-office as well. This kind of superficial difference in social organization has no deep significance, and, if such snippets of information are over-emphasized by repetition and exploitation in dialogues, students may well develop the attitude that the Americans or the British persist in doing things in odd ways for no apparent reason. This type of factual information can also become outdated overnight as a result of a shift in social organization or habits. (Note, for instance, the tremendous increase in the number of "fast-food" eating places, where there is a limited menu, very short preparation time, and no table service; and a similar increase in "pre-prepared" foods in the supermarkets, as more and more women take jobs outside the home.)

True cultural understanding means an appreciation of basically different attitudes and values which are reflected in the things people do, but which are not necessarily explicitly stated. It is difficult to work such concepts into short situational exchanges without oversimplifying and stereotyping social behavior.

The following dialogue,[34] obviously for students with some experience in reading, does convey a basic American value which is reflected in many aspects of individual and social life.

C23 At the Supermarket

(A woman from a foreign country goes grocery shopping and runs into some problems.)

SUPERVISOR   I'm the supervisor. Can I help you?
CUSTOMER   Yes. I need just one egg, but the clerk won't sell it to me.
SUPERVISOR   That's right. It's necessary to buy at least half a dozen.
CUSTOMER   But why? I don't want *six* eggs; I just want *one*.
SUPERVISOR   Selling eggs singly isn't profitable. And the idea is for the store to make a profit.
CUSTOMER   It bothers me that I can't buy the quantity I want.
SUPERVISOR   You don't understand. Running a supermarket is very complicated.
CUSTOMER   So is grocery shopping, in case you don't realize it.
SUPERVISOR   But look at the variety here. It's possible to buy almost anything.
CUSTOMER   Anything except one egg, you mean.

Commentary

1. Reflected in this dialogue is the role of the profit motive in American culture and in particular the tendency to reduce the amount of human labor (usually the most costly item) in business operations in order to make a larger profit. Reducing the use of human beings in marketing leads to the prepackaging of goods (and hence to the necessity of buying goods in fixed amounts) and in general to a reduction in individual attention and service. Furthermore, the American's dependence on the automobile and on a lot of storage space for goods in the home means that the fixed quantities sold often seem to visitors from other countries to be relatively large quantities.

2. Does the language of the dialogue strike you as consistently idiomatic and natural? (See checklist below.)

* Examine some textbook dialogues which purport to convey some understanding of American or British culture. Analyze the cultural content in the following terms: Is the cultural content of a superficial nature, reflecting interesting but insignificant aspects of behavior or social organization, or are the features portrayed surface indicators of deeper attitudes and values?

CHECKLIST FOR ORIGINAL OR REWRITTEN DIALOGUES

1. Do I intend this to be a grammar-demonstration, a conversation-facilitation, or a recreational dialogue?

2. Is the conversation interesting and natural? Do the participants say something worthwhile? Have I avoided the question-answer-question-answer format?

3. What points of grammar (or conversational items) do I wish students to assimilate?

4. Is my list so ambitious that it has made the dialogue stilted and unnatural? What can I omit while still achieving my purpose? (See C18.)

5. Can I increase the redundancy to make the conversation more natural? (See C2.)

6. Can I include more expletives and rejoinders to make it sound more spontaneous? (See Chapter 4: G44.)

7. Are the levels of language I have used appropriate and consistent? (See C5.)

8. Is the dialogue of a reasonable length for classroom use and exploitation? (Is it open-ended? Should I rewrite it as a spiral series?)

9. Are individual utterances short enough to be assimilated or, alternatively, do they break naturally into useful segments?

10. Have I re-entered lexical items, idioms, and grammatical structures from previous dialogues to refresh the students' memory?

11. In how many ways can this dialogue be exploited? (See below.)

12. Does the situation lend itself naturally to interesting or amusing recombinations? Is it likely to stimulate students to produce their own recreational dialogues or skits?

Dialogue exploitation

The dialogue as a teaching technique has come in for much criticism because it has been used unimaginatively and its full potential ignored. There is more than one way to use a dialogue. In fact, the possibilities are so extensive that one could actually exploit each dialogue differently for a whole semester, if one wished.

DIALOGUE MEMORIZATION

The most criticized way of teaching through dialogues has required of all students that they memorize every dialogue completely and thoroughly (and this often for dialogues of fifteen or twenty sentences) and that they be able to recite the whole sequence on demand. This type of activity is time-consuming and tedious and gives indefensible importance to a particular sequence of utterances. As a result, students are at a loss when they do not hear the precise cue they are expecting. They become discouraged and exasperated by the mistakes they make in recalling memorized materials—mistakes which have nothing to do with their comprehension and assimilation of the material.

As has been noted earlier, there is no need for memorization of *grammar-demonstration dialogues*. A certain amount of repetition to ensure correct, fluent production is sufficient. Thorough exploitation with variety, in the ways suggested below, paralleled by as much grammatical explanation as the students need, will ensure understanding of the principles behind the structures used, while judicious practice in their meaningful use in all kinds of variations of their original setting will prepare students to use them perceptively in utterances of their own creation. Similarly, vocabulary will be retained more thoroughly if used frequently in various contexts.

Conversation-facilitation dialogues, which are short and full of expressions of wide applicability, may be memorized to the point where the useful segments, rather than the original sequence, are immediately available for use. Meaningful variations of the sequence will be welcomed as signs of real assimilation of the material. Recall may be aided by the use of a series of pictures on film, flashcards, or transparencies for overhead projection. Some teachers in the early stages like to have a native-language translation readily available when the student momentarily forgets the sequence of the dialogue; others reject this aid, preferring to concentrate on direct association of utterance and action.

WAYS OF PRESENTING AND LEARNING FROM THE DIALOGUE

With imagination the teacher can vary ways of presenting the dialogue. There are *five aspects* of the dialogue activity which need to be provided for if the energy expended is to yield any fruit in terms of the students' growing ability to function freely in the language. For each aspect, we have suggested a number of possible activities. Teachers will select from among them those that are consistent with their general approach.

1. Some *setting of the scene* to arouse student interest in the content of the dialogue and facilitate comprehension of the language used.

For example: acting out of the conversation, with appropriate props, in the native language (if this is consistent with the teacher's attitude toward the use of the native language as an aid in beginning classes), or else through mime; discussion of the content of the dialogue with the help of pictures, slides, flashcards, projected diagrams, maps, plans; discussion of some aspect of life or some social situation for which the dialogue will supply a cultural contrast; some classroom language activity of the direct method or Gouin type (C11–13) which relates to the content of the dialogue; some preparing of the semantic area through discussion or through a competition or game; the recounting in English of an incident or anecdote of related interest, or the showing and discussion in the native language of a cartoon or a series of stick figures related to the theme. For a *grammar-demonstration* dialogue: the raising of some questions about the grammatical problem to arouse interest in its manifestations in the script and as a stimulus to the students to find out for themselves how the rule works.

2. Some technique for *focusing student attention* on the meaning of the interchange.

For example: students may be asked to listen to the whole dialogue on tape several times as a listening comprehension exercise, with opportunity between each hearing for group piecing together of the meaning; students may listen to the dialogue as they watch a series of slides, or look at a series of sketches illustrating the content of the interchange; students may be supplied ahead of time with a set of questions for which they should find answers as they listen to the dialogue; sometimes, for variety, students may be given the written script of the dialogue to peruse and ask questions about before listening to it without the script.

3. Some *familiarization* of students with the actual utterances in the dialogue through an activity which makes cognitive demands on them.[35]

For example: as students in the initial stage repeat the lines of the dialogue to develop fluency in their production, they take roles, group speaking to group or class to teacher, until they can handle the material with reasonable efficiency; after hearing an utterance two or three times, students try to reconstruct it as a group endeavor; the teacher writes the material on the board and gradually erases sections to see if students are repeating meaningfully and can supply the erased portions (erasures increase in length). For a *conversation-facilitation* dialogue: some students mime the dialogue while the class supplies the words; students go off in pairs and practice taking roles, testing each other on knowledge of the material; students act out the roles on an individual basis or as group presentations.

4. Some *formal manipulation* of the material in the dialogue, exploiting the useful expressions in a *conversation-facilitation* dialogue or the morphological and syntactic items in a *grammar-demonstration* dialogue.

For example: directed dialogue or guided conversation (see C24); group recombinations for similar but slightly different situations; chain dialogue (see C25). For *grammar-demonstration* dialogues: analysis of rules demonstrated in the material, leading into intensive practice through the various kinds of oral exercises described in Chapter 4. For *conversation-facilitation* dialogues: items of the dialogue may be used as personal questions to students who either answer for themselves or pretend through their answers to be someone else (the teacher or other students guess who they are); the teacher, or a student, establishes a situation by a remark and another student responds with a suitable expletive or rejoinder:

A   I can't eat with you. I don't have any money./I haven't got any money.
B   Too bad! (or That's a shame!)

For a given expletive, the student creates an utterance:

A   *Hey! What d'you know!*
B   Hey! What d'you know! They've painted their house blue!

A   *Excuse me*
B   Excuse me, could you please tell me where the post-office is.

5. Some ways in which the dialogue material can be used in the *creation of new utterances and new dialogue* expressing the students' own whims, feelings, and imaginings. The suggestions below encourage students to draw on anything they know from previous dialogues, from group conversation or from reading, in preparing their versions. (They should, however, be discouraged from seeking extra vocabulary in dictionaries at this stage.)

For example: the creation of a similar situation in another setting (the irate shopper demanding money back for a faulty appliance becomes the irate air traveler demanding a refund for a ticket, or a householder trying to get rid of a door-to-door salesman becomes a television viewer trying to cut off a telephone advertiser); group preparation, using a series of pictures of a different setting and a climactic utterance (*But it's broken!*) as a basis for a dialogue with a similar dénouement to the one already studied. See also suggestions for *Recreational Dialogues*, under *The Dialogue as a Culminating Activity*, below.

DIRECTED DIALOGUE OR GUIDED CONVERSATION

The teacher prompts pairs of students to reproduce sections of the dialogue. Directed dialogue may be conducted in several ways.

C24   (Working from C20)
   a. TEACHER TO STUDENT A (in the student's native language)
                    Ask B where (s)he's going.
        STUDENT A   Where're you going, Terry?
        TEACHER TO STUDENT B   Tell A you're going to lunch.
        STUDENT B   I'm going to lunch.

b. TEACHER TO STUDENTS A & B (in the students' native language) You meet each other in the corridor and one of you asks the other where (s)he's going. The other replies (s)he's going to lunch.

> STUDENT A   Where're you going, Terry?
> STUDENT B   I'm going to lunch.

c. TEACHER TO STUDENT A (in English) Ask Terry where (s)he's going.
> STUDENT A   Where're you going, Terry?
> TEACHER TO STUDENT B (in English) Tell Bobby you're going to lunch.
> STUDENT B   I'm going to lunch.

Commentary

Directed dialogue is more difficult than most teachers realize because it involves a transformation of the teacher's cue for which students must be well prepared. Any potential usefulness is often negated by the amount of time devoted to the pure mechanics of the performance. *It is sometimes helpful to perform the operation several times in the students' native language to accustom the students to the procedure before using any of the approaches suggested.*

d. TEACHER TO STUDENTS A & B (in English) You meet in the corridor and one of you asks the other where (s)he's going; the other responds that (s)he's going to have lunch.

> STUDENT A   Where're you going, Terry?
> STUDENT B   I'm going to lunch.

Commentary

Here the language of the directions is more complex than the language, possibly memorized, of the response. This can make the exercise confusing and difficult for an elementary-level student.

CHAIN DIALOGUE

This is a challenging and amusing way for students to practice retrieval of many expressions and structures they have learned. It can begin with very recent material (for instance, a response pair from C20), but should soon develop into a competition to think up questions and answers of all kinds.

C25 TEACHER TO A   Where're you going, Terry?
                A   I'm going to lunch.
             A TO B   Would you like to come with us?
                B   Fine.
             B TO C   Where'll we go?
                C   Let's go to the movies/cinema.
             C TO D   Do you like movies/films?
                D   No, I prefer television.
             D TO E   How old are you?
                E   I'm fourteen.
             E TO F   What about you?

Rubbishing the dialogue

As a variation of the chain dialogue, but with a similar aim of developing flexibility by drawing on all kinds of expressions which the students have acquired, one team of students (Chris) undertakes to keep to the utterances in the dialogue recently studied, the other team (Pat) thinks up possible responses other than those learned. (Later the teams exchange roles.) Students try to remain within the bounds of what they have learned but may ask the teacher occasionally for a few new expressions, thus adding to their repertoire things they would like to say. (Since this is a satirical approach there is no need for the resulting sequence to be semantically probable.)

C26 (Based on C20)

CHRIS   Hi, Pat.
  PAT   Hello. I don't believe we've met. (*or* There must be some mistake *or* I beg your pardon, were you talking to me?)
CHRIS   Where're you going? To the movies/cinema?
  PAT   No, I'm not going any place. (*or* No, I'm going to bed; *or* What business is it of yours? *or* What in the world are movies?)
CHRIS   Would you like to come with me?
  PAT   Don't be ridiculous! (*or* Great! Let's go! *or* No, I don't think so; *or* Sure, if you'll buy the tickets!)

THE DIALOGUE AS A CULMINATING ACTIVITY

It has become customary to think of the dialogue as an introductory teaching technique, but it can also come at the end of a unit of study, whether dialogues are or are not used as a technique in the body of the lesson. In this case, it demonstrates in operation in a realistic situation what has been studied analytically. It is then enjoyed as an opportunity to express oneself in language and structures which are now familiar. This is the place for the *recreational dialogue*, or *skit*.

As a bridging activity, the *recreational dialogue* should have as its starting point a situation for which the students have some vocabulary and expressions available to them. "Situation" here is used in its broadest sense: a person alone in a house who hears a strange noise outside the window experiences a similar nervous reaction to a person watching a spider weave its web from the ceiling to a shelf of his bookcase and may very well exclaim in the same fashion: "Gosh! What'll I do?"

Most students need the stimulus of seminal ideas such as the following, which take them from the shelter of the cove further and further into the open sea.

1. Skits may be based on an adaptation of the type of situation in the dialogue they have just been studying: two people discussing their meal in a restaurant become the seven dwarfs grumbling about the meal Snow-White has prepared; two people meeting in a supermarket become a boy meeting a girl at the school dance.

2. Students are given one side of a conversation which is not explicit and are asked to create a dialogue. Different groups act out their versions.

C27   A   Pardon me, but what have you got there?

      B   . . . .

      A   I've never seen anything like that!

      B   . . . .

      A   You really like things like that?

      B   . . . .

      A   Excuse me, but I'm afraid I've got some work to do.

3. Students are given a response-pair beginning: *A: Who told you that? Your sister? B: No. She wasn't even home.* They extemporize a response-pair completion (or prepare a longer completion). Students should not strive each time for wit, which requires fairly sophisticated manipulation of language, but rather for a sensible conclusion.

C28   RACHEL   Who told you that? Your sister?

      DICK   No, she wasn't even home.

      RACHEL   But I saw her on the balcony!

      DICK   No, that was my mother. They look alike.

4. Students are given a punch line and different groups work out short skits leading up to it. (*But it's already left!* or *No, no! Not me! please!*)

5. Skits are based on a list of words providing basic elements (*a train, an old lady, two students on holiday, the border between two countries, a customs officer, a little white envelope, the next day*).

6. Students prepare puppet plays using the particular settings of recent dialogues (*a restaurant, a bank, grandma's house*). Timid or reticent students will often express themselves in the voice of a puppet.

7. Students create original dialogue arising from an ambiguous picture or a cartoon without caption. The pictures chosen should show an obviously emotional situation, a predicament involving two or more people, or some incongruity.

8. Students invent dialogues based on problems caused by differences in everyday living in the United States or Britain; e.g., a foreign visitor in an American hamburger-restaurant is presented with a large roll filled with meat, melted cheese, and salad—but the restaurant provides no knife and fork; problems of two tourists trying to find an acquaintance in an apartment building/block of flats (*bell, buzzer, caretaker, nameplate, elevator/ lift, first floor/ground floor*).

The Cummings device[36]

One attempt to link structural practice and lexical exploration to communication is Stevick's Cummings device, based on the two-utterance communication. Stevick says, "The shorter a dialog, the less unexplained, confusing clutter it contains."[37] As a technique for moving from manipulation of structures to communication at each learning step, the Cummings device merits a place in this section on bridging activities.

"Cummings device" is Stevick's preferred term for his earlier "microwave cycle" which he describes as follows:

The . . . format itself, in what we may a little wryly call its "classical form," contained a basic utterance (usually but not always a question) and from four to eight potential answers or other appropriate rejoinders. If the basic utterance and the rejoinders are well chosen, they can lead to almost immediate real or realistic . . . conversation in class, and are also likely to find use in real life outside of class. At the same time, new structures and new vocabulary can be kept to a minimum.

A . . . "cycle" was divided into an M-phase and a C-phase. *M* stood for *m*imicry, *m*anipulation, *m*echanics and *m*emorization, and *C* for *c*ommunication, *c*onversation, and *c*ontinuity. Within the M-phase, the first section usually introduced the answers or rejoinders, often in the form of a substitution drill with a separate column for cue words. The second section contained the question(s) or other basic utterance(s). The C-phase combined the elements of the M-phase with each other and, ideally, with material from earlier lessons, to form a short sample conversation.[38]

The C series is so designed that lexical items are easily substitutable (substitutable items being placed in parentheses as a guide). As Stevick explains,

it is only through this kind of "delexicalization" that one can get away from content words chosen either at the whim of the textbook writer, or for their high frequency in the language as a whole, and that one can insure the use of the content words that are of high frequency in the student's immediate surroundings. In this way, through localization and personalization of vocabulary, we improve the likelihood that language *study* will be replaced by language *use*, and that language *use* will become a part of the group life of the students.[39]

The usefulness of this technique is that the teacher who has mastered the principle can derive Cumings devices, as need and interest suggest, from any materials—lessons in books, newspaper articles, material heard on tape, radio, or film track, or ongoing communicative activities. As with any device, it is intended, not as the whole of the course, but as one among the many possible activities which provide variety for student learning.

C29 *The Cummings device*

M-1

	Jean works in the city.
We	We work in the city.
Bob and Mike	Bob and Mike work in the city.
every day	Bob and Mike work every day.
eight hours a day	Bob and Mike work eight hours a day.
You	You work eight hours a day.
Susan	Susan works eight hours a day.
in an office	Susan works in an office.

M-2 Do you work every day?
No, I don't work every day.

M-3 Where do you work?
When do you work?
How many hours a day do you work?

C-1 A Do you work in (an office)?
  B No, I don't work in an office.

  A Does Betty work in (an office)?
  B No, she works in (a store/shop).

  A Do you work (on Thursdays)?
  B Yes, I work (every day).

C-2 A Where do you (work)?
  B I work (in the city).

  A Do you work (in Chicago)?
  B Yes, I do.

A   When do you (work)?
B   I work (every day).

A   How many (hours) a (day) does Henry (work)?
B   He works (eight) (hours) a (day).

A   How many (days) a (week) do you work?
B   (Five) (days) a (week).

C-3   A   Do (you) work (in Chicago)?
B   Yes, (I) do.

B   Do (people) work (eight) (hours) a (day) here?
C   No, (they) work (seven) (hours) a (day).

Note that in the C (Communication) phases the questions will be personalized: names and activities used will be those of members of the class.

Stevick warns his readers that the device "is not a theory, nor a method, but only a format,"[40] that there are a number of pitfalls to be avoided in writing individual cycles (these are discussed in Chapter 6 of Stevick, 1971), and that no course should consist of just one format. "Procedures and systems and approaches," he says, "supplement one another more than they supersede one another."[41]

THE CUMMINGS DEVICE AND CULTURAL INFORMATION

In C29, questions and answers refer to general activities of daily life in any society. The device can also be used to interest students in differences between daily activities in their own country and in English-speaking countries. The following types of information could be incorporated in a Cummings device based on question forms.

C30   In the United States you can buy candy and cigarettes in a drugstore. In Britain you can often buy sweets at a newsagent's. Can you get free road-maps at gas-stations in the United States? Where can you buy guide-books and maps in Britain? (In a bookshop or at a newsagent's.)

*   Try to construct a Cummings device incorporating the type of information in C30.

Oral reports

Up to this point most of the bridging activities discussed have involved questions and answers, short statements and comments, requests, and exclamations. Another important facet of communicating includes describing, narrating, and explaining, all of which involve more sustained speech. Very early in the language course, students should have opportunities to practice these skills, taking as topics whatever suggests itself in the course of their reading or classroom activities. Reading passages, dialogues, sets of pictures, films, magazines, or class discussions of aspects of the country, its achievements, and the people who live in it provide basic vocabulary and ideas from which the students fan out in a creative way.

1. Reports at first are *short* (four or five sentences), later expanding as the students gain in confidence and experience. Students are always encouraged to ask the presenter questions about details of the report.

2. Initial efforts may be combined ones. Students in small groups construct their reports orally, with one student writing the group production on a chalkboard while the others criticize and improve on it until all are satisfied. When the class is next reassembled, a spokesman for the group gives the description or narration orally, without referring to a script, and students from other groups ask questions. (The role of presenter is taken by different members of the group on successive occasions.)

3. In Lenard's verbal-active method, oral compositions play an important role.[42] She reiterates to her students a slogan which (translated) reads: "*An excellent composition is original, imaginative, and accurate. A dictionary? No, no, absolutely not.*"[43] After the composition has been thoroughly discussed and worked over orally in class, it is written out and corrected by the teacher. "There is no point," Lenard says, ". . . in permanently recording . . . anything that has not reached its best possible form."[44]

We may add that, at least by the intermediate level, teachers need to give students help in the effective use of the dictionary and some oral reports can then be devised as demonstrations of successful dictionary search. (See Chapter 9: *Exploring the Dictionary*.) In these cases, presenters explain in simple English paraphrases any specialized vocabulary they have used, thus developing another useful skill.

4. Early reports may be guided in a number of ways.

a. A sequential series of questions is provided on what has been read, viewed, or discussed, or on a similar, but personalized, situation.

C31 You want to park your car at a parking meter. What kind of money do you need? You have only a dollar bill. What do you do? What may happen if you don't put money in the meter? What is a "motorcycle cop"? What does he do? Are you always allowed to park at a parking meter? You may find that your car is gone. Why? What happens at rush-hour? What signs should you look for when you want to park?

With general questions such as these, the students' answers become very diverse; e.g., instead of getting change for the meter, a student may decide to park somewhere else; or he may take a chance and not put money in; he may find his car is gone because it has been stolen or because it has been towed away.

   b. Students are given a series of pictures with no questions attached, the interpretation being left entirely to their imagination or invention.

   c. A framework of key words forms a skeleton outline.

C32 You are going to take a trip by plane.

   Preparations — car — parking — baggage/luggage — ticket — passenger lounge — newspaper — two young lovers — a disagreeable young man — two sailors — announcement of flight — boarding — departure.

   d. Persons, places, or things in the students' own environment lead to mystery descriptions for which the other students guess the referent.

   5. A simple form of oral report is a regular *Show and Tell* session, where students of their own volition share with their classmates things they have discovered about the United States, Great Britain, English-speaking Canada, Australia, New Zealand, Singapore, Hong Kong, Jamaica, the Bahamas, or other English-speaking areas, and show objects imported from these countries, stamps, postcards, maps, menus, objets d'art, and bric-à-brac brought back by touring relatives.

   6. Oral reports are an essential part of learning about the great figures and artistic, scientific, and social achievements of the people as well as their pleasures and aspirations in daily living; students prepare individual and group presentations as a culmination to their research on specific topics.

   7. At more advanced stages, many opportunities arise for students to explain and discuss what they have been reading, hearing, or seeing in films, or to discuss topics of general interest arising from these or from current events in the news.

Situation tapes

   Cartier[45] reports experimentation with situational conversations on tape for individual practice. The students hear the voices of two or more persons who are ostensibly conversing with them. The interlocutors on the tape call each other by their names and soon the students feel that they know them and that they are actually being spoken to. Spaces are left for the students to record their parts of the interchange. Each conversation is so designed that the students are led to make replies that are consistent with its drift, while still choosing what they actually wish to say and the way they wish to express it. After recording their responses, the students listen to the completed conversation and then re-record it as often as they wish until they are satisfied with their part. (After all, we always think of that clever response after the crucial moment has passed.) The context can also be filled in with visuals. No monitoring or correction is supplied, the students being perfectly free to express themselves on their personal tapes to the best of their ability. In this way, the less confident students are able to practice real communication without the embarrassment of expressing themselves inadequately in front of others.

C33   Roger and David happen to meet you in front of a theater/cinema.

The student is shown a picture of the theater/cinema, with the name of the film being shown and a notice stating the times at which it will be shown. Italicized speeches are on the tape. A blip* indicates when the student is expected to reply.

ROGER	*Hello, how's everything? Are you going to see this?**
STUDENT	Yes, they say it's rather good.
or	No, I'm just going for a cup of coffee.
or	Yeah, I've got nothing else to do.
DAVID	*My sister told me it was terrific.*
ROGER	*I don't know anything about it, personally. Do you?**
STUDENT	Some of my friends have seen it.
or	No, I don't know anything about it either.
or	No, I've never even heard of it before.
ROGER	*Well, what do you want to do, David?*
DAVID	*I don't care. I just like watching the girls go by.*
ROGER	*Let's all go to this film. Are you waiting for somebody?**
STUDENT	Well, yes, actually, I'm waiting for a friend of mine.
or	No, I have no plans, really.
DAVID	*We're in no hurry. Feel like having something, Roger? What about a cup of coffee?*
ROGER	*Good idea. What time does the next show begin?**
STUDENT	In about ten minutes, I think.
or	At seven o'clock, it says here.
or	It's beginning now . . .

* Imagine you are visiting San Francisco. Try to make up a series of taped utterances for a situation tape. Then see whether different kinds of responses can be inserted without destroying the coherence of the sequence.

2
Autonomous interaction

Returning to the schema C1, we observe the gap between skill-getting and skill-using. Some indications have been given of ways in which production or pseudo-communication activities can become bridging activities, facilitating and stimulating autonomous interaction. (See also Chapter 4: Oral Practice, Type B exercises, p. 138.)

The crossing from bridge to shore, however, will not necessarily take place without encouragement. Many students will remain on the bridge, rather than face the unprotected autonomy of real communication, unless they are given opportunities very early to develop confidence and self-reliance through frequent, pleasant incursions into autonomous territory. In other words, such students will prefer the safety of the structured exercise and develop a nervous attitude toward the unstructured which will be hard to change. Our students must learn early to express their personal intentions through all kinds of familiar and unfamiliar recombinations of the language elements at their disposal. The more daring they are in linguistic innovation, the more rapidly they progress.[1] This means that priority must be given to the development of an adventurous spirit in trying to convey one's meaning to others in the foreign language.

How can we develop this necessary confidence and self-reliance? We must create, and allow to develop naturally, opportunities for our students to use the second or foreign language for the normal purposes of language in relations with others—as Birkmaier puts it, "to use language in a natural, useful way, in a significant social setting."[2] Such activities link listening and speaking, since, without ability to comprehend the speech of others, "communication" becomes an uninteresting and frustrating one-way street. In some approaches, activities such as those described in this section are the chief preoccupation. Even where this is not so, they must be given time and place if students are to communicate in uninhibited freedom.

Categories of language use

Students need situations where they are on their own (that is, not supported by teacher or structured exercise) trying to use the foreign language to exchange with others messages of real interest to them. Yet we cannot send students off in groups or pairs and tell them to interact. *Motivation to communicate* must be aroused in some way. We must propose, or encourage students to develop, activities which have an intrinsic interest for them—activities in such natural interactional contexts as the following: (1) establishing and maintaining social relations, (2) expressing one's reactions, (3) hiding one's intentions, (4) talking one's way out of trouble, (5) seeking and giving information, (6) learning or teaching others to do or make something, (7) conversing over the telephone, (8) solving problems, (9) discussing ideas, (10) playing with language, (11) acting out social roles, (12) entertaining others, (13) displaying one's achievements, (14) sharing leisure activities.

These types of interactional activity lend themselves to various patterns of individualization, with students naturally seeking out partners with whom they feel at ease. Maslow[3] has shown that each individual has a hierarchy of needs to be satisfied, rising from physiological needs through the needs for feelings of security, belongingness, esteem (of others and for oneself), and self-realization. These are reflected in complex interrelationships within any group. Since genuine interaction springs from the depths of the individual personality, all of these needs affect student reactions in a truly autonomous situation. For these reasons, only the students themselves know whether personally they feel more at ease with a fluent speaker who can help them along, a less fluent speaker whose lesser ability encourages them in their own efforts, or a good listener who inspires them with confidence. Some students, by their nature, interact very fully with few words. Students thus form their own small, natural-affinity interactional groups which select or generate activities as the group becomes a compatible unit.

An imaginative teacher and involved students will think of many absorbing and exciting interactional activities. Listed below are some expansions, by no means exhaustive, of the possibilities for language use within each category and some sample activities which would lead to the use of language in the terms of the category. Naturally, once an activity becomes truly autonomous, the student automatically draws on elements from other categories, e.g., while making something (category 6), a student may over-turn a container of paint and apologize (category 1), then solve a problem by suggesting how such a situation could be avoided by a different arrangement of working space (category 8).

All of the activities suggested will obviously not be possible for all students from the earliest stage of learning. The teacher will *select and graduate activities to propose* from these categories, so that the attitude of seeking to communicate is developed early in an activity which is within the student's growing capacity. An impossible task, which bewilders and discourages students too early in their language learning, is just as inhibiting of ultimate fluency as lack of opportunity to try what they can do with what they know. The sample activities within each category are broadly labeled E (Elementary), I (Intermediate), and A (Advanced). This is obviously not a hard-and-fast guide since the maturity, capabilities, and goals of groups are so diverse.

1. ESTABLISHING AND MAINTAINING SOCIAL RELATIONS

(E)   Greetings between persons of the same and different age and status, introductions, wishes for special occasions, polite enquiries (with attention to the permissible and the expected questions in the culture), making arrangements, giving directions, apologies, refusals; (I) excuses, mild rebukes, conventional expressions of agreement and polite disagreement, encouraging, discouraging, and persuading others; (A) expressing impatience, surprise, dismay, making promises, hedging (the gentle art of non-communication), teasing.[4]

Conversation capsules or *mini-incidents* can be developed by interaction groups to demonstrate how to handle various situations. These need not be lengthy. Students learn appropriate gestures as they enact the situations.

(E)   Answering the door and politely getting rid of an unwanted caller; calling on the phone with birthday greetings, congratulations on a successful achievement, an enquiry about the health of a friend, or to make some arrangements; interacting at a party with people one does not know very well; enacting urgent situations (fire, drowning, street attack) which require quick vocal responses with set phrases; (I) welcoming visitors at home, customers in a shop, or clients in an office.

(A)   These uses become inextricably interwoven within other activities. Reality is achieved when students are able to greet, escort, and entertain an English-speaking visitor to some class activity or visit in English-speaking homes; or, in a foreign-language situation, interact in English with an exchange student or teacher or a visitor to their town, visit an English-speaking area, if possible on a family-exchange basis, or engage in an informal activity of category 14.

2. EXPRESSING ONE'S REACTIONS

Students can be put in real or simulated situations where they have to react verbally throughout a television show, at an exhibition of pictures or photographs, during a friendly sharing of slides, or during the showing of an animated cartoon. (In these cases the clever or amusing remark, instead of being frowned upon as presumptuous, is welcomed, as long as it is in English.)

3. HIDING ONE'S INTENTIONS

(I)   Each student may be given a mission which must not be revealed under any provocation, but which must be carried out, if at all possible, within a given period of time. This activity carries purposeful use of the language beyond course hours as students try to discover each other's missions. (E) Selekman[5] has developed for this category a game called *Super Spy*. One group forms a team of spies who decide on a mission. Each spy goes to a different group, the members of which try to find out the assigned mission through astute questioning. The group which is successful first then explains how their spy's mission was discovered. This activity also involves (5), (8), and (13).

4. TALKING ONE'S WAY OUT OF TROUBLE

Simulated or real situations of increasing verbal difficulty should be set up, where students must use their wits to extract themselves from a dilemma, e.g., giving non-answers to an inquisitive neighbor anxious to know the origin of a loud noise heard in the middle of the night; redirecting the course of an awkward or embarrassing conversation; answering the complaint: "By the way, I called you last night on the phone, as we'd arranged, but no one was home" without revealing where one was or what one was doing.

5. SEEKING AND GIVING INFORMATION

a. *Seeking information* on subjects for which students have some basic vocabulary. (A) Finding out specialized vocabulary for a special interest can be part of this type of interaction, particularly in connection with (6). (I) Students may be sent to find out specific information from a monolingual English speaker in the school, or an informant who pretends to be monolingual, or the students seek the information from English speakers outside of the course or the school. The information may be useful for activities in categories (1), (6), (8), or (12).

b. *Giving information* (E and I) about oneself, one's family background, the area where one lives, one's career aspirations, vacation preferences, pet peeves; (I and A) about some subject in which one is proficient (e.g., a student may be giving information to other students learning to do or make something, perhaps explaining what he or she is doing while doing it).

Combining a. and b. (E and I) All kinds of classroom opportunities arise for students to wonder why and ask the teacher or each other. Students should be encouraged to ask questions in English about what they are to do and to seek information about customs and institutions of English-speaking peoples. If a new student has joined the class, if there is a new baby in the family, if some student has returned from a vacation or a summer job, or if someone saw an accident on the way to school, other activities should be suspended while students ask about it in English. *Simulated settings* like bank or airline counters, customs desks, shops, or restaurants may be used to expand the school setting. Advertisements from magazines can give an initial fillip to the interaction, with students enquiring about advertised services. As a basis for asking and answering questions or giving directions, students may use air schedules, customs forms, or menus written in English, or maps and brochures from an English-speaking country which have been brought home by traveling relatives or the teacher, or obtained from tourist or cultural services. The *interview technique* also combines these two aspects of information-sharing. (A) The interview may be based on social roles adopted by the participants, thus linking (5) with (11). The results of the interview may be written up for a wall newspaper, as a link with writing practice.

6. LEARNING OR TEACHING HOW TO DO OR MAKE SOMETHING

Here, language is associated with action. The possibilities for increasing the interest and motivation of students of all kinds of abilities and interests are limitless. It is the basic technique of foreign-language camps and should be incorporated automatically into the programs of English-language clubs. On a smaller scale it can become part of a regular course. The pressure of intensive courses is certainly relieved by sessions in the language where students actually work with real-life materials and activities (sports, hobbies, crafts, physical exercise, dances).

7. CONVERSING OVER THE TELEPHONE

This is always difficult in a new language because of the distortions of sound, interference, and lack of situational, facial, and body language clues to meaning. It should, therefore, be practiced early. The students should learn to use a phone book from an English-speaking country and, in a second-language situation, make actual calls enquiring about goods, services, or timetables for transport.

The help of monolingual, or presumed monolingual, contacts outside the course should be enlisted. Some retired teachers, incapacitated persons, and older persons living alone who know English well would enjoy talking over the phone regularly with enthusiastic students. These outside aides should be instructed to act strictly as monolinguals[6] and should be informed of the specific nature of the student's assignment. Where no such outside help is available, teachers will act as informants for (A) students from their colleagues' classes, and (A) students will act as informants for (E) and (I) students.

The telephone practice is usually associated at the beginning with (6) or (8). After several calls to the same person, however, students seem to relax and begin to enjoy this opportunity to talk about all sorts of personal activities and problems to a sympathetic listener and this encourages natural self-expression in English.

8. PROBLEM SOLVING

The problem should require verbal activity for its solution. It may involve (5) or (6), even (3), (4), (9), or (10).

a. (E) Such well-known games as *Twenty Questions, Who Am I?, Who and What?, Animal-Vegetable-Mineral,* and their derivatives are popular. One student thinks of something (or someone, or an historical incident . . .), the others try to guess what it is with the fewest possible yes-no questions. (See G43.) (I and A) These games can become very sophisticated as versions of television panel series like *I've Got a Secret, To Tell the Truth* (where three people pretend to be the person who performed some particular acts and the students try to decide which one is telling the truth), and *What's My Line?* (where the questioners try to decide the occupation of the person being questioned).

b. (E and I) Selekman has experimented with a game called *Guilty Party*[7] where one student is accused by the group of an unspecified crime which he must discover through a series of questions (When did I do this? Where did I do it? Why did I do it? Did anyone help me? . . .) After discovering the nature of the crime, the accused must attempt to defend himself to seek an acquittal. (A) This game can be played after a study of the American or British legal system and incorporate relevant features of the administration of justice in certain English-speaking areas.

c. (E and I) Lipson,[8] in an attempt to focus the students' attention on the *content* of the sentences they are producing, has worked out materials which take up the principle of the well-known type of puzzle:

A, B, and C live on X, Y, and Z streets.
A works in an office.
B is a lawyer.
C stays home while his wife goes to work.

The people on X street all work in factories.
The people on Y street are all single.
The people on Z street all own their own businesses downtown.

On which streets do A, B, and C live?

Lipson's materials are about hooligans who steal in factories, conduct themselves badly in parks, like to smoke on trolley buses, and are often uncultured people (uncultured people never wash). Later we find out that hooligans are of two types: those who conduct themselves badly in parks never wash, while those who steal in factories like to smoke on trolley buses. The plot thickens when we find out that there are two gangs of hooligans, Borodin's and Gladkov's: Borodin steals at Gladkov's factory and Gladkov at Borodin's. This complicated background leads to questions such as the following:

Which hooligans often wash?	Hooligans who steal at factories
	OR
	hooligans who don't conduct themselves badly in parks . . .
When does Borodin steal at his own factory?	He never steals at his own factory.
Why not?	Borodin steals at Gladkov's factory.
What does Gladkov do when Borodin is not stealing?	As far as I know, Gladkov steals at Borodin's factory. . . .

Both Selekman[9] and Lipson[10] report that students become so involved in these problem-solving activities that their verbal participation becomes really creative and personally meaningful. As Lipson puts it: "What often happens is that members of the class start arguing with each other, and the teacher steps aside and lets the argument run."

d. (A) Problem-solving activities may be associated with some project for another course. Students may want to find answers to such questions as the following:

(i) Do the British and the Americans feel the same way about the role of NATO?
(ii) How exactly is Southern fried chicken, *or* Yorkshire pudding prepared?

The answer to (i) may be sought through library research, listening to speeches, interviews with British and American visitors, reading of newspapers and magazines, and finally classroom discussion of what each student has gleaned, thus interweaving (5), (8), (9), and (13). Question (ii) may require some of the same procedures, along with experimentation in the kitchen (6).

9. DISCUSSING IDEAS

(E and I) Factual details of things read, seen, or heard provide a basis for discussion. Mystery stories are useful. Cultural differences are most likely to provoke lively discussion. Since students at the (E) and (I) stages are at a disadvantage in such discussions because of the teacher's wider command of the language, the teacher must refrain from taking over and doing all the talking. At these levels, topics for discussion are normally kept to areas for which the students know some vocabulary and expressions. Otherwise, they come after a project of research into the area or students are provided with some written or recorded material from which they can acquire the necessary English terms for use in the discussion.

(A) Students decide on controversial subjects they wish to discuss, prepare their points for discussion, but make their remarks without a written script; two groups prepare the same topic and discuss it with each other while students from other groups ask questions; one student takes a viewpoint and tries to convince other students that this viewpoint is tenable.

Stevick's *microtexts*[11] are useful as starters. A short text in English on any subject may be selected by teacher or students. This text is distributed, shown on the overhead projector, or written on the chalkboard; students then discuss and elaborate on the details of the text and any implications of it. The text should not be more than fifty words in length, or, if delivered orally, should not take longer than thirty seconds to relate. With experience, teachers and students can draw an astonishing amount of interesting discussion from almost any text. Possible microtexts are (E) a menu, a concert program, an airline timetable, selections from letters from English-speaking correspondents, or a paragraph from a newspaper about the official activities of some leading political figure; (I) newspaper accounts of the dog that saved its master during a fire, a bank robbery, two children lost in the mountains, a recent Nobel Prize winner, a swing in fashions for dress or hair styles or selected letters from *Ann Landers, Dear Abby,* or some other heart-throb columnist; (A) accounts of recent decisions on American or British domestic or foreign policy (editorial comments from two different English-language newspapers or from an English-language newspaper and one in the student's own language may be compared); suggested changes in the Cambridge examinations; the development of alternative schools in some cities of the United States; the latest approaches to the drug problem; letters to the editor raising interesting questions.

10. PLAYING WITH LANGUAGE

Newspapers and magazines have for years published regularly all kinds of word games (crossword puzzles, acrostics and double-crostics, vocabulary expansion quizzes), books on language enjoy a perennial popularity, and magic and esoteric works continue to mesmerize devotees. From early childhood people are fascinated by language. This natural love of language can be exploited in the language class.

(E, I, A) *Scrabble* games encourage students to enlarge their vocabulary.

(E) Nonsense and counting rhymes may be learned by heart and recited for fun. Songs with repetitive refrains are popular. Students like to learn onomatopoeic expressions (animal cries, rain dripping, doors banging) and these can be used in games and classroom drama.

(I) Oral construction, in groups, of crossword and other language puzzles can stimulate much discussion in the language, particularly when the construction becomes complicated in the final stages. *Charades* provide amusing themes for classroom dramatization. Students take a two-syllable word (*highway*) and for each syllable they improvise a short episode which brings in the word it represents (*high/way*). They then act out an episode which brings in the complete word (*highway*) and students guess which word it is. (Other possibilities are: *bay/bee/baby*; two segments: *under/take/undertake*; *enter/prize/enterprise*; compounds: *shop/lift/ shoplift*; or three or more syllables: *lamb/men/table/lamentable*.

(A) Students may seek out and discuss word origins, word histories, and borrowings. They may look for and discuss words which have developed different meanings in British and American English (e.g., *biscuits*, *pavement*) and different words which are used in these varieties of English to describe the same thing (e.g., *hood/bonnet*; *trunk/boot*; *line/queue*). They may become interested in tracking down words from their own language which have been incorporated into English and finding out when these were first borrowed (e.g., *orange* from Arabic, *pajamas* from Hindi, *Sabbath* from Hebrew, *curfew* from French, *peccadillo* from Spanish).[12] They may also search their own language for words borrowed from English and list these according to historical periods and special fields of knowledge or areas of technical activity.

At this level too, students may begin to take an interest in specific variants of the English language (e.g., the accent and common expressions of dialects in different regions of the United States, in Britain, Canada, Australia, and New Zealand, as well as Jamaican and Indian English.)

11. ACTING OUT SOCIAL ROLES

Psychologists point out that we are constantly taking on different roles and the style of language which goes with them.

Dramatic improvisation is an excellent technique for eliciting autonomous interaction. Situations and participating characters are suggested in a very sketchy fashion. Students are allowed a short time to plan what they will do before they enact the scene, improvising the dialogue as they proceed. Several groups or pairs may improvise the same situation with very different results. Even inhibited students feel free to express themselves when they are being someone else in a recreational activity.

(E) Students act out roles in which they can use expressions learned in (1).

(I and A) Situations are proposed which represent various social settings with characters of different occupations, relationships, and levels of authority.

a. The job interview with a timid (or over-confident) applicant.

b. The overbearing bureaucrat and the applicant for a visa extension.

c. The landlady trying to find out all about the reticent new tenant on the fourth floor.

d. The hippie son asking his very proper father for money.

e. The cocktail party at the Embassy: the vapid female talking about nothing at great length or echoing what other people say (*You know this is the very first time I've ever been invited to the Embassy./Really? You're here for the very first time?*); the boastful type (*I'm X, you know, the author of all the best sellers. Of course you've read my great mystery thriller: Deep in the Heart of Texas?*); the parallel monologue (A: *My daughter was married this morning.* B: *Really? I have three sons.* A: *She married a telecommunications engineer.* B: *Oh, yes. My oldest son is studying medicine*); the ignoramus talking to the Nobel Prize winner . . .

f. Situations based on proverbs.

g. Well-known political figures or characters in films or television programs may be mimicked in familiar situations.

12. ENTERTAINING OTHERS

Students should be given the opportunity to use their natural talents for singing, making music, or acting as host for a radio call-in program or a television talk show. Groups of students may prepare and present radio or television commercials. (These may involve more or less talking interspersed with mime, and are, therefore, very suitable for the early stages of a course.) A complete radio or television program with news, situation comedy, commercials, weather report, interview, give-away show, sports, song and dance routine, and national anthem may be prepared for presentation to another class, for a Fourth of July or Queen's Birthday celebration, for an Open Day, or for a school assembly.

13. DISPLAYING ONE'S ACHIEVEMENTS

(E, I, and A) Students may tell the group about what they did in (3), (4), (5), (6), or (8), or present and explain special projects, which will often be interdisciplinary, e.g., the study of an aspect of art, music, architecture, or history. (A) As a climax to (9), groups may present their different viewpoints in a full-scale debate.

Some kind of public presentation can become a regular culminating activity to draw together many individualized interaction projects.

14. SHARING LEISURE ACTIVITIES

Students should have the opportunity to learn, and become proficient in, the games and diversions of English-speaking people. They should be able to participate in verbal competitions. Where there are special activities traditionally associated with festivals or national holidays, students should be able to engage in them at the appropriate time: decorating the Christmas tree and singing Christmas carols, celebrating Guy Fawkes Day or Hogmanay, rolling eggs at Easter, dressing up for trick-or-treat at Halloween, preparing a Thanksgiving dinner.

Much autonomous interaction takes place at the English-language students' club or at class excursions and picnics. Visits are arranged to see exhibitions of American or British paintings, to eat at restaurants which serve English or American specialties, to see films in English (without subtitles) or to attend performances by visiting theatrical companies. Groups within a class may take turns preparing typical meals and inviting the others. In a foreign-language situation, schools may invite English-speaking exchange students. English-speaking residents of the district or visitors passing through should be invited to talk with classes on a formal or informal basis. Students should undertake to show their town or their school to English-speaking visitors or tourists on a regular basis.

At the advanced level students often opt for *purely oral courses* to perfect their ability to communicate. For these courses, activities such as those described above which plunge students into normal uses of language are essential.

✱ Take three of the categories listed and for each try to think of three more activities which would lead to these particular normal uses of language. If you are studying this book in a class group, have a brain-storming session to see what you can add to the suggestions given above.

Situations of utterance[13]

Frequently, programs are designed to prepare students to interact in specific professional or vocational settings. Research is being conducted, for instance, into the type of language used between doctors and patients, factory supervisors and operatives, social workers and persons in need of their assistance. Howatt points out that designing a course which prepares students to interact in specific roles in real-life situations requires that the course designer "first discover what activities the job entails and what part is played in these activities by language of different kinds. He must decide how much emphasis is to be placed on talking and how much on reading or writing. He must find out what topics come up often enough to be worth discussing in class and he must also bear in mind the kind of people the pupil will eventually have to deal with."[14]

The Council for Cultural Co-operation of the Council of Europe (CCC) has published "an analytical classification of the categories of adult needing to learn foreign languages" which is intended "to provide a starting-point for a description of linguistic situations" in which persons in these occupations will have to use English.[15]

The CCC classification breaks down the actual activities in which persons of specific occupations will need to employ, to varying degrees of proficiency, the skills of understanding, speaking, reading, and writing a foreign language. Actors, musicians, and dancers, for instance, will need, among other things, to be able to understand and give stage directions and instructions; office supervisors will need to be able to read written documents in the fields with which they are associated, to draft reports, and to write letters; guards, conductors, air hostesses, and stewards will be required to understand a language of everyday communication in order to give information and attend to the comfort and security of passengers; while waiters and bar personnel will be required to understand and speak, not only a language of everyday communication, but a quite specialized language as well.[16]

A breakdown of this type is equally applicable to adolescent students who have a specific career goal in mind. Persons in any occupational category will operate more efficiently if they have a greater command of the language. However, in many programs in adult basic education or in connection with vocational training they may have to settle for less. Analyses like these can be very helpful in designing activities and simulated situations which focus on the needs of the students. Students can then extemporize and practice using what they know in a realistic and purposeful way.

As used by the contributing experts of the Council for Cultural Co-operation of the Council of Europe, "situation of utterance" is not a simple concept like acting out the ordering of a meal in a restaurant or the buying of a ticket at an airport.[17] It includes "the sum of those extra-linguistic elements that are present in the minds of speakers or in external physical reality at the moment of communication . . . [which] play a part in determining the form or the function of the linguistic elements"[18] and also the particular spatio-temporal situation in which speaker and hearer are interacting[19] in order to produce some result, whether purely psychological or concrete. The use of situations of utterance is intended to make language learning "a process of acquiring a new aid to action."[20] In this way, they have great potential for motivating students to engage in autonomous interaction.[21]

Improvement, not perfection
CORRECTION OF ERRORS IN AUTONOMOUS INTERACTION

It is during intensive practice exercises, or construction practice, that immediate corrections may be made. Even then, we should not jump in before our students have had time to think and often to correct themselves. Our task is to make our students conscious of possible errors and to familiarize them to such a degree with acceptable, rule-governed sequences that they are able to monitor their own production and work toward its improvement in spontaneous interaction. In interaction practice we are trying to develop an attitude of innovation and experimentation with the new language. Nothing dampens enthusiasm and effort more than constant correction when students are trying to express their ideas within the limitations of their newly acquired knowledge of the language. Teachers who are non-native speakers of the language know that they are very often fully conscious of a mistake they have just made, even mortified by it, but unable to take it back. We should be happy when our students have reached the same level of awareness of acceptable usage, since it means they are becoming autonomous learners as well as autonomous speakers.

The best approach during interaction activities is for the instructor silently to note consistent, systematic errors (not slips of the tongue and occasional lapses in areas where the students usually acquit themselves well). These errors will then be discussed with the students individually at a time when the instructor is helping them evaluate their success in interaction, with particular attention to the types of errors which hinder communication. Teachers will then use their knowledge of the areas of weakness of a number of students as a basis for special emphases in instruction and in review. In this way, we help students focus on what are problem areas for them as they learn from their mistakes. Steady improvement will come only from individual motivation and purpose: that personal desire to perfect one's communicative effectiveness which is stimulated by genuine interest in what one is doing.

WHAT LEVEL OF CORRECT SPEECH CAN WE EXPECT FROM OUR STUDENTS?

The first question we must ask ourselves is: How do native speakers frame their utterances when they are thinking only of expressing their meaning?

C34 (Caller talking to a radio disk jockey on a call-in program about increases in the fees for cable television).

> CALLER: Of course/ of course/ that's what I'm/ I'm sayin'/ it was/ a big rip-off/ they're not giving you what they/ they they totally/ told you/ what they were going to give you/ really/ . . . I feel bad for people who are/ elderly people

who/ that's their only enjoy/ you know enjoyment/ and I feel that/ even two dollars a month/ I mean let's face it/

DISK JOCKEY: Well, here's the thing you know uh/ the cable antenna/ brings you uh/ a very clear and good/ signal as you know/ uh/ I would say this/ it really does get down to this/ if a person feels that they cannot/ uh/ afford to have this kind of service/ they have uh/ alternatives/ I mean you can/ you can get a different kind of a hookup that's all/

CALLER: Right/ you can have it taken out/ right/ but I mean/ you know it sounded so great when they came in and everything/ and/ uh/ I'm sure people in Methuen Andover and North Andover's getting just as good a reception as anything. . . .[22]

Commentary

This passage, transcribed from a taped conversation, shows clearly how we feel our way toward the most effective framework for expressing our meaning, leaning heavily on hesitation and transition expressions (*uh, really, you know, I mean, let's face it* . . .) and repetitions (*I would say this, it really does get down to this* . . .); searching around for the best way to present our meaning (*they're not giving you what they/ they totally/ told you/ what they were going to give you*); changing our minds in midstream about what we want to express, so that we have to switch from one type of structure to another (*that's what I'm/ I'm saying it was a big rip-off*); leaving sentences unfinished (*I feel that/ even two dollars a month/ I mean let's face it*); and neglecting number agreement as we develop our thought (*if a person feels that they cannot afford* . . .). Note that we do not make basic errors in morphology or word order. (In *I feel bad for people who are/ elderly people who/ that's their only enjoyment* the switches and changes indicate hesitancy in formulating a sentence which will express the speaker's precise meaning; within the segments the syntax is perfectly normal.) The repetitions also help our listeners to process each segment at the speed of utterance by providing redundancy to reinforce the meaning they are extracting.

It is clear that we cannot expect our students always to speak English in well-formed sentences in the heat of personal expression, when they do not do so in their native language. We must also expect students to hesitate, restructure sentences, and make sudden changes of lexical choice which may temporarily affect agreements of person and number in the immediate vicinity. These imperfections are important only if they affect comprehensibility.

THE SI LINE

Stevick draws to our attention an interesting fact about simultaneous interpreters. "These remarkable individuals," he observes, "perceive both lexical meaning and grammatical form, and come out with their own reformulations in the other language after only a few seconds delay. Even as they speak, they are taking in new data for interpretation . . . But if they are to continue, there is a line that they dare not cross: they must not become personally involved in what they are saying. Once the content of the message begins to make a difference to them, they lose the power of speaking and listening at the same time."[23] Stevick calls this boundary the SI (simultaneous interpretation) line: "Above it," he says, "lie grammatical form and dictionary meaning; below it lies everything that matters to speaker and listener."[24]

In view of this psychological phenomenon we have no reason to be surprised that students engaging in genuine interaction make many slips which we know they would not make in structured activities. Correcting them immediately and frequently will force students, for self-protection, to keep their attention above the SI line and will result in speech which is more carefully correct but which never goes beyond the banal and the obvious. This is surely not our goal.

INDIVIDUAL DIFFERENCES

Because of the personal nature of autonomous interaction, the participation of particular students will naturally be consistent with their personalities. Some people are temperamentally incapable of interacting by means of a babble of words; to expect them to do so is to force them back into pseudo-communication and into mouthing memorized phrases. The quality of the interaction will be judged by other criteria: ability to receive and express meaning, to understand and convey intentions, to perform acceptably in all kinds of situations in relations with others. The means by which the student attains these desirable goals will be a function of personal learning strategies. We can allow these full play through the provision of a wide choice of activity options, but we cannot determine for others what they shall be.

THE INDIVIDUAL TEACHER

Some non-native teachers feel inadequate to the demands of autonomous interaction activities because of insufficiencies of training or a long period of time away from the teaching of the language. Just like their students, such teachers grow in skill and confidence as they participate. In a non-authoritarian approach teachers accept and acknowledge their weaknesses, drawing as a compensation on their ability to stimulate interesting activities and involve others. Their students then accept the teacher as a member of a group which is learning together.[25] From year to year the teacher's control of the language improves, especially if tapes of authentic native speech are used regularly to supplement the teaching, and every opportunity is taken to listen to English on the radio, or on the sound tracks of films, and to speak it in contacts with colleagues in the school, at professional meetings, and *especially in the classroom*. Teachers of English who are anxious to improve their English also read for pleasure modern books and plays in English to keep themselves in contact with the contemporary spoken and written forms of the language. What they do not know, they encourage their students to find out, or, better still, together with their students they find it out cooperatively. Teachers of English should also make every effort to join in professional visits to English-speaking areas, or to go on their own. If finances are the problem here, they organize groups of students for such a visit and cover their own expenses by accompanying the group as guide and informant. Many a poorly prepared teacher has overcome such inadequacies. The essential is the determination to do so.

3
Listening

Essential to all interaction is the ability to understand what others are saying. Even in the native language many people are poor listeners, whether through weak powers of concentration, egocentrism, or short auditory memory. Yet it has been estimated that of the time adults spend in communication activities 45 per cent is devoted to listening, only 30 per cent to speaking, 16 per cent to reading, and a mere 9 per cent to writing (and these data are from a pre-television, pre-talking-picture, pre-dictaphone era).[1] Apart from communicative interaction, much of the enjoyment in second- or foreign-language use comes from listening activities—watching films and plays or listening to radio broadcasts, songs, or talks by native speakers. Even in class students learn a great deal from listening to their teacher, to tapes or records, or to each other.

It is noteworthy that some students who do not excel in other areas of foreign-language use achieve a very high level of success in understanding spoken messages. It has been suggested by some researchers that there is a special listening comprehension factor,[2] but this has not yet been fully characterized. Even in life situations many people become skilled, in their own or another language, in understanding registers, dialectal variations, and complexities of structure which they cannot produce in their own speech. Troike[3] has called this a difference between receptive and productive competence. Students with special skill in listening comprehension should be encouraged and given opportunities to go beyond others in this area which is especially suitable for individualized work. They should also be rewarded in final grading with full consideration for this skill in which they excel.

Listening is a complex operation integrating the distinct components of perception and linguistic knowledge in ways which are at present poorly understood.[4] Psychologists have tried to explain this phenomenon from several viewpoints, each of which can give us some clues to our students' problems in listening to a foreign language and suggest ways of structuring effective materials for practice and enjoyment.

The schema C1 brings out the cognitive nature of listening which involves *perception* based on *internalized knowledge* of the rules of the language. Students have to learn to abstract from a stream of sound units which machines cannot as yet be programmed to identify, to assign these to categories, and to attribute to them functions in relation to other units, so that an intelligible message may be constructed from what they are hearing. While they are doing this, they are anticipating the import of the message, holding segments already identified in their immediate memory and readjusting their interpretation of earlier segments in accordance with the final message *as they understand it.*

In this context the phrase "as they understand it" is basic because listening is not a passive but an *active process of constructing a message* from a stream of sound with what one knows of the phonological, semantic, and syntactic potentialities of the language. Even in our own language we often "hear" what was never said. This becomes an even more frequent occurrence in a language we are still learning. It is this active process of message construction which has been labeled *reception* (or comprehension of the message) in C1. The two terms *perception* and *reception* represent the two levels[5] of practice required to improve systematically the student's skill in interpreting messages intended by speakers.

Models of listening processes

Some linguists[6] maintain that knowledge of the same system of grammatical rules of a language is basic to both listening and speaking. Some psychologists, on the other hand, believe the rules we apply are different and that we employ perceptual strategies[7] for surface scanning of what we are hearing, stopping to penetrate to underlying relations only to resolve ambiguities or untangle complexities. Despite their theoretical divergence, interesting insights can be derived from various linguistic and psychological schools of thought, each of which emphasizes a different facet of the complicated processes of listening and receiving messages.

In this section, we will discuss in detail (A) the role of uncertainty and redundancy in Cherry's theory of communication, (B) Neisser's active processing of a message, and (C) Bever's strategies of perceptual segmentation (with which we will link Schlesinger's semantic-syntactic decoding).

A. The uncertainties of a spoken message

Cherry[8] says, "Communication proceeds in the face of a number of uncertainties and has the character of . . . numerous inductive inferences being carried out concurrently."

He lists these uncertainties as:

1. Uncertainties of speech sounds, or acoustic patterning. Accents, tones, loudness may be varied; speakers may shout, sing, whisper, or talk with their mouths full.

2. Uncertainties of language and syntax. Sentence constructions differ; conversational language may be bound by few rules of syntax. Vocabularies vary; words have many near-synonyms, popular usages, special usages, et cetera.

3. Environmental uncertainties. Conversations are disturbed by street noises, by telephone bells, and background chatter.

4. Recognition uncertainties. Recognition depends upon the peculiar past experiences of the listener, upon his familiarity with the speaker's speech habits, knowledge of language, subject matter, et cetera.

Here we have in a nutshell many of the problems our students face in the comprehension of speech, each of these being compounded where a language other than our native language is involved. "Yet," Cherry continues, "speech communication works. It is so structured as to possess redundancy at a variety of levels, to assist in overcoming these uncertainties."[9] In C2 we examined some of the redundancies of spoken, as opposed to written, English. It is time now to examine a specimen of completely unedited, authentic speech, uttered in a natural situation by a person who had no idea that what she said would ever serve any pedagogical purpose. (This passage will reinforce the impressions gained from C34.)

EDITED AND UNEDITED LISTENING COMPREHENSION MATERIALS

In preparing materials and activities for listening comprehension we do not give enough consideration to the differences between edited, or artificially constructed, messages and an authentic output of speech in natural interaction. As a result of such editing we often make the listening comprehension materials we record, or present to the students orally in class, much more difficult to comprehend than we realize. The difference is like that between listening to a prepared and polished scholarly paper read verbatim and the free interchange of unprepared discussion which follows the paper and usually makes the speaker's ideas seem much clearer.

C35-37

The following edited and unedited discussions of the same subject will illustrate this difference. The unedited version is taken from a taped discussion with a friend of one of the authors.

The speaker is discussing the problems faced by immigrants, who have had traumatic experiences in their earlier lives, when they settle in a new country.

C35   Edited content of the remarks of the taped speaker:[10]

> You realize how hard it is for them to come into a new country. One lady I worked for had missed out on the gas chambers four times. She's really wonderful but she's still very insecure. She locks the back door all the time. She finds it very hard to believe nothing's going to happen to her in Australia. It's a very interesting story to listen to. These people are very wary of you for about six months and they don't trust anybody. It's very hard for me to understand why they can't forget the past when I haven't gone through it myself. I suppose you shouldn't judge people.

C36   The following passage, transcribed from the original tape, shows how the same ideas were expressed in authentic interaction. Slashes indicate the position of the pauses in delivery. No attempt has been made to insert punctuation, which is a convention of written language.

> You really / you realize / uh you know how hard it is / for them to come into a country / uh / where they've come from you know I worked for one lady / and um / four times she'd missed out on the uh gas chambers / four times / and you know / she's she she really is / really wonderful / but she's still very / insecure you can tell / she locks the back door all the time / you know she finds it very very hard / to to believe that nothing's going to happen to her in Australia / but it's a her very interesting story to listen to / the people you know / after they / they're they're very wa- you know wary of you / for about six months / and they don't trust anybody / but gee uh it's / very very hard to / um / understand / uh you know / wh- why they can't um / sort of / forget the past / I can I can realize how hard it is for them / but I just sort of you know / I always I suppose if I'd gone through it myself I would uh / it's hard to judge / you shouldn't / you know judge people I suppose

C37   If we set C36 and C35 out in parallel columns we see much more strikingly how much verbal redundancy has been eliminated even in such a col-

loquially expressed version as C35. For C36 a separate line has been
allotted to each breath group.

C36	C35
You really	
you realize	You realize
uh you know how hard it is	how hard it is
for them to come into a country	for them to come into a new
uh	country.
where they've come from you	
know I worked for one lady	One lady I worked for
and um	
four times she'd missed out on	had missed out on the
the uh gas chambers	gas chambers four times.
four times	
and you know	
she's she she really is	She's
really wonderful	really wonderful
but she's still very	but she's still very
insecure you can tell	insecure.
she locks the back door all the time	She locks the back door all the time.
you know she finds it very very	She finds it very hard
hard	
to to believe that nothing's going	to believe nothing's going to hap-
to happen to her in Australia	pen to her in Australia.
but it's a her very interesting story	It's a very interesting story to listen
to listen to	to.
the people you know	These people
after they	
they're they're very wa- you know	are very wary of you
wary of you	
for about six months	for about six months
and they don't trust anybody	and they don't trust anybody.
but gee uh it's	It's
very very hard to	very hard
um	
understand	for me to understand
uh you know	
wh- why they can't um	why they can't
sort of	

forget the past	forget the past
I can I can realize how hard it is for them	
but I just sort of you know	
I always I suppose if I'd gone through it myself I would uh	when I haven't gone through it myself.
it's hard to judge	
you shouldn't	
you know judge people I suppose	I suppose you shouldn't judge people.

Commentary

Although the edited version C35 retains the conversational flavor of C36, C35 eliminates repetitious segments which merely elaborate the thought content in minor ways while the speaker is seeking the most effective way to express her idea (*I can realize how hard it is for them, I suppose if I'd gone through it myself, it's hard to judge*); conjunctions or prepositions indicating a direction of sentence structure which is not followed through (*after they / they're very wary*); hesitation expressions (*sort of, um, uh*), conversational tags and formulas (*you know*), and false starts (*I just sort of you know / I always I suppose if I'd gone through it myself*). It also regularizes syntax which does not observe the accepted restraints (*it's a her very interesting story to listen to*). Thus in a well-meaning attempt at improving the "disorderly" output of C36, the editor has provided in C35 a version which would demand much more concentrated effort in listening than the authentic speech of C36. *As with speaking, we may well be demanding more of our foreign-language listeners in the exercises we present than is demanded in native-language listening.*

Authentic materials like these are easy to obtain where English-language radio programs can be recorded. Unfortunately, classroom teachers who are in a foreign-language situation often have problems of poor reception for such stations. The following suggestions may help in such cases:

1. When visiting English speakers and English-speaking exchange students are temporarily at hand, teachers should seize the opportunity to tape-record general conversation with the visitors. Suitable excerpts from the tapes should then be shared among groups of schools.

2. Cultural services of the appropriate embassies and consulates should be bombarded with requests for tapes of radio discussions, informal chats,

and film soundtracks, until an awareness is created that these are the types of materials our students need.

3. Exchanges of tapes should be encouraged between classes in local schools and classes of a similar age in schools in English-speaking countries. (These are sometimes called *twinned classes*.) The classes in both countries should be encouraged to send each other unedited tapes—not of prepared talks, but of free discussion in English among members of the class on aspects of their daily lives and their likes and dislikes. To obtain such authentically expressed tapes requires a change of attitude on the part of teachers who often expect a class exchange tape to be a perfectly orchestrated performance. The native English-speaking classes should be encouraged to ask questions of their English-learning friends about those sections of the tapes which they did not understand. In this way the learners of English will not only gain much pleasure and information from the tapes, but will also become more conscious of the way inaccurate production hinders comprehension.

4. Individual students should be encouraged to begin tape exchanges with correspondents in English-speaking countries, along the lines of the more conventional letter exchanges.

Listening to authentic tapes recorded by native speakers who are not teachers provides one of the best opportunities for students to have real contact with the life and thought of English-speaking people, whether from the United Kingdom, the United States, Australia, Canada, New Zealand, or other English-speaking areas. Through these tapes, learners of English encounter the normal and the natural, even the trivial, much more than in the reading of newspapers, magazines, novels, plays, and short stories, all of which tend to choose as subjects the exceptional, the sensational, the idealized, or the eccentric in order to arouse and maintain interest.

RECOGNITION UNCERTAINTIES

Listeners construct a message from what they are hearing according to certain expectations[11] based on:

—what they know of the language, not only syntax and lexicon, but usage in these areas for different styles of language (see C5);
—their familiarity with the subject under discussion;
—the knowledge of the real world that they share with the speaker (through which the latter can assume certain things which have not been expressed);
—their acquaintance with or assumptions about the personal attitudes and interests of the speaker;
—their observation and interpretation of the circumstances of the utterance, including what has preceded it;
—their understanding of the cultural context in which it occurs;

—their reading of paralinguistic cues (speed of speech, length of pauses, loudness, pitch, facial expressions), gestures, and other body language which differ from culture to culture.[12]

Listeners impose a syntactic structure on what they are hearing and this arouses further expectations about what is to come. Sometimes a succeeding segment proves to be incongruous with their syntactic expectations and this forces them to reconsider and project a different syntactic structure, in other words, to resolve the ambiguity.

For these reasons, ability to receive messages aurally becomes more refined as knowledge of the potentialities of the grammatical system increases.

C38   1. *Angela likes music better than her dog.*

Commentary

a. The hearer, anticipating the usual English order of subject-verb-object in the final elliptical segment of the sentence, may process this information as:

Angela likes music,
her dog likes music,
but Angela likes music more than her dog likes music.

The hearer, knowing something about the behavior of dogs, is not surprised, then, when the speaker goes on to say:

In fact, the poor thing dashes off to the back of the kitchen and howls as soon as she starts up the record-player.

b. If, instead of this, the speaker adds something like:

In fact, the poor thing is always wandering around the building looking for attention,

the hearer who processed the sentence as in a. has to pause for a moment and readjust the processing. Again, since he knows something about the behavior of dogs, he readjusts his interpretation of the syntactic structure of what he heard to provide the information:

Angela likes music
Angela likes her dog,
but Angela likes music more than she likes her dog.

c. The hearer may not need to hear a further utterance in order to assign the appropriate structure to this sentence. Context will supply all the clues that are necessary if he is in a situation where he can observe the behavior of Angela and her dog.

2. *All hippies don't vote.*

This colloquial sentence is truly ambiguous out of context because either of the possible interpretations is plausible:

a. All members of the class we call "hippies" do not vote (that is, no hippie votes);

b. Not all members of the class we call "hippies" vote (that is, some hippies vote but not all hippies vote).

In these cases, the listener must hold the utterance in immediate memory while comparing it with the context or the circumstances of the utterance before assigning it a disambiguating structure.

* Discuss the two possible syntactic structures of the following:

C39   Visiting professors can be an embarrassment.
The cat feels cold.
He published an English translation of a Japanese poem that is hard to understand.

Ignorance of the cultural context can be an impediment

C40   (A) Two students, Dale and Dwight, are in the supermarket.

DALE: Look at the price of those steaks, will you! They just go up and up!
DWIGHT: It's all the grain going out of the country that does it.
DALE: We should keep our grain for our own producers, if you ask me! We'll all be vegetarians soon!
DWIGHT: Well, don't blame me! I'm from Massachusetts!

Commentary

A student could understand every word of this interchange and yet miss the intensity of feeling and emotional overtones which it conveys to a contemporary American.

1. *The subject matter.* Young Americans have grown up to expect an abundance of excellent steaks at very reasonable prices. Not only is broiled steak a favorite dish all the year around, but it is considered normal fare

for summer barbecues. Its price is then a matter of considerable concern to young people with limited incomes.

2. *The shared knowledge* of the two participants. When Richard Nixon was President he concluded the first deals to sell U.S. grain to the Soviet Union. This caused a shortage of grain on the American market and raised prices for the grain which remained. Large sections of the beef cattle industry normally fatten their steers on grain. During this period, some farmers deliberately destroyed beef cattle as a protest, maintaining that they could not afford to raise them for the market. Others raised fewer cattle for beef. The price of steak rose steadily. As a result, many students could not afford the steaks to which they were accustomed. Since even hamburger (made from lower quality beef) rose in price, many students found themselves forced to change their eating habits and eat much less meat. Dwight's last remark refers to the fact that Massachusetts was the only state in the Union whose delegates did not vote for Richard Nixon for the second term of his presidency. His remark is an adaptation of a bumper sticker which was popular among residents of Massachusetts during the tense Watergate period when Richard Nixon was forced to resign from the presidency: "Don't blame us! We're from Massachusetts."

3. *Language clues. Will you!* and *if you ask me!* are expressions of exasperation. *Don't blame me*, even as a quotation, would be an inappropriate reaction in such an exchange unless Dale's voice had been conveying strong feeling. In spoken form, tone of voice would convey some of this significance. If the person speaking were visible (on film, for instance) facial expression and body movements would help in the interpretation of this emotional element.

C41 (A) *News Report: CBS*
The Government in Guatemala ordered a quick burial of all those killed in yesterday's disastrous earthquake. The Red Cross says there may be as many as 3,000 dead, although no one knows for sure, and that 15 out of every 100 bodies are not being identified. Some 3,000 people are reported to have been injured in the quake. The quake shook most of Guatemala, most of Central America, and parts of Mexico. The most destruction is in the northwest section where authorities now estimate 800 died. The homeless are dependent on the government for food. Foodlines are set up every few blocks. While there is fresh water in three-fourths of the capital, in the northwest section the police are patrolling the supply and authorities, fearing an epidemic, ordered a mass burial for the last of the earthquake victims in the capital.[13]

Commentary

1. This news report is in a mixture of *formal* and *consultative* styles. Since the announcer wishes his listeners to feel they are being addressed he intersperses among more formal announcements (e.g., *The Government in Guatemala ordered . . .*; *some 3,000 people are reported to have been injured*) less formal utterances like *no one knows for sure.*

2. News broadcasts like this are more difficult to follow linguistically than the natural, informal speech of C36, because many of the rephrasings which provide redundancy of content have been eliminated and a more specialized vocabulary is employed (e.g., *authorities now estimate, foodlines are set up, police are patrolling the supply*). On the other hand, they are delivered in a more deliberate tone, with clearer enunciation, and distinct pauses at major syntactic boundaries. Notice in this newscast how key words are repeated in close juxtaposition in case the listener has not heard a word clearly (e.g., *yesterday's disastrous earthquake . . . in the quake. The quake; for food. Foodlines*), and the major news item in the first sentence is repeated in the last sentence.

3. Radio commentaries are often easier to follow than newscasts because they discuss a single subject for some time, whereas a complete newscast moves rapidly from one subject to another.

4. *Place names and personal names* given orally can hinder recognition considerably (see also C42). Students need instruction in recognizing names of people who are frequently in the news. (Names like Young, Callaghan, and Mao Tse Tung are pronounced in other languages quite differently from their accepted pronunciation in English.) If newscasts are made available within the week in which they were broadcast, familiarity with recent events of international significance will provide conceptual background for recognition of many of the names of people and places.

World geography lessons with English wall maps and guessing games with names of famous persons in the accepted English oral form are helpful as associated activities when newscasts are being used as listening comprehension material. The students and the teacher should also keep a file of clippings from English-language newspapers and magazines. These give background information, with the specialized vocabulary needed, for current preoccupations in the international sphere, as well as in English-speaking countries.

5. The difficulties faced by the students on first hearing a newscast can be diminished by encouraging them to relisten to the recording of the broadcast until they have comprehended the gist of the discussion.

Equally important for the comprehension of radio broadcasts is *recognition of numbers and dates.*

C42 (A) *News Report: CBS*

There's been another disastrous nursing home fire in the Chicago area—the second in a week. Smoke and flames from a fourth floor room of the 9-story Cermak House in suburban Cicero killed 6 persons. 26 were hospitalized. Most of the 475 patients, though, didn't have to be evacuated because of sophisticated equipment that stopped the fire from spreading by automatically closing doors. An electrical malfunction is suspected as the cause of that fire. In New York City, a night-time apartment house fire on Manhattan's West Side took 10 lives; 7 were children. 10 other persons were hospitalized.[14]

Rapid recognition of numbers and dates is indispensable to modern communication. One has only to think of common situations like asking the operator for telephone numbers, requesting airline and train schedules, changing travel plans, and understanding prices, rates for service, final accounts, bank balances, exchange rates, current dates, dates of birth, times for performances, or document numbers. With the multiplication of computerized services, more and longer numbers are becoming a part of everyday life, the latter often involving also rapid recognition of the *names of letters of the alphabet.*

Practice in attentive listening to numbers is provided in games like Bingo, in dictation of series of numbers of increasing complexity, and in competitions where events must be selected from lists of multiple-choice items to correspond with dates given orally. The alphabet should be learned early and students should become adept at recognizing the oral spelling of new words and names letter by letter. This skill can be very useful to foreigners in communication situations where they are being introduced to people with names which are unfamiliar to them.

PRACTICAL APPLICATIONS

1. Activities to *prepare the learner conceptually* for the type of content in a listening exercise are valuable in helping students develop expectations and project possible meanings.

2. Listening comprehension materials should preferably be well *integrated thematically* with the rest of the learning program; otherwise, discussions of a related subject may be necessary to stimulate the student's thinking. For example, sharing ideas on the way one feels when surrounded by strangers in a strange place would prepare the students for listening to C36; a prior discussion of the work of national and international relief

agencies would make C41 more comprehensible; discussion of some aspects of the current American educational scene makes comprehensible a conversation among mothers who are anxious about their children's safety in school; at a more elementary level, practice in telling the time in English prepares for a tape where several prospective travelers are making enquiries at an airline counter.

3. Students may be encouraged to project, to think ahead to reasonable completions, by games which test their alertness in detecting tricks in the completion of sentences.

Keeping Tabs on the Speaker is a team game which forces the student to think of the meaningful use of learned phrases or facts by dislodging them from their familiar settings. It may be given orally or on tape.

At the elementary stage, simple narratives may capitalize on common errors in meaning which students are making in everyday phrases they have learned in dialogues or classroom conversation. (For instance, elementary students often confuse *How are you?* and *How old are you?* or *Where do you live?* and *When do you leave?*) Groups of students can prepare these narratives to try out on other groups. The team preparing the narrative gets points for each item missed by the opposing team.

One, or two, narrators read the prepared narrative expressively, not pausing or indicating in any other way where there are anomalies. When students interrupt to point out an anomaly and are able to give an appropriate replacement, their team scores a point.

C43 (E) With anomalies italicized:

That morning, I went out alone. My brother *who was with me* asked me:
"By the way, *Miss*, how old are you?"
"*Very well*, thank you, I said. "What time is it?"
"*It looks like Newport*," I replied.

Commentary

If each utterance begins, as in the last two utterances, with an inappropriate segment, the position of the error becomes predictable. Students preparing narratives should be alerted to avoid clues such as positional regularity, alternation of correct/incorrect, and so on.

(I) Attention to detail to overcome the lulling effects of expectation can also be encouraged in listening to factual material. In C44 below, some of the facts will be known to the students from a lesson in geography; the effect of this lesson will be to create expectations which may make it difficult for them to "hear" some of the discrepancies. Once again a point is awarded to the team of the student who detects a fantastic or incorrect fact and can supply a suitable replacement for the offending segment.

C44 (I)

Statements read	Replacements
Liverpool is a very busy seaport *about seventeen miles* from London.	*about a hundred and seventy miles or a long way*
Few ships come into the port of Liverpool.	*Many or a lot of*
Every day many *sheep* sail out of this great port.	*ships*
They leave the *decks* of Liverpool for all parts of the *sea*.	*docks world*

Commentary

The narrator must be careful not to accentuate slightly the incorrect word or look as though a response is expected at a certain point. Because of the phonetic similarity in some cases (*sheep/ship*), and the fact that other words belong to the same semantic field (*many/few*), students' expectations will often lead them to think they have heard something which makes sense in the context.

B. The active process of constructing a message: stages of perception[15]

1. PERCEIVING A SYSTEMATIC MESSAGE

In listening comprehension *we first learn to perceive that there is a systematic message rather than accidental noise in a continuous stream of sound.* We learn to recognize a characteristic rise and fall of the voice, varying pitch levels, recurrences of certain sound sequences which may seem somewhat like those of our own language, yet strangely different. We may then be able to tell that we are listening to a specific language even though as yet we do not understand it. At this stage, we must make an elementary segmentation of what we hear in order to retain it in our memory. Even with gibberish or a completely unknown tongue, we must segment in some way in order to repeat or memorize it. Many of the amusing things little children say result from their idiosyncratic segmentation of what they do not fully understand. (This is the stage called *Identification* in the chart of activities for listening comprehension, C67).

Prolonged listening as an introduction to language study

Students are often plunged into trying to produce utterances in a new language too soon. As a result, they approximate these to the phonological system of their own language without having any feeling for the distinctiveness of the new language.

It has been suggested by some that learning a new language should begin with a prolonged period of listening to the language without attempting to produce it. Prolonged listening to a strange language, which is not associated with visuals, action, or some intellectual exercise to help in identification of meaning, can become boring and will not necessarily lead to advantageous results. Babies hear a great deal of language around them for a long time before they speak, but always associated with persons, places, objects, actions, and bodily needs so that they gradually focus on segments of it which are functional in their living space.

The *total physical response* approach encourages early attentive listening with physical action to demonstrate comprehension, but with no attempt at production.[16]

C45 In the form of the game *Simon Says* this approach has always been with us:

TEACHER OR STUDENT: Open your book
Students do not react.
TEACHER OR STUDENT: Touch your head.
Students do not react.
TEACHER OR STUDENT: Simon says: Touch your head.
Students touch their heads . . .

C46 In its more developed form, students learn to perform progressively more complicated series of actions, still without any attempt at production. This has been shown to produce a high rate of retention.[17]

Students move from simple imperatives (*write*; *stand up*) to short directions (*go to the door*; *write on the blackboard*), then to more complex directions (*go to the teacher's desk and put a book on it*), and finally to novel directions combining utterances already heard (*go over to the window, pick up the book, put the book on the teacher's desk, and sit down on the chair*).

Some practice of this type should be included in all early lessons, no matter what approach is being used.

Discriminating sounds which change meaning

1. Gattegno, it will be remembered, encourages early listening to tapes and disks of different languages, so that the students gradually come to *recognize characteristics of the language they are learning*. This is useful practice in identification. The classroom teacher can introduce this element without much difficulty by playing tapes of English songs and readings of poetry as background in the elementary classroom—in intervals before classes begin, while students are engaged on projects, over amplifiers to set the atmosphere for the beginning of a language laboratory session, or in

a listening room or a listening corner of the classroom. This strategy encourages individual students to listen for the pleasure of the sounds. Some students will pick up parts of the songs, particularly refrains, purely by imitation, as some opera singers do, thus learning to segment what they are hearing. This is pure perception, not reception of a message. Documentary films may be shown with the original English sound track, even before students can be expected to understand it, to familiarize the ear with the sound-aura of the language. After hearing a great deal of the language in this way, students will be far less inhibited about pronouncing words so that they really sound like English.

2. Various types of *aural discrimination* exercises are given in Chapter 5. Some of these exercises can be worked into aural discrimination games and competitions which involve listening practice. They should be continued at the intermediate level to keep students alert to sound distinctions which affect meaning.

C47 *Correct me*

Groups of students, or the teacher, prepare stories into which they work words which are inappropriate in the context but could be confused with the appropriate word if the listeners were not paying careful attention to sound distinctions. The student who has the best pronunciation, or the teacher, tells the story orally. A point is awarded to each student who notices an inappropriate word and is able to give the appropriate substitute with correct pronunciation.

In the sample text below, incorrect words are italicized and correct words are given in parentheses.

(I) Olive goes out one day to do her shopping. At the supermarket she looks carefully at the *prizes* (prices) on all the packets because she's a good *chopper* (shopper). She buys some bread, some meat, and then some *bins* (beans) for supper. She almost forgets that she needs a *point* (pint) of milk, and, of course, some *river* (liver) for the cat. At a display counter, *he's* (she's) given some cheese. It's a new kind, but she doesn't like the *test* (taste) of it. It's too mild. She decides to *pie* (buy) some chicken *soap* (soup) because it's a *gold* (cold) day. Her basket is now *fill* (full) so she goes to *pray* (pay) for what she has in her basket. She doesn't have to wait *wrong* (long), so very soon she's on her *why* (way) home to prepare her evening *mill* (meal).

2. IMPOSING A STRUCTURE

In the second stage of perception, we identify in what we are hearing segments with distinctive structure—segments which seem to cohere. These segments may not be distinguishable by machine because it is at this stage that *we impose a structure on what we are hearing according to our knowledge of the grammatical system of the language.* The more we know of a language the more easily we can detect meaningful segments, such as noun phrases, verb phrases, or adverbial phrases. Our experience with our own language makes us expect such structural segmentation. For this reason, we may segment incorrectly at first with a language with a very different structure. (It is interesting to note that in psychological experiments subjects rarely report hearing ungrammatical sentences, and when asked to repeat ungrammatical utterances they correct them, which indicates that they are imposing known structures in constructing a message from the sound signal.)

This early segmentation determines what we will remember of the actual sound signal. It is a process of *selection.* The identification of meaningful "chunks,"[18] or syntactic groupings, reduces the load on our memory. Just as it is easier to remember nine numbers in three groups (382 965 421), so it is easier to remember *I can see him / across the road / in his garden* as three syntactic groupings, or meaningful chunks, rather than as ten separate words, even if we are not sure of the lexical meanings of some of the words.

If we have segmented incorrectly or heard inaccurately we will retain what we think we have heard because we will have no further access to the sound signal after echoic memory has faded. (Echoic memory is estimated to last a few seconds only. It is during this interval that we can still readjust our segmentation, as discussed in C38).

Practical application

Except in specialized courses, listening comprehension is not usually practiced in isolation from other language-learning activities. Some common classroom techiques help students develop their ability to hear language in organized chunks (or to segment according to syntactic groupings).

1. The *backward buildup* technique is frequently used in the memorization of conversation-facilitation dialogues. Each utterance to be memorized is divided into syntactically coherent segments. Students learn the last segment with correct end-of-utterance intonation, then the second-last followed by the last, and so on.

C48   An utterance such as *There's a nice little restaurant down by the station* would be memorized in imitation of the model as follows:

down by the station.
a nice little restaurant down by the station.
There's a nice little restaurant down by the station.

In this way students move from a new segment to a segment they already know and this makes for more confident recitation.[19] (Note that each segment and each combination of segments in C48 could be useful on its own.)

2. *Dictation* is useful when well integrated with other learning activities. Dictation also involves listening to language segmented in meaningful chunks. Students in the early stages should be encouraged to repeat the segments to themselves before trying to write what they think they have heard. This gives the students practice in imposing a construction on the segment before they write it, thus increasing their short-term retention of the segment.

3. Oral exercises which require students to vary syntactic segments purposefully provide practice in "hearing" language in syntactically coherent chunks. (See Chapter 4: G9-G21.)

4. *Information Search*, a kind of spot dictation, gives practice in detecting syntactic cues to segmentation. In this activity, students are asked to listen to a sequence of sentences, writing down only the segments which answer certain questions with which they are supplied beforehand. The passage is given orally several times and students write down the segments which answer particular questions as they comprehend them, that is, after the first, the second, or the third hearing. This encourages attentive listening for specific segments that fulfill certain syntactic functions, e.g., who? where? what?

C49 (E) It's the first of April. It's nearly one o'clock.[20] Elizabeth is in school. She's sitting in her usual place in the third row. Her friend, Julia, is sitting in front of her. The afternoon class is about to begin. Elizabeth takes out of her pocket a little piece of paper on which she has written "Kiss me." Very gently, she pins it to the back of Julia's dress.

Questions supplied	*Segments to be written*
1. What day is it?	the first of April
2. What time is it?	nearly one o'clock
3. Where is Elizabeth?	in school
4. Where is she sitting?	in the third row
5. Where is Julia?	in front of Elizabeth
6. Has the class begun?	No, the class is about to begin
7. What does Elizabeth take out of her pocket?	a little piece of paper with "Kiss me" written on it.
8. Where does she put it?	on the back of Julia's dress

5. *All Ears.* Inexperienced students need practice in listening for certain *syntactic signals* which must be recognized without hesitation in rapid speech because their presence or absence significantly affects meaning.

Important among these are the *contracted forms of the auxiliaries* which signal time relationships and aspect. The English speaker's habit of suppressing the *release of most final consonants*, which is even more evident in mid-sentence, adds to the problems for the learner of English. Consequently, many students find it difficult in rapid speech to hear the differences between *I've seen her, I'll see her,* and *I'd see her* (and even *I'd have seen her*) and have the same difficulty with *he can* and *he can't, he must* and *he mustn't,* or *he ought to do it* and *he oughtn't to do it.*

In this game, the students are divided into two (or three) teams, A and B (or C). The students listen to a series of utterances given at normal speed only once, with the abbreviated forms and reduced vowels of familiar style. After each statement the teacher points to a student in team A who must reassert the fact in the statement in short form, in the affirmative or the negative as in the original (see C50 below). If the student does not respond within two seconds the teacher points to a student in team B, and then, without repeating the utterance, to another student in team A (or in team C) if necessary, until the appropriate answer has been elicited. The turn then goes to the second team, irrespective of who supplied the correct answer (and then to the third or back to the first). The student who was originally designated receives two points for a correct answer; a backup student receives one point.

C50 (I)

Teacher's statement	Student response
1. Elizabeth must sell it.	Yes, she must.
2. I'll see her, you know.	Yes, you will.
3. I can't swim tomorrow.	No, you can't.
4. I'd have eaten it.	Yes, you would have.
5. I've seen her, of course.	Yes, you have.
6. He'd hide it, naturally.	Yes, he would.
7. She can try it now.	Yes, she can.
8. He oughtn't to tell her.	No, he oughn't to.

A variation of this game *Today or Tomorrow?* draws attention to *signals of tense.* Students mime an action in the present tense, but clap or tap with a pencil when they hear the *'ll* of futurity (*I'll, he'll*) or the auxiliary use of *going to* (*gonna*) in the immediate future. Students making wrong reactions are progressively eliminated.

C51 (E and I)

We'll get up early today.
On Sundays, we sleep till ten.

We'll wake up and we'll look out the window.
I'm going to wash straight away.
I'll brush my hair for ten minutes.
I clean my teeth in the morning and I dress carefully.
Here come my little sisters. They're going to get washed next.
They'll stay in the bathroom for an hour. . . .

* Work out a game to train for recognition of the various intonation patterns.[21]

3. RECIRCULATING, SELECTING, RECODING FOR STORAGE

At the third stage of perception we recirculate material we are hearing through our cognitive system to relate earlier to later segments and *make the final selection* of what we will retain as the message. In this way, we follow a "line of thought." We then *recode what we have selected for storage in long-term memory.*

Rehearsal or recirculation of material perceived

1. Unfamiliar language elements which are being held in suspension and recirculated while decisions are being made as to the composition of the entire message impose a *heavy load on the short-term memory*. Sometimes the short-term memory becomes overloaded and some of these segments have to be discarded in order to leave room for the absorption of new segments. It should not surprise us, therefore, if inexperienced listeners, at an elementary or even intermediate stage, declare that they understood everything as they were listening but are unable to recall what they understood. At this stage students may be able to recognize from multiple-choice items or true-false questions details of what they heard, whereas they would not be able to give a full account of the message without this help.

2. *Many different aspects of a listening text may be retained* by students and these may not always be those elements the teacher expected. Students often need some guidance as to the facets of a message on which they should concentrate for the purpose of the exercise. This guidance in selection, which relieves the memory of some of the burden of detail, can be supplied by preliminary discussion or questions (given orally, or in writing).

3. At the elementary stage, students may be provided with questions with multiple-choice items *before* they begin listening. They should be encouraged to mark a tentative choice during the first hearing and confirm this on the second or third hearing. Teachers should remember that this method combines listening with reading. They should take care to see that the multiple-choice items supplied are short and expressed in language simple enough for the level of the students concerned. The items should not

reproduce verbatim any sections of the material for listening practice, since this makes the task merely one of recognition, not comprehension.

4. Although some people consider that providing written questions is a *mixing of modalities* which raises doubts as to whether one is testing listening comprehension only, several other facts must be kept in mind.

a. *Oral questions* cannot be absorbed during the process of listening to other material. (Psychological studies show that we filter out competing oral stimuli when the material to which we are listening demands careful attention.)

b. Oral questions given before or after the listening material add a further aural exercise to the one being evaluated. (Students may have understood the exercise, but not the questions on it.)

c. Oral questions asked *after* a listening exercise of some length require the retention of details over a period of time. They therefore test not only immediate comprehension but long-term retention. The same observation may be made about oral questions asked *before* listening to an oral narrative, or dialogue, as a guide to selection. These will need to be repeated after the material has been heard. Otherwise, we are evaluating not only listening comprehension but also retention and recall. The use of oral questions is, therefore, more appropriate at the intermediate level. (For the special problems of short listening comprehension items, see *Designing Multiple-Choice Items for Listening Comprehension*, below.)

d. At the elementary level, the problem of oral versus written questions is often solved by the *use of pictures*. Students are asked to circle the letter corresponding to the picture which best represents what they are hearing. They may also be asked to complete a diagram or picture according to oral directions or to mime what they are hearing.

5. When the attention of students is directed to particular aspects of the listening task they will not retain in their memory material they do not require for this specific purpose, except incidentally. With C47, for instance, students may very well comprehend as they proceed and make correct decisions about the inappropriate items and appropriate replacements, yet still not be able to say at the end what the complete narration was about. After the C47 exercise has been completed, the passage should be read as a whole, with the appropriate replacements, as practice in comprehension of a complete narrative.

Note that since *the processes involved in fluent reading and in listening are similar,*[22] students will have the same problem in reading. A common test of reading has been to ask students to read a passage aloud with careful attention to diction, phrasing, and intonation. Students performing well on this task will not necessarily be able to answer questions on the content of what they have just read, without first being given the opportunity to reread the passage silently. With their attention concentrated on identifying meaningful segments, interrelating these in sentences distinguished by certain intonational patterns, and pronouncing individual words and groups of words comprehensibly, these students may have engaged their cognitive system in too much activity to be able also to recirculate segments and recode them for long-term storage.

6. When students have selected segments for the construction of the message they are extracting, they will no longer have access to the rejected segments (unless these were recirculated as alternatives and retained because the student was in doubt). If students have misunderstood the tenor of the message, the solution is not to question them further in an attempt to extract the correct message. They should be given some indication of where they misinterpreted the message and the opportunity to hear it again, so that they can construct a new version of it.

7. It is a mistake to make all listening comprehension exercises tests with strict limitations. Students should be *allowed during practice to listen to material as often as they need to* until they are able to "hear" and retain the content. Relaxed conditions, with no feelings of apprehension, are essential, since emotional tension greatly affects, our ability to "hear" a message. Students should have frequent opportunities to listen to material purely for the pleasure of comprehension without the threat of grading.

8. *The recirculation of material in the memory takes place during the pauses in speech*, so the pauses are vital. In normal speech, pauses are lengthened by hesitation expressions (*uh ... um ... er ...*), whereas in edited speech, or careful speech, these extensions of the pauses are missing. This allows less processing time for the listener. Speech which appears "too fast" to the inexperienced listener should be "slowed down" by lengthening slightly the pauses between segments, rather than by slowing down the delivery within the segments. An unnaturally slow delivery distorts the natural sounds and flow of the language, making it more difficult for the students later to accustom themselves to a normal speed of delivery.

Recoding of material for storage in long-term memory

We store what we hear in long-term memory in a simplified form. In common parlance, *we retain the gist of what was said*, that is, the basic semantic information, rather than the actual statements with all their complications of structure.

C52 We may hear the following discussion of the relative virtues of peanut butter and chicken soup.

Two stories, which could have had tragic endings, ended happily recently. One little boy who was lost in New York's Central Park was found tired and hungry, but fortunately he wasn't hurt. Two little girls accidentally locked themselves in a bathroom in an apartment building in Virginia. They were tired and hungry too when someone finally found them.

The thing that struck me about the reports of these two incidents was the first meals of these youngsters. They had no sooner reached home than their mothers sat them down and gave them a meal: the girls had peanut butter sandwiches and milk; the boy had peanut butter sandwiches and strawberry soda pop.

What's the great thing about peanut butter? In my day, it was chicken soup.[23]

C53 If asked what this passage was about, a student might come up with a series of statements like these:

Two stories about lost children ended happily recently.
A little boy got lost in a park.
Someone found the little boy.
He was tired and hungry.
He was quite all right fortunately.
Two little girls locked themselves in a bathroom.
Someone let the little girls out.
The little girls were tired and hungry too.
The little girls' mother gave them peanut butter sandwiches and milk.
The little boy's mother gave him peanut butter sandwiches and soda pop.
The narrator's mother would have given him chicken soup.

Commentary

1. In reducing what was heard to a set of factual statements, the student has produced *a series of simple active affirmative declarative sentences* (SAAD's to the psychologist). This is the basic type of sentence in most grammars. Facts in this form are the easiest to recall because all relationships are reduced to Subject-Verb-Object, with some adverbial modifications.

2. A set of basic utterances like these is quite *redundant* in that much information is repeated from sentence to sentence. This provides associational tags which make it easier to retrieve all the information about any one aspect, as in the following examples:

C54 What was the story of *the little boy?*

A little boy got lost in a park recently. He was found all right fortunately. He was tired and hungry. His mother gave him peanut butter sandwiches and soda pop.

Or: What was the story about *the little girls?*

Two little girls locked themselves in a bathroom in an apartment building. Someone found them and let them out. They were tired and hungry. Their mother gave them something to eat. She gave them peanut butter sandwiches and milk.

3. Note that *a certain amount of the information in the original has been dropped*. Without looking back to check the details, our reader, like the student listener, may very well not recall, for instance, that it was in New York's Central Park that the little boy was lost, that the soda pop he was given was strawberry flavor, or that the narrator noted at the beginning that the two stories could have had tragic endings. In preparing questions which require retrieval of information from long-term memory, teachers should keep in mind how this information is stored and *focus on the central line of thought and the basic facts*, rather than on peripheral detail.

Where there is ambiguity, listeners, by reducing the message to its basic elements, interpretatively clarify relationships between what they have assimilated and what they are hearing.

C55 A listener hears:

What annoyed Rupert was being investigated by the local police.

He recodes this information for long-term storage as:

    A. The local police were investigating Rupert.
       This fact annoyed Rupert.
or B. Something annoyed Rupert.
       The local police were investigating this thing.

If he has selected interpretation A for recoding for storage, this is what he will recall and he may even argue forcefully that this is what was said, as listeners do in native-language communication situations. After he has constructed interpretation A from what he has heard, interpretation B will be accessible to him only if a contiguous segment forces him to readjust interpretation A while he is still recirculating what he heard through his short-term memory.

Since psychological experiments and empirical intuition seem to indicate that recoding is basic to long-term memory storage, *we can help our students develop efficiency in listening comprehension*, and in retention and recall, by:

1. presenting them with an outline of the main ideas in basic SAAD sentences before they listen to a structurally complicated version;

2. by asking them to state in basic SAAD sentences what they have retained of a listening comprehension exercise;

3. by asking questions on the text which require SAAD sentences as answers.

The teacher's expectations

We cannot expect students to extract and retain from foreign-language listening material more than they do in the native language. Experiments have shown that average-ability adults recall a very low percentage of the possible information from broadcast talks (about 20 percent when they were not aware that they were to be tested, 28 percent when they knew they were to be tested). Other studies suggest that college students comprehend about half of the basic matter of lectures. The degree of listening efficiency on any particular occasion depends, of course, on the type of material and its organization, the interest the material holds for the listener, the way it is presented (speed, audibility, variations in tone of voice, situational relevance), and even such factors as the acoustics of the room and the emotional state or physical fatigue of the listener. Nevertheless, "evidence on the ability of people to be trained in listening makes it clear that many people listen below capacity"[24] in the native language. We may expect a higher degree of concentrated attention to a listening exercise which is not in the native language because students are aware of its difficulty for them, but *we must not look for total or near-total recall of detail.* In order to correct any unrealistic expectations, it is often useful to try a listening comprehension exercise out on a native speaker before giving it to foreign- or second-language learners.

* Reduce the basic facts in the following text to SAAD sentences and write some questions which would extract from the listener this series of related facts, rather than a few isolated details.

C56 *Rapid reading*

The trick with a book, a newspaper, a magazine, a business report, or even a stock market prospectus is to get what is inside the covers out—without the bother of turning all those pages. Since no one has mastered this trick as yet, or at any rate mastered it to any great degree, most people are consigned to the tedium of page turning.

Along came the rapid readers with the promise that they had a method where you could virtually flip the pages, as though you were watching a movie.

In other words, you can read passively instead of actively.

But this is obviously not reading, any more than going to the movies or watching television can be called learning. No lawyer who has prepared an important brief wants a rapid-reading judge nor have I noticed since the proliferation of rapid-reading teachers that there has been any noticeable improvement in understanding the income tax forms.[25]

C. Strategies of perceptual segmentation

For the psychologist Bever, "the internal logical relations are a major determiner of perceptual segmentation in speech processing."[26] This view aligns well with that of the linguist George Lakoff, of the generative semantics group, that logical categories and logical classes provide the natural basis for grammar and, therefore, ultimately of language use.[27] In other words, since our experience of the real world has taught us to expect such functions as agents, actions, objects, and place, time, and manner modifications,[28] we identify these in what we hear.

Bever has identified four strategies[29] which we seem to employ in the perception of speech.

1. First of all, we tend to segment what we hear into sequences which could form *actor-action-object . . . modifier* relations. This segmentation strategy Bever calls Strategy A. Clearly, for this elementary segmentation, we need to be able to identify, at least approximately, syntactic groups. Fortunately, languages generally supply a certain number of surface indicators of function or syntactic cues. In this way, we separate out different clauses within the sentence.[30] This aspect of perceptual segmentation has already been discussed as stage two of the active process of constructing a message and exercises have been proposed for developing this ability in a new language.

2. In English, we learn to expect the first $N . . . V . . . (N)$, that is, noun . . . verb . . . optional noun, *to be the main clause* (that is, to set out the overriding idea of the sentence) unless morphemes like *if, when,* or *before* warn us that we are dealing with a subordinate clause. This Segmentation Strategy B carries over to some other languages, although it will not necessarily apply to all. Where the native language of the students differs from English in this respect, they will need to learn to adopt this strategy in listening to English speech. Students will also need to learn to interpret rapidly cues to subordination such as those mentioned above (and many others: *although, since, after,* and so on). At the advanced level, they should be able to recognize such deviations from the usual pattern as the not uncommon way of opening a sentence in more formal listening materials with a participial construction (verb + *ing*), as in *Reading between the lines, we infer that the candidate is being less than frank; Opening the conference, the President made the following observations.*

3. In applying Strategy C, we seek the meaning by *combining the lexical items* in the most plausible way. Thus, *the dog bit the man* is easily comprehended, whereas *the man bit the dog*, not being consistent with our normal experiences of the real world, gives us pause. We may "hear" it as *the man was bitten by the dog*, but be forced to reprocess it as subject-verb-object when later segments make it clear that something unusual has happened. Alternatively, we may ask the speaker to repeat the statement.

4. Sometimes there is no specific semantic information to guide us in assigning relationships. We then fall back on a primary functional labeling strategy, based on the apparent order of lexical items in a sentence—Strategy D. We assume that any *noun-verb-(noun), NV(N), sequence* represents the relations *actor-action-object*. It is for this reason that we understand the active construction *the dog chased the cat* more quickly than the passive form *the cat was chased by the dog* which will often be heard as *the cat chased the dog,* especially by children. In the case of a passive of this type, which allows for reversal of roles, later information will cause us to pause and reprocess the utterance syntactically. We then search for cues (passive form of the verb, agent *by*-phrase) which indicate the order *logical object-verb-logical subject.*

SEMANTIC-SYNTACTIC DECODING

Schlesinger has called the process of relying at first on semantic expectations and resorting to syntactic processing only in doubtful cases *semantic-syntactic decoding.*[31] In summary, we perceive the semantic cues and rapidly assign these such roles as actor (or experiencer or instrument), action, object, or modifier according to our knowledge of the real world. It is when our initial interpretation does not fit into the developing message that we pause to analyse syntactic cues to function.

Because of this initial tendency in listening to take the easier road of semantic decoding, students with an *extensive vocabulary* can often interpret a great deal of what they hear by sheer word recognition and logical reasoning. A person listening to a news broadcast might identify the following lexical items:

C57 ...snow...Northern California...good...farmers...San Francisco... biggest snow...89 years...surprise...drought...bad...California... yesterday...San Francisco...Catholics...asked...pray...rain...morning...woke...snowing...biggest snow...San Francisco...century... snow...mountains...short...winter...sports...again...ski...paralysed...ranchers...sold...cattle...agriculture...California...three million dollars...snow...rain...finally...come.[32]

With this basic information, their knowledge of similar situations, and their powers of inference, the students would probably have little difficulty deducing the following facts:

C58 The huge snowfall in Northern California is good news for farmers out there. In San Francisco the biggest snowfall in 89 years came as a surprise. The drought has got so bad in California that yesterday in San Francisco Roman Catholics were asked to pray for rain. This morning when San Franciscans woke up it was snowing—the biggest snow in San Francisco this century laid a couple of feet of snow in the Sierra Nevada mountains which had been woefully short. Winter sports can finally get going again. Ski resorts had been paralyzed. Ranchers had sold off their cattle prematurely. Agriculture in California had lost three hundred million dollars before the snow and the rain which has finally started to come.

* As an exercise in introspection try to remember which of Strategies A–D you employed in your perception of the meaning of C57.

AURAL RECOGNITION VOCABULARY

Since combining lexical items in a plausible way plays such an important role in listening comprehension, attention should be given to the building of an extensive aural recognition vocabulary.

For many students, particularly above the elementary level, the greater part of their vocabulary is acquired in association with reading and writing. It is not surprising, therefore, that many of them have problems in recognizing by ear the words they already know in graphic form. Not only do they have to cope with many oddities of sound-symbol correspondence (*cough / through / dough / thorough / bough / enough*) but they are often uncertain about the correct position of stress (*difficult; permít / pérmit*) and this causes them to puzzle about a word they really know quite well. They also have difficulty recognizing words derived from words they have often met in their reading (or in speaking practice). Because of the nature of the reading material usually found in early textbooks they are often not familiar with the rapidly disseminated vocabulary of contemporary technology, science, politics, and social diversions (*pipeline, jumbo jet, supersonic, blue jeans, jazz* and *rock*): words which may very well be present already in their own language as borrowings. Many of these are pronounced in a sufficiently different fashion in English from what the students are accustomed to in their native language to seem like new words to them. There is also the problem of the reduction of unstressed vowels and the running together of many words in rapid speech.

To develop confidence in aural recognition of words originally encountered in graphic form, students need to understand and apply constantly the rules of sound-symbol correspondence in English. Although these rules may at times seem a little complicated (see R27), there are many easily learned regularities and these, with the common irregularities, need to be practiced orally at frequent intervals. Knowledge of such rules often helps students visualize the probable spelling of a seemingly new word and so relate it to what they know. This is an ability which is important to a student who has been accustomed to learning the language graphically or who by modality preference is visually oriented.

All kinds of practice techniques and competitions can foster transfer from visual to aural recognition and from aural to visual.

1. Clearly *comprehensible pronunciation of all new words* should be expected as they are encountered, so that the student's ears are kept tuned to a high pitch. This is particularly important beyond the elementary level, where students and teacher often relax their efforts to perfect pronunciation and intonation. It is no wonder, then, that so many students fail to recognize words pronounced so differently from the classroom norm.

2. Flashcards should be made of *groups of words which follow certain rules* of sound-symbol correspondence and competitions organized with points allotted to the first person who gives the correct pronunciation for the series, e.g.,

fight, sight, light;

mate, gate, late;

boy, toy, joy.

Later, more rigorous competitions can be conducted with the words isolated from the series and presented in short sentences.

3. Conversely, students should hear words in short sentences and be asked to *identify* which of the *spellings* on three cards represents the word they heard, e.g.,

/sɪt/   site, sit, seat;

/hət/   hut, hat, hate.

4. Students should be shown cards of words in *special problem groups* and drilled in their pronunciation, e.g.,

/ɪ/   ship, chip, dip (which must not be confused with *sheep, cheap, deep*);

/ʊ/   look, foot, wood (often pronounced by students as in *Luke, food, wooed*).

5. *Spelling bees* may be conducted to arouse enthusiasm for a high level of performance. Words are given in sentences, then repeated in isolation, or in short word-groups, for the student to write down, e.g.,

"Better" is the comparative form—*comparative*;

He swore an oath—*oath*.

Students making mistakes are progressively eliminated until a champion is found.

6. Spelling bees may be paralleled by *pronunciation bees*. Sentences are flashed on the screen or wall by overhead projector, or are shown on flashcards, and elimination contests are conducted for acceptable pronunciation, e.g.,

Look at the *dawn*—/dɔn/.

Note: Items for both 5 and 6 should be kept to words students may be expected to meet. Common words with irregular pronunciation will be introduced, e.g., *women*. Any unfamiliar word which follows regular sound-symbol correspondence rules is admissible, e.g., *dungeon, prosperous, intentional, gigantic*. Teams may work out elimination lists to try out on each other.

7. *Spot dictation* is useful at the elementary level; continuous dictation passages are useful at higher levels.

8. Students should be trained in the changes in pronunciation and stress pattern as one moves *from a root word through various derivatives and compounds*. They should be encouraged to make up their own series. Each series admissible must follow regular sound-symbol correspondence rules, e.g.,

simple,   simply,   simplicity,   simplification,   simplify.
/símpəl/ /símpliy/ /sɪmplísətiy/ /sɪmpləfəkéyšən/ /símpləfay/
derive,   derivative,   derivation.
/dəráyv/ /dərívatɪv/ /dɛ̀rəvéyšən/

9. Students should be given regular practice in finding and interpreting *pronunciations and stress patterns in dictionaries*. Teaching phonetic symbols for recognition purposes can arouse interest in this exercise. The system taught should be that used by the dictionary the class will be using. (For the system used in this book and other commonly used systems, see Appendixes A and B.)

10. If students are to understand radio newscasts and documentary films they should be given regular training in the aural identification of the *contemporary vocabulary for matters of international preoccupation*, e.g., /pəlúwšən/ *pollution*;   /riysáyklɪŋ/ *recycling*.

Some people will object that the above recommendations relate the aural too closely to the graphic and that aural vocabulary should be learned only by ear. This may be advisable for specialized aural courses, although, even in this case, student modality preferences must be allowed some play. Most intermediate and advanced language classes have multiple aims. Students who have been trained to depend on visual information need the liberating realization that there are predictable relationships between the pronunciation of a word and its written form. In this way, what they have learned in one modality can become available to them in the other, and the students' limited processing capacity will be used more economically and efficiently.

Macro or micro?

With listening, as with all other aspects of language learning, we must keep in view the final goal of *macro-language use* (the ability to use language holistically for normal life-purposes). *Micro-language learning* (the learning of elements of language and their potential combinations) is only a means leading to this end.

In the macro context, listening can be evaluated only by response: How do listeners react emotionally? How do they respond? Verbally or by action? Do they do what they have been asked or told? Do they use the information offered? Do they fill the supportive role of the listener? (In other words, do they utter, at appropriate intervals, agreeing or consoling interpolations, exclamations of surprise, or tut-tutting noises?—such expressions in English as *Right! Oh my! Is that so? No! Really? You don't say!, Good grief! uh-huh* or *mm* to indicate they are still at the end of the line.) Do they laugh or smile at the right moments? Are they absorbed by what they are hearing?

Because micro-language learning is more easily assessed than macro-language use, there is a tendency to think of the evaluation of listening comprehension in terms of multiple-choice and true/false items. Certainly these can play a useful part in directing the students' efforts in listening and helping them assess the accuracy of their comprehension. The importance of the understanding of fine detail at crucial points in some aural tasks cannot be ignored, since puzzlement can cause an emotional or cognitive block, which overloads channel capacity so that the student loses the thread. On the other hand, there are students who tackle aural comprehension almost heuristically with considerable success. Students who can cope with macro-language use practically from the start may be wasting their time on micro-tests of detail. Other students need the developmental, step-by-step approach and their needs should not be neglected. Even for the latter, however, functional comprehension in real situations must be the ultimate criterion.

For these reasons, listening comprehension is particularly suited to individualized arrangements, with students working at their own level and their own pace. Teachers should assemble all the materials they can find in *developmental listening kits*, each containing micro-training exercises for particular purposes, but culminating in a macro-activity. Students should be encouraged to work their way through a series of these kits in their own manner and at their own pace. Taking one's own time is important in listening, where individuals require differing lengths of time for processing. Students who are capable of doing so should be encouraged to jump from macro activity to macro activity, until listening to the new language becomes for them natural and effortless. Eventually most students will reach the stage where their listening is completely integrated with communication activities of the kind outlined in Chapter 2.

We must place students in situations where listening comprehension plays an essential role, then see how they cope. Macro-language evaluation should be related to the normal uses of listening in life-situations:

1. as part of a purposeful communicative interchange;
2. for receiving direction or instructions;
3. for obtaining information;
4. for the pleasure of an activity like watching a play, a film, a television show, or a fashion parade, or listening to a sports commentary, a newscast, or a group discussion on the radio;
5. for participating in social gatherings (listening to small talk, listening to others conversing, and so on).

Any items in the B and D sections of the *Chart of Listening Comprehension Activities,* C67, are appropriate for macro-language assessment.

ASSESSMENT OF MICRO-LANGUAGE LEARNING

Many aspects of micro-language learning have already been discussed in this chapter (discrimination of sounds and stress which change meaning; recognition of intonation patterns, syntactic segments, and word groups with high frequency of occurrence; aural vocabulary recognition). Any activities in the A and C sections of the *Chart of Listening Comprehension Activities,* C67, can be adapted to micro-language testing.

One of the commonest forms of assessment of this developmental phase of listening comprehension is the use of *multiple-choice questions,* yet the preparation of this type of test holds many pitfalls for the inexperienced.

The test items often consist of *short questions or comments in isolation,* like those in C59, for which students choose appropriate rejoinders (sometimes completions) from multiple-choice options.

C59   1. Where are you going this morning?
        2. What's the time, John?
        3. What's that over there?

In natural interaction, there is a context for such short utterances which helps in the interpretation of the fleeting sounds, e.g., place, time, relationship of the person speaking to the person addressed, previous utterance, gesture of pointing or eyes turned in a certain direction, facial expression of exasperation, surprise, or expectancy. If the person addressed is taken off-guard, the interlocutor frequently makes a circumstantial comment before repeating the question, thus bringing it into focus, e.g.,

C60   A. Where are you going this morning?
        B. What did you say?
        C. It's very early. Where are you going this morning?

Materials writers often seem not to realize that isolated short utterances are more difficult to "hear" correctly than longer, contexualized segments.

In real life, the responses which would actually occur to such short non-contexualized utterances may well be some of the options considered "incorrect" by the writer of the multiple-choice exercise. Choosing the "appropriate" response then becomes a question of reading the mind of the item-writer or the corrector of the exercise.

C61 Circle the letter corresponding to the most appropriate response to the question you hear.

Recorded voice: Where are you going this morning?
    A. I'm just coming back from the station.
    B. To church. Would you like to come too?
    C. Me? I'm going to write letters.
    D. I'm just waiting for a friend.

Any of the above is an "appropriate response" in a certain context.
    A. *I'm just coming back from the station.* (I may be walking along the street, but I'm not *going* anywhere. I'm *coming back.*)
    B. *To church. Would you like to come too?* (The "appropriate response" anticipated.)
    C. *Me? I'm going to write letters.* (I'm not going anywhere this morning. I've got far too much to do here at home.)
    D. *I'm just waiting for a friend.* (I may look as if I'm waiting for the lights to change so that I can cross the road, but I'm not.)

As any experienced teacher knows, students who dispute the grading of such short multiple-choice items can often justify their choices quite logically. Some kind of context should be built into every listening item.

C62 (Cf. C59.)
    1. You're putting on your coat! Where are you going this morning?
    2. I'm hungry. What's the time, John?
    3. What's that over there? Across the road.

Students should also be given opportunities from time to time to select more than one "appropriate response," adding a brief note indicating a possible context. This encourages projection of expectations of the kind provided also in *Situation Tapes* (C33).

The following passage for listening which gives a detailed context would actually be easier than a short, non-contextualized utterance (if we exclude clichés and sentences students have heard over and over again in class):

C63 (1) *Recorded voice:*

It was such a hot day. The water was cool and clear. Everyone was swimming and splashing in the waves. Philip was lying quietly in the shade under a big rock, letting the sand run through his fingers. Out at sea, a ship was sailing for England. What was Philip doing?

Choices supplied: A. He was on a ship going to England.
B. He was swimming in the sea.
C. He was resting on the beach.
D. He was throwing sand at a big rock.

The recorded passage contains a number of associated concepts which provide clues to the correct answer. Students who have understood some parts clearly, but not all, have more opportunity in a longer passage like this to reconstruct by intelligent guessing those sections they did not comprehend fully.

DESIGNING MULTIPLE-CHOICE ITEMS FOR LISTENING COMPREHENSION

Many of the problems of multiple-choice items discussed in Chapter 7 (in the section: *Assisting and Assessing Reading Comprehension,* p. 241) apply also to multiple-choice items for assessing listening comprehension. There must be no ambiguity in the choices. The correct choice should not repeat word for word some sentence in the listening text. The correct choice should not depend on comprehension or non-comprehension of one unusual vocabulary item. Where there is a series of questions on one passage, the correct choices should not form an obvious sequence which students can detect without understanding the passage (a later item can sometimes supply the answer sought in an earlier question, if the writer of the item is not careful). Care must be taken to see that the items do not test powers of logical deduction, or ability to recognize exact paraphrases, rather than actual comprehension of the passage.

Apart from the general problems of preparing multiple-choice questions, items for listening comprehension present problems peculiar to this modality. The items have to be prepared in such a way that they give a clear indication of what the student "heard", that is, constructed personally from the sound signal. Item-writers must be able to imagine themselves in the place of the neophyte and reconstruct what the latter may be "hearing." For these reasons, it is difficult for native speakers to construct suitable choices for listeners who are not very familiar with English, unless they have had considerable experience with the specific problems such listeners experience.

It is useful to analyze what types of confusions one is anticipating on the part of the listeners by the choices one proposes. If there is no pre-dictable rationale for a certain choice, it can be considered a "donkey item" which will be chosen only by a student who interpreted almost nothing of the sound signal. There should never be more than one "donkey item" in each set and this particular item must be very plausible, if it is to be selected at all. Unless it has some obvious relationship to the rest of the set, or reechoes closely what was heard, even the donkeys will shy away from it.

C64 (E) *Recorded voice:* In your family, everyone works a lot. Do you some-times take a rest on Sundays?

> *Choices:*   A. Yes, we all work on Sundays.
> B. Yes. Some days we're tired after our long walk.
> C. Yes, Sunday is just like the rest of the days.
> D. Of course. We watch television on Sundays.

Commentary

A. The student who chooses A

1. identifies the question form *Do you* which usually requires a yes/no answer and a pronoun response of *I* or *we*;

2. recognizes the words *everyone works* (possibly *your family* as well) *on Sundays* (which provides some associative context);

3. misses several words in the actual question (*take a rest*). Since she has not understood the question, she chooses an item which assembles the elements she has heard in a plausible way.

B. The student who chooses B

1. identifies the question form *Do you?* which usually requires a yes/no answer and a pronoun response of *I* or *we*;

2. confuses *works a lot* with *walks a lot*;

3. confuses *Sundays* with *some days*

4. has probably understood "your family" since he chooses an item with "we" as a response.

The student has not, however, understood the question. He chooses an item which would provide a sensible answer to a possible question relating the elements he thought he heard.

C. The student who chooses C has understood neither the statement nor the question, but the C response picks up the words he has recognized at the end of the sound sequence and which he has retained in his short-term memory (*rest . . . Sundays*). C is a "donkey item" in that it makes no pretense at answering the question.

   D. The student who chooses D has selected the most appropriate response. It refers to an activity (*watching television*) which comes into the category of restful occupations, without repeating any elements of the question except the time element: *on Sundays*. It thus tests apprehension of meaning, while avoiding the possibility that the student is not comprehending but merely selecting the choice with the most items in identical form.

C65 (I or A) I really wonder what's coming over Americans these days. Any Saturday evening in summer the suburbs are filled with a penetrating blue smoke. The outdoor chefs are at it again. Just when we've advanced from wood-burning stoves and smoky kitchens to nice, clean, electric cookers and microwave ovens, we all go outside to sit on the grass and eat burned steaks from paper plates that bend and drip all over our clothes. Or, worse still, the flies and mosquitoes drive us inside to eat our barbecued hamburger on the kitchen table. This, I suppose, is progress.

   Which of the following statements is true, according to what you have just heard?
   A. In summer Americans employ chefs to cook the meals outdoors and serve them in the kitchen.
   B. In summer, Americans like to cook and eat some of their meals in the garden.
   C. Americans eat their meals from paper plates in a kitchen full of flies and mosquitoes.
   D. Only the rich have electric cookers in America. The poor eat hamburger which they cook over a wood fire.

Commentary

An aditional source of error in this example may be the student's lack of knowledge of the American way of life.

   A. This choice would attract a student who knew very little about the way Americans live and had understood very little of what was said. It echoes the words "in summer," "outdoor," and "chefs." "Kitchen" is an elementary word he has no problem recognizing. He feels comfortable with this statement which repeats precise elements from the text.

   B is the correct choice. It draws elements from several sentences and requires comprehension of a sequence of ideas.

C. This could be a derogatory statement about "progress"—technological advance associated with good, old-fashioned dirt. For a student who understood very little except that some people were eating off paper plates and who had caught the words "flies," "mosquitoes," and "kitchen," this could be a plausible choice.

D. This choice reflects a common misconception about America in many poor countries—that it is a country of very rich people who have all the luxuries and very poor people who are deprived of these things. There are enough precise elements from the text (electric cookers, hamburger) which are associated with "the American way of life" in the minds of people in other countries, and other elements in the statement like "cook," "wood" and "fire" which are implied by many expressions in the text (chefs, kitchens, cookers, ovens, steaks; smoke, wood-burning, barbecued). For a student who had not understood the drift of what she heard, this is a definite possibility. Apart from precise expressions from the text (electric cookers, hamburger), the statement is expressed in simple English which would be understood by a weaker student.

* *Analyze* in similar fashion the anticipated reactions of the students who will choose the various alternative responses proposed in the following listening comprehension exercise.

C66 You say he's gone already? But it's only six in the morning!
A. Yes, he'll be ready to go at six.
B. Yes, he's often sick in the morning.
C. You know he always takes the 6:30 train.
D. No, I don't want to go at six in the morning.

C67 *Chart of listening comprehension activities*[33]

In the following chart, the activities are divided into four learning stages:

A. *Identification:* perception of sounds and phrases; identifying these directly and holistically with their meaning.
B. *Identification and selection without retention:* listening for the pleasure of comprehension, extracting sequential meanings, without being expected to demonstrate comprehension through active of language.
C. *Identification and guided selection with short-term retention:*[34] students are given some prior indication of what they are to listen for; they demonstrate their comprehension immediately in some active fashion.
D. *Identification and selection with long-term retention:* students dem-

onstrate their comprehension, or use the material they have comprehended, after the listening experience has been completed; or they engage in an activity which requires recall of material learned some time previously.

Elementary level (E)

A. IDENTIFICATION (E)

Macro

1. Listening to tapes of various languages to detect the language one is learning.
2. Listening to songs and poems for the pleasure of the sounds (in classroom, listening room, or listening corner).
3. Songs and poems played over loudspeakers in the language laboratory for atmosphere.
4. Hearing original sound tracks of documentary films before being able to understand them.

Micro

5. Aural discrimination exercises.
6. Short-phrase discrimination with pictures.
7. Listening to segments of dialogue to be learned.
8. Responding with miming actions to segments from dialogue learned or from classroom conversation.
9. Responding with flashcards to names of letters of the alphabet.
10. Backward buildup in imitation of a model (C48).

B. IDENTIFICATION AND SELECTION WITHOUT RETENTION (E)

11. Games involving miming of words and phrases learned.
12. Listening to conversation-facilitation dialogues, songs, or poems already learned.
13. Listening to retelling of stories already read, reacting in some way to variations from the original.
14. Listening to a conversation which is a variant of a dialogue studied.
15. Listening to an anecdote based on reading material studied.
16. Teacher gives some background information on a topic, then tells an anecdote, or describes an experience.

With visual

17. Listening to a description of pictures or slides.
18. Listening to an anecdote, story, or dialogue illustrated with a flannelboard.
19. Listening to a *Show and Tell* oral report.

With action

20. Total physical response activity or *Simon Says* (C45-46).

21. Obeying classroom instructions.

22. Listening to simple narration, raising hands whenever a color (or occupation, or kind of food, etc.) is mentioned.

23. *Letter Bingo:* Letters of the alphabet are called randomly; each student checks these to see if they are in the word he has in front of him; the first student who has checked all the letters of his word wins.

24. *Number Bingo:* Numbers are called randomly; students check these numbers against numbers on cards they have been given; the first student with all of his numbers correctly checked wins.

C. IDENTIFICATION AND GUIDED SELECTION WITH SHORT-TERM RETENTION (E)

With visual

25. Discrimination of numbers, dates, and times of day by pairing ones they hear with multiple-choice items, clockfaces, lists of famous events, or flight schedules.

26. Learning a dialogue with vanishing techniques (see *Dialogue Exploitation* in Chapter I, p. 35).

27. True/false questions supplied beforehand; the student listens to variation of a dialogue or story read and checks answers.

28. Multiple-choice answers supplied beforehand; the students listen to a dialogue or story using recombinations of vocabulary and structures learned, and check appropriate answers.

With action

29. Miming the actions in a story being narrated.

30. Obeying complex classroom instructions for class exercises and tests.

31. Completing a diagram according to instructions.

With speaking

32. Directed dialogue (C24).

33. Group piecing together of a new dialogue from initial hearings.

34. Participating in Cummings device (C29).

35. Participating in Gouin series (C11-13).

36. Participating in verbal-active series (C15).

37. *Who is it? What is it? Where is it?* (guessing who, what, or which place is being described by teacher or student).

38. Intensive practice exercises varying syntactic segments (see Chapter 4).

39. Taking part in Lipson-type puzzle exercises: see *Categories of Language Use* 8 in Chapter 2, p. 51.

40. Running commentary: listening to a story and giving the gist at the end of each sentence in SAAD's (see C52-53).

With writing

41. Writing down words which are dictated letter by letter.

42. Writing from dictation series of numbers of increasing length and complexity.

43. *Information Search* (C49): writing down segments which answer particular questions.

44. Dictation: students repeat to themselves what they think they heard before they write it.

45. Spot dictation (R26).

D. IDENTIFICATION, SELECTION, AND LONG-TERM RETENTION (E)

46. Listening to a continuation of a story (with the same vocabulary area, same setting, and same characters).

47. Listening to a story different from, but with similar vocabulary to, one already read.

48. Listening to a conversation similar to one studied.

49. Listening to skits prepared by other students.

50. Listening to dramatizations of stories read.

51. Listening without the text to the expressive reading (on tape, by the teacher, or by a student) of a poem already studied.

52. Listening to other students reciting poems in a poetry competition.

53. Checking answers to aural questions given before or after a passage for listening.

54. Checking appropriate choices for multiple-choice continuations (or rejoinders) given orally after a listening passage.

With speaking

55. Listening to a story, then giving the gist at the end in SAAD's (see C52-53).

56. Answering questions orally on a passage just heard.

57. Responding to others in spontaneous role-playing.

58. Listening to and discussing oral reports of other students.

59. Chain dialogue. (C25).

60. Rubbishing the dialogue (C26).

61. Acting out learned dialogues with others (paraphrasing the sense rather than repeating by rote).

62. Learning and acting a part with others in a skit or original dialogue.

63. *What's my Line?:* student mimes a series of actions, others ask yes-no questions until they have guessed what the student does for a living.

With writing

64. Students answer questions in writing after they have listened to a story or conversation.

65. Students write down what they have learned from another student's oral report.

66. Cloze test[35] on content of what has been heard (W28).

Intermediate level (I)

A. IDENTIFICATION (I)

1. Aural discrimination of small sound distinctions which change meaning of sentences.

2. Recognition of the characteristics of a familiar level of speech with reduced vowels, and words run together, syllables omitted (e.g., *going to* as /gɔnə/) through listening to authentic informal speech on tapes, disks, or film sound tracks.

With visual

3. Aural recognition of English pronunciation of names of foreign personalities and places (supplied on scrambled lists).

4. Aural recognition of English words which exist as borrowings in the native language of the listener. The students identify these rapidly from scrambled lists.

With action

5. Recognition of aural indicators of tense: *Today or Tomorrow?* (C51) —tapping for future tenses, miming present tenses.

With writing

6. Demonstrating recognition of words dealing with contemporary international, scientific, technical, political, and social affairs which are similar in English and the native language of the student and writing these down.

B. IDENTIFICATION AND SELECTION WITHOUT RETENTION (I)

7. Listening to a complete reading of a story studied in sections.

8. Listening to a dramatization of a story read.

9. Listening to the acting out of scenes from a play read.

10. Listening to a disk or tape of the reading, by an English-speaking person, of a short story, poem, or extracts from a novel.

11. Listening to a version in SAAD's before listening to a more complicated version (see C52-53). No questions are asked.

12. Listening to a teacher or another student telling an amusing incident which happened on the way to school or at school.

13. Listening to a news item told by the teacher or another student.

14. Listening to the teacher or another student giving background information for a news item.

15. Listening to the teacher or another student giving background information for reading or for a class or group project.

16. Following the line of discussion in a group conversation.

17. Listening to English songs.

With visual

18. Listening to a presentation of slides of some aspect of British or American culture, history, or visual arts.

19. Watching and listening to a documentary film on some aspect of life in an English-speaking country.

20. Watching and listening to the final showing of a scholastic film (with a background of contemporary British or American culture) which has already been studied in class.

21. Listening to a story as one is reading it silently, to improve fluent reading techniques.

With action

22. Following directions for classroom organization.

C. IDENTIFICATION AND GUIDED SELECTION WITH SHORT-TERM RETENTION (I)

23. Selecting from aural choices completions for sentences heard.

24. Listening to oral compositions of other students.

25. Listening to skits and spontaneous role-playing of other students.

26. Students discuss news beforehand; then listen to newscasts to find answers to certain questions raised.

27. Students listen to exchange tapes and correspondence tapes.

28. *What am I describing?* (guessing an object described by a fellow student). Alternatives: *Where am I? Who is it?*

With visual

29. Students are provided with multiple-choice or true/false questions beforehand, then they check answers as they listen, or immediately afterwards.

30. Students choose among written completions for sentences given orally.

31. Students practice reading aloud with a tape model: each student reads a segment, listens to the model reading, then rereads the segment.

32. Students watch films of which they have previously studied the sound track or a synopsis.

33. Students watch films in which they are looking for specific cultural details, certain interactions of characters, or particular developments of the story.

With action

34. Following instructions for making something.

With speaking

35. Providing oral sentence completions at the end of longer and longer sequences.

36. Students hear questions beforehand (they do not see them). They then hear the passage, hear the aural questions again, and give oral answers.

37. The student gives spontaneous responses on *Situation Tapes* (C33).

38. *Correct Me* (C47): noting inappropriate words in a story given orally and suggesting appropriate replacements.

39. *Twenty Questions:* group asking of eliminative yes-no questions to discover the name of a famous person selected for the game. Alternatives: *Who and What?* (guessing a famous person and an object one associates with that person); *Animal-Vegetable-Mineral* (similar to *Twenty Questions,* but the item being guessed is not necessarily a person and there is no limit to the number of questions which may be asked).

40. *Not yes! Not No!:* group elimination game where students are asked all kinds of questions which they may answer in any way they can, so long as they never use *yes* or *no.*

41. *All Ears* (C50): quick-fire response to syntactic cues.

42. Oral spelling bees.

43. Fulfilling the supportive role of the listener (*Really? . . . You don't say! . . . uh-huh . . .*).

With writing

44. Written spelling bees.

45. Spot comprehension: students are given incomplete statements about the content of what they will hear; after listening, they fill in the blanks with the missing details, expressed in short phrases.

46. Dictation: gradually increasing the length of the segment to be retained.

47. Taking dictations containing information on cultural matters already

discussed, like famous sayings of leading historical figures, famous anecdotes most English-speaking children know, e.g., George Washington and
the cherry tree (American); Robert the Bruce and the spider (British).

48. Taking down dictated notes on the lives and achievements of historical figures, painters, musicians.

D. IDENTIFICATION, SELECTION, AND LONG-TERM RETENTION (I)

49. Listening without a script to readings of plays studied.

50. Listening to a part of a play for which the students will develop
impromptu continuations later.

51. Listening to episodes of a mystery serial. (The teacher can con
struct these from the dialogue in a detective story and have this material
recorded by several speakers. Sound effects add reality.)

With speaking

52. Answering aural questions asked after a long listening passage.

53. Group conversations and discussions on an assigned topic.

54. Preliminary discussion for preparation of oral compositions.

55. Questions and discussion after listening to other students' oral compositions.

56. Participating in spontaneous skits and role-playing.

57. After listening, answering in SAAD's questions asked on the
passage (see C52-53).

58. Listening to a passage, then giving the gist in SAAD's.

59. Listening to a mystery story without hearing the conclusion; then
discussing possible explanations.

60. Taking map journeys (C14).

61. *Guilty Party* (discovering the crime of which one is accused and
defending oneself).

62. Participating in simulated telephone conversations or authentic telephone conversations with monolingual, or presumed monolingual, English
speakers.

63. Interviewing visiting native speakers of English to find out who
they are, what they do, what they think, and so on.

64. *I've Got a Secret:* discovering the secret a fellow student is con-
cealing (the secret may be career plans, weekend plans, what irritates the
student most, etc.).

65. *To Tell the Truth:* three students pretend to be the person whose
unusual experiences are recounted at the beginning; other students try to
find out by questioning who is the real Mr. or Ms. X.

66. *Charades:* see *Categories of Language Use* 10 in Chapter 2, p. 54.

67. *General Knowledge Quizzes:* students can choose such categories as American or British history, institutions, contemporary life, current events, language, literature, art, music, sport, exploration, famous men and women.

68. *Keeping Tabs on the Speaker* (C43-44) as a test of cultural information.

69. Listening to and discussing exchange and correspondence tapes.

70. Taking part in general conversation at English-language clubs, tables, or camps, at celebrations of festivals, or during study abroad or family-exchange programs (during summers or school terms).

With writing

71. Listening to a passage and then writing the gist in SAAD's (see C52-53).

72. Listening to a mystery story which stops before the conclusion, then writing an explanation.

73. Listening to a segment of dialogue, then writing a composition which gives it a context and a conclusion.

Advanced level (A)

A. IDENTIFICATION (A)

1. Aural discrimination of features of rapid spoken style, regional accents, and levels of language, through listening to authentic tapes, films, radio broadcasts, or plays.

With writing

2. Transcribing and retranscribing tapes of unedited authentic speech until the students have recorded it all (to learn, through personal observation, characteristics of unedited speech and tune the ear to understand it).[36] The students play back any sections of the tape as often as they wish.

B. IDENTIFICATION AND SELECTION WITHOUT RETENTION (A)

3. Listening to a sequel to a passage read.

4. Listening to recordings of plays and poems already studied.

5. Listening to scenes from other plays by the playwright studied in class.

6. Listening to other poems by the poet studied.

7. Listening to debates and panel discussions by fellow-students.

8. Listening to English-language newscasts for personal information and pleasure.

9. Listening to commercials recorded from English-language short-wave broadcasts or mock commercials prepared by fellow-students.

10. Listening to recordings of popular songs.

11. Continuing tape correspondence with an English-speaking friend.

C. IDENTIFICATION AND GUIDED SELECTION WITH SHORT-TERM RETENTION (A)

12. Listening to a student presentation of a mock radio program, call-in program, or television talk show.

With visual

13. Watching English-language films.

14. Listening to a student presentation of a fashion parade.

With speaking

15. Listening to lecturettes by other students on aspects of British or American civilization, culture, or literature and asking questions.

16. Listening to an aural text and recording answers to questions on the text.

17. Group conversations with visiting native speakers of English.

18. Micro-texts: see *Categories of Language Use* 9 in Chapter 2, p. 53.

With writing

19. Students practice taking notes on classroom lecturettes, first with an outline of points to be covered, then without guidance.

20. Dictation: students are expected to listen to and retain whole sentences before writing.

D. IDENTIFICATION, SELECTION, AND LONG-TERM RETENTION (A)

21. Listening to lectures by visiting speakers of English on aspects of contemporary life in English-speaking countries.

22. Watching performances of English-language plays by visiting actors.

23. Watching performances of plays in English by the school English club or on the invitation of other schools.

24. Listening to recordings of group conversations of British or American speakers discussing subjects of interest.

25. Listening to readings of plays not studied previously.

With visual

26. Extracting different lines of thought from a listening passage: listening with one set of printed questions, then listening again with a different set of questions.

27. Visiting a show of American or British art and listening to a commentary in English.

With action

28. Seeking information from documentaries, tapes, and records for group projects or class discussions.

29. Listening to lengthy instructions for a task one has to perform.

30. Learning to cook American or British dishes from oral instructions.

31. Visiting a restaurant which serves American or British cuisine, discussing the menu with an English-speaking waiter, and eating an American or British meal in company with other English-speaking students.

32. Making preparations for an English-language festival with a British or American exchange student, or teacher, who explains what to do in English.

33. Activities at an English-language club, English-language camp, or during a study abroad tour.

With speaking

34. As much of the lesson as possible is conducted in English.

35. Listening to a passage and recording oral answers to questions about it.

36. Listening to recordings of plays, poems, and speeches and discussing them afterwards.

37. Learning songs in English from recordings.

38. Learning a part for a play from a recording made by professional actors.

39. Group conversations and discussions on cultural subjects which students have researched, on films they have seen, or on books and journals they have read.

40. Discussion of newscasts in English.

41. Asking questions at lectures by visiting speakers of English or exchange students.

42. Talking on the telephone with native speakers of English, seeking information for projects or for reporting back to class.

43. Interviewing visiting, or local, speakers of English or exchange students to find out information about their way of life, attitudes, and institutions for a group project on contemporary American or British culture.

44. Watching an English-language film and being able to discuss afterwards questions which require aural comprehension, rather than kinesic or visual interpretation.

45. Engaging in debates and discussions on controversial subjects.

46. Showing English-speaking visitors around the school or town.

47. Listening to a story which members of the class will dramatize spontaneously later.

48. Listening to tapes of radio discussions with English-speaking authors and civic leaders, or speeches by political figures, and discussing these in the context of contemporary life.

49. Listening to newscasts in order to act as daily or weekly reporter for the class.

50. Taking part in such competitions as Intermediate activities 61, 64, 65, and 67.

51. Reconstruction of the text: As a preliminary study of the differences between spoken and literary language, leading later to explication of the text or commentary on a literary text (also called literary analysis or literary appreciation) students listen to a poem or short literary extract and, with the help of systematic questioning from the teacher, reconstruct it orally.

With writing

52. Taking dictations containing information related to cultural subjects being researched.

53. While listening to a speech, lecture, or taped discussion, students take notes for use with a group project.

54. Listening to a speech, lecture, or taped discussion and writing afterwards a summary of the main points, for use with a group project.

55. Reconstruction of the text: After having done 51, students reconstruct the text in writing, individually or as a group, and then compare their version with the original as an exercise in stylistics.

56. As an ambitious project for a class in which listening comprehension is a major objective, or as an independent study project: students listen to British or American broadcasts to draw out information on differences between these cultures and their own. They write up the results of their research in English. (Much can be learned from the types of news reported and what this conveys about the interests and preoccupations of English-speaking peoples; the types of goods advertised on English-language commercial stations and the way they are advertised; the kinds of interviews conducted, and with whom; the types of music played on different stations; the subject matter of comedy hours, situation comedies, and popular songs, and the types of questions asked by listeners.)

* Does the situation in which you are teaching English, or intending to teach English, represent a second-language or a foreign-language environment? In this situation what possibilities exist, or could be developed by you, to provide better opportunities for your students to listen to authentic, natural English speech? In what ways can you encourage them to seek out for themselves contacts with English-speaking persons or further opportunities to hear English spoken?

4
Oral practice
for the learning of grammar

Deductive or inductive?

At some stage students must learn the grammar of the language. This learning may be approached *deductively*, (in which case students are given a grammatical rule with examples before they practice the use of a particular structure) or *inductively* (students see a number of examples of the rule in operation in discourse, practice its use, and then evolve a rule from these examples with the help of the teacher; or they see a number of examples, evolve a rule from these examples with the help of the teacher, and then practice using the structure). In either of these approaches, there is a phase wherein students practice the use of grammatical structures and apply the various facets of grammatical rules in possible sentences. This subject is discussed in greater depth in Chapter 8.

Oral exercises

In many classrooms, the greater part of grammatical practice has always been in writing. Here, we are concerned with the contribution that can be made by oral practice exercises of many kinds. In this chapter, we shall:

1. examine types of exercises traditionally found in textbooks and see which ones are suitable for or can be adapted to oral practice;

2. study examples of more recently developed drills and exercises and discuss their features;

3. categorize, exemplify, and discuss six types of oral practice exercises (repetition, substitution, conversion, sentence modification, response, and translation exercises).

Traditional types of exercises

Although the examples in this section are taken from books published years ago, they show almost in caricature many features which can still be found in books currently in use. It is hoped that through recognizing the patent absurdity of these aspects of the presentation of grammar and grammatical exercises teachers in training and practicing teachers may become much more sensitive to the subtler forms in which these defects still appear.

1. GRAMMAR RULES AND EXERCISES

If we examine older textbooks we find that many of them set out a *grammatical rule*, with a few *examples* of its use. The rule may be expressed in a traditional terminology for English grammar with which students may or may not be familiar or it may use terminology carried over from the grammatical system of the native language, as in G3. (In more recent books the terminology may be that of some contemporary system of grammatical analysis which is quite new to most of the learners.) In a laudable attempt at comprehensiveness, the writer may make the particular rule under discussion appear more complicated than it need be for a language-learner.

G1 (a) A grammar for French students learning English states that there are four genders in English:

masculine (all nouns for males) : *a boy, a bull, a cock*;
feminine (all nouns for females) : *a girl, a cow, a hen*;
common gender (all nouns which may be used for both males and females) : *child, cousin*;
neuter (all nouns for things and for animals for which one does not precisely state the sex) : *table, pen, bird*.[1]

Commentary

1. Later in the book from which G1(a) has been taken, there are sections on personal pronouns, possessive adjectives and pronouns, and reflexive pronouns, all of which give indications as to how to handle masculine, feminine, and neuter nouns. Nowhere is the "common" category

mentioned again and no indication is ever given as to what the student should do with this apparently important piece of information. How, then, is one to refer to a noun of "common gender"? A more modern approach is to apply the term *dual gender*[2] to the many words which may be used to refer to either males or females, e.g., *doctor, teacher, cousin, cook*. This term at least gives the student the hint that either *he* or *she* may be used. The term *common* would then be reserved for a much smaller and much less important class for which *he/she/it* may all be appropriate (e.g., *child*), although context usually dictates this choice fairly clearly for the speaker. With *child*, for instance, *it* is reserved for very young children, usually not personally known to the speaker, e.g., "That baby next door! It screams all night!"

2. The examples given show indefinite articles with masculine and feminine nouns, but not with common gender and neuter nouns. Does this mean that one should say in English: *I saw a little boy* and *I saw a red hen*, but *I saw little child* and *I saw red pen?* This is a perfectly legitimate question for a student to raise after reading this grammatical explanation. Here we see one of the weaknesses of using *fragments as examples* to illustrate rules.

3. Although the writers of this textbook were apparently trying to be comprehensive, they have ignored what has been called *collective* gender[3] for words like *family* which may be referred to as *they*, e.g., "With *their* likes and dislikes, *they're* a funny family." This category would probably be much more useful for the learner of English than the rather imprecise "common gender." We are not suggesting that an elementary grammar should deal with all the complications of English grammar, but that emphasis should be laid on those aspects which will be *most useful* in providing the students with forms within which to express their own meanings in creative utterances. Simplicity within the bounds of true function is certainly preferable to multiple categorizations.

After the rule has been stated, *exercises* are usually given for practice in the application of the grammar rule.

G1   (b) What gender are these nouns?
A duck, a widow, a lad, a cousin, a harness, a well, a husband, a fool, a marquess, a wind, a ship, a bee . . .[4]

Commentary

1. Since the words in the exercise are unrelated to any reading passage or wider context in the book, this exercise presumably involves looking

up each word which is unfamiliar in a bilingual dictionary and deciding from the native-language equivalent whether or not a sex can be assigned to it. This is time-consuming and a mechanical, mindless chore when it is unassociated with the use of the words in any meaningful context.

2. The words seem to have been chosen quite haphazardly. There is no attempt at relating words in collocations. *Harness* and *marquess* were presumably included because the endings could mislead the less conscientious student, who had tired of turning the pages of the dictionary, into thinking they were feminine on the analogy of *actress* and *princess*. (The inevitable comment about ships being referred to as *she* was supplied on the previous page of the book from which this example has been quoted. The question may well be raised as to whether this fact about usage assigns "feminine gender" to ships.)

3. Since this exercise clearly involves the use of a bilingual dictionary, native-language conventions for gender may well mislead the unwary student.

G2   In the same book from which G1(b) was taken, we are told that inanimate objects can always be personified in English, but that, since the names of things are undifferentiated by gender, it is the sense that determines the pronoun to be used. The feminine, we are told, expresses ideas of beauty, softness, charm, and tenderness; the masculine expresses ideas of strength, nobility, terror, and ugliness.[5]

Exercise: Complete, paying special attention to personified objects:

a. Mount Everest raises _____ head above the clouds.
b. The Thames brings life and wealth to London, _____ favourite child.
c. Why should I fear Death? _____ will end my sufferings.
d. In my difficulties, hope never left me: _____ was my comfort and helped me through.
e. War, the scourge of mankind, was tearing the world in _____ dreadful claws.
f. The stormy sea was raging and _____ roar drowned our voices.[6]

Commentary

1. There is nothing about the rule in G2 which can be termed "grammatical," although it appears in a very widely used book which contains the word "grammar" in its title and the rule is set out under the general heading "Gender." It is a subjective interpretation of English usage which is based on *cultural stereotypes* of masculinity and femininity. For most of the

examples in the exercise, a native speaker of English would normally use
its. If pressed to choose a gender, most native speakers would hesitate and
then give very personal reasons for their final choice of gender. (Is snow-
capped Mount Everest to be considered beautiful or strong and noble? Ask
yourself similar questions about the other examples in the exercise.)

2. This very controversial exercise would be even further complicated by
the images (and, in some cases, genders) which the native languages of the
students associate with *sea, death, war, mountains,* and *rivers.* (A student
digesting this "rule" may well be mystified by the strange inconsistency of
speakers of English who then apparently use *she* for ships, engines, motors,
tanks, and trains, as stated a few lines earlier in the book.) G2 is a further
example of how *so-called "grammar rules"* can make the learning of a
language much more complicated than it need be.

3. We may also note in the exercise the very varied vocabulary and the
diversity of structure which students must comprehend before they can
make their choice between *he* and *she.*

G3 Change into the 3rd person singular of the preterite:

I am a boy; I get up at 7 a.m.;
I wash and dress myself; when I am ready,
I go to school where I say my lessons.
I come back at 10 and do my home-work.[7]

Commentary

This is an example of an *unnecessarily tricky* exercise which appeared in a
book for francophone students.

1. The students note that these five items have to be changed from the
present tense form to the preterite (a grammatical term transferred from
the students' native-language grammar and originally from Latin grammar). These students may not notice (or may notice) that the exercise
also involves a change from the first person singular to the third person
singular, a fact which is immaterial as far as the verbs are concerned, since
the past tense forms are the same for both persons.While the students
are concentrating on the verb forms, as the wording of the instruction
seems to imply they should, they may well make slips in such associated
changes as "*he* says *his* lessons" and "*he* does *his* homework." In other
words, the *probability of errors not necessarily due to ignorance of the verb
forms* (the point of the exercise) is greater here than in an exercise in

which the students are asked to concentrate on one aspect of grammar at a time. How will such incidental slips affect the allotment of marks for the exercise?

2. Furthermore, although the instruction requires only a change to the third person singular form with no mention of masculine, feminine, or neuter, the first sentence in what is apparently connected discourse is "I am a boy." This is presumably *an implicit instruction* to give third person singular masculine forms throughout. Since this extra requirement affects the use not only of pronoun subjects but of possessive and reflexive forms as well, why was this instruction not given explicitly and unequivocably at the beginning? (The strangeness of the last sentence in relation to the rest of the passage may well raise doubts in the minds of the students that all of these sentences are intended to show a coherent connection.)

Since this series of items appeared on the test paper of an important province-wide examination, it is clear that questions like those raised above are not of minor significance.

G4 (i) Change into the passive voice:

a. They asked what they had to do.
b. He spoke only when they spoke to him.
c. The knights watched over the sword day and night.[8]

Commentary

1. An evident fault here is *imprecise instructions*. There are no indications as to which verbs in these sentences should be changed into the passive form. Sentence (a) may be rewritten as "They were asked what they had to do," or "They were asked what had to be done," or "They asked what had to be done," all three renditions changing the meaning of the original sentence to a greater or lesser degree. Was this the intention of the constructor of the exercise? It is hard to tell. Students unable to read the teacher's mind may well get (a) wrong, even though they know very well how to form the English passive.

2. Similarly, because of vague instructions, the conscientious student may write for (b) "He was spoken to only when he was spoken to by them," thus producing a nonsensical sentence, or "He spoke only when he was spoken to by them," which is very clumsy in English.

3. "The sword was watched over by the knights day and night" for (c) is also inelegant in English.

4. Constructors of grammatical exercises should make sure that,

—instructions are precise;

—the sentences which result from proposed conversions are probable and felicitous sentences in English;

—the vocabulary content of the sentences is not so unnecessarily varied as to cause extra burdens of comprehension for the student who is concentrating on a grammatical operation.

G4 (ii) Turn into the interrogative form:

1. You do not remember me.
2. He obeyed his master.
3. They came by boat or by train.
4. She knocks at the door.[9]

Commentary

There are five interrogative forms possible for (1) and eight possible for (4). Apart from not knowing precisely what is required, students have, within the compass of four short sentences, to deal with interrogation in present and past tenses, in the negative and in the affirmative, and in three different persons and two numbers.

All of these exercises from traditional textbooks are *teacher or textbook directed*. They leave no place for student creativeness, for enjoyment, or even mild interest. They give the students no opportunity to develop their ability to use English for normal communication.

2. FILL-IN-THE-BLANK EXERCISES

These exercises are found in textbooks which profess to teach aural-oral skills as well as in texts oriented to written practice in grammar. They are discussed here because they are often used for oral practice in the classroom. (As written exercises they are examined in detail in Chapter 8.)

G5 Insert, *a, an,* or *one* in the blanks in the following sentences to make correct English sentences:

a. _____ of my greatuncles was at Gettysburg.
b. Is that _____ amethyst pendant?
c. _____ high-speed computer is always expensive.
d. This is _____ university of great renown.
e. I telephoned _____ of my friends.

Commentary

1. This exercise does not require students to read and understand even one complete English sentence. All they need to do is to look at the spelling of the word that follows the blank and obey the following rules: if it is a word beginning with a consonant or a vowel that is pronounced like a consonant, insert *a*; if it is a word beginning with a vowel or mute *h*, insert *an*; if it is the word *of*, insert *one*. Thus the exercise is completed rather like a crossword puzzle.

2. Items are quite *unconnected semantically* and contain complications of unfamiliar vocabulary and concepts which encourage the students to close their minds to all else but the blank to be filled.

3. With this type of exercise, students often jot down the *replacement in isolation* in their exercise books. Unless the teacher is careful, students will respond with words in isolation (*one, an, a, a, one*) even when the exercise is completed orally. In either case, they do not hear or say a complete English sentence at any stage. Since the student is "learning the rules" one by one in disconnected material, it is unlikely that there will be any high degree of transfer to a spontaneous utterance, without further practice of a different nature.

G6 Include in the sentence given the word in parentheses, making any necessary changes to indicate possession:

a. The (cat) tail was very short.
b. Where is the (boys) dormitory?
c. I have (Marilyn) pencil.
d. Harry looked at the (church) report.
e. The (men) coats were wet.

Commentary

1. As written practice, this exercise encourages students to *find answers for segments*. Students need only to check to see whether the word in parentheses is singular or plural and, if plural, whether it ends in an *s*, adding only '*s* or ' to the word supplied, as the case may be. They do not need to read or understand the complete sentence.

2. As an oral exercise, these five sentences may seem to require only the same choice betwen one form for the singular or for the plural not ending in *s*, and another for the plural ending in *s*. Beneath the deceptive simplicity of this choice, however, is hidden the *complication in spoken English* of the possessive morpheme, with its allomorphs /s/, /z/, and /ɪz/ which

are dependent on phonetic environment. This aspect of spoken English requires practice, of course. The writer of this exercise, however, has clearly had the written differences between the singular and plural possessive forms in mind and has not taken into account the fact that in an oral exercise it would be impossible to know whether the student intended to say *boy's* or *boys'* in (b), since they are pronounced identically. A difference of this type, which is purely a written phenomenon, should be practiced only in a written exercise, since it is irrelevant in speech.

3. Students are confronted with *incorrect English sentences* which may be impressed on the minds of some students, particularly since they contain faults that many non-English speakers commit (e.g., *the cat tail*). The original sentences cannot reasonably be given orally and the less attentive student may not notice the slight difference in the correct form, *cat's tail*, supplied by a fellow student or the teacher.

4. Sentence (d) seems to require a *conversion which is optional* depending on the context. *Church report* is perfectly acceptable in many contexts, as in *the church report is not ready yet,* but is not necessarily the best choice in all cases, e.g., *I was shocked by the budget scandal at St. Paul's, yet the church's report didn't mention it.*

5. With vocabulary connected with things in the classroom, or in pictures on the wall or in the textbook, practice of possessive forms can be more effectively carried out through a *rapid oral exercise* in which students are asked questions like: Q: *Is this your book?* (R: *No, it's Martha's book*); Q: *Is this Pat's pen?* (R: *No, it's Jack's pen* or *No, it's Jack's*); or Q: *Is this the church's roof?* (R: *No, it's the church's steeple*). The teacher should make it clear that all answers must contain a possessive form. (See also G12.)

G7 Fill in the blanks in the following sentences with *some* or *any*, depending on the context:

a. Give her _____ food.
b. Don't speak to _____ strangers on the way.
c. She hasn't _____ friends.
d. I always take _____ magazines with me.

Commentary

1. In this exercise the student must reflect more than in G6, where the rest of the sentence does not affect the decision to be made about the possessive segment as it does here.

2. The student *does not see incorrect forms* in print.

3. The student must *pay attention to the complete sentence* and identify its form (affirmative? negative?) before making a decision about the correct word to fill the blank.

4. This exercise, even more than G6, is normally a *visual* task (blanks cannot be spoken by the teacher). If the teacher attempts to give the items orally, with a slight pause for the blanks, normal English intonation is shattered. Furthermore, the exercise as given here would be misleading in oral form, since some sentences like these are acceptable with no inserted word (e.g., *Give her food!*). Students may very well gain the impression, not intended by the teacher, that *Give her . . . food* (with a slight pause for emphasis) is an incorrect English sentence.

5. If the answers are said aloud with their full context, students at least articulate a complete English sentence. Otherwise, they rush through, rapidly "filling in the blanks."

6. Items again are unconnected and *uninteresting*. The choice to be made for affirmative and negative imperatives could have been exploited more efficiently, allowing some place for student innovation, by devising a rapid oral exercise in which students ask each other to do or not to do various things, with orders like: *Give me some pencils; Don't give her any pencils;* or *Give her some pieces of chalk,* to which an enterprising student can retort: *I don't want any pieces of chalk.* This encourages students to begin talking to each other in English from the earliest lessons.

3. REPLACEMENT EXERCISES

G8 Replace the italicized word with the noun indicated, making any necessary changes.

a. Your *sister*? I didn't see her. (*brother*)
b. Does the *mayor* park his car here? (*actress*)
c. I've served your *breakfast*. Now eat it. (*eggs*)

Commentary

1. The student sees or hears a complete *English sentence* and responds with a complete English sentence.

2. The exercise can be given orally, in which case the instructions will be changed as follows: "Listen carefully to each sentence and the noun I will give you after the sentence. As you repeat the sentence, insert this new

noun in an appropriate position, making any other necessary changes."
This is actually close to the substitution drill technique of G9. However,
because of the continual changes in structural formation, tenses, and lexical
content in successive sentences, it would be difficult to hold the sentences in
the memory while making the substitutions orally. For this reason, it is
essentially an exercise for written practice. In the next section we shall
see how by observing certain restrictions it could be transformed into an
oral exercise.

Systematic oral practice exercises
1. PATTERN OR STRUCTURE DRILL EXERCISES

These types of exercises are found in most contemporary textbooks and on
language laboratory tapes. They are designed for rapid oral practice in
which more items are completed per minute than in written practice. Some
teachers mistakenly use them for written practice, thus giving students a
boring, tedious chore.

Pattern drill exercises are useful for demonstrating the operation of certain structural variations and familiarizing students with their use. They
serve an *introductory function.* They are useful only as a preliminary to
practice in using the new structural variations in some *natural interchange,*
or for review and consolidation of the use of certain structures when
students seem in doubt.

When pattern drills are used, it is important that students understand the
changes in meaning they are effecting by the variations they are performing.
Sometimes a grammatical feature has been encountered in listening or
reading material or in a dialogue. Its functioning has been observed,
experienced, or explained, and a rapid drill is now conducted to familiarize
the students with the use of this grammatical feature in various contexts.
Sometimes a *demonstration* pattern drill introduces the grammatical
feature, which is then explained before being practiced again in a drill
sequence which requires thoughtful reconstruction by the student.

Intensive practice exercises or drills are useful for learning such formal
characteristics of English as tense forms (not tense use), irregular forms of
verbs, pronoun choices, and so on. These drills may be of many types and
of varying degrees of complexity, as we shall see in this chapter.

Teaching series

G9 Repeat the model sentence you hear. In successive sentences replace the
last word by the cue words given, making any necessary changes. You will
then hear the correct sentence. Repeat it if you have made a mistake.

(The correction and the repetition of the correct response will be given here only for the first item, as a demonstration of the technique.)

a.   MODEL SENTENCE   Do you see my father? He's over there.

CUE   Brother

RESPONSE BY STUDENT   Do you see my brother? He's over there.

CORRECT RESPONSE CONFIRMED   Do you see my brother? He's over there.

REPETITION BY STUDENT OF
CORRECT RESPONSE (IF DESIRED)   Do you see my brother? He's over there.

FURTHER CUES   (uncle, son, George, Mr. Smith . . .)

b. Do you see my sister? She's over there.
(aunt, mother, Mary, Mrs. Smith . . .)

c. Do you see my car? It's over there.
(house, church, school, cat . . .)

d. Do you see my children? They're over there.
(friends, cousins, students, classmates . . .)

e. Do you see my orange trees? They're over there.
(boxes, books, dogs, roses . . .)

f. Do you see my grandparents? They're over there.
(girlfriend, truck, skis, husband, customers . . .)

Commentary

1. This is called a *four-phase drill*. When the student does not repeat the correct answer after the model, it is referred to as a *three-phase drill*. The fourth phase provides useful practice for the student who has made a mistake. The third phase (confirmation of the correct response) is usually included on a laboratory tape, but it can become irritating in class when students are giving correct responses smartly. It should be used only when needed.

2. In this exercise there is a *fixed increment*, that is, a segment which is repeated in each utterance in a series. Here, it is *Do you see my* . . . , which makes it possible to introduce many different nouns of various genders, in both singular and plural forms. The noun substituted acts as a cue for the subject pronoun in the second segment which also has a terminal fixed

increment: *over there*. These two unvarying segments reduce the memory load for the students and allow them to concentrate on the minimal changes they are being asked to make. Fixed increment segments of this type are usually retained during *six to eight items*, especially when a new structure is being learned.

3. The sentences used are *short,* thus lightening the memory load.

4. The *lexical content is restricted* to vocabulary with which the students are familiar so that they can concentrate on the structural rule they are applying.

5. Each sentence the students utter is one which could *possibly appear in conversation.*

6. There is *no ambiguity in the exercise.* The instructions are clear and each item is so composed that only one response will be correct. This makes it possible for the acceptability of the response to be confirmed by a correct response given by the teacher or the voice on the tape. This is particularly useful when the student is working individually with a recorder or in a language laboratory.

7. (f) is *the testing phase* of the drill. In a complete exercise it will range over the five possibilities in random order in eight (or more) items. Through it the students can see whether the rules they are internalizing produce correct sentences and the teacher can tell whether the students need further practice of specific variations of the feature they have been learning.

8. Note that each item must be selected carefully so that its number or gender is quite clear. Words like *sheep* or *teacher* would be ambiguous as cues in the testing phase (f) because both *it* and *they* would be possible responses to *sheep* and both *he* and *she* would be possible responses to the cue *teacher*. In (a)—(e), this problem should not arise because the model sentence given by the teacher or taped voice will make it clear to the student whether the particular set of items is concentrating on singulars or plurals, masculines, feminines, or neuters. After a few items, students expect the rest of the set to follow the pattern demonstrated by the model item. (Instructions usually indicate to the student when a testing phase is to be presented.)

9. It will depend on the age and maturity of the students and the intensiveness of the course whether this series is presented gradually over a period of time or practiced in one lesson.

10. Since words are grouped according to gender and number, the operation of the drill can become mechanical and cease to be useful, because students are no longer concentrating on the grammatical point at issue. It should not be continued beyond the point where students have

acquired familiarity with the forms. At that stage, they are ready to produce utterances of their own creation, using the forms they have been learning.

Patterned response

The drill in G9 would be *less monotonous* and the students would be participating in a *more realistic* way if the response were not a simple repetition with substitution, but required an answer form.

G10 a. Practice with the model (students repeat sentences demonstrating the structural model):

Do you see my father over there?
Yes, he's across the road.

b. The drill continues, following the same pattern:

CUE	Do you see my uncle over there?
RESPONSE	Yes, he's across the road.
(Confirmation)	

CUE	Do you see my son over there?
RESPONSE	Yes, he's across the road.
(Confirmation)	

CUE	Do you see my sister over there?
RESPONSE	Yes, she's across the road.
(Confirmation)	

Chain drill

A *final practice* at the end of this series can be a chain drill on the following pattern: each student in turn invents an utterance and produces a cue for the next student. Students should be encouraged at this stage to be as original as they can within the limitations of the pattern.

G11

STUDENT A TO STUDENT B	Do you see my father over there?
STUDENT B	Yes, he's across the road.
(TO STUDENT C)	Do you see my friend over there?
STUDENT C	Yes, she's in front of the bank.
(TO STUDENT D)	Do you see the apple trees over there?
STUDENT D	No, they're not apple trees . . .

This chain drill can be a *team game*, each team gaining a point for each correct link in the chain (with a limit being set to the time for reflection to keep the game moving smartly). The chain passes to the other team each time an error is made or a student fails to respond within the time allowed.

Patterned response in a situational context

> A drill of this type is more interesting and has more reality if it is given a *situational* context and students can add a comment of their own.

G12 Context can be provided by the use of objects in the classroom, the view from the window, or pictures. The drill is conducted first in choral fashion with students referring to things pointed out by the teacher (*Do you see the trains in the station? Yes, they're over there*). Then the drill moves to individual response, with students pointing out people or things to each other (*Do you see my new pencil? Yes, it's blue; Do you see the doctor? Yes, he's in front of the hospital*).

Finally a *game* develops. Team points are awarded for correct answers to the question *Do you see X?* Students understand that the answer must contain a pronoun to replace the noun in the question. They respond with such expressions as *Yes, they're in the corridor* or *No, it's under the book.*

With a little practice and some choral responses at the beginning, a game of this type can proceed as smartly as an oral drill, yet the students are producing utterances of their own. Swift response can be elicited by pausing a short time for one student to reply, then moving to another if the student is still hesitating.

> Successful completion of an oral drill does not guarantee that the students will use the correct form in *autonomous production*. Students must try to express themselves outside of a framework which forces them to produce certain answers.

G13 The lesson may conclude with the students asking each other questions: *In your bedroom, do you have a carpet/have you (got) a carpet?*[10] (*Yes, it's blue and red*); *Does your grandmother live here?* (*No, she's in Lincoln*). Alternatively, they may play a game such as *I'm thinking of X. Describe X.* Students guess: *You're thinking of a book; it's red*, or *You're thinking of a girl; she's fat* . . . until they find the right answer.

> Suggestions for encouraging autonomous production are given in Chapter 2.

* Try to write a series of drills to teach and test the *object forms of the pronouns* or the use of *the question words: who* and *what.* Think of *situational contexts* in which these could be practiced and *games* which would produce the same types of responses as a drill. Then see if the types of games you have invented work smoothly by trying them out on other students.

2. SUBSTITUTION OR VARIATION TABLES

Oral drilling can also be performed with the use of variation or substitution tables[11] such as the following.

G14

My	father		a	lawyer
Her	mother	is		doctor
His	friend		an	architect
Our	sister			actress
Your	cousins		—	mechanics
Their	neighbors	are		engineers
	brothers			farmers

Commentary

1. This is a *mixed drill* and presumes some prior learning of specific structural items either in dialogues, reading material, oral work in the classroom, or earlier more restricted drills on the determiner forms of the possessive pronouns (sometimes called possessive adjectives[12]) and the singular and plural forms of the verb *be* in the third person. The drill then focuses on contexts which involve choice in the use of the indefinite article. It serves a useful purpose in drawing together in a systematic way what has been learned and what is being learned. (See also W1–3.)

2. The drill may be conducted with the complete table in front of the students in an initial *learning phase*. The teacher points to various items on a chart, or on a diagram on the chalkboard, to elicit different combinations from the students. In the second or *testing phase*, the students work from a table where items have been jumbled and columns 3 and 4 have been left blank.

G15

Her	friend			farmers
Our	neighbors			doctor
Their	father			actress
My	sister			engineers
Your	brothers			lawyer
His	cousins			architect
	mother			mechanics

Finally students move on to practice with items not on the original chart, and here suggestions from G12 for *applications in situational contexts* will apply.

3. If, as is usually the case, the items are related to dialogue or reading material already studied, the variations may be taught *without a chart* by using *flashcards or pictures* of characters familiar to the students. In this case, column 1 will be restricted to third person possessive pronouns which will be cued by descriptions of the picture: *John's father: his father . . . ; Mary's and John's cousins: their cousins. . . .* After considerable practice in this purely aural-oral fashion, students will then look at the chart in their books.

4. As with G9, this practice with variation tables is preliminary learning of grammatical structures. It must be accompanied by more extensive, and more spontaneous, applications of the variations in some form of *personal interchange* between students and teachers. (See G13.)

Six groups of oral exercises

For each type of exercise in this section a brief description with an example will be given, some comments will be made on common faults to be avoided in constructing such exercises, and some English structural features for which this type of oral exercise would be useful will be listed.

Oral exercises fall into six groups: repetition, substitution, conversion, sentence modification, response, and translation exercises.

1. REPETITION OR PRESENTATION DRILLS

In simple repetition drills, the instructor gives a model sentence containing a particular structure or form to be manipulated and the students repeat the sentence with correct intonation and stress. Repetition drills are not, in one sense, a special category of exercise which will be used for practicing certain types of structure; they represent, rather, a commonly used technique for familiarizing the student with the *specific structure,* with the *paradigm,* or with the *procedure for the practice.* For this reason they are sometimes called *presentation drills.* They are useful as *introductory material,* but it must be remembered that from mere repetition, no matter how prolonged, the student will learn little except the requirements of the drill.

G16   MODEL   Where is the station?   Oh, I see it.
        STUDENT Where is the station?   Oh, I see it.

        MODEL   Where is the cab driver?   Oh, I see him.
        STUDENT Where is the cab driver?   Oh, I see him.

        MODEL   Where are the shops?   Oh, I see them.
        STUDENT Where are the shops?   Oh, I see them.

Commentary

1. This example highlights one of the defects of many repetition drills: their unreality and lack of application to the students' situation. Unless the students are looking at a picture showing a scene in a city, G16 could become completely mechanical,[13] with students attending only to the cue words *it, him, them,* or merely repeating them absentmindedly with the rest of what is fed to them. In this case, the structure could just as easily be presented with nonsense words: *Where is the doplin? Oh, I see it; Where is the daplin? Oh, I see her.* The students might actually find the latter procedure more amusing since it might focus their attention, through curiosity, on the cues in the drill.

2. If students are to use in other situations the object pronouns being demonstrated, they should be concentrating on the meaning of what they are saying. Some reality can be introduced by referring to objects the students can see and having them point to them as they respond: *Where is the cupboard? Oh, I see it; Where are the readers? Oh, I see them.*

2. SUBSTITUTION DRILLS

Commonly used types are simple substitution, double substitution, correlative substitution, and multiple substitution drills.

a. *Simple substitution drills* have been demonstrated in G9.

b. *Double substitution drills* are similar to simple substitutions in that the student has no other operation to perform apart from substitution of a new segment in the place of an existing segment. There are, however, two slots into which the new segments may be inserted. The signal which indicates to the student which is the appropriate slot for a new segment is the structure of the segment in relation to the structure of the complete sentence. Double substitutions require the student to be more alert than do simple substitutions because they continually change the wording (and, therefore, the meaning) without changing the structure. They are *still mechanical*, however, because each segment is usually signalled in such a way that it can be substituted in the correct slot without the student necessarily understanding its meaning.

G17 MODEL SENTENCE If I find it / I'll give it to you.
     CUE *If you want it*
    RESPONSE *If you want it* / I'll give it to you.
     CUE *he'll sell it to you*
    RESPONSE If you want it / *he'll sell it to you.*
     CUE *If you request it*
    RESPONSE *If you request it* / he'll sell it to you.

CUE *he'll send it to you*
RESPONSE If you request it / *he'll send it to you.*

Commentary

1. The pattern of activity the student learns is "substitute in alternate slots, retaining the new segment for two responses (as in the sequence: *AB, CB, CD, ED, EF* . . .)."

2. If the instructor makes clear what elements are being manipulated (in this case "present tense in the *if* clause: future tense in the principal clause"), students will find this type of substitution useful for familiarizing themselves with the correct tense form for the correct slot in the utterance. Students will, however, need a more demanding type of activity that forces them to decide where to put each segment according to the meaning they wish to convey if the teacher is to be sure that they can really use the pattern in communication. This may take the form of an innovative *chain drill* (G11), a *game*, or a *structured interchange* (where the students invent conditional statements themselves).

c. In *correlative substitution drills* each substitution requires correlative changes to be made elsewhere in the model sentence. (See G9 f.)

G18 MODEL SENTENCE *He* brings *his* lunch.
               CUE *You* . . .
        RESPONSE *You* bring *your* lunch.
               CUE *Jane and Mary* . . .
        RESPONSE *Jane and Mary* bring *their* lunche*s.*

This type of drill is useful for learning such things as possessives, reflexives, the *-s* ending of the third person singular verb in the present tense, the changing forms of the verb *be*, irregular verbs, the inflection of the verb after relative pronouns, the forms of the plural and possessive morphemes, and certain sequences of tenses in related clauses.

With a little imagination, this type of drill can be used to practice styles of language (see C5).

G19   MODEL Hi/hello, Bill. How's it going?
        CUE Mrs. Murphy
   RESPONSE Good morning, Mrs. Murphy. How are you?

CUE Dr. Smith
RESPONSE Good morning, Dr. Smith. How are you?
CUE How's everything?
RESPONSE Hi/hello, Sammy. How's everything?

Correlative substitution can be made *more realistic* by designing the cue with a natural-sounding tag which elicits a response that completes a conversational interchange.

G20 CUE I'm drinking coffee for breakfast. What about *Jim?*
RESPONSE *Jim's* drinking coffee for breakfast too.
CUE I'm eating eggs for breakfast. What about *you two?*
RESPONSE *We're* eating eggs for breakfast too.

This type of tag can also be used to elicit changes in reflexive pronoun forms:

G21 CUE I really hurt myself. What about Mary?
RESPONSE Mary really hurt herself too.
CUE Jim really enjoyed himself. What about you two?
RESPONSE We really enjoyed ourselves too.

d. *Multiple substitution drills* are a *learning/testing device* to see whether students can continue to make a certain grammatical adjustment they have been learning while they are distracted by other preoccupations —in this case, thinking of the changing meaning of successive sentences so as to make substitutions in different slots. In order to make the substitutions in the appropriate slots, students have to think of the meaning of the whole sentence, which changes in focus with each substitution. For this reason, students need to be very alert to perform this exercise successfully.

After study and practice of *much* and *many* with count and uncountable nouns the following multiple substitution drill could be used:

G22 MODEL SENTENCE She brings too many pencils to school.
CUE *Peter*
RESPONSE *Peter* brings too many pencils to school.
CUE *money*
RESPONSE Peter brings *too much money* to school.
CUE *takes*
RESPONSE Peter *takes* too much money to school.
CUE *library*
RESPONSE Peter takes too much money to *the library.*

CUE *books*
RESPONSE Peter takes *too many books* to the library.
CUE *Students*
RESPONSE *Students* take too many books to the library.

The last response, which requires a correlative change not related to the main focus of the exercise, as well as the expected substitution, provides a challenge for an enthusiastic class which enjoys showing how much it has learned.

3. CONVERSIONS

The term *transformation* has long been applied to the types of exercises in which such operations are performed as changing affirmative sentences into negative sentences, statements into questions, simple declarations into emphatic declarations, active voice into passive voice, or present tense statements into past tense statements. Exercises like these have been the staple of foreign-language classes for many years. Some of these processes happen to parallel what are known as "transformations" in transformational-generative grammar (e.g., negativization, passivization, and the interrogative transformation); others do not, but when they do this is usually more of a coincidence from the point of view of the constructor of the exercise than a derivative relationship. The term "transformation" is, therefore, misleading to some people because of a presumed intentional connection with transformational-generative grammar. For this reason, the term "conversions" will be used for exercises in changing sentence type, in combining two sentences into one, in moving from one mood or tense to another, in changing word class (e.g., replacing nouns by pronouns), substituting phrases for clauses or clauses for phrases (e.g., adverbial phrases for adverbial clauses, infinitive phrases for clauses), or substituting single words for phrases or phrases for single words (e.g., adverbs for adverbial phrases, adjectives for adjectival phrases).

These are conversions rather than substitutions in that they require the use of a different form (frequently with a correlative change), a change in word order, the introduction of new elements, or even considerable restructuring of the utterance. They are useful for developing flexibility in the selection of formal structures for the expression of personal meaning.

a. *General conversions*

In our discussion of the construction of common types of conversions and the weaknesses to be avoided, we will use examples based on the asking of *questions*. Interrogative forms are among the most frequently used in the language, and practice with them can easily be given *a situational context* and *a personal application*.

G23 Change the following statements into questions.

    CUES   a. John and I are sitting in the classroom.
              b. I am a student.
              c. The actress lives in Canada.
              d. My aunt and uncle have their breakfast early.
              e. Margaret does her shopping on Thursdays.
              f. We can work together.

Commentary

1. This traditional type of elementary conversion exercise requires the student to attend to a number of different aspects of the formation of yes-no questions in a very few items. In these six items the student is required to use subject-inversion with *be*, *do*-periphrasis with single and with plural subjects (nouns and pronouns), and with main verbs including *have* and *do*, and subject-inversion with a modal. This is a formidable task for an elementary-level student.

2. When (a) and (b) are converted into questions they produce utterances which have close to zero probability of occurrence, yet such sentences can still be found in books in use at the present time in many parts of the world. (f) is a more useful item because it does produce a question which could be of use to the students at a later stage.

3. (c), (d), and (e) illustrate a common tendency for exercises of this type to range over any and all topics, and into any vocabulary area, with no meaningful coherence. This may not appear to be a grave fault, but it deepens the impression of many students that language study is mere manipulation of words and has no reality or relevance.

In the six sentences in G23, students are *tested* for their knowledge of a mixed set of interrogation rules. The exercise should, therefore, come after a *series of learning exercises,* in which the students encounter various aspects of the conversion and practice them step by step. Each exercise in such a series will consist of six or more sentences (with familiar or interesting vocabulary) which after conversion will produce questions formed on the same pattern and semantically related, as in the following:

G24 Convert the following statements into questions according to the model:

    REPEAT Peter has a new car.
             Does Peter have a new car? / Has Peter (got) a new car?
      CUES a. Teresa has a new car.
             b. The car has a radio.

   c. She likes to drive.
   d. Students drive fast in this city.
   e. They stop at stop signs.
   f. You park in a parking lot.

A *complete series on yes-no question formation* would include a set on the placing of *be*, GB *have* (in some senses), or any auxiliary before the subject, sets on the *do*-periphrasis with the simple present or past tense forms of verbs including *do* (and GB certain senses of *have*), a set on the differences in behavior between the modals *can* and *have to,* a set eliciting questions in statement form with rising intonation (*You are coming too?*), and several sets with tag questions (*He drives fast, doesn't he?*). Naturally, negative questions with the use of the contracted form of *do* + *not*, or of *be, have,* or another auxiliary + *not*, would receive special attention (*Doesn't he know? Aren't I invited? Isn't he an Australian? Wouldn't you like one?*). Some review sets would be interpolated. Study of several of these aspects, though naturally not all of them at once, would have to precede a mixed exercise of the G23 type.

The great *advantage of oral exercises,* apart from their obvious role in helping students develop facility in producing correct forms in sequence while using their speech organs, is that so much more practice can be accomplished in the time available. This allows for step-by-step progression through a series of rules. The practice sets will normally be spread over several lessons. The amount of subdivision within these sets and the number of sets presented at any one time will depend on the level of instruction, the maturity of the students, and the intensiveness of the course. For elementary classes, the forms necessary for simple communication will be enough. For more mature students, discussion of the various possibilities can reduce the necessity to proceed by one-feature-at-a-time practice.

Situational and personal application. Another set of grammatical rules commonly practiced through conversion exercises is the series determining the form and position of pronouns which occur as direct and indirect objects of the verb. Most textbooks resort here to the replacement in sentences of nouns by pronouns: "Paul gave *his father* the books" becomes "Paul gave *him* the books"; "Paul gave his father *the books*" becomes "Paul gave *them to* his father", and "Paul gave *his father the books*" becomes "Paul gave *them to him*", paralleling the alternative non-pronominalized form: "Paul gave the books to his father".

Conversion exercises like the following are also used.

G25 Listen carefully to each of the following sentences and replace by pronouns in the appropriate form and position the words which are repeated. You may need to add a preposition.

> MODEL Paul gave his father the books. His father.
> RESPONSE Paul gave him the books.
> CUES a. Janet read her mother the letter. Her mother.
>   b. Janet read her mother the letter. The letter.
>   c. Michael repeated the words to his friend. The words. . . .

While these rules for the form and position of the pronoun objects are being learned, students can also learn the difference in choice of preposition for actual and intended recipient. This can be taught by a reverse conversion exercise, where students are given cue sentences like *I gave her a car* to be converted into *I gave a car to Janet* and *I made him a sweater* to be converted into *I made a sweater for John.*

In every case where a series of rules is involved, the number of exercises necessary for assimilating these rules thoroughly through conversion practice alone would be very extensive. The number of exercises can be shortened considerably by judicious explanations of grammatical functioning. Those conversion exercises which are then retained can be made more vivid by associating structure with action. Students may be asked to respond to instructions and questions by making statements of their own invention, as in a normal conversational interchange, along the following lines:

G26 (I)   Don't give Albert that book. I'm not going to give it to him.
Give Shirley that picture. No, I'm going to give it to Stephen.
Did you make a bag for Martha? No, I made her this necklace.
Did she make you a present? Yes, she made a cushion for me.

Commentary

1. If students prepare ahead of time they can come to class with instructions and questions for each other which will require quick-wittedness in responding and cause quite a lot of amusement for the class.

2. *A mixed practice* of this type presumes preliminary sequential learning, but it is very effective in providing for *review of an integrated set of rules.* Conducted orally, without hesitation, it enables the students to absorb the rhythm of the sequences. This is an aid to memory which is

quite lost if students constantly write out their responses—editing and re-editing their first attempts as they "put the objects in the right place" in a conscious, artificial way. Other considerations apart, it is more fun for the students and the teacher.

b. *Combinations*

Combinations are a form of conversion exercise which has also been used for many years. It involves a process which reflects certain features of transformational grammatical analysis and can be very illuminating in differentiating some aspects of the rules. For instance, students often have difficulty in understanding when the relative pronoun *that* must be retained and when it can be omitted. Let us analyse two sentences with relative clauses which begin with *that* and try to see in which contexts the omission of *that* is permissible and what are the underlying reasons for this difference.

1(a) I saw the man that you photographed.
1(b) I saw the man you photographed.
2(a) I saw the man that fell off the horse.
2(b)*I saw the man fell off the horse.

If we examine 1(a), we find it combines two underlying sentences:

I saw the man,
you photographed the man,

in both of which *the man* occurs as a direct object of the verb. The relative pronoun *that* in 1(a) replaces one occurrence of *the man* as direct object, the subjects of the two underlying sentences, *I* and *you*, being clearly stated.
Sentence 2(a) also combines two underlying sentences:

I saw the man,
the man fell off the horse,

but here *the man* is the object of the first sentence and the subject of the second sentence. *That* in 2(a) replaces one occurrence of *the man* (the case in which *the man* is the subject of the subordinate clause). As a result, if *that* is omitted, we are left with one clause in which the subject is not clearly stated, as in 2(b). Since it is not permissible to omit *that* when it is the subject of the clause, 2(b) is not an acceptable sentence in English (as is indicated by the convention of marking it with *).
Often the relative clause is embedded in the sentence as in 3 and 4.

3(a) The man that you photographed built the house.
3(b) The man you photographed built the house.
4(a) The man that built the house came to see me.
4(b)*The man built the house came to see me.

In the sentences with asterisks, the unacceptable sentences in English, the omission of *that* causes problems of aural perception. Bever points out that, when listening, we tend to perceive clauses, not single words, as we segment the message.[14] He also maintains that we expect the first noun-verb-noun we hear in English to be the main clause and to represent actor-action-object, unless some linguistic signal tells us otherwise (see Chapter 3: *Strategies of Perceptual Segmentation,* p. 87). If the rule in English permitted the omission of *that* in every case, we would have no signal to block our perception in 4(b) that *the man built the house* was the main clause. In 3(b) this problem does not occur because *you* following *the man*, that is, NN, acts as a signal that we are not hearing the complete main clause first.

Asking students to combine two underlying sentences by using a relative pronoun is moving from a deeper level of structure to surface structure. Taking a surface structure sentence and examining its underlying components can be very useful in identifying the real functions of elements of the surface structure. In this way what are often taken to be identical structures are found to be quite distinct, as in the classic examples:

5. John is eager to please.
   John is eager,
   John pleases somebody.
6. John is easy to please
   John is easy,
   Somebody pleases John. [15]

Students often wonder why some clauses seem to be combined with *that* and some with *what* when in both cases we may have subordinate relative clauses. An analysis into underlying components makes the distinction quite clear:

7. He sees the damage that you have done.
   He sees the damage.
   You have done the damage.

One occurrence of *the damage* as object may be replaced by *that* as in 7, or *that* may be omitted as in 8:

8. He sees the damage you have done.

In 9, we have a different situation:

9. He sees what you have done.
   He sees A.
   You have done A.

Here, the repeated object is something unspecified. In this case both occurrences of the unspecified something are represented in the surface structure by *what* which cannot, therefore, be omitted.

The following oral exercises, G27–28, require more active construction of sentences with relative pronouns than the traditional fill-in-the-blank exercises of the type:

Fill in the blanks in the following sentences with *that* where it is essential. Leave the blank where *that* may be omitted.

I gave him the book _____ he wanted.

G27 Combine each of the following pairs of sentences into one acceptable sentence, using *that* or omitting *that* where it is possible to do so. Make the first sentence the main clause.

a. Give me the keys.
   I left you the keys.

b. The car is over there.
   I bought the car yesterday.

c. Don't close the door.
   The door has just been painted. . . .

G28 (1)   Combine each of the following pairs of sentences into one acceptable sentence, using *what* or *that*, as is appropriate. (You may omit *that* where it is permitted.)

a. The mother accepted it.
   Her daughter brought it.
   RESPONSE The mother accepted what her daughter brought.

b. The neighbor refused the money.
   I offered him the money.
   RESPONSE The neighbor refused the money that I offered him.
         OR The neighbor refused the money I offered him.

The procedure of combining sentences to form one utterance can also be used for creating dependent phrases beginning with present participles (*he arrived at the station: he went straight to the ticket office—Arriving at the station, he went straight to the ticket office*), or with prepositions such as *before* and *after*. (Where one clause will be subordinate to the other, it must be clear to the student which of the two sentences to be combined will be the main clause and which the dependent clause. Sometimes temporal relationships will make this clear.)

c. *Restatement*

Restatement is another useful kind of conversion exercise.

G29 One frequently used type of *directed dialogue* is a restatement exercise. (See also C24 c.)

> CUE Tell George your name is Ronald.
> RESPONSE George, my name is Ronald.
> CUE Ask Alice where she's going.
> RESPONSE Where are you going, Alice?
> CUE Ask her to wait for you.
> RESPONSE Wait for me, please.

A series of this type is usually based on a dialogue which has been learned, but all kinds of restatements can be invented to practice different grammatical features. A realistic note is added if one student pretends to be giving directions to a third party by telephone, while a second student is supplying the necessary information (*Tell her to take Route 123 . . .*).

G30 A *running commentary* by one student on what another student or the teacher is saying softly gives practice in restatement of direct speech in indirect speech form.

> (I) STUDENT A I've just arrived but I'm leaving in a few minutes.
>   STUDENT B She said she had just arrived but was leaving in a few minutes.
>   STUDENT A Why are you looking at me like that?
>   STUDENT B She asked me why I was looking at her like that.

Another type of replacement (sometimes called a *contraction*) consists of replacing a longer expression with a shorter expression (e.g., a clause with a prepositional phrase, a prepositional phrase with a noun phrase, a relative clause with an infinitive construction) or a fuller expression with a more elliptical one, while retaining the basic meaning.

G31 (I) a. Restate each of the following sentences replacing the relative clause with an infinitive construction of similar meaning.

> 1. I need a desk *that I can put my books on.*
>   RESPONSE I need a desk *to put my books on.*
> 2. If they had a house *they had to pay for* they'd save.
>   RESPONSE If they had a house *to pay for* they'd save.

b. Restate each of the following sentences replacing the words italicized with a noun phrase.

1. She recognized *that she had made a mistake.*
   RESPONSE She recognized *her error.*
2. *The man who owns the car* lives across the road.
   RESPONSE *The owner of the car* lives across the road.

Contraction exercises can be used to teach the use of *ellipsis* in familiar speech;[16] as in the following example.

G32 (I or A)   You are talking informally with close friends. For each of the sentences you hear give the familiar elliptical form.

a. I've got a lot of fruit here. Do you want any?
   RESPONSE Gotta lot of fruit here. Want any?
b. I'm sorry I can't come. I'm afraid I've caught a cold.
   RESPONSE Sorry I can't come. 'Fraid I've caught a cold.
c. What a crowd there is! It must be the last train!
   RESPONSE What a crowd! Must be the last train!

* List for yourself other areas of English grammar for which some form of restatement would be a suitable exercise and try to think of ways in which this restatement can be incorporated into a natural communication activity.

4. SENTENCE MODIFICATIONS

Sentence modification exercises are of three kinds: expansions, deletions, and completions.

a. *Expansions*

Expansions serve two purposes. Type A requires strictly grammatical manipulation and is useful for learning such things as the position of adverbs. It can be teacher or student directed. Type B is more spontaneous; it gives students the opportunity to create new and original sentences from a basic sentence, often in an atmosphere of competition.[17] Students should be encouraged to spice the exercise with humorous items.

Type A expansions. Students often have problems with the appropriate placing of adverbs and adverbial expressions in an English sentence. This question is very complex.[18] Nevertheless, at some stage, students will need to be familiar with at least the following rules for placing adverbs of manner, place, time, and frequency in normally stressed sentences. Students will learn later that they may be given other positions for reasons of emphasis or contrast (information focus), or in formal written language, and that a few adverbs do not necessarily conform to these rules.

1. Adverbs of manner and place (*awkwardly, well, there*) usually appear after the verb or after the direct object, if there is one (he climbed *awkwardly*; he chewed it *well*; he left it *there*). Exception: *quickly* may be used in a time sense (he *quickly* gave up: he *soon* gave up).

2. Adverbs of time and expressions like *once, twice,* usually occur at the beginning or at the end of the sentence (or clause), the end position being the more common (I'll see you *tomorrow*; *tomorrow* I'll take you to the beach; they saw the film about Everest *twice*). Exception: *still* (he is *still* selling toffee apples).

3. Adverbs of frequency come after the auxiliary, or modal used with another verb, but before simple forms of verbs (he's *rarely* in; he has *seldom* replied; he can *never* understand; he *sometimes* stays longer). *Sometimes* may appear at the beginning or end of the sentence (*sometimes* he says funny things; he says funny things *sometimes*). Exceptions: with *used to, have to* (I *seldom* have to tell her twice). At times the auxiliary or modal is used as a simple form (he *never* is; I *rarely* can).

This complex set of rules can be practiced very effectively in an oral expansion of Type A:

G33 (1)

BASIC SENTENCE She left the house
CUE early
RESPONSE She left the house early.
CUE rarely
RESPONSE She rarely left the house early.
CUE last year.
RESPONSE Last year she rarely left the house early.

Many other grammatical features can be practiced in a Type A expansion:

G34 Insert in the sentences you hear the expressions supplied in the cues.

BASIC SENTENCE He bought a book.
CUE old
RESPONSE He bought an old book.
CUE stained
RESPONSE He bought a stained old book

CUE history
RESPONSE He bought a stained old history book.
CUE medieval
RESPONSE He bought a stained old medieval history book.

Type B expansions provide students with the opportunity to create new sentences from a basic frame by expanding the frame as they wish, as often as they wish. In this type of practice no two students would produce exactly the same answer.

G35   CUE The man crosses the street.
STUDENT A The tired old man crosses the busy street.
STUDENT B The busy business man crosses the main street hurriedly twice a day.

A Type B expansion may be conducted as a *chaining activity,* with each student in succession adding a new element to the sentence until a limit seems to have been reached. At that stage, a new chain begins with another simple sentence.

b. *Deletions*

Flexibility in manipulating structures can be developed by reversing processes.

Type A deletions, which are the reverse of Type A expansions, provide further variety in practice.

G36 Delete the negative elements in the following sentences, making any necessary changes.

CUE They haven't any coffee.
RESPONSE They have some coffee.
CUE She didn't come.
RESPONSE She came (*or* She did come.)
CUE You came, didn't you?
RESPONSE You didn't come, did you?
(*or* You came, did you?)

Type B deletions serve a less useful purpose than Type B expansions. Expansions require students to decide at which point in the sentence to insert additional information of their own choosing. Deletions of extra information usually require only formal changes, as practiced in Type A deletions. For this reason deletions are not creative.

c. *Completions*

In completions, part of the sentence is given as a cue and the students finish the sentence either with a semantically constant segment in which some syntactic or morphological change must be made according to the cue (Type A_1), with a suitable segment which is to some extent semantically governed by the cue (Type A_2), or with a segment of their own invention (Type B).

Type A_1 completions.

G37 (I) In the following exercise you will hear the model sentence: *If I see him I'll tell him.* Throughout the exercise, you will retain the same concluding notion, varying the segment from future tense to conditional as the introductory segment changes.

MODEL SENTENCE If I see him I'll tell him.
CUE If I saw him . . .
RESPONSE If I saw him I'd tell him.
CUE If you took it . . .
RESPONSE If you took it I'd tell him.
CUE If you left . . .
RESPONSE If you left I'd tell him.
CUE If she comes . . .
RESPONSE If she comes I'll tell him.

Type A_2 completions.

G38 (I) In the following exercise you will hear the model sentence: *He gave me back my pen because he preferred his.* Throughout the exercise you will retain a concluding segment similar in meaning to *because he preferred his*, but as the introductory segment varies you will vary the person referred to in the concluding segment.

MODEL SENTENCE He gave me back my pen because he preferred his.
CUE I gave you back your eraser . . .
RESPONSE I gave you back your eraser because I preferred mine.
CUE We gave her back her colored pencils . . .
RESPONSE We gave her back her colored pencils because we preferred ours.

Commentary

With an exercise involving a correlative change of this type, it is usually advisable for the student to repeat two, or even three, items with the instructor at the beginning in order to be sure of the kind of manipulation required.

A Type A₂ completion is very useful for *vocabulary learning:*

G39 Complete the following statements with the appropriate occupational term, according to the model:

> MODEL A person who drives a cab is a *cab driver.*
> CUE A person who builds houses . . .
> RESPONSE A person who builds houses is *a builder.*
> CUE A person who sells meat . . .
> RESPONSE A person who sells meat is *a butcher.*

Type B completions. A Type B completion allows students to make their personal semantic contribution within a syntactically fixed framework. It is useful for practicing such things as restrictive and non-restrictive relative clauses (also called defining and nondefining); the various possibilities with infinitive constructions (*he was the first man to leave the refinery*; *she came to Tokyo to learn Japanese*; *it was good of you to book the room for us,* etc); correct prepositions to use with phrasal verbs, the use of the infinitive with or without *to*; or the addition of clauses or phrases expressing purpose (I opened the window / *to let the air in*; I left the note / *so that you would know where I was*).

G40 (I)   Invent a completion containing an infinitive construction for each sentence you hear, according to the model: He was the second man . . . He was the second man *to ask her that question.*

> CUE She has decided . . .
> RESPONSE She has decided to marry him.
>   *or:* She has decided not to marry him.
>   *or:* She has decided to leave the country.
>   *or:* She has decided to take a job . . .
> CUE You needn't . . .
> RESPONSE You needn't go to school today.
>   *or:* You needn't pay me yet.
>   *or:* You needn't tell me your secrets. . . .

Commentary

In a Type A₁ completion on the use of infinitive constructions the concluding segment would remain the same throughout the exercise, except for the appearance or non-appearance of *to*, with the cue supplying the new semantic content: I refused / *to talk to them*; you needn't / *talk to them*; my mother made me / *talk to them*; she doesn't want / *to talk to them*). An exercise of Type A₁ may precede the Type B exercise above to familiarize students with the required structures or to refresh their memories. All practice should, however, move toward Type B exercises where students supply something of their own invention and then go beyond Type B to *creative practice*, like that described in Chapter 2 under *Autonomous Interaction*, p. 47.

* Look for other areas of grammar for which sentence modifications would be useful and try to think of original ways of presenting them which draw close to the real purposes of communication.

5. RESPONSE PRACTICE

In one sense all oral exercises are forms of response practice. In the particular type referred to here, *question-answer* or *answer-question* procedures are used, or students learn to make appropriate conventional responses to other people's utterances (*rejoinders*).

a. *Question-answer practice*

Ability to ask questions with ease and to recognize question forms effortlessly, so that one can reply appropriately, is of the essence of communication. It has always been a basic classroom activity. Unfortunately, much question-answer material is very stilted, questions being asked for the sake of the form, without attention to their real interest to the student. The structure of questions can be practiced through conversion exercises. Question-answer practice is useful for such things as forms and uses of tenses, various kinds of pronouns, and cleft sentences which make clear the informational focus (e.g., *It was my book she took*). It is most frequently associated with a picture, slide, or film, reading material, some project or activity, or a game. It can, however, be carefully structured for language-learning purposes. Since the form of an appropriate answer is nearly always a reflection of the question, teachers can elicit the forms and uses they want by skillful construction of the questions. In the following series, for instance, successive questions elicit the use of different tenses from the student, yet the communicative interaction develops naturally.

G41 (1) (The students have been reading about or viewing a film of the adventures of a group of young people in Boston.)

Q. Why didn't they come home before midnight?

A. They didn't come home because there were fireworks over the river. It was the Fourth of July.

Q. Do you often stay out late at night?
A. No, I go home early because I'm always hungry.

Q. Perhaps when school starts you'll stay out later.
A. Probably. I'll be working back in the library then.

Q. What would you do if your mother stopped getting dinner for you because you were always late?
A. I'd ask her for some money to buy hot dogs or hamburgers.

Commentary

The development of this type of interchange is not predictable, but the alert questioner can keep on switching the conversation to a different time perspective. The same type of approach can be developed at the elementary level through discussion of an action picture.

Many *situations* can be created in the classroom for the asking of questions and the obtaining of answers.

G42 With a simulated telephone link, all kinds of situations can be invented which elicit questions and answers from students.

1. Student A calls student B on the phone. Student B asks questions until he or she is able to identify the person calling and the purpose of the call.
2. Student C calls student D to get some information on a special subject. Student D has an English-language travel brochure, a menu, or a collection of advertisements from which to give the information requested.

b. *Answer-question practice*

Only too frequently the teacher asks all the questions, yet in a foreign-language situation it is more commonly the language learner, or foreign visitor, who needs to be able to ask questions with ease. Certainly, in a natural conversation, each participant passes freely from the role of interlocutor to respondent. Answer-question practice takes place when the teacher, or some student, has the answer and the others must find out what it is. This type of exercise takes place naturally and interestingly in such games as *Twenty Questions, Animal-Vegetable-Mineral,* and *Who and What?*

G43 In *Twenty Questions* one person (A) thinks of someone or something. By asking eliminating questions to which A may reply only yes or no, the players narrow the field of possibilities until they are able to guess the person or object in question. Only twenty questions may be asked before the game is lost.

   Animal-Vegetable-Mineral is similar except that the first eliminations are in these three categories and the number of questions is not limited.

   In *Who and What?*, A thinks of a person and an object typically associated with this person. Forms of questions will be more varied than in the first two games because A may give information, while trying to do this as ambiguously as possible. When the students have guessed the person, they must guess the object associated with this person (e.g., the school janitor and his keys; Winston Churchill and his cigar).

c. *Rejoinders*

   In every language there are conventional ways of responding to the utter-ances of others which ease social relations and make continued communica-tion less effortful: ways of agreeing, disagreeing, expressing pleasure, as-tonishment, surprise, displeasure, or disgust, ways of responding to another person's monologue so that one appears to be participating, and ways of acknowledging replies to one's questions. These responses are frequently not taught in any systematic way to students of English, with the result that the latter often offend, either by not contributing as they should to an interchange or by contributing too forcefully or pedantically. Some re-joinders will be learned incidentally because the teacher will use them frequently; others can be practiced in an oral exercise from time to time.

G44 (I)   Listen to the following sentences and respond to each with an appropriate exclamation or rejoinder. (This exercise uses GA forms.)

> CUE   Didn't get the job. Just got there as the manager went off to lunch.
> RESPONSE   Tough luck!
> CUE   See you at two at the bus stop.
> RESPONSE   OK.
> CUE   Thought I'd never see Dennis again. Then I go into this building and there he is waiting for the elevator.
> RESPONSE   No kidding.

Commentary

This mixed exercise is, of course, a review and presumes preliminary learning of appropriate rejoinders, either through a series of exercises on particular rejoinders or through the teacher's continual use of them in class. Rejoinders learned artificially, out of context, are easily forgotten.

Students should be encouraged to intersperse them liberally through their communication activities, always being conscious of the level of intimacy at which they are appropriate.

* Begin keeping a list of frequently used rejoinders and warnings so that you can employ them yourself in class and teach them to your students. Your list might include such GA and GB expressions as *Sorry! Pity! Tough luck! Tough break! Right! OK. It's OK. Good Lord! Look out! Mind out! Not bad! Too bad! Really? You don't say! Is that so? You're welcome. Wow! Fantastic! No! Don't bother. What a shame! No way! I'm sorry.*[19]

6. TRANSLATION EXERCISES

Translation exercises have slipped into disfavor in recent years. This is not because translation itself is reprehensible. In fact, it is a natural process with many practical uses. Unfortunately, for many teachers it became an end, rather than a means for improving the student's control of the structure of the language. As a result, many translation exercises became tortuous puzzles, in which four or five complicated structural features would be carefully intertwined within one sentence. The question of translation, and how it can be used most effectively, is discussed in depth in Chapter 9.

The habit of translating everything one hears or says (or reads or writes) can become a hindrance to fluency. Many students do not realize that it is possible to learn to comprehend and think in a new language directly; hence the need for procedures which encourage and develop this ability. For these reasons translation exercises, if used at all, should be used sparingly, and then only for linguistic features which it is difficult to practice entirely in English.

Oral translation drills can be useful where the students learning English share the same first-language background. A series of sentences in the native language is given to elicit rapid formulation of equivalents in English. The series may be designed so as to elicit a series of utterances in a tense being practiced (e.g., he's coming, they're going, we're eating, etc.), a series using irregular forms which need constant checking (e.g., he went, they wrote, I spoke, she swam, etc.), position of pronoun objects (particularly where this contrasts with native-language usage), position of adverbs, and so on.

Oral translation drills differ from old-fashioned "sentences for translation," designed as written exercises, in several significant ways.

1. Since the native language serves solely as a stimulus for the production of authentic utterances in English, only natural idiomatic utterances that the student could conceivably find useful in communication are used (e.g., he went home early).

2. Stimulus sentences in the native language are *short*, centering exclusively on the grammatical feature being practiced (e.g., I gave it to him; I told her).

3. Stimulus sentences remain within a *familiar vocabulary range* so that the student's attention is not distracted from the grammatical feature being practiced.

4. Oral translation drills do not encourage students to look for one-to-one equivalences between the native language and English by distorting the native-language stimulus to bring it closer to the English form the teacher wants the student to produce. Instead, they require students to produce an utterance in English which is *semantically equivalent* to the native-language stimulus. In this way they encourage students to think in English. They are particularly useful for practicing distinctively British or American idioms (e.g., I wouldn't put all my eggs in one basket; What on earth do you think you're doing! I've had it).

5. Although stimulus sentences are short, they are not fragments, but *complete utterances* providing a clear demonstration of usage. Instead of being asked to translate simple forms of the verb in isolation, whether regular or irregular, students are presented with more likely utterances, such as: he left yesterday, she went to the post office.

6. As with other oral drills, oral translation drills provide practice of *one grammatical feature* consistently through six or seven items before the drill moves on to a related feature or to a further complication of the same feature.

7. After several drills developing familiarity with a certain feature, a *mixed drill* may be given (as in G9).

8. Oral translation drills, other than mixed drills, provide a stimulus for quick production of verb *forms* for particular tenses, *rather than for the use of these tenses*, which is more complicated and should be practiced in other ways (see Chapter 8). When the use of tenses is being practiced, moving from the native language to English can be very misleading because expressions of time relationships and aspect rarely show sufficient correspondence from one language to another.

9. Oral translation drills are *useful for quick review*—for refreshing students' memories and pinpointing persistent inaccuracies. Conducted at a brisk pace, they do not give the students time to pore over the English equivalents and edit them, as written exercises do.

* Discuss with other teachers or teacher trainees who have students with the same native-language background as your students the implications of points 1–9 for oral translation drills using that language as a stimulus. Design a series of stimulus sentences in that language which will meet the criteria given.

Simultaneous interpretation

When some grammatical features are well learned, oral translation drills for review may be placed in a more realistic setting by giving individual students the opportunity to act as English-speaking simultaneous interpreters for the poor monolingual "non-English-speaking" teacher or a fellow-student. With classroom-laboratory facilities, an authentic simultaneous interpreting situation can be staged. The passage for interpretation will be carefully prepared by the teacher so that it is possible for the student to interpret successfully. (It can also be designed to elicit certain features, for instance, specific tenses, indirect speech, or modals.) Other students will be asked to comment on the success of the interpreting and have the opportunity to improve on it. This type of activity is also suitable for recording in the language laboratory.

✳ Form small groups of students interested in different types of oral exercises.

1. Find examples of the selected type of oral exercise in textbooks, workbooks, or laboratory manuals, and discuss whether or not they are well constructed.

2. Try writing an exercise of this type for a structural feature for which it is appropriate.

3. Try your exercise out on the class to see if it is effective.

4. Take some poorly constructed oral exercises of this type, rewrite them in a more effective form and then try them out on other students.

5
Teaching the sound system

Understanding descriptions of phonological systems: a little terminology[1]

The discussion in this section draws on certain concepts of structural linguistics that have proved to be helpful in teaching the sounds of a new language. In order to follow the discussion in this chapter, the reader needs to be familiar with certain commonly used terms. The sounds we make are *phones*. Although the number of phones that can be produced by any individual speaker is practically unlimited, only certain sounds are recognized by the speakers and hearers of a particular language as conveying meaning. The smallest unit of significant or distinctive sound has been called a *phoneme*. A phoneme is actually an abstraction rather than a concrete description of a specific sound. Any particular phoneme comprises a group or *class* of sounds that are phonetically similar but whose articulations vary according to their position relative to the other sounds which precede or follow them. The environmentally conditioned variants of any particular sound occurring in complementary distribution are *allophones*. "In complementary distribution" means that these sound variants are regularly found in certain environments where they do not contrast with each other, e.g., variant A may occur perhaps only in medial position between vowels, whereas variant B always occurs in initial or final position.

In *articulatory phonetics*, we study the positions of the organs of speech, e.g., the tongue, lips, or vocal cords, in the production of different sounds. These articulatory descriptions can help us when we are trying to produce unfamiliar sounds. In speech, however, the organs are in continual motion,

149

so that sounds may vary slightly as they are produced in association with other sounds or are given differing degrees of stress. This variation must remain within a certain band of tolerance if it is not to hinder comprehension, that is, if the phonetic variants are still to be recognizable to a listener familiar with that language as manifestations of the same phoneme.

The concepts mentioned above can help the teacher to understand and define problem areas which speakers of one language encounter when attempting to learn another. For example, in this system, the difference between /l/ and /r/ in English is a phonemic difference, as shown by the fact that *It's light* and *It's right* have different meanings which are signalled only by the change of the element /l/ to /r/. The phoneme /l/ in many varieties of English, however, has two allophones, the *clear* or *bright* [l] and the *dark* (velarized) [ł], which occur in different environments ([l] before vowels and /y/, and [ł] after vowels and /r/), and which are, therefore, in complementary distribution. Since these varying sounds always appear in certain environments they may be termed allophones of the phoneme /l/. For these varieties of English, the allophones are not merely accidental variants, since they do not alternate with each other in the same position but have each a clearly defined distribution. (Note that, as in the discussion in this paragraph, it is customary to use slashes /l/ for phonemic representations, but square brackets [l] for phonetic or allophonic representations.)

The recognition of the phoneme is basically a psychological process which results from experience with a particular language. Many English speakers do not notice the difference between [l] and [ł] in their own language, because these sounds are non-distinctive in English, that is, they do not clearly differentiate one word from another. They are, however, aware of the difference between /l/ and /r/. On the other hand, speakers of Japanese and Chinese may not distinguish /l/ and /r/ in their first experience with English, because they identify them with sounds which are not distinctive in their language.

It is a mistake to assume, however, that it is only unfamiliar distinctions at the phonemic level that pose problems for language learners. Both English and French have two sets of stop phonemes, /p, t, k/ and /b, d, g/, as in English *pan, tan, can*; *bun, done, gun* and French *pan, tant, quand*; *ban, dans, gant*. The two sets are often represented as distinguished in both languages by the feature of voicing, and in fact the principal allophones of /b, d, g/ are voiced in both languages. But the presence or absence of voicing is not necessarily the feature which is most important in the production or perception of these sounds in every environment. In initial position in stressed syllables, English /t/ is voiceless, but it is also aspirated, or followed by a puff of air. The /t/ of *stop,* which is not in initial position, is voiceless but not aspirated. [tʰ] and [t] are thus said to be allophones of the phoneme /t/ in English. French /t/ does not have the aspirated variant [tʰ]: it is always unaspirated. If a French unaspirated [t] is used in English where an aspirated [tʰ] is expected, it may sound to English speakers like /d/, even though it is not voiced, *tie* sounding like *die*. The reverse situation may also occur: English speakers sometimes think the French are perversely calling the famous dish a *guiche*, rather than a *quiche*, because the lack of aspiration of the French initial consonant is, to English ears, a cue for the perception of an initial voiced stop, in this case English /g/. Thus the identification of a feature as distinguishing two phonemes, as voicing is often shown to do on charts of English consonants, does not imply that it is the only feature which can cause misunderstanding in a certain environment. There are often associated features to which foreign learners must pay attention. Prator and Robinett make the point as follows. Unintelligibility may be regarded as *"the cumulative effect of many little departures from the phonetic norms of the language. A great many of these departures may be phonemic; many others are not. Under certain circumstances, any abnormality of speech can contribute to unintelligibility."*[2]

Contrastive analysis and error analysis

Recognition of the importance of the student's native language in new-language learning has led to the development of the field of research known as *Contrastive Analysis*. There are now numerous scholarly analyses which compare the structure of English with that of another specific language. Many of these include a discussion of the pedagogical implications of the comparisons drawn.[3] Other books discuss the theoretical and practical issues involved in contrastive analysis (giving many examples of such comparisons).[4]

Some linguists and applied linguists have challenged the assumptions of what has been called the "strong" version of the contrastive analysis hypothesis: that a thorough contrastive analysis of two languages (to the extent that the present state of linguistics allows languages to be comprehensively and systematically compared) can reliably predict all the problems a learner of one language can experience in learning the other and will therefore provide a scientific basis for constructing teaching materials.[5] As in other related fields, current research is emphasizing the importance of investigating language *learning* (what first and second language learners actually *do* in the process of acquiring control of a language) as opposed to language *teaching* (what the teacher can do to help the learning process). We can learn much from the types of errors students actually make. A "weak" version of the contrastive analysis hypothesis would take observed errors and try to explain them by reference to contrastive data. However, not all sources of difficulty and error can be explained as native-language "interference". Errors provide evidence of the student's knowledge of the language at a given stage (what Selinker has called an "interlanguage") and of the strategies being employed in learning the language.[6] Systematic errors are an important source of information to the student and teacher alike, because they represent the learner's current hypotheses about certain aspects of the language and provide the teacher with the information necessary to help the student revise these hypotheses.

In spite of criticisms of an unwarranted dependence on contrastive analysis, however, teachers continue to find its insights useful in understanding their students' problems, and in helping their students to understand what is to be learned. An awareness of the differences between the new and the native languages can lead students to realize which of their native-language speech habits can be transferred to the new language without unduly affecting comprehensibility and which cannot. It seems desirable, then, that teachers be familiar with the significant differences between the English sound system and that of the language or languages their students habitually use if they are to help them acquire a pronunciation acceptable and comprehensible to a native speaker of English.

Generative phonology

In *generative phonology*,[7] sound systems are not described in terms of phonemes (a concept generative phonologists do not consider useful), but of *distinctive features*. These features are binary, that is, either present $(+)$ or absent $(-)$, which enables the phonologist to represent the phonological system of a language by a feature matrix. Features are described in terms which may be *articulatory* (taking into account such things as place and manner of articulation), *acoustic* (referring to information detectable by technical instruments), or *perceptual* (e.g., syllables or stress). Generative phonologists are attempting to establish a set of *universal* distinctive features which may be used to characterize the sounds of all languages. To the generative phonologist the pronunciation of a word is a surface representation resulting from the application of transformational rules to an abstract underlying form. This approach has brought to light some interesting relationships between surface sound realizations and traditional spelling systems.

The study of the correspondences between English spelling and English sounds is, of course, not new, but traditionally it has confined itself mainly to making rules for the pronunciation of monosyllabic words on the basis of their spelling, e.g., *i* has the "short i sound" (/ɪ/) when followed by one or two consonants (as in *tip, tick*); it has the "long i sound" (/ay/) when followed by *e* or a consonant plus *e* (as in *tie, tide*). The pronunciation of multisyllabic words is occasionally treated in English-language texts, sometimes with generalizations. More usually, learners of English are provided with lists of words with specific stress and vowel patterns, rather than rules which they can actually use in determining the pronunciation of a new word.

Principles drawn from generative phonology are now being applied in English-language teaching for the formulation of rules for the pronunciation of multisyllabic words. Dickerson has shown that certain rules formulated in Chomsky and Halle's *Sound Pattern of English,* although too difficult for use in most English-language classes, can be "translated into teachable and learnable generalizations"[8] for determining the stress pattern of a word, the quality of its stressed and unstressed vowel letters, and the pronunciation of its consonant letters. Pencil-and-paper exercises out of class prepare for oral practice in class.

Using rules of this type requires some grammatical understanding since it depends on recognition of parts of speech as well as of spelling patterns. An example given by Dickerson of a stress rule for multisyllabic words which uses spelling cues is the following: when students look at a verb such as *provide, represent,* or *develop,* the question they ask is: Does the last syllable consist of the spelling pattern ⟨VC⟩? (⟨V⟩ and ⟨C⟩ represent vowel and consonant letters.) If the answer is yes, stress the syllable to the left of the final syllable (devélop); if the answer is no, stress the final syllable (províde, represént).[9] This approach is suitable for adults at the intermediate or advanced levels, but not for children or beginners.

Variation and change in English

Like other widely spoken languages, English exists in a great variety of forms. While native speakers, either consciously or unconsciously, adjust to differences in vocabulary, grammar, and pronunciation, students of a foreign language at any stage may be baffled by a particular item they "know" but do not recognize in its variant form. Variation in native speech has many possible sources but regional and social differences and the situational level of speech (see C5) are of particular significance to the student of English.

Extensive studies have made available a great deal of information about regionally and socially differentiated forms of the language. Teachers particularly interested in such studies should consult Raven McDavid, Jr., "The Dialects of American English," in W. Nelson Francis, *The Structure of American English* (New York: The Ronald Press Company, 1958), pp. 480–543; Carroll E. Reed, *Dialects of American English* (Cleveland: World Publishing Co., 1967); William Labov, *The Study of Nonstandard English* (Urbana, Ill.,: National Council of Teachers of English, 1970); David L. Shores, ed., *Contemporary English: Change and Variation* (Philadelphia: J. B. Lippincott Co., 1972); or H. Orton and E. Dieth, *Survey of English Dialects* (Leeds: E. J. Arnold, 1962).[10]

Even in the classroom the student of English will be confronted with variations within the same variety, for teachers adjust their enunciation and speaking tempo to the mood of the situation and the reaction of the class. The teacher's style may vary from slow, careful articulation to informal, conversational speech. In rapid conversation, words tend to be omitted or changed by consonant loss and by reduction or loss of vowels, and there is more assimilation and linking, e.g., (General American) /²wânə trâyətə ³gín³ ||/ (Want to try it again?), /²ən jôyðə ³šów læs nâyt³||/ (Enjoy the show last night?). (See Chapter 1, pp. 7–9.)

The choice of the kind of English to be taught will depend on several things: the variety the teacher uses, the variety used in the surrounding community, the goals of the students in studying English, and the resources (texts, tapes, other English speakers) that are available.[11]

TWO VARIETIES OF ENGLISH: MAJOR DIFFERENCES BETWEEN THE PHONOLOGICAL
SYSTEMS OF GENERAL AMERICAN AND GENERAL BRITISH ENGLISH[12]

Both within and outside of North America and the British Isles, there are various kinds of "standard English," sometimes in competition with each other. The varieties of English that will probably concern the majority of teachers are General American (GA), and General British (GB). The following distinctions should be familiar to teachers of English.[13]

1. *Stress, intonation, and juncture.* The main features of these systems are the same for these two standard varieties of English, with some noticeable exceptions.

a. *Stress patterns:* In the set of words ending in the suffixes *-ary, -ery, -ory,* GA has a tertiary stress on the vowel in the next-to-last syllable, and GB has no stress (or weak stress) on the vowel in the next-to-last syllable (GA: sécretàry; GB: *sécretary*).

b. *Intonation patterns:* Contrast (GA): Are you quite sure? with (GB):
Are you quite sure? Marckwardt describes the chief differences as follows:

For one thing, the range of the British sentence, the distance from the highest to the lowest tone, is generally greater. Moreover, the British sentence reaches a high tone either at the very beginning or soon after, and then the tone descends gradually until the final terminal juncture, with its accompanying intonation turn, is reached. In contrast, the American sentence maintains a fairly level tone until just before the termination.[14]

2. *The consonant systems of GA and GB.*
The chief differences here are in the allophones and distribution of the /t/, /d/, and /r/ sounds. For the most part, the allophones of /t/ and /d/ are the same in GA and GB. In one position, however, /t/ and /d/ share a characteristically American allophone: between vowels, when the following

syllable is not stressed, these phonemes are often realized as a flap (rather than a stop) called a flap *t*: phonetically [ɾ]. Bowen describes the flap *t* for GA as follows:

... in a word like *pretty* the tongue begins low in the mouth and then rises rapidly and flicks past the alveolar ridge behind the upper teeth. The resulting "brush past" is the flap /t/.[15]

This is a common American pronunciation of the medial consonants in words like *city, better; body, wedding.* In addition, a flap *t* is often used in such words as *enter, hurting, harder,* where phonetically the segment before the flap may be simply a nasalized or retroflexed vowel. In GA, a flap articulation may also occur in word final position before a stressed initial vowel in the following word, as in *it is, at all, faded out.* The flap *t* accounts for the frequently-noted homophony of such pairs as *latter* and *ladder* or *kitty* and *kiddy* in the speech of many Americans.

The flap *t* is very much like the flap *r* in some other languages, such as Spanish, and in fact closely resembles the flap *r* sometimes used intervocalically in British English. (The phonetic similarity between the American flap *t* and the British flap *r* explains why writers wishing to represent British speech for American readers will occasionally write *very* as *veddy*, which would commonly be pronounced [vɛ́ɾi] in GA.)

More generally in GB, /r/ before vowels is pronounced with little or no friction, with the tip of the tongue raised so that it is just behind (but not touching) the tooth ridge, and with the edges of the tongue against the back teeth.[16] Before another consonant or in final position in GB, orthographic *r* is not pronounced in the manner just described. It may be represented as a lengthening of the preceding vowel (*hard* /haːd/, see note 17) or as a centering glide (*hear* /hɪə/). (It is interesting to note that the hesitation form /ə/, commonly spelled *uh* in American writing, is often spelled *er* in British writing. This has led to the introduction of the word *er*, pronounced /ər/, in American speech, as in "I er don't know what to say.") In both of the positions indicated above, GA has the retroflex glide or liquid consonant /r/, phonetically [ɚ]. (See p. 158 for a further description of this phenomenon.)

3. *The vowel systems of GA and GB.*

a. In GA, retroflection is the distinguishing feature of the central-vowel element in syllables usually transcribed /ər/, as in *her, bird,* or *over*: phonetically they are simply [ɚ]. In addition, the retroflex [ɚ] of GA may give a retroflexed quality, sometimes called "r-color," to the vowels it follows, as in *arm* or *ford.* Contiguous lateral and nasal consonants (such as /l/, /n/) also affect vowels, causing dipthongization in monosyllables, as in [bɪəł] for *bill,* and nasalization, as in [dɛ̃n] for *den.*

b. The main differences between GA and GB lie in the central and back vowels, as can be seen from the following chart[17] of GA and GB vowel phonemes:

GENERAL AMERICAN

Simple vowels

ɪ sit		ʊ book
ɛ set	ə *ago*	ɔ bought
	cut	saw
æ sat		
	a *fa*ther	
	not	

Diphthongs

iy meet		uw boot
ey mate		ow boat
	ay buy	
	aw out	oy boy

GENERAL BRITISH

Simple vowels

ɪ sit	ɜ bird	ʊ book
ɛ set	ə *ago*	ɔ bought
		saw
æ sat	ʌ cut	
	a *fa*ther	o not
	dart	dog

Diphthongs

iy meet		uw boot
ey mate		ow boat
	ay buy	
	aw out	oy boy
ɪə here		ʊə poor
ɛə there		

c. The "separation by a common language" that exists between speakers of American and British English results not simply from these differences in the vowel system itself, but also from the fact that a given lexical item may not be pronounced with the "same" vowel sound in both GA and GB, even where technically the correspondence between the two systems may permit the word "same" to be used. A chart[18] reveals more clearly the kinds of differences that can occur at this level:

	Gen. Am.	Gen. Brit.
bad		æ
	æ	
path		
part	ar	a
father		
	a	
lot		
		o
dog		
	ɔ	
caught		
short	ɔr	ɔ
shore	owr	

Note: The pronunciation of items with final *-og* is very unstable in GA, not only within a dialect but within an individual's speech. A given item may be pronounced with /a/ one time and /ɔ/ another, e.g., *hog* /hag/, /hɔg/. There is other evidence that the contrast between /a/ and /ɔ/ is weakening: in at least one dialect area it does not exist, see McDavid in Francis (1958), p. 520. In other areas it is often difficult to observe in the speech of young people. GA speakers who maintain a contrast between /ow/ and /ɔ/ in most positions often lose it before /r/: *shore* and *short* have the same vowel for these speakers. (The loss is parallel to the widespread loss of /ey/ɛ/æ/ contrasts before /r/, as in the well-known *Mary, merry, marry* triplet.) The low back vowel area is relatively unstable in British speech as well. In the introduction to CPD, Lewis says (p. xvi) that he has not given as an alternative GB pronunciation "the 'saw' vowel," /ɔ/, "in such words as *soft, loss, frost, cloth*, etc now extremely unusual (except in *off*) in speakers under retirement age in Great Britain (though still the predominant type in America)."

Articulatory descriptions and empirical recommendations

Articulatory descriptions for the production of a particular sound, using terms like those in the previous sections, are useful for the preparation of the teacher. They make clear to young teachers what they themselves have been doing, perhaps intuitively rather than consciously, in the pronunciation of English. They can be used to highlight the types of articulatory difficulties students may be expected to encounter in learning to speak English. The teacher does not usually give such descriptions to the students at the introductory stage (although they may be helpful for remedial work and of interest to older students or to students learning a third language). Instead, from their knowledge of the articulatory data, teachers develop empirical recommendations to help their students produce sounds they do not seem to acquire easily by imitation.[19] (This subject is discussed in more detail below under *Remedial Training,* p. 172.)

TEACHING AN AMERICAN ENGLISH /r/

We may take as an example of a sound which often proves difficult for speakers of other languages, the American English /r/. In teaching students to produce this /r/, we begin by considering sources of difficulty in the students' native language. According to Bowen, the commonest source of difficulty with this sound is that "it is not common among the world's languages";[20] a sound like it will rarely be found in the students' native language, yet in languages using the Roman alphabet the letter *r* is very common. This leads to a second source of difficulty—what the Politzers call "orthographic interference."[21] Students who have already learned to use the Roman alphabet to represent one language, and are now seeing English as well as hearing it, will tend to associate sounds from their earlier experience with Roman letters. Teachers should be aware of these possible sources of interference, and should be able to describe the incorrect articulations which their students produce in order to compare what these students are doing with what they should be doing. Empirical recommendations such as those that follow can then be developed on the basis of this comparison.

Prator and Robinett's advice for the production of an American /r/ is as follows:

S1 "A large majority of English-speaking people . . . pronounce it with both sides of the tongue touching the back part of the tooth ridge and the back teeth. *It is important to note that the tongue tip does not touch anything*; the middle of the tongue, including the tip, is lower than the sides, and the air goes out through the channel formed between the middle of the tongue and the roof of the mouth. The lips are slightly open. The glide, the characteristic /r/-sound, is produced as the speech organs move to this position from a vowel, as in *are* /ar/, or away from this position to a vowel, as in *red* /rɛd/. In whatever direction the movement may end, *it always begins by a motion toward the back of the mouth*. More than any other factor, it is this retroflex (toward the back) motion that gives the English /r/ its typical sound. The tongue tip rises a little and is curved backward, while the sides of the tongue slide along the back part of the tooth ridge as along two rails.

"Pronounce the vowel /a/. As you do so, curve the tip of your tongue up and slide the sides of the tongue backward along the tooth ridge, and you should have no difficulty in producing a perfect American /r/."[22]

Bowen gives the following description of the American /r/:

S2 "The retroflex /r/ is typical in American English. It is similar to the /l/ in having the back of the tongue relatively low in the mouth. The tip is curled high toward the back of the mouth, but not touching anywhere. This American variety has sometimes been called a growled /r/. Actually the /r/ is very much like a vowel, and when it follows /ə/ the effect is a /ə/ with retroflection (tongue tip curled back) added."[23]

From these descriptions it is clear that the main features of an American /r/ are: 1. having the tongue in a central position, as for the vowels /ə/ or /a/; 2. having the tongue tip curled back; 3. having the back of the tongue low and the edges of the tongue against the back part of the tooth ridge. What is perhaps equally helpful to the student in these descriptions is the negative advice: don't let the tongue tip touch anything. Keeping the tongue tip free and out of contact with any other part of the mouth means that there will be no friction or flap; whether pre- or post-vocalic, the sound will be a vocalic glide.

S3 In helping students to pronounce an American /r/, teachers might begin with Prator and Robinett's instructions, "Pronounce the vowel /a/. As you do so, curve the tip of your tongue up. . . ."[24] They might then add the admonition, "Don't let the tip of your tongue touch anything!"

For students whose native language has a uvular *r*, Prator and Robinett have the following recommendation:

S4 "This [uvular] type of *r* is also a glide, characterised by movement of the speech organs, but to produce it the tongue slides a little forward, rather than backward, and the muscles of the soft palate are tensed. Students who find it difficult to avoid this type of *r* in English should concentrate on the *backward* movement of the tongue and making the uvula and soft palate (the soft back part of the roof of the mouth) remain motionless and relaxed."[25]

Such sets of directions are quite different from articulatory descriptions expressed in technical language. Teachers should understand the physical basis for the correct production of sounds. They should then think of ways in which, through the execution of familiar movements, the student can be led to produce the unfamiliar movement required for a particular sound. These instructions are empirical recommendations.

✱ 1. From your knowledge of American or British English articulatory movements, work out empirical recommendations for inducing students to make correct /p/, /t/, and /k/ sounds, aspirated (as in *pool, tool,* and *cool*) and unaspirated (as in *spool, stool,* and *school*); and to distinguish between voiced and voiceless consonants at the ends of words (*pays* from *pace*; *cab* from *cap*). Be sure to consider the lenis articulation of the voiced consonants and the greater length of vowels preceding them, and remember that the so-called voiced consonants are often phonetically unvoiced in this position.

2. Chinese, Japanese, Korean, and Thai speakers have difficulty pronouncing /r/ in English because sounds resembling the allophones of English /l/ and /r/ are allophones of a single phoneme in their native languages. Work out empirical recommendations to help overcome this difficulty. Consult Prator and Robinett (1972), p. 97, and Bowen (1975), p. 52, for further information on this problem.

Teaching English sounds as a system

Teachers often concentrate on correct articulation of those distinctive English sounds which do not exist in the students' native language (the so-called "difficult" sounds), while allowing students to produce near-equivalents from their native language for the rest. Unfortunately, incorrectly articulated consonants affect the production of vowels just as incorrect vowel production affects the contiguous consonants. Similarly, rhythm and intonation have a striking effect on the articulation of segmental elements. Use of correct English stress and pitch patterns will help to improve the production of vowels and consonants.

EFFECTS OF THE INCORRECT PRODUCTION OF POST-VOCALIC /l/ AND /r/

The common characteristics of the English consonants /l/ and /r/ are that they are produced with a minimum of friction and with the back of the tongue relatively low in the mouth.[26] The general position of the tongue is in fact the same or close to that required for pronouncing /ə/. The movement of the tongue to this central and mid position after front vowels helps to give these vowels their characteristic diphthongal quality in monosyllables, as in *ill* and *air*. The "clear *l*" allophone, [1], which may be the sound students bring from their native language, and which is possible in some positions in English (e.g., before front vowels, as in *let*), will not have this diphthongizing effect. Nor, generally, will a flap, trilled, or uvular /r/. The characteristic glide to a mid central tongue position which marks the pronunciation of /l/ and /r/ after front vowels in GA leads Prator and Robinett to represent such words as *kill* and *fear* as /kɪəl/ and /fɪər/.[27] Attention to the frictionless, vocalic character of these consonants will also help the students' pronunciation of another kind of sound, the weakly stressed syllabic consonants of *little* [lɪɾ], *saddle* [sǽdɫ̩] or [sǽɾ], *kennel* [kʰɛ́nɫ̩], GA *what're* [(h)wɔ́ɾɚ], and *dinner* [dínɚ].

EFFECTS OF CORRECT RHYTHM AND INTONATION

The characteristic rhythmic pattern of English speech is that of a few, regularly spaced, strongly stressed syllables interspersed with weakly stressed syllables. (See Chapter 1, *Stress Patterns in English*, p. 9). If teachers insist on a clear contrast between strongly and weakly stressed syllables from the beginning, and present the clearest possible rules for assigning phrase and word stress, they will help students acquire English closely resembling native speech not only in this single feature. Putting heavy stress on a few syllables may make it easier for some students to lengthen and diphthongize the vowels of these syllables. (They may still, of course, have to be *taught* to do these things: length and diphthongization are automatic accompaniments of stress only for those speakers whose language experience has led them to make this combination.) Correspondingly, weakly stressing other syllables will facilitate the production of reduced vowels, syllabic consonants, and other kinds of consonantal weakening (e.g., devoicing and non-release of consonants). In similar fashion, early and continuous insistence on correct intonation contours can help to connect them to stress and juncture patterns, and to promote automatic control of the interrelated systems. The use of the appropriate rhythm and intonation patterns makes students' speech sound much less foreign and more English, frequently compensating for other faults of pronunciation.

* The above discussion of the English sound system is illustrative only and by no means exhaustive. Be sure you are aware of and able to help your students with specific pronunciation problems caused by their native speech habits, by experience they have had with other languages, or by orthographic interference.

Aural discrimination

Students confronted with strange sounds will at first tend to perceive them as variants of the categories of sounds with which they are familiar in their native language. If this continues, it will, of course, affect comprehension, but it will also hinder the development of a near-native pronunciation. Students who are not aware of the existence of certain distinctions of sounds are unlikely to produce these correctly, except by chance on random occasions. When they are able to "hear" the differences, that is, discriminate between sounds aurally, they can work toward perfecting these distinctions in their own production.

English sounds which have no counterpart in the native language will at first be difficult for students to distinguish. Such sounds will usually be perceived as a familiar sound. Native speakers of French will tend not to perceive the difference between /s/ and /θ/ and between /z/ and /ð/: *sink* and *think* will be homophones for them, as will *Zen* and *then*. Native speakers of Greek will not distinguish /s/ from /š/ or /z/ from /ž/: *see* and *she, bays* and *beige* (/beyž/) will sound alike to them.

English sounds for which there are *apparently similar sounds in the students' native language* may pose problems as great, or even greater, than those for which there are no corresponding sounds. Native speakers of French, Spanish, and Greek (among other languages) will tend to hear the English /iy/ of *seat* as though it were the same as their native-language sound /i/, as in French *site*, or Spanish *pica* or Greek σπίτι /spiti/. The English /uw/ of *boot* will seem very like their native-language /u/. They will have difficulty distinguishing these English diphthongs, /iy/ and /uw/, from the simple vowels /ɪ/ and /ʊ/, as in *mitt* and *book*. This problem is different from the /s/š/ identification mentioned above since French /s/ is an acceptable substitute for English /s/, whereas French /i/ is *not* an acceptable substitute *either* for English /iy/ or for English /ɪ/: using French /i/ incorrectly makes *beat* sound like *bit*, and *bit* sound like *beat*.

Sounds of English which occur also in the students' native language but with a different distribution will pose further discrimination problems. The sound [ŋ] occurs in Greek and Spanish, but only as an allophone of /n/ (e.g., before velar consonants): it is not phonemically distinct in these languages as it is in English. Students of Greek and Spanish language backgrounds will have difficulty in perceiving the difference between the final consonants of *thin* and *thing* or the medial consonants of *singer* and *finger*. German resembles English in having a set of voiced consonants phonemically distinct from a voiceless set. The voiced set does not, however, occur in word-final position. Hence German speakers have difficulty in distinguishing such English pairs as *cup* and *cub, seat* and *seed, place* and *plays*. The consonant sequences /sp, st, sk/ occur in Spanish and Turkish, but only medially, not in initial position in words. Spanish speakers will tend to hear *school* and *a school, state* and *estate* as homophonous sequences. In Japanese, consonant sequences resembling English clusters occur word-initially, but they may also be pronounced as, and are regarded as, two syllables.[28] Hence Japanese speakers may not distinguish *sport* and *support, scum* and *succumb*.[29]

AURAL DISCRIMINATION PROBLEMS

Exercises may be designed to help students discriminate sounds which are causing them difficulty, once the kind of problem involved has been identified. Particular English sounds should be differentiated both from closely related English sounds and from sounds in the students' native language which may be interfering with their perception.

Just how much difficulty a particular student may have in distinguishing one sound of English from others depends on a number of factors, such as individual sensitivity to distinctions of sound, the pronunciation of the teacher, and how carefully the student happens to be listening at the time. As a rule, the students are first taught to discriminate a problem sound from a similar sound in English, or from an interfering sound in their native language. If the students' inability to distinguish the sound persists because of confusions with other sounds, then the number of discrimination exercises is increased to cope with this complexity. Problem areas in English which involve one or more discriminations for speakers of specific languages are illustrated in examples S5–9. In the diagrams accompanying these examples, the sounds to be discriminated are connected by arrows. The various discriminations involved in each example are numbered. Readers will wish to develop their own examples for the particular problems arising from differences between English and the sound systems of the native languages of their students.

1. A simple discrimination

S5 (1)   Eng. /w/⟵————————⟶ German /v/
                      (1)

The student learns to discriminate between the rounded, frictionless semivowel and the voiced labiodental fricative. (Note that this discrimination may be complicated by orthographic interference if a written script accompanies the exercises.)

2. Distinguishing an English sound which does not exist in the student's native language from two interfering sounds.

S6

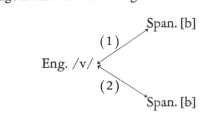

The Spanish student learns to discriminate the English /v/ of *very* and *ever* ([v]) from the Spanish [b] of *vaca* and also from the [b] of *lobo*.

3. Distinguishing two English sounds which do not exist in the student's native language from a sound to which the student tends to assimilate them.

S7

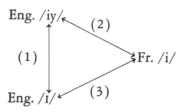

The French student learns to discriminate the English /iy/ of *seat* from the English /ɪ/ of *sit*, and to recognize that both of these differ from the French /i/ of *site*.

4. Distinguishing one English sound from three interfering sounds in the student's native language.

S8

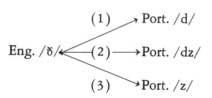

Quite frequently the sequence /dz/ is mistakenly used by Portuguese-speaking learners of English as a closer approximation to English /ð/ than the more obviously inadequate /d/ or /z/.[30]

5. Distinguishing two English sounds from each other and each of these from certain interfering sounds in the student's native language.

S9

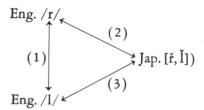

The Japanese student has to learn to distinguish the English /r/ of *row* from the English /l/ of *low*, and to recognize that both of these differ from the variants of Japanese /r/, e.g., [ř, ɭ] which are retroflex and lateral flaps.[31]

* Continue the comparison between the sound systems of English and another language with which you are familiar. Select three discrimination problems students of that language might have in learning English, and represent them diagrammatically. In your experience, do students of that language background actually have the problems that the comparison predicts?

TYPES OF AURAL DISCRIMINATION EXERCISES

These exercises are necessary only when discrimination problems become evident. Often they serve remedial purposes. Which types of exercises and how many are used at a time, and how these are interspersed with production exercises, will vary according to the needs of a particular group of students at a particular time. Usually, after some aural discrimination exercises, students will be encouraged to produce the sounds themselves to demonstrate what they have observed. If confusions are still evident, more aural discrimination exercises may be tried.

The sounds /iy/ and /ɪ/, which are easily confused by students of many language backgrounds, will be used for demonstration purposes in the following examples. These sounds may be identified and practiced separately, discriminated from each other and from interfering sounds from the students' native languages, and finally produced in close proximity (as in *eat it, kiss me, dim screen, clean dish, even if, skip a beat, steal the pill*).

Type 1: Identification of the sound, e.g., /ɪ/

The sound will have been encountered in dialogue or conversational narrative, or in oral work in the classroom, in an utterance like: *Mrs. Smith lives here* or *Where is it?*

1. The sound in a familiar context.

S10 Listen carefully to these sentences:

a. Where is it?   a. Come in.
b. Where is it?   b. Come in.
c. Here it is.   c. Come in, Mrs. Smith.

2. The sound in single words.

S11 d. live, sit, if, finish.

3. The sound in a larger context.

S12 How many times do you hear the sound /ɪ/ in the following sentences?

e. Come in, Miss Mitchell.
f. Finish quickly.
g. Turn it in.

Type 2: Minimal pair technique
      1. Discriminate between similar sounds in English and (Spanish).

S13 Listen to the difference between the English /ɪ/ and the Spanish /i/.

    a. *fin*/fin
    b. *bit a*/vira
    c. *pick a*/pica

      2. Discrimination between similar sounds within the English phonological system.

S14 The sound /ɪ/ is not the same as /iy/. Listen carefully to the differences between the following pairs:

d. bit/beet	g. bin/bean
e. rid/reed	h. hill/heel
f. live/leave	i. pitch/peach

Type 3: Same-different exercises
    Listen carefully to the vowel sound in these pairs of words and tell me (or: mark on your answer sheet) if the two vowel sounds are the same or different.

      1. English/Spanish

S15 (For English /ɪ/ vs. Spanish /i/):

    a. *it, it*   (same)
    b. fin, *fin*   (different)
    c. vida, vida   (same)

S16 (For English /iy/ vs. Spanish /i/):

    d. *feel a,* fila   (different)
    e. *beat a,* vira   (different)
    f. *seen, seen*   (same)

      2. English/English

S17 (For English /iy/ vs. English /ɪ/):

    g. eat, eat   (same)
    h. feel, fill   (different)
    i. bin, bin   (same)
    j. fist, feast   (different)
    k. litter, liter/litre   (different)

S18   l.   For the list, for the list   (same)
        m. Where's the peel?, Where's the pill?   (different)

      With English/English discriminations it is possible to use larger contexts than single words as long as the only difference in sound is the change of vowel.[32]

Type 4: Differentiation exercises
        You will hear three sounds numbered 1, 2, and 3. Write down (or: tell me) the number of the one which is different from the others.

          1. English/Spanish

S19   (For English /iy/ vs. Spanish /i/):

a. 1. *si*	2. *si*	3. see	(3)
b. 1. *fila*	2. feel a	3. *fila*	(2)

S20   (For English /ɪ/ vs. Spanish /i/):

c. 1. *sin*	2. *sin*	3. sin	(3)
d. 1. *fila*	2. fill a	3. *fila*	(2)

          2. English/English

S21   (For English /iy/ vs. English /ɪ/):

e. 1. sit	2. seat	3. seat	(1)
f. 1. for the least	2. for the least	3. for the list	(3)

S22   *Variation*
      In the following group of words, one does not have the same vowel sound as the others. Make a check mark for each word as you hear it, crossing the one which has a different vowel sound from the others:

    g. stiff, if, *reef*, cliff, biff. (Student marks / / X / /)
    h. read, heat, *his*, crease, ease

Type 5: Rhyming exercise (combining aural discrimination and production)

S23   Listen to the following word and give me as many words as you can think of which rhyme with it:

    TEACHER   meet
    STUDENTS   eat, seat, fleet, ~~fit~~, ~~bit~~, beat, complete, repeat.

* Construct items similar to those in Types 2, 3, and 4 of this section to help students discriminate:

1. English /a/ from English /ə/ʌ/;
2. English /uw/ from English /ʊ/.
3. Either of the above pairs, or another pair of closely related sounds in English, and an interfering sound in another language with which you are familiar.

Production
INTRODUCTION OF THE ENGLISH SOUND SYSTEM

Should the learning of a language begin with a series of lessons on the sound system? This is the approach of some textbooks. Usually, when this is done, little attention is paid to the usefulness of the words in which the sounds are produced or whether they will be used in classwork in the early lessons. A systematic treatment of English sounds can call forth such pairs as *ether, either; ruching, rouging*—words which do indeed illustrate important contrasts in the English consonant system, but not all of which are necessarily of much use to the beginning student. An approach which begins with practice on lists of words illustrating and contrasting English sounds may be acceptable for highly motivated adult learners to whom the rationale of the teaching has been explained, but it is unwise for elementary, junior high school, or senior high school classes. It can become boring, and its relevance is not understood by the students, who are anxious to be able to say something practical in English.

In the early lessons, the students can be introduced to the whole array of English sounds which they try to repeat after the teacher before being drilled carefully in particular problems of pronunciation. Sentences like the following are frequently the first the student learns: *Hello, Jack. How are you?* /²hə³lów¹ | ²ǰǽk² || ²hàw ³á(r)yuw¹#/. These five words contain eleven (GB) or twelve (GA) different sounds, of which only one, /h/, is repeated. Students might be expected to have difficulty with several of the sounds (initial /h, y, ǰ/; /r, l/; the weakly stressed /ə/ and the diphthongs). A normal reply, *Fine, thanks. How are you?* /³fáyn¹ | ¹θǽŋks² || ²hàwə(r) ³yúw¹#/ introduces six more sounds (as well as a contrasting intonation pattern), making a total of seventeen or eighteen distinct sounds. This shows the impracticability of trying to keep the early material within the limits of a certain number of sounds if natural, usable utterances are to be learned. Sentences such as *Ellen never let Eleanor tell* or *Sue used to use two tools* which are artificially constructed to introduce only one or two vowel sounds at a time may have some place in laboratory drill, particularly of a remedial nature, but their utility is limited in developing conversational interchange. Tongue-twisters like *She sells sea-shells by the sea-*

shore, for practicing the /s, š/ contrast, or like *Peter Piper picked a peck of pickled peppers,* for practicing aspirated stops, may be used for relaxation in the classroom and to focus attention on a particular problem. Repetition of such concentrated conglomerations of one sound gives some practice in the correct articulation of the sound. This, of itself, does not ensure equally successful transfer to utterances where the sound is more sparsely distributed. The sound will need to be practiced in many contexts if it is to reappear correctly articulated in spontaneous utterances.

EARLY TEACHING OF THE SOUND SYSTEM

Language learning usually begins either with the simple dialogue, useful expressions for classroom interchange, or a conversational narrative in the textbook. As students listen to the teacher or model, their ears become attuned to the overall system of sounds of the language and its characteristic rhythm, stress, intonation, and juncture. *Approximations to correct pronunciation* are sought in everything the students reproduce, without insistance on perfection at every point since this is too discouraging for them at this early stage.

Problem sounds are singled out at intervals in the first few weeks and practiced, with attention to acceptable and comprehensible production.

1. The teacher begins with *short phrases* from current work; then, if necessary, isolates *specific words,* gives practice in *a specific sound,* returns to the practice of words and then to *the complete phrase,* moving, e.g., from *in the house* to *the house,* to *house* and, if absolutely necessary, to /aw/, then rebuilding to *house, the house,* and finally to *in the house.*

Students may be asked to produce the sound in isolation a few times if they are having trouble with it, but not for long. Most sounds are rarely heard in isolation, and students must become accustomed to the slight variations which occur when sounds are made in association with other sounds.

2. Sounds should be practiced in various positions in the phrase, so that students become familiar with the effects of phrase stress on sounds (pitch change, lengthening), and of weak stress on certain classes of words (consonant loss, vowel reduction).

S24 How *áre* you? (/ar/a/ under phrase stress)
How *are* yóu? (/ər/ə/ with weak stress)

How are *yóu?* (/yuw/ under phrase stress)
How *áre you?* (/yuw/ /yʊ/ with weak stress; (yə/ in informal speech)

Can he sée *her?* (/kəniy/, /ər/ə/ with weak stresses)
Yes, he *cán.* (/kæn/ under phrase stress)
Hĕ can see *hĕr.* (/hiy/, /hər/hɜ/ under contrastive stress).

3. When the teacher senses that students would profit from intensive practice in specific pronunciation problems, the training should move from *identification* of the sound (associated with aural discrimination of similar sounds, where necessary, as in S6–21), to *imitative production*. When imitative production is well advanced, the practice moves to *guided non-imitative production* (where the exercise is so structured that the student is induced to produce the sound without first hearing the model). The goal must be *autonomous production* of the correct sound in non-structured contexts.

During intensive training in the production of a certain sound, it is helpful for students to hear a correct model after they have produced the sound themselves. They need to be sensitized to the differences between their own production and the desired pronunciation if they are to improve in unsupervised practice. Where their own production has been faulty they should correct it immediately, while they still retain the auditory image of the model. (The four-phase format of G9 is often employed for this reason.)

STAGES OF INTENSIVE PRACTICE

1. Identification. Student listens.

S25 MODEL In the book . . . the book . . . in the book . . . the book . . . the book . . . in the book.

2. Imitative production.

S26 MODEL   In the book.
     STUDENT   In the book.
     MODEL   In the book.

Students repeat after the model to correct their production or confirm it.

A similar four-phase format continues while the students imitate *the book, book, the book, in the book,* thus practicing the sound in narrower contexts and then producing it once more in the larger context.

The practice moves on to such expressions as:

S27 I need a book; Please open your book. (under phrase stress)
My book is on the table; Is your book at home? (secondary stress)
He's going to buy a Spanish book; I need an English book. (tertiary stress)

3. Guided non-imitative production.

S28 TEACHER Where's your book?
STUDENT My book is on the desk.

TEACHER What's that? Your English book?
STUDENT No, that's my history book.

TEACHER Ask John where his book is.
STUDENT John, where's your book?

4. Autonomous production.

S29 An interchange takes place between students, with the students themselves selecting the way they will ask the questions or answer them.

Where's your book?
My book is at home.

What book is that?
That's my English book.

What color is that book?
That book is blue (or) It's blue.

What are you reading?
I'm reading my English book (or) My English book.

Is that a good book?
No, it's a terrible book (or) No, it's terrible.

Can I borrow your book?
No, I'm using my book (or) No, I'm using it (or) Certainly (or) Where's yours?

If the interchange is truly autonomous, students will occasionally produce sentences which do not contain the sound being practiced.

In the early lessons it is not only particular sounds which are practiced, but also patterns of stress, intonation, and juncture. (Make sure you are familiar with American or British usage in these areas.)[33]

WHAT DEGREE OF PERFECTION SHOULD BE EXPECTED IN THE EARLY STAGES?

Practice should concentrate on errors of pronunciation which would hinder comprehension, e.g., [liv] for [lɪv] in *where do you live?* and errors which force students into other errors (like those discussed under *Teaching*

English Sounds as a System). The teacher will need to return again and again, in an unobtrusive fashion, to correct persistent faults which clearly affect comprehension or acceptability by native speakers, while continuing to encourage the improvement of the overall standard of pronunciation.

Remedial training

A distinction must be drawn between the types of exercises suitable in the very early stages, when the student knows only a little of the foreign language, and appropriate exercises for remedial training at a later stage. At first emphasis is laid on distinctions which are likely to cause problems of comprehension. Later, advanced students often need intensive practice in the production of certain problem sounds or sequences of sounds to correct a "foreign accent."

Remedial work at an advanced level usually takes the form of a *systematic review of the English sound system*. At this stage, students have a wide-ranging vocabulary and considerable knowledge of grammatical structure. After a certain number of retraining drills (see S35–38), exercises can be used which exploit the students' knowledge of the language, eliciting from them the sounds being reviewed while they are concentrating on grammatical conversions and manipulations (see S39).

REMEDIAL PRODUCTION EXERCISES

Exercises of this type are usually constructed on a contrastive basis, highlighting problems of interference from sounds in the student's native language which are close to the English sounds being practiced and from other English sounds which to the student appear similar to the particular sounds to be produced (see S5–9). The remedial exercises in production may be preceded by *aural identification exercises* in which the sound is used in short utterances which are meaningful.

1. Remedial production exercises are frequently preceded by *articulatory instructions* for the correct production of the sound, with warnings about native-language habits which interfere with correct articulation. These are sometimes accompanied by photographs or diagrams showing the recommended position of the speech organs. (Articulatory information can, of course, be supplied without the use of technical terms. In the instructions below, *alveolar* and *aspirated* can be omitted and the explanations of these terms used instead.)

S30 *Articulatory instructions for the production of an English /t/, initially in stressed syllables and after initial /s/*

In most positions English /t/ is an alveolar stop, i.e., the breath stream is stopped briefly as the tip of the tongue touches the alveolar ridge. Syllable-initial /t/, as in the word *top*, is *aspirated* when the syllable is stressed (that is, a puff of air is emitted when the air flow is released). After syllable-initial /s/, as in the word *stop* (stressed or unstressed), the /t/ is *unaspirated*, resembling in this position a French or Spanish /t/ in its manner of articulation.

These articulatory instructions are often accompanied by *empirical recommendations* for achieving the correct articulation or for testing whether the sound is being correctly produced.

S31 *Empirical recommendations: English aspirated and unaspirated /t/*

Hold a piece of paper (or a lighted match) in front of your mouth as you say English *tone* or *tool*. The paper (or the flame) should be blown by a puff of air emitted with the /t/. Now say *stone* or *stool*: the paper (or flame) should move very little.

S32 *Articulatory instructions for the production of English /æ/*

English /æ/ is a low, front, unrounded vowel. The tongue is lower in the mouth and farther back than for /ɛ/, but not as far back as for /a/. It is a simple vowel, not a diphthong, but in American English it may be diphthongized in monosyllables under phrase stress (compare the /mæt/ of *What's a mat?*, which may be [mæət], with the /mæt/ of *What's a mattress?* [mæt-]).

S33 *Empirical recommendations: English /æ/*

The most obvious way of helping students produce this sound is to ask them to imitate the teacher's production of a word or series of words with /æ/, such as *pat, bad, gas, bag*, followed by a word or series with /ɛ/, such as *pet, bed, guess, beg*. The students can also be asked to observe the teacher's mouth: What happens when the teacher pronounces pairs like *beg, bag; pat, pet; bed, bad; gas, guess; fellow, fallow*? The mouth is wider open for /æ/ than for /ɛ/. Students may also notice that syllables with /æ/ are often longer and more diphthongized.

Students can be asked to imitate the sound of a sheep or goat. While this may instantly transport the class to a rocky mountain slope, it can produce some very creditable /æ/ sounds. It may also, of course, make students feel that it is an inherently humorous or ridiculous sound. But it will demonstrate that they can produce the sound, and that it may even exist in their native repertory, if only in animal noises.

Note: A very noticeable difference between GA and GB is the GA use of /æ/, the "short *a*" sound, in a group of words in which GB uses /a/, the "broad *a*": *laugh, half, bath, pass, dance.*[34] In general, the words in which this alternation occurs are those in which *a* is followed by the voiceless fricatives /f/, /θ/, /s/, or by /n/ plus a consonant. There are about 150 commonly used words in this group. In a situation where both GA and GB are used, the teacher should be aware of this alternation.[35]

2. Production exercises *should not begin with the sound in isolation.* This is useful only when articulatory movements are being practiced. English sounds rarely occur in isolation. A few English sounds are words (/ey/ or /ə/: *a*; /ay/: *I*) and some are exclamations (/ow/: *oh*; /a/: *ah*; /ɔ/: *aw*; /aw/: *ow*; /uw/: *oo*; /š/: *sh*) or reduced forms (/iy/: *he* as in the phrase *has he?*). Except for these and the names of some letters, English sounds normally occur in combinations. The various relationships into which a sound enters modify it slightly, and it is these natural sequences which must be learned. Production exercises begin, then, with the *sound in single words or short phrases* which demonstrate the various environments in which it can occur. For instance, a consonant may be practiced in initial, medial, and final positions and in association with certain other consonants; a vowel may be practiced under varying degrees of stress and after or before certain consonants. This is the stage of *imitative production.* The words in which the sounds are practiced should be words which students can use, rather than nonsense words.

S34 *Relationships in which the consonant /t/ may occur*

a. table, tell, top, tooth, took, attack (*initial in a stressed syllable,* followed by various vowels)
b. try, twist; star, strong (in *initial consonant clusters*)
c. Atlantic; later, button, bottle; after, testing, instant; country, construct (*medial* in various relationships)
d. lift, act, thanked, searched, against, tests, attempts, ants, dance (in *final consonant clusters*)
e. tomorrow, today (*initially in an unstressed syllable*)
f. eat it, sit down, let go, at last, night-time, night rate (*word-final, with various releases*)

S35 *The vowel /ow/ in various positions*

a. go, coat, rode, open, patrol, supposing (stressed)
b. window, tomor*row*, omit, toma*to* (unstressed)

The above examples also provide practice in pronouncing /ow/ in conjunction with various consonants. (If the students are reading the words as they practice them, they should be reminded that not all the letter *o*'s in the examples are pronounced /ow/, and that most weakly stressed syllables have the vowel /ə/. Students should be practicing correct stress patterns in these exercises, even though the focus is on a particular vowel or consonant sound. See *Effects of Correct Rhythm and Intonation*, p. 161.)

3. The sound is then *practiced in short sentences,* also in various environments and stress and intonation patterns. This is still imitative production.

S36 *The consonant /t/ in short sentences in various environments*

   a. Take two, please.
   b. Let's eat.
   c. Write a letter.
   d. Did it cost a lot?
   e. Don't tell me.
   f. Try to lift it.
   g. He wants to meet her.
   h. Once in ten months. GA: /wônts in tên mônts/;
      GB: wʌnts in tên mʌnts/.

4. Remedial exercises often practice *two similar sounds at the same time* in order to highlight auditory and kinesthetic differences, since it is oppositions and contrasts within the sound system which make a language meaningful.

S37 *Vowel contrasts* are demonstrated in such pairs as:

   a. He's hitting it: he's heating it.
   b. It's a good book: it's good food.
   c. Where's the dock?: Where's the duck?

S38 *Consonant contrasts* are demonstrated in the following pairs:

   a. Here's the pill: here's the bill.
   b. He's racing it: he's raising it.
   c. It's a staple: it's a stable.
   d. She bought the rope: she bought the robe.

5. Exercises are next introduced which, through some form of grammatical manipulation, force the students to *produce the sound unmodeled.* This is guided non-imitative production.

S39 *Vowel production*

a. A change of *he takes it* from the simple present to the past tense forces students to produce a sound /ʊ/ in *he took it*, while concentrating on the grammatical manipulation they are asked to perform.

b. A change of *a house* from the singular to the plural forces students to produce the voiced /z/ of the stem and the syllabic plural suffix of *some houses.*

6. The sound is then practiced in *longer utterances,* in mixed environments, or in sections of discourse. In this way the effects of proximity to other sounds in characteristic sequences and the influence of intonation, stress, and juncture are more fully experienced. This practice need not be purely repetitive and imitative. It can take the form of a structured conversational exchange, so designed as to induce the student to produce certain sounds.

S40 *The consonant /ŋ/*

a. What are you thinking about?
   I'm thinking about studying English.

b. Let's sing something.
   What'll we sing? (or) Let's sing "Home on the Range."
   What shall we sing?

c. Do you want anything else?
   No, nothing, thanks (or) Yes, something interesting to read.

In application practice of this type, there is no need to concoct sentences loaded with a particular sound, like: Which ring finger is longer and stronger? Such artificiality makes students overconscious of what the exercises demand of them and the resulting production is no real indication of what they will produce autonomously.

7. Sounds may finally be practiced *in a formal context* such as *the reading of poetry or literary prose,* which can be contrasted with the reading of informal material. These reading styles contrast with both casual and careful speaking styles. It is important that students learn the differences among the various styles of speaking and reading orally. (See also Chapter 1: *Style of Language*, p. 14, and Note 1.8, p. 357.)

If a passage is read after a model this is merely imitative production. If it is later read by the student alone, this is guided non-imitative production.

8. There is a place for some *anticipation practice*. Students read each section first before hearing it read by a model. They then have the opportunity to reread this section and continue reading the next section before again hearing the model. This can be done as spaced reading on tape, provided that the natural pauses between word groupings are as obvious as in the following passage of simple conversation.

S41 /iy-ɪ/ *contrasts*

STUDENT	How long have you lived here?
MODEL	How long have you lived here?
STUDENT	How long have you lived here? asked Mrs. (/mɪsɪz/) Smith.
MODEL	. . . asked Mrs. Smith.
STUDENT	. . . asked Mrs. Smith. I've lived here for six weeks, said Tina.
MODEL	I've lived here for six weeks, said Tina.
STUDENT	I've lived here for six weeks, said Tina. Where do you live?
MODEL	Where do you live?
STUDENT	Where do you live? I live on Mill Street, near Lincoln.
MODEL	I live on Mill Street near Lincoln.
STUDENT	I live on Mill Street, near Lincoln, in that big rooming house for women.
MODEL	. . . in that big rooming house for women.

9. The ultimate goal of this type of remedial practice is for students to demonstrate control of the sound they have been practicing while they are engaging in *autonomous production* in conversation.

* *Questions to discuss* in class or with other teachers.

1. Should remedial production exercises be conducted with book open or with book closed? (What has been your own experience?)

2. Why do you think nursery and counting rhymes like S42 are often used for pronunciation practice?

S42 One, two,
Buckle my shoe.
Three, four,
Shut the door.
Five, six,

Pick up sticks.
Seven, eight,
Lay them straight.
Nine, ten,
A big fat hen.
Eleven, twelve,
Dig and delve.

3. How would you help a student correct the following faults? Putting
a vowel before or in the middle of initial consonant clusters /sp, st, sk/
(/ɛspiyk/ for /spiyk/; /səkuwl/ for /skuwl/); pronouncing *singer* as
though it rhymed with *finger*; pronouncing *good* as though it rhymed with
food; giving equal stress and citation-form vowel quality to all the syllables
in an utterance, e.g., /hwɛ́r dúw yúw lív/ instead of /(h)wɛ̂rdəyə lív/ or
/wɛ̂əduyu lív/.

4. Which do you consider the most useful for practicing sounds: poems
or prose extracts? Why?

* *Find some short poems* which would be useful for practicing certain types
of sounds. They must be attractive and simple in content, with vocabulary
and structures appropriate for the level at which you propose to use them.
A certain amount of repetition of lines, or segments of lines, will make
them more useful, particularly if this involves alliteration of a feature
to be practiced or assonance involving vowels requiring special attention.
Short lines are an advantage if you wish the poem to be memorized.

STIMULATING INTEREST IN REMEDIAL PRONUNCIATION PRACTICE

If students need corrective training but have become bored with the usual
sound production exercises, this remedial work can be associated with the
study of a phonemic or phonetic system of transcription for English. As
students concentrate on learning which sounds are represented by which
symbols and as they endeavor to write down dictated passages in phonemic
or phonetic symbols, they become more sensitive to fine distinctions of
sound. The reading aloud of passages in phonemic symbols can be a
useful remedial production exercise. The transcribing of passages back into
normal written English draws the students' attention to the relationships
between the English sound and spelling systems.[36] These new intellectual
interests often stimulate motivation to improve pronunciation where "more
pronunciation exercises" would fail.

Similarly the organization of a poetry recitation competition, the production of some short one-act plays by different groups for a festival or an inter-school social gathering, or the exchange of letter-tapes with English-speaking correspondents will make students conscious of the need to improve their pronunciation. Oral presentations can also stimulate students who need remedial work in this area.

MONITORING ONE'S OWN PRODUCTION

When working with tapes on their own, students have difficulty in detecting their errors of pronunciation. Aural discrimination exercises help students refine their ability to perceive distinctions.

To make them more conscious of these distinctions in their own production, students may be asked to read on to tape a series of aural discrimination exercises of Types 3 and 4 (S15–21) and then, later, to use this recording as an exercise, comparing their final discrimination decisions with the original script from which they recorded the exercise.

Students can be encouraged to evaluate their progress in perfecting their pronunciation by marking their weaknesses and their successes on a *pronunciation checklist* (S43).

1. When *working with tapes,* students should keep the checklist beside them as a guide to the features of the English sound system to which they should be attentive.

2. If the practice session is monitored, students should mark on the checklist the weaknesses in pronunciation which the monitor has drawn to their attention, so that they may concentrate on improving their production of these features.

3. Monitors should keep a cumulative record on a pronunciation checklist for each student, so that at each session they may refresh their memory of the weaknesses they have already drawn to the attention of particular students. In this way some faults can be emphasized at one session and others at another, thus making maximum use of the short time available for giving attention to the needs of individual students.

4. If pronunciation tapes are checked from time to time by the teacher, comments may be entered on a duplicate pronunciation checklist for the student's consideration when recording.

The following checklist[37] is not exhaustive. A particular language background may make some items irrelevant, whereas students of another language background may require additional items. The native language of the students will play an important role in determining which vowel and consonant contrasts are serious problems that merit special attention.

S43 *Sample Pronunciation Checklist*

Features for Attention	Estimate of Quality (E, A, or U) *	Monitor's Comments or Personal Notes on Progress
General Features		
1. Lax muscular control.		
2. Central tongue position.		
3. General legato articulation.		
4. Stress- (rather than syllable-) timed rhythm.		
Vowels		
5. Lengthening, diphthongization under phrase stress.		
6. Reduction to /ə/ or /ɪ/ under weak stress.		

GA	GB		
7. /iy/	7. /iy/		
8. /ɪ/	8. /ɪ/		
9. /ey/	9. /ey/		
10. /ɛ/	10. /ɛ/		
11. /æ/	11. /æ/		
	12. /ɜ/		
13. /ə/	13. /ə/		
	14. /ʌ/		
15. /a/	15. /a/		
16. /uw/	16. /uw/		
17. /ʊ/	17. /ʊ/		
18. /ow/	18. /ow/		
	19. /o/		
20. /ɔ/	20. /ɔ/		
21. /ay/	21. /ay/		
22. /aw/	22. /aw/		
23. /oy/	23. /oy/		
	24. /ɪə/		
	25. /ɛə/		
	26. /ʊə/		

Features for Attention	Estimate of Quality (E, A, or U)*	Monitor's Comments or Personal Notes on Progress
Vowel Contrasts (GA and GB)		
27. /iy/ɪ/[†]		
28. /ey/ɛ/		
29. /ɛ/æ/		
30. /uw/ʊ/		
31. /ə/a/ (GA); /ʌ/a/ (GB)		
32. /ow/ɔ/ (GA); /ow/o/ɔ/ (GB)		
Consonants		
Stops:		
33. ⁻/p; b/[‡]		
34. /t; d/		
35. /k; g/		
Affricates:		
36. /č; ǰ/		
Fricatives:		
37. /f; v/		
38. /θ; ð/		
39. /s; z/		
40. /š; ž/		
41. /h/		
Nasals:		
42. /m/		
43. /n/		
44. /ŋ/		
Liquids:		
45. /l/		
46. /r/		
Semivowels:		
47. /w/		
48. /y/		

Features for Attention	Estimate of Quality (E, A, or U) *	Monitor's Comments or Personal Notes on Progress

Consonant Contrasts

49. Voiceless voiced pairs, e.g., /p, b/; /t, d/; /k, g/; /č, ǰ/; /f, v/; /θ, ð/; /s, z/; /š, ž/.
50. Stop or affricate and fricative with same or similar point of articulation, e.g., /p, f/; /t, θ/; /b, v/; /d, ð/; /č, š/; /ǰ, ž/; or fricatives with similar points of articulation, e.g., /θ, s/; /s, š/; /ð, z/; /z, ž/.
51. Postvocalic nasals, e.g., /ræn/, /ræŋ/.
52. /l/r/;
    /v/w/;
    /y/ž/ǰ/.

Other Consonant Problems

53. Extra vowel before or between consonants in clusters or after final consonant, e.g., /ɛstæmp/ or /sətæmp/ or /stæmpə/ for *stamp*.
54. Inflectional endings: /-s, -z, -t, -d/.
55. "Silent" consonants, e.g., ha*l*f.

Stress

56. Word stress: primary, tertiary, weak (or zero).
57. Phrase stress: normal, (main or primary), secondary, tertiary, and weak; contrastive.
58. Phrase stress correlated with intonation contour.

Features for Attention	Estimate of Quality (E, A, or U) *	Monitor's Comments or Personal Notes on Progress
Intonation (For pitch levels, see p. 350.)		
59. Short statement.		
60. Long statement (including 232|).		
61. Yes-no question.		
62. Information question.		
63. Choice question.		
64. Series.		
65. Exclamation and interjection.		
Juncture		
66. Phrase juncture: # (final fall, fade-out of voice).		
67. Phrase juncture: || (final rise).		
68. Phrase juncture: | (utterance medial, voice and pitch sustained).		
69. Internal juncture: open /hìy mâyt ráyt/		
70. Internal juncture: closed /šíykən trâytə síyɪm/		

* E = Excellent (near-native); A = Acceptable (but not yet perfect); U = Unacceptable (needs attention).

† between sounds indicates that these sounds should not be confused in pronunciation, e.g., /iy/ɪ/.

‡; indicates grouping because of similarity of place of articulation.

＊ Use this checklist to evaluate a recording of your own speech in English.

You will have to ask another student, a fellow teacher, or your instructor to evaluate points 1 and 2 for you by watching you. Later, discuss in class how the list can be adapted for use with particular native language backgrounds, and how it might be improved. Is it too long for practical use? Could certain categories be evaluated together?

＊ Sometimes teachers (and students) use, for initial or final evaluation of pronunciation, a recording of a passage such as the following, which was specially written to include most of the features in the sample checklist. Try to evaluate a recording by one of your fellow students of this passage.

$S44$ *Evaluation Passage*

Study the following passage carefully for three minutes to see that you understand the development of the dialogue, but do not make any marks on the paper. Read the passage clearly and expressively into the microphone with your tape recorder set at Record. Do not read the names JOE and BETTY in capital letters at the left.

JOE   Where are you going, Betty?

BETTY   Hello, Joe. I'm going shopping. I've just moved and I need some things for my room. Would you like to come with me, or are you going to work?

JOE   Thanks, I'd like to come. I want to buy a few things, too.

BETTY   I'm going to look for a chair, a rug, and perhaps a picture.

JOE   A rug? How big? Did you measure your room?

BETTY   Oh no. I'm only going to get a little one. A big one would be very expensive. I haven't got much money.

JOE   I haven't either. First let's go along to that old shop—the one near the railway station.

BETTY   O.K. My boyfriend told me that was a good place to start.

II
THE WRITTEN WORD

6
Reading I:
purposes and procedures

Most students learning English expect to be able to read the language sooner or later. Their personal desires and expectations vary from wanting to be able to read Shakespeare, Hemingway, or a scientific journal to being able to read a tourist brochure or advertisements on roadside billboards. Fortunately, reading is a completely individual activity and students in the same course may be reading at very different levels of difficulty in English, just as they do in their native language.

To be able to read in English in the sense of extracting meaning from a graphic script is not an aim in itself. Each student's aim is to be able to extract something specific—something of interest to him or to her—and this must be kept in mind from the beginning. Many an English textbook in days gone by started the student reading with such inanities as:

R1 I am a student. I am in the classroom. I am studying English. This is my book. It is blue. It is an English book.

Reading activities should, from the beginning, be directed toward *normal uses of reading*. We read normally:

1. because we want information for some purpose or because we are curious about some topic;
2. because we need instructions in order to perform some task for our work or for our daily life (we want to know how an appliance works, we are interested in a new recipe, we have forms to fill in);

3. because we want to act in a play, play a new game, do a puzzle, or carry out some other activity which is pleasant and amusing;

4. because we want to keep in touch with friends by correspondence or understand business letters;

5. because we want to know when or where something will take place or what is available (we consult timetables, programs, announcements, and menus, or we read advertisements);

6. because we want to know what is happening or has happened (we read newspapers, magazines, reports);

7. because we seek enjoyment or excitement (we read novels of all kinds, short stories, poems, words of songs).

Activities for developing reading skill should exploit these natural desires and impulses, preferably by supplying something which cannot be readily obtained in the native language: something which is interesting, amusing, exciting, useful, or leads to pleasurable activity.

R2 A quick check of some commonly used textbooks reveals as reading material:

Long *dialogues*, which tend to be stilted and too obviously contrived to illustrate particular points of grammar which are to be taught in that unit (e.g., the *going-to* future, order of modifiers, modal auxiliaries).

Lengthy *prose passages* about life in a college town in the United States, full of descriptions of the small actions people perform from day to day, and the places where they live, work, and play, with no unusual happenings to relieve the monotony. Because such texts are frequently constructed to introduce an unrealistic number of particular structures and vocabulary items, they become dull and rambling.

Many of the reading passages lack the flashes of humor and whimsy that could make the learning experience more enjoyable for both student and teacher, and the student's reaction may well be: *What a boring book!*

* Look at the reading material in several elementary and intermediate textbooks and class this material according to the normal uses of reading. Mark in each case whether it is interesting in content, amusing, exciting, useful, or promotes some activity.

There are various ways of approaching the teaching of reading. The approach will be selected according to the objectives of the students. Teachers now realize that students must be attracted to the learning of another language by the assurance that they will be able to attain the kind of competence they themselves are interested in, rather than being "put through the mill" according to someone else's preconceptions of the ideal English-language course.

Five possible objectives for a reading course are: reading for information; reading of informal material; fluent, direct reading of all kinds of material; literary analysis; and translation of texts.

A. Reading for information

Some students may wish to learn merely to *extract certain kinds of information from English texts* (scientific, historical, political, philosophic, economic, sociological). They wish only to learn to *decipher,* to break the code sufficiently for their purposes. Courses of this type appeal particularly to students in the senior years of high school and they fulfill the needs of some undergraduate and graduate students. Such courses are also useful to adult learners who wish to pursue a particular subject beyond the limits set by their own language.

Courses (and materials) can be designed to teach students to extract information from texts with only a recognition knowledge of basic grammatical relations[1] and of the commonly used function words (determiners, prepositions, conjunctions, pronouns, common adverbs, interrogative and negation words)—words which commonly emerge among the first two hundred words in frequency lists. The students can then achieve their purpose with the help of specialized dictionaries of terms used in their particular fields of interest. Students can be taught to guess audaciously at the content. They then discuss the reasons for their guesses and reasons for the inaccuracy of some of these guesses.[2] From the beginning students read texts of interest to them, carefully selected to provide a gradation of difficulty. In a course of this type the students do not want, nor expect, to learn fine points of pronunciation or aural-oral or writing skills, nor do they want to learn to read directly and fluently in the new language for pleasure. They gain their satisfaction from their ability to draw the information they want from the text rapidly, without attention to style.

These students need the following skills:

1. *Complete control in recognition of points of grammar which impede comprehension of the written language.*

R3   One such problem area in English is the recognition of relative clauses. Unwary students may not realize that a relative clause may have no introductory relative word; hence, they may misinterpret sentences like the following:

The lady Betty mentioned never appeared.
It is not hard to prepare food children like.

❋ List five other points of *recognition grammar* which could cause problems for the learner of English.

2. *Knowledge of word formation* which will help them to recognize the functions and nuances of meaning of words derived from the same radical.

R4 They should be able to separate *prefixes and suffixes* from the radical and recognize the part of speech that is indicated by the suffix, as in the following examples:

convenient, inconvenient
understand, misunderstand
exist, coexist
interest, interesting
kind, kindness
bear, bearable, bearer
discreet, indiscreet; polite, impolite; legible, illegible; regular, irregular
sane, sanity; vain, vanity
red, redden; black, blacken; strength, strengthen

R5 They should be able to extract meaning from compound forms like the following:

traffic light, tablecloth, landowner, tape deck
breakthrough, takeoff, shootout
overflow, update; downpour, backlash, take-home pay
footwear, carwash
homemade, hand-woven

It is especially important for students to learn that compound meanings in English are frequently expressed by placing separate nouns side by side, e.g., bank account, hour hand, employment opportunities.

❋ Make up some word games which would develop sensitivity to word families and compound words, e.g., competitions in listing derivatives and compounds, in constructing as many words as possible from letters supplied, in extending radicals with affixes to make new words.

3. *Practice in recognizing English words which they already know, sometimes in a disguised form.* The native languages of the students may

share many words with English. These may be either cognates (words descended from a common ancestor, e.g., German *apfel*, English *apple*), borrowings from English which have been completely assimilated in pronunciation and applied to similar but not necessarily identical phenomena (e.g., French *le sandwich*, English *sandwich*), or English words more recently adopted in their original form in the student's native language as designations for distinctively American or British phenomena (e.g., the words *test, baseball,* and *jazz* are used freely in a number of languages). Whatever the source of the shared words, the differences between the spelling or writing systems of English and those of the students' native languages may obscure the correspondence. (See *A Different Script,* p. 196).

R6 a. English *theorem*, Greek θεώρημα; English *philosophy*, Greek φιλοσοφία.
A Greek student learning to read English can be helped by knowing that Greek θ normally corresponds to English *th* and Greek φ normally corresponds to English *ph*.

R7 a. English *wake*, German *wachen*; English *sight*, German *Sicht*.
A German student will find it useful to know that German *ch* often parallels English *k* or *gh*.

b. English *war*, French *guerre*; English *William*, French *Guillaume*.
A French student will find it useful to know that French *gu-* sometimes parallels English *w*.

c. English *fact*, Italian *fatto*.
The Italian student who has some knowledge of the relationship between English consonant clusters and Italian double consonants will not need to look on *fact* as a new and unknown word.

Students whose native language shares cognates with English should be made aware of the kinds of cognates that occur. They should also learn that the areas of meaning the cognates cover and the ways they are used in the two languages, that is, their distribution, often do not coincide.

R8 English *He can't support her*; French *Il ne peut pas la supporter*. The most likely meaning of *support* in the English sentence is *maintain* or *provide for*. *Supporter* in the French sentence means *stand* or *endure*. (English: *He can't stand her*).

Many cognates are disguised by historical change, as in R7, but often these disguises are thin and systematic enough to warrant the attention of the reader.

R9 a. English *s-*, *es-*, or *ex-* often equal French *é-* (before *t* or *c*) :

strange,   étrange
establish,   établir
extend,   étendre
scarlet,   écarlate

b. English *p* or *v* often equal German *f*, *ff*, or *pf*:

hope,   hoffen
pipe,   Pfeife
shovel,   Schaufel

c. English noun endings in *-ty* often correspond to Spanish endings *-dad* or *-tad*:

society,   sociedad
liberty,   libertad

* If the class is familiar with a language that has cognates with English, share notes on other regular features of the cognates or disguised cognates that you have observed or can discover.

4. *Recognition knowledge of the most frequent "false friends."* Two languages may share cognates which are easily recognizable but whose meanings have diverged. Students need to have a recognition knowledge of these words and they should keep their own cumulative lists of them with a short sentence illustrating the use of each in English.

R10 "False friends"

English *become*—German *bekommen*
Although these two words have a common origin and look alike, they have diverged in meaning. German *bekommen* now means *receive*.

English *advertisement*—French *avertissement*
Here again the French student learning English may be misled, because in French *avertissement* means *a warning*. *Advertisement* in French is *annonce*, similar to the English word *announce(ment)*, but again different in meaning.

These divergences often continue through a series of false associations as in the following set from Spanish:

R11

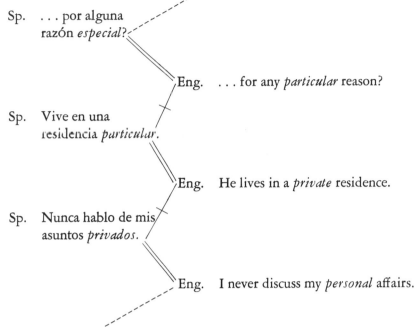

Sp. ... por alguna razón *especial*?

Eng. ... for any *particular* reason?

Sp. Vive en una residencia *particular*.

Eng. He lives in a *private* residence.

Sp. Nunca hablo de mis asuntos *privados*.

Eng. I never discuss my *personal* affairs.

✱ 1. Make a list of "false friends" from your native language or the languages spoken by your students (they will enjoy helping you).

2. Try to develop sets like R10 from the language you know best to English.

5. *Recognition knowledge of the most frequent borrowings into English from non-cognate languages.* It may be interesting and helpful for students whose language has been a source of English words to compare the areas of meaning and the formal correspondences of these words in the two languages. (*Pajamas/pyjamas*, for instance, has changed its meaning as it has traveled from Persian and Hindi to English. For further examples, see R13.)

WHAT DO WE DO ON THE FIRST DAY?

As with all teaching, the way the students are oriented toward the course at the beginning can be crucial to their progress. In a course where students are reading for information they should be *given confidence* from the first lesson that they will be able to read English without difficulty in a very short time. This is possible very early if texts are used which take advantage of widely-known English words and of cognates, where these exist. (For students whose first language uses a different script, see *A Different Script*, p. 196.)

The teacher should *explain to the students the techniques* that will be employed to extract meaning from the text and impress on them that they must acquire rapidly a *recognition knowledge of basic grammar* and an automatic knowledge of *common relational words*, like prepositions, conjunctions, adverbs and pronouns, so that these no longer impede their extraction of meaning. They must also learn thoroughly the *most frequently used nouns and verbs* so that these can provide a framework for guessing the meaning of new words from the context. Very early, they must begin a *personal list of words* which often cause them to pause, as well as of specialized vocabulary of interest to them.

A PLAN FOR THE FIRST LESSON

1. Begin with all the English words you and your students can think of which are commonly used in the students' native language. Among them might be such words as:

R12 football, film, television, radio, astronaut, airport, picnic, guitar, electron, bar, tennis, telephone, camping, sandwich, hot-dog, jet, rock . . .

As you write each word on the chalkboard, pronounce it in English and ask students to repeat it after you. The length of the list will impress the students with the number of English words they already know.

2. Point out that English has borrowed words from many languages. Some of these words have been borrowed by many other languages as well to form a kind of "international" vocabulary. Find words which English has borrowed from the native language(s) of your students or which are shared borrowings or derivatives in both English and the native language(s), and prepare a few simple sentences using these. Give the students the sentences to read. (Try to design your sentences so that you can point out incidentally simple English function words like: the, a, an; in, of; and, but.)

R13 From Italian: Papa photographed the carnival from the balcony.
                      The gondolier assassinated the colonel with his pistol.
                      After the opera they consumed some spaghetti.

     From Arabic: They sat on a sofa in an alcove of the harem.
                      We study algebra, but not alchemy.
                      She likes sherbet, but she doesn't like alcohol.

From Hindi: The pundit lived in a bungalow.
        She covered the cot with chintz and folded the pajamas.
        The coolie caught the thug.[3]

Alternatively, with students whose native language is of Romance or Germanic origin, or who have already learned a language from one of these families, the next step could be to initiate a short discussion on the history of the English language with its intertwined Anglo-Saxon (Germanic) and Norman-French (Latin) origins (and many subsequent borrowings). The teacher will show how English speakers tend to use the two strands in parallel, so that the reader will often see two quite different words which have the same meaning, the informal word occurring in both speech and writing, while the formal equivalent is found mainly in the narrative, descriptive, and expository sections of a text.

R14 *Informal* Germanic strand: start; leave; end.
    Formal   Latin-derived strand: commence; depart; terminate.

  3. Give some further sentences to show that, while the forms of English words change very little, word order is important in conveying the meaning.

R15 The little girl looked at the birds. The birds looked at the cat. The cat looked at the birds. The little birds looked at the little girl. (This sequence should be illustrated with simple sketches on the chalkboard to make the meaning clear.)

The position in the sentence, not the form of the words, tells us which phrase is the subject, or actor, and which is the object. The usual order in English is subject-verb-object. (If the students share a common native language, particularly one which relies on inflections rather than word order for distinguishing subject-verb-object, give contrastive examples from their language to show how important word order is in English.)

  4. At this point the few changes in the form of words in R15 may be discussed. Ask students what differences they have observed in the singular and plural forms. (Here the sketches on the board will help.) Point out the invariant form of the definite article and the adjective.

  5. Write on the board a present tense version of R15.

R16 The little girl looks at the birds. The birds look at the cat. The cat looks at the birds. The little birds look at the little girl.

Tell the students that R15 referred to past time. R16 refers to present time. Ask them what differences they see in the verbs. Discuss the past tense inflection. Then reemphasize the importance of word order by drawing attention to the confusingly identical -*s* ending of the plural noun and of the third person singular of the verb in the present tense.

6. The first lesson should end with a group deciphering of 'a short passage with a great number of English words which are widely used in other languages, so that the students can leave the class "knowing how to read English already."

A passage like the following would be suitable:

R17 After the film, the students walked to the drugstore. Some of them wanted cigarettes or chewing-gum; some wanted magazines or paper-backs. But they all wanted something to eat, and they all sat down at little tables. Young Americans all wear blue-jeans and T-shirts or pullovers, and they order hamburgers or hot-dogs and Cokes or coffee. But are they all alike?

At Table 1, they talked about sports. They all liked basketball and tennis, but one student said, "I don't like football." Another said, "I don't like American football, but I like soccer. Let's have a game tomorrow."

At Table 2, a student said, "That film had great music! I liked that guitar!" Another student said, "They play that music on the radio. I'll make you a recording of it on my cassette."

At Table 3, the students talked about their holiday. One said to another, "I'm going by plane, and then I'm going to hire a car for the weekend. Why don't you come with me?" The other said, "Are you a millionaire? I'm broke. And I've lost my passport and I haven't got a visa. I'm going to stay home and watch television."

At Table 4, the students talked very loudly. One was saying ". . . communism or democracy . . . ," and another was saying ". . . inflation and the energy crisis . . . ," and another was saying ". . . missiles against guerilla warfare. . . ." Everybody heard them, but nobody listened to anybody else.

7. As preparation for the next lesson, ask the students to make a list of expressions, slogans, trade names, hotel names, quotations, and proper names borrowed from English which are in common use in their language(s). Since such borrowings frequently become adapted to the host language both in pronunciation and nuance of meaning, comparing them with the original English expressions will provide excellent material for pronunciation practice and further incidental teaching.

A DIFFERENT SCRIPT

For students who are accustomed to a different script from English (Thai, Japanese, Arabic, Hindi, etc.) the Plan for the First Day will become the Plan for the First Two Days. Steps 1 and 2 will be sufficient for the first day. R12 and R13 form an excellent introduction to the English printed script, particularly for the late adolescent and adult students for whom the Reading for Information approach is designed.

The first lesson will begin with Step 1: listing words in the first language which are borrowed from English. These will be supplied by the students and written on the board in the script the students know with the English printed script in a parallel column. After about ten words have been listed and pronounced orally several times, students will be asked to note similarities and try to pick out symbols which represent certain sounds. This approach is not as haphazard as it may seem: *pipeline, missile, satellite, hijacker, blue-jeans, whisky,* and *smog* (where appropriate) already account for 21 letters out of the 26 in the English alphabet. (Students are being trained to recognize symbols for approximations to sounds, not to pronounce or spell English words. This is a specialized course with a primary objective—extracting information from printed materials—and this precise and limited objective must be kept in mind.) While students are learning to recognize the symbols for specific sounds, the teacher will give them practice by adding to the list suitable English borrowings and words from the students' first language which have been borrowed into English, asking for approximations to the pronunciation (see R13). For some less-frequent letters, well-known names from the entertainment field and other international areas can be useful, e.g., Kojac, Zsa Zsa Gabor, Qantas, New York. Opportunities will be seized to point out the appearance of letters which are not pronounced individually but indicate pronunciation of a segment, e.g., *ph*antom jet, satellit*e*. Clearly this introductory lesson will not be sufficient for mastery of all the details of the script, but it will provide sufficient background for pressing ahead with the Second Day, Steps 3–6, pp. 195–96. For reading purposes, a new script is best learned through use, through purposeful problem-solving. The details will become clear as they are needed. (See also *Writing a Different Script*, p. 266.)

ACTIVITIES IN THE READING FOR INFORMATION CLASS

As soon as the students have acquired some skill in extracting information from an English text they may begin to work in small interest groups, in pairs, or individually, according to temperament, as a supplement to large-group guidance on aspects of written English. As time goes on, the proportion of small-group or individual work will increase. Large-group activity is gradually reduced to those occasions when students feel the need for further help in specific areas.

Every possibility for encouraging autonomous activity should be explored. One such avenue is the preparation of group projects centered around special interests. Students in the project group may fan out in exploratory reading for a certain period in order to report back and establish a list of what is worthwhile reading for all members of the group. Alternatively, students may assign each other specific articles or sections of books on which the readers will report back to the group (in their native language if the group is of a homogeneous language background) for a sharing of the information gathered.

Once the students acquire confidence in approaching English-language texts on their own, the class rapidly individualizes its activities, with students seeking out specific types of reading materials in which they are interested. The task of the teacher is to be available to help and to draw to the attention of the students interesting articles in contemporary English-language magazines which the students may purchase themselves or read in the library. The teacher should also be ready with suggestions of illustrated books in English with interestingly written texts and varied content which the students can find in local libraries and bookstores. Books of this type lead the student on because of the intrinsic attraction of the subject matter. In this way, students can become interested in seeking out information in English in order to explore in depth subjects of their own choosing and they thus develop the habit of using their newly acquired skill purposefully.

ENGLISH FOR SPECIAL PURPOSES (ESP)

This term is used where English is being learned with some specific vocational or educational purpose in mind. (See also *Situations of utterance*, p. 56.) Students may be preparing to study specialized subjects in the English medium at undergraduate or graduate level, in their own country or abroad, or they may wish to be able to use with a minimum of effort textbooks, reference books, or scholarly journals and reports available to them only in English. For such students, the first two of the normal uses of reading (p. 187) are the most important. The recommendations already made in this section, Reading for Information, apply to English for Special Purposes, but the following additional observations are pertinent. These will be considered under the heading of certain fundamental questions which should be discussed in relation to specific situations.

1. *What should be selected as the subject matter for an ESP class,* particularly when the group of students is not homogeneous in interests and intentions? "Physical and Biological Sciences," "Humanities," "Social Sciences," "Engineering and Technology" as terms are of very little use in deciding what material will be useful to particular students. An astrophysicist has quite different interests from a microbiologist, and a nuclear engineer is not a bridge-builder.

2. *What lexical knowledge is of most use to the particular group of students in whom you are interested?*[4] They will need to know the general

English vocabulary in common use and a specialized vocabulary. The latter will vary widely according to field of interest and may frequently involve terminology with which the English teacher, who usually studied in the humanities or a Faculty of Arts, is only vaguely familiar, if at all, since knowledge and the terminology associated with it is proliferating at such a rapid pace. ESP teachers must see that dictionaries for specialized fields are readily available.

3. *Who should teach the ESP course?* A specialist in the English language or a specialist in the major field of the students who has a good grasp of English? Or should this be an area for team-teaching? When the English-language specialist teaches the course, the students often understand the real meaning of the text better than the teacher does, once the mystery of the strange words is penetrated. This is clearly a situation for cooperative learning,[5] students learning from the teacher and the teacher learning from the students. It is also an area where individualized or group projects are useful (see pp. 197–98).

4. *What grammatical constructions should be emphasized?* There has been some research into the types of structures which are used more frequently in certain types of writing in the sciences, in economics, in history, and in other fields, but results are far from conclusive. Do economists tend to use the conditional and comparatives and superlatives more frequently than others?[6] Do experimenters in the sciences use the simple present or the present progressive more frequently? Do discursive writers in scientific and technical fields use the passive voice more than creative writers do? Corbluth feels that "there are certain linguistic characteristics in most expository, intellectual, or academic English (the English of any subject that can be studied) which distinguishes it from ordinary colloquial English (chat) on the one hand and from literary or imaginative English on the other."[7] He speaks "of the way a piece of writing logically coheres, partly through the use of connectives (*however, therefore, on the other hand, for example, moreover*) and partly through semantic means. A writer of this kind is typically defining, exemplifying, proving, contrasting. . . . If a student works on *any* examples of such intellectual discourse, they will be relevant to his needs."[8] This should be encouraging to teachers of ESP while they await more conclusive research results and the incorporation of these results into available materials.

Corbluth also notes that ESP teachers usually choose for their classes "models of clear and lucid exposition," whereas much scientific writing (or writing in any field) is "badly organized, turgid, unclear—poor English, and poor scientific English."[9] What should be the reaction of the ESP teacher to this real situation?

5. *How is comprehension to be tested?* The class exercises and tests in ESP courses should be of an active and participatory character. Multiple-choice questions, carefully drafted, may be useful for testing the students'

ability to detect nuances of meaning which derive from structural subtleties. Technical translation is a specialized craft which should be expertly taught to those who require or desire it (see Chap. 9: *Translation*, p. 325). For the normal purposes of the ESP course, students should be required to draw out important points from larger passages, either in the form of succinct note-taking or summarizing, or in order to provide answers to thought-provoking questions on the text. This parallels more closely the ultimate purposes for which the students are in the class.

* Discuss the adequacies, inadequacies, and special problems which you have observed in the teaching of English for Special Purposes and make specific proposals which could be implemented to improve the program with which you are (or have been) associated.

B. Reading of informal material

Some students, more interested in English for interpersonal communication, may want only to be able to *read correspondence, notices, newspaper headings, and advertisements*. For these a course emphasizing listening and speaking will be complemented with practice in reading informal English materials and in writing informally, with some study of the clichés of officialese and popular journalism. These students will need to be most familiar with the simple present (*I live*) and simple past (*I lived*), and with present and past progressive (or continuous) (*they are leaving, we were eating*). They will know the present perfect (*she has arrived*), and the main uses of the modal auxiliaries (*I must go; he might come; can I help you?* etc.) The past perfect (*I had finished*) and perfect progressive (*he has been reading, he had been reading*) will be less important for them, and their knowledge of such constructions as the past conditional (*if he had come, I would have told him*) and such forms as the subjunctive (*I insist that he go*) will be limited to passive recognition. They will need the *going-to* future more frequently than the future with *will*. They will not often encounter complicated structures such as introductory participial constructions (*Entering the room suddenly, he saw* . . .) or nominalized clauses (*his telling you that* . . .). In other words they will read English written in the informal style they use in speech rather than in a formal literary style. Their reading will thus reinforce their speech patterns.

The earlier stages of reading development described later in this chapter will prepare this group for their objectives.

C. Fluent, direct reading of all kinds of material

Students who want to learn to use English flexibly in all modalities, who hope to be able to pick up a novel, a biography, a newspaper, or a magazine (light or serious) and read the contents fluently for pleasure, as well as being able to communicate orally and in writing, will require a course which provides balanced development of all language skills. It is to this group that the six stages of reading development described in this chapter and the next apply. This is the group which aims at attaining the stage of reading directly in English without mental translation and without constant recourse to a dictionary.

D. Literary analysis

Some of Group C will wish to develop also the skill of in-depth analysis of literary material which requires considerable refinement of perception of nuances and choices in language. For this they require special training.

Teachers interested particularly in the preparation of this group are referred to: "Literature in TESL Programs: The Language and the Culture," John F. Povey, *TQ* 1 (1967): 40–46, and "The Literature Lesson," Bruce Pattison, *ELT* (1964): 59–62, both reprinted in Allen and Campbell (1972); "The Times and Places for Literature," F. André Paquette et al., in *Foreign Languages: Reading, Literature, Requirements,* ed. T. E. Bird (*NEC*, 1967), pp. 51–102; *The Teaching of Foreign Literatures,* theme of *MLJ* 56, 5 (1972); and for high school level: S. Dunning and A. B. Howes, *Literature for Adolescents: Teaching Poems, Novels, and Plays* (Glenview, Ill.: Scott, Foresman & Co., 1975); D. Burton, *Literature Study in the High School,* 3d ed. (New York: Holt, Rinehart, and Winston, 1970); M. Ryan, *Teaching the Novel in Paperback* (New York: Macmillan, 1964); and A. Purves, ed., *How Porcupines Make Love* (Lexington, Mass.: Xerox, 1972).

E. Translation

Other students may want to *translate English texts* accurately into their own language. This is an art which requires a sophisticated knowledge of the native language as well as of English. A course with finesse of translation as its objective will concentrate on fine distinctions of syntax and vocabulary and contrastive aspects of sentence and paragraph formation. The perfecting of pronunciation, fluency in oral communication, and composition in English will not be emphasized. Translation for scientific and industrial purposes requires a more than superficial acquaintanceship with many fields and much experience with the many dictionaries available for the specialized vocabularies of medicine, physics, engineering, chemistry, electronics, business, and so on. Translation of literary works requires a sensitivity to nuances and subtleties of meaning, speech registers, and levels of style in English and a perceptive awareness of the flexibility and potentialities of the original language. Such a course can be engrossing for those with a special fascination for language, but tedious and frustrating for any who are not in the course of their own volition. Translation is discussed more fully in Chapter 9.

Each of these five objectives is, of course, legitimate. In designing or selecting reading materials and learning activities, the teacher needs to keep clearly in mind the specific purpose toward which the course, or a particular student's interests, are directed.

The remainder of this chapter will concentrate on the needs of Group C (which covers in its earlier stages the needs of Group B, and from which Group D and some of Group E will later emerge). Some of what is said about this program for progressive development of reading skill can be adapted also to certain aspects of courses for Group A. Teachers of the latter group will take from the discussion what seems appropriate to the needs of their specialized course.

Lexical, structural (or grammatical), and social-cultural meaning

The reader must learn to extract from the graphic script three levels of meaning: lexical meaning (the semantic implications of the words and expressions), structural or grammatical meaning (which is expressed at times by semantically empty function words, but also by interrelationships among words, or parts of words), and social-cultural meaning (the evaluative dimension which English-speaking people give to words and groups of words because of their common experiences with language in their culture). When we consult a dictionary we find an *approximation of lexical meaning*, usually in the form of a paraphrase. Where a synonym is given, this frequently has a non-matching distribution of meaning, e.g., for *deceitful* the synonym *misleading* may be given, yet every use of *misleading* does not imply the *intention to* deceive which is an essential element in *deceitful*. A study of grammar rules and experience with language in action help us to apprehend *structural meaning*. It is *social-cultural meaning* which is most difficult for a foreigner to penetrate. This is meaning which springs from shared experiences, values, and attitudes. When this type of meaning is not taken into account, or when students interpret an English text according to their own cultural experiences, distortions and misapprehensions result. Living among English-speaking people for a long period will give a student, or a teacher who is not a native speaker of English, an insight into this aspect of meaning, but the average student will need at first to depend on footnotes and the teacher's explanations. As vicarious experience of American or British or Canadian or Australian life and attitudes increases through much reading, the student will come to a deeper understanding of the full meaning of many texts.[10]

R18   In the following passage the writer describes some lunch-time customs of Americans. Readers of English around the world are familiar with the

American *drugstore*, both from frequent descriptions and depictions of it and from its recent appearance in replica in many countries. The meaning of *cafeteria*, an eating place where one collects one's meal on a tray and then sits down at a table to eat it, may not be so well-known as *drugstore*, and for speakers of some languages the word is a real "false friend" (see R10). It is not, however, rich in cultural significance. On the other hand, the significance of the word *lunch* in the United States can be comprehended fully only by a person familiar with American social life.

A lot of people pack their own lunch at home and bring it to work. It's a good way to save money. If you only have a half hour or forty-five minutes for lunch, it's a good way to save time, too. It's especially convenient for people who are dieting or who can only eat certain things for medical reasons.

The majority of people, however, probably go someplace where they can buy their lunch already prepared. Next to bringing your own lunch to work, the fastest and cheapest way to eat is to go to the lunch counter of a drugstore. Cafeterias may be a little or a lot more expensive, but they're also fast, and you don't have to leave a tip.[11]

Lunch has a *lexical meaning. AHD* defines it as "1. A meal eaten at midday. 2. The food provided for this meal" (p. 775). But even knowing these meanings, a person not familiar with American working and eating habits may miss the full connotational meaning of the word. The idea of only "a half hour or forty-five minutes for lunch" may seem strange to people accustomed to a two-hour break in the middle of the day, when one can go home or to a restaurant for a substantial and leisurely meal, and even stranger to people who expect to have not only a large meal but a rest after it before returning to work in the mid or late afternoon. The emphasis in the paragraph on saving both time and money may correspond to what is now often referred to as "American efficiency," but the idea of packing up a lunch in a paper bag at home and bringing it to work with you may seem to many students to be carrying efficiency too far. A person who has not lived in the United States may not know that "bringing a lunch" is not in itself a mark of being either a school-child or a member of a low social class: office workers, factory workers, managers, college professors all may do it. Another aspect of *lunch* is that, while speed and economy may be desirable, sociability and professional contact are often important elements too. Americans often have lunch with friends, associates, or colleagues and frequently count on discussing matters connected with their work or on "doing business" during the meal (cf. the expression "There's no such thing as a free lunch"). For most Americans, *lunch* as part of the working day and working world contrasts with *dinner*, which is the largest meal of the day, eaten at home with the family in the early evening. The American housewife normally does not cook a real meal at lunch time (cf. the woman who said, "I married my husband for better or worse, but not for lunch"). Dinner is the meal she takes pains with, and dinner time is often the only time a family is together. The *social-cultural meaning* of *lunch* can be understood only by a student who has learned something of the way of life of the average American.

Structural meaning:

R19 . . . Next *to* bringing your own lunch *to* work, the fastest and cheapest way *to* eat is *to* go *to* the lunch counter . . .

Understanding structural meaning is, of course, a prerequisite to penetrating any text. In the sentence above, the various instances of *to* lack to a greater or lesser degree the precise lexical meanings of content words like *counter*, yet they are essential if the sentence is to be understood; they show structural relationships between parts of the sentence and may therefore be said to have *structural* or *grammatical meaning*.

Word counts and frequency lists

A number of lists of the most frequently used words in written English have been published. The two best known word counts are *The Teacher's Word Book of 30,000 Words* by Edward L. Thorndike and Irving Lorge (1944)[12] and *A General Service List of English Words* by Michael West (1953).[13]

The Thorndike-Lorge *Teacher's Word Book* (TWB) presents data from three words counts and a semantic count, based on four different samples of various kinds of printed English of at least four and a half million running words each.[14] The sections of the book most useful to language teachers are Parts I and V. Part I is a list of 20,000 words (those occurring at least once per million words), each followed by five indicators of frequency. The first indicator is a summary figure: the number of occurrences of the word per million up to 50 occurrences. (Words occurring between 50 and 100 times per million words are marked A; those occurring more than 100 times per million words are marked AA. There are 952 A words and 1,069 AA words.[15]) The other four indicators give the frequencies of the word for each of the four counts. Part V lists the 500 most frequent and the 500 next most frequent words.

Michael West based his *General Service List* (GSL) on the 2,000 words of *The Interim Report on Vocabulary Selection*,[16] which was prepared as a basis for English language teaching materials, and on two *semantic counts* (one by Thorndike and Lorge and another, of the 570 commonest words, by Lorge). These are counts which "establish the relative frequency of the occurrence of the different meanings" of words with more than one meaning.[17] For each word is given the number of times it occurs in the count of 5 million words, and then the frequency of the various meanings in terms of percentages of these occurrences. According to West, the "chief values of the list are that it shows:

(1) how very heavy is the learning-burden of the major words compared with all the others, and how very much the learner's task may be lightened by cutting out everything which is not really essential, especially in those heavy words.
(2) how much less frequent and less important are the minor items of words than one would have expected . . ."[18]

A third word list which has had considerable influence in the teaching of reading at the elementary level in the United States, and should therefore be of particular interest to teachers of English in bilingual programs, is the Dolch *Basic Sight-Vocabulary* of 220 words (BSV).[19] Sight words are words whose meaning the reader grasps so rapidly that they "do not seem to come between him and the meaning at all."[20] The 220 words in the list, according to Dolch, are "so common in all reading matter that all children should know them instantly by sight."[21] This list consists of words common to three other lists widely-used in the teaching of elementary reading and "is called 'basic' because it includes the 'service words' that are used in all writing, no matter on what subject":[22] conjunctions, prepositions, pronouns, adverbs, adjectives, auxiliary verbs and some regular verbs. No nouns are included in the basic sight vocabulary. Dolch considers that nouns are in a different category because each relates to a special subject matter.[23]

This basic character of the 220 words means that they are important for learners of English as a second or foreign language. For non-native speakers, any second-language text contains more unknown words than for native speakers who know most of the words orally and have, therefore, merely to recognize them in the text. First-language readers, in drawing semantic information from what is before them, lean heavily on the content words, very few of which are in this basic vocabulary, pausing to verify, when in doubt, by looking more carefully at the function words. To second- or foreign-language readers in the early stages, this rapid recognition of the "important" words (which convey the burden of the message) as opposed to the "basic" words (which hold the network of meanings together) is not available. If they are ever to learn to read

English fluently with rapid comprehension, they need to learn which words to know so well that they do not need to focus on them until they find themselves in difficulties (that is, the function words and some very common verbs, adjectives, and adverbs).[24] When the unknown content words pose real problems, the function words aid the inferencing process by establishing a framework (the ____ of the ____ was ____ on the ____ by the ____).

In the preparation of reading materials for foreign learners, writers and publishers often use their own lists, "based ultimately on the work of Thorndike, Lorge, and West, as all word lists must be,"[25] at least for the present. L. A. Hill, for instance, has prepared five lists for use by the Oxford University Press in preparing second-language materials: 500, 750, 1000, 1500, and 2075 headword vocabularies.[26] A set of vocabularies at five levels of 1000 words (from 1000 to 5000) is the basis for the *Ladder Series* (LS).[27] This series consists of books simplified to these five levels and a *New Horizons Ladder Dictionary*[28] of 5000 words to accompany them. Two word lists are included in *The Key to English Vocabulary* (KEV)[29]: a list of 230 function words, and a 2000-word vocabulary list. These lists are of interest to our readers because they have been designed "for use in controlled-vocabulary reading materials, with learners of English as a second language specifically in mind."[30]

Despite the usefulness of frequency lists in the preparation of reading materials, no one would claim that a 3000-word or even a 5000-word vocabulary (however carefully selected and basic it may be) is sufficient for fluent reading of all kinds of texts. Specialists in teaching a second or foreign language make a clear distinction between "service" words (words of the highest frequencies) and "special content" or "local" words (sometimes called *topical, utility,* or *personal* vocabulary).[31] The latter is the group of words which at any level of reading ability will draw the interest of the student and provide much of the specific information of the text, but which are too specialized to be among the few thousand most frequent words. Keniston says that special vocabulary items dealing with technical subjects and other "environmental" words "are most effectively learned by experience or from special lists compiled to meet a particular need."[32] (See also *English for Special Purposes*, p. 198.)

R20 As an example of this distinction, on reading the sentence: *My little brother, who had gone behind a tree, suddenly called out, "I've found a spider!"* a student is more likely to be interested in the word *spider* (which does not appear in GSL or Hill's 2075-headword vocabulary) than in words such as *my, a, little,* or *call* (all in GSL and BSV and among the commonest 500 in TWB). *My, a, little,* and *call* belong to the service or frequency vocabulary; *spider* might be added to the student's "special" words, the personal utility vocabulary learned in a situation where spiders are relevant.

Knowledge of a basic vocabulary will ensure that students know the most widely used words which provide the framework of any sentence, thus revealing to them a set of relationships which will serve as a basis for "intelligent guessing" or "inferencing" when they encounter unfamiliar content words. (Example R24 demonstrates this process.) Each student will need, then, to build his or her own *personal* or *topical vocabulary* from reading materials, and for this students should be encouraged to keep individual notebooks in which they copy words they wish to remember, setting them out in short sentences demonstrating their use in context.

How an unfamiliar text appears to a student

In the following discussion, the opening paragraphs from the first chapter of *The Crocodile Dies Twice*, by Shamus Frazer,[33] will be used for demonstration. The full text is given at the end of this section (R25). Readers should refrain from referring to it until they have worked through this section, in order to get the feeling their students may have on being confronted with this text for the first time.

R21 Text from *The Crocodile Dies Twice* as it would appear to a student knowing only the 220 words of BSV. On the right are additions and deletions to be made to the text if the student has learned only the 230 function words of KEV, expanded to include the other forms of the verbs in the list (e.g., *are, was*, from *be*). Numbers refer to the order of blanks in the line. Names and places specific to the text have been placed in parentheses; the capital letters signal their special role to the reader.

The ＿＿ ＿＿ in (Singapore) are very ＿＿
in the ＿＿. There are not many ＿＿ about and
the ＿＿ are made by ＿＿ and not ＿＿. You   omit *made*
＿＿ the ＿＿ of ＿＿ in the ＿＿, the ＿＿
of the＿＿, the ＿＿ of ＿＿ in the ＿＿ and
the ＿＿ of the ＿＿.
    In the ＿＿ ＿＿ ＿＿ ＿＿ and the ＿＿   (2) add *more*
and ＿＿ ＿＿ ＿＿. ＿＿ ＿＿ ＿＿ into the
＿＿. (Chinese) ＿＿ and ＿＿ ＿＿ to ＿＿
around the ＿＿ where ＿＿ is played. They   omit *played*
＿＿ and ＿＿ and make a ＿＿ of ＿＿. The   omit *make*
＿＿ ＿＿ are full of the ＿＿ of ＿＿ and the   omit *full*
＿＿ of the ＿＿ in (Chinatown). The ＿＿ are

_____ _____ the _____, but they are not as _____ as   (2) add *than*
they are in the _____.

    It does not look like a _____ where _____ _____   omit *look*
can _____, at any _____ of _____. But it was here,
one _____, that _____ _____ _____ to (Ali bin
Mustapha). It was the _____ of an _____ which
_____ three _____.

R22 Text from *The Crocodile Dies Twice* as it would appear to a student knowing the first 500 words of TWB and recognizing certain derivatives and less
frequent meanings. Notes on these forms appear in the correspondingly
numbered sections of the commentary following the passage. (Words
derived from but not in the TWB 500 list are italicized.)

    The _____ Gardens in (Singapore) are very _____ in the mornings.
There are not many people about[1] and the sounds are made by _____ and
not men. You hear the _____ of _____ in the _____, the _____ of the _____,
the *movements*[2] of _____ in the trees and the sound of the _____.

    In the _____ more people _____ and the _____ and _____ become _____.
Cars _____ _____ into the Gardens. (Chinese) _____ and children begin to
_____ around the place where _____ is played. They talk and _____ and
make a _____ of _____. The city streets are full of the _____ of _____ and
the cries[3] of the men in (Chinatown). The Gardens are _____ than the
streets, but they are not as _____ as they are in the mornings.

    It does not look like a place where anything _____ can happen, at any
time of day. But it was here, one morning, that something _____ happened
to (Ali bin Mustapha). It was the *beginning*[4] of an _____ which *lasted*[5]
three weeks.

Commentary

    1. *About:* might not be understood in this adverbial use, which makes
up only two per cent of the occurrences of the word in West's semantic
count.

    2. *Movements:* could be guessed from knowledge of *move* and context;
it will be easily recognized by students from a Romance language background.

    3. *Cries:* might cause difficulty for students not familiar with the *-y/-ies*
alternation and knowing the meaning of "cry" only as "weep."

    4. *Beginning:* would probably be easily understood as a noun derived
from the verb, especially as a definite period of time follows.

5. *Lasted:* the verb is much rarer than the adjective (ten per cent of occurrences compared to eighty-four per cent); it might not be understood here, although "three weeks" following it would help.

R23 This passage shows how the text from *The Crocodile Dies Twice* would look if the 220 words of BSV and the 230 function words of KEV were omitted.

_____Botanical Gardens _____ (Singapore) _____ _____ quiet _____
_____ mornings. _____ _____ _____ _____ people _____ _____ _____ sounds
_____ _____ _____ animals   men.   hear _____ splash _____
fish _____ _____ lake, _____ music _____ _____ birds, _____ movements
_____ monkeys _____ _____ trees _____ _____ sound _____ _____ insects.
_____ _____ afternoons _____ people arrive _____ _____ animals _____
insects become quiet. Cars drive slowly _____ _____ Gardens. (Chinese)
amahs _____ children begin _____ gather _____ _____ place _____ music
_____ _____. _____ talk _____ shout _____ _____ _____ _____ _____ noise.
_____ city streets _____ _____ _____ _____ smell _____ petrol _____ _____
cries _____ _____ men _____ (Chinatown). _____ Gardens _____ quieter
_____ _____ streets, _____ _____ _____ _____ _____ quiet _____ _____ _____
_____ _____ mornings.
        _____ _____ _____ _____ _____ _____ place _____ _____ frightening
_____ happen, _____ _____ time _____ day. _____ _____ _____ _____,
_____ morning, _____ _____ frightening happened _____ (Ali bin
Mustapha). _____ _____ _____ beginning _____ _____ adventure _____
lasted _____ weeks.

Commentary

Here we have a clear demonstration of the indispensability to precise meaning of function words such as articles (*the, a, an*), prepositions (*in, by, of*), pronouns (*they, it*), conjunctions (*and, but, where*), words used for negation and comparison (*not, as*), and common verbs (*be, make, look*). Yet clearly R23 gives us much more information than R21. Neither function words alone nor content words alone enable us to divine clearly what is taking place, although the content words of R23 enable us to piece together the possible meaning more than do the function words of R21.

R24 This passage shows how the text from *The Crocodile Dies Twice* would look to a student knowing the 1000 most frequent words of TWB. Numbered blanks in the text are discussed in the commentary below.

If the words of LS–1000 are known, the following words would be added to the text (the numbers after the words indicate the numbered blanks in the text into which they would be inserted): *quiet* (1, 8, 15), *fish* (3), *lake* (4), *music* (5, 10), *slowly* (9), *noise* (11), *smell* (12), *quieter* (14). Three additional words in the text do not appear in LS–1000, although their component parts do: *afternoon(s), anything, something.*

The _____ Gardens in (Singapore) are very _____¹ in the mornings. There are not many people about and the sounds are made by animals and not men. You hear the _____² of _____³ in the _____⁴, the _____⁵ of the birds, the movements of _____⁶ in the trees and the sound of the _____⁷.

In the afternoons more people arrive and the animals and _____ become _____⁸. Cars drive _____⁹ into the Gardens. (Chinese) _____ and children begin to gather around the place where _____¹⁰ is played. They talk and shout and make a lot of _____¹¹. The city streets are full of the _____¹² of _____¹³ and the cries of the men in (Chinatown). The Gardens are _____¹⁴ than the streets, but they are not as _____¹⁵ as they are in the mornings.

It does not look like a place where anything _____¹⁶ can happen, at any time of day. But it was here, one morning, that something _____¹⁷ happened to (Ali bin Mustapha). It was the beginning of an _____¹⁸ which lasted three weeks.

Commentary

Once readers are familiar with the function words and common verbs, and have a recognition knowledge of some additional basic vocabulary, they can usually work out the meaning of most of the remaining words in a passage by intelligent guesswork or inferencing. How this might be done for the unknown words represented by numbered blanks in R24 will now be discussed. (The numbers in the commentary refer to the numbered blanks in the text.) Inferences which may be drawn will be indicated by an asterisk. We will assume that the title of the story has been explained (e.g., with reference to a picture on the title page). This knowledge and the pictures on the outside and inside covers of the book from which this passage has been taken establish the scene as tropical and near water.

1. The intensifier *very* should suggest an adjective, and the first clause of the next sentence gives a clue as to which one. (The last clause of the second sentence might make *quiet* less easy to guess, but the rest of the paragraph establishes the atmosphere of human silence.)

2.–4. These are difficult to identify precisely if none of the three words is known. However, *sounds* and *hear* indicate that 2 refers to *some kind of sound of 3: *some kind of animal (because sounds of animals, not men, are heard here); 3 are *in* something, *probably not trees, because the next phrase refers to *birds* and the phrase after that is *in the trees*. We know from the title that there is probably water at hand, so the reader may infer *the sound of something in the water. In any case, there is enough information elsewhere for this to be left vague for the moment.

5. Taking a cue again from *hear*, the reader readily infers *song of the birds, *singing of the birds. This is sufficient for the moment. Later, the reader encounters the same word at 10, *something which is played and which children gather round to listen to. The step from *song* to *music* is not far.

6. *Animals that move about in trees in the tropics, (*monkeys?).

7. This might be guessed by a process of elimination: what other kinds of "animal" sounds are left? We have something in the water, birds, animals in the trees; we are left with *something in the air (not birds), perhaps *insects.

9. *-ly* should be recognized as an adverb ending. How do cars usually drive in parks? *Slowly.

10. See 5 above.

11. Once *shout* is known, the inference is easy: they make a lot of *noise.

Students should be taught to reason in this way about the probable meanings of words with which they are not familiar, instead of rushing to look in a dictionary.

* Work out inferences in a similar fashion for blanks 12–18 in R24. (Do not look at R25 until you have worked out possible inferences and discussed them with others in your class.)

R25 Complete text from the opening paragraphs of *The Crocodile Dies Twice* (S. Frazer). Parentheses indicate glosses not in the original text.

The Botanical Gardens in Singapore are very quiet in the mornings. There are not many people about and the sounds are made by animals and not men. You hear the splash of fish in the lake, the music of the birds, the movements of monkeys in the trees and the sound of the insects.

In the afternoons more people arrive and the animals and insects become quiet. Cars drive slowly into the Gardens. Chinese amahs (nurses) and children begin to gather around the place where music is played. They talk and shout and make a lot of noise. The city streets are full of the smell of petrol (gasoline) and the cries of the men in Chinatown. The

Gardens are quieter than the streets, but they are not as quiet as they are in the mornings.

It does not look like a place where anything frightening can happen, at any time of day. But it was here, one morning, that something frightening happened to Ali bin Mustapha. It was the beginning of an adventure which lasted three weeks.

Six stages of reading development

To help students develop progressively their ability to read more and more fluently and independently materials of increasing difficulty and complexity, six stages of reading development are recommended. Materials in English of an appropriate level of difficulty for each stage are presented and discussed, and suitable activities are suggested for reinforcing the developing reading skill and for ensuring a clear grasp of the meaning of what is read. More detailed discussion will be found in *Teaching Foreign-Language Skills* (Rivers, 1968), pp. 221–37.

The six stages do not represent six levels of study (in the sense in which Brooks used this term).[34] Stage One may begin after the first oral presentation of a short dialogue, or after some active learning of simple actions and statements in the classroom context, or in simulated situations. Should teacher and class prefer it, Stage One may be postponed to allow for two or three weeks of entirely oral work. This is often the case with younger students. As soon as students acquire some familiarity with sound-symbol correspondences in English and the word order of simple sentences, they pass from Stage One to Stage Two (reading of recombinations of familiar material). For a while Stage Two may alternate with Stage One. A more mature group of students, already adept at first-language reading, may pass rapidly through Stages One and Two and move on to Stage Three (reading of simple narrative and conversational material which is not based on work being practiced orally). Some textbooks plunge the student directly into Stage Three at the beginning, particularly if development of reading skill is the primary objective. Progress through Stages Three, Four, and Five becomes a largely individual matter as students outpace one another in ability to read increasingly complicated material.

Stage One: Introduction to reading

The introduction to reading will be very short or longer depending on the age of the students and the intensive or non-intensive nature of the course.

Students learn to read what they have already learned to say either in short dialogues, in informal classroom conversation, or through the oral presentation of the initial conversational narrative. Questions require only recognition of material in the text.

The major emphasis is on the identification of *sound-symbol correspondences* so that students perceive in graphic form the meanings with which they have become familiar in oral form.

Reading is an integrated part of language study, not a specialized activity. At this stage:

Reading is linked with listening.

Students learn to segment an oral message[35] (that is, to identify its phrase structure groupings) and then try to recognize these groupings in graphic form.

Reading is linked with speaking.

Students learn to say a few simple things in English and then to recognize the graphic symbols for the oral utterances they have been practicing. The script helps them to remember what they were saying, to see more clearly how it was structured, and to learn it more thoroughly. It also provides further variations of these utterances for them to use orally.

Reading is linked with improvement in pronunciation (including intonation).

Students practice correct production of sounds and appropriate phrasing as they learn to associate symbols with sounds.

Reading is linked with writing.

Students consolidate sound-symbol associations through dictation or spot dictation exercises. They confirm this learning by copying out, with correct spelling, sentences they have been learning. They write out sentences associated with pictures and use, as practice in reading, what their fellow students have written. Teacher or students write out instructions which others read and then put into action.

R26 *Spot Dictation*

Spot dictation enables the teacher to focus the attention of the students on the correct spelling of certain words and on slight differences in the spelling of near-homographs. It is a testing device to encourage the mastery of the spelling system, as contrasted with word recognition. Sometimes students write the words separately, sometimes in blanks on a partial script.

The teacher reads a complete sentence to the class so that the students hear the word in context.

TEACHER   Peter has a friend who lives in the city.

The teacher then repeats a word or a particular group of words which the students write down.

TEACHER   *who lives* . . . (Students write *who lives.*)
TEACHER   Peter has a friend who lives in the city.
          His name is Robert.

His name . . . (students write)
His name is Robert.
Robert doesn't like music.
doesn't like . . .
Robert doesn't like music.
But he likes books.
he likes . . .
But he likes books.

Reading is linked with the learning of grammar.

Students see in written form what they have been learning orally and consolidate their grasp of grammatical structure.

Reading is linked with learning about language.

Students become conscious of differences between the surface structure of English and that of their native language. Students take language universals for granted because they are universals, e.g., the fact that sentences consist of noun phrases and verb phrases. They tend to expect other features to be universals too. Many surface differences are more clearly observable in written language, e.g., the forms of pronouns and other function words which are reduced in unstressed positions in pronunciation (*he*———/iy/ in *but he* . . . ; *to*———/ə/ in *want to*).

Reading is linked with learning about the culture of the speakers of the language.

The written script in textbooks should be accompanied by illustrations and photographs which elucidate many aspects of the life and customs of the people and add new meaning to even the simplest of exchanges in the foreign language. Even culturally neutral material (see Rivers, 1968, p. 275) becomes more alive when the student sees how everyday situations vary in other cultures and have a different import. Some time should be spent from the earliest lessons in arousing the students' interest in American and British life and attitudes. (As reading skill develops and students read more widely, this particular link becomes more and more important.)

RECOGNITION OF SOUND PATTERNS REPRESENTED BY THE GRAPHIC SYMBOLS

The student beginning to read English will have to recognize many spellings for one sound, many sounds for one spelling, and the role of "silent" letters.

R27   1. The sound /iy/ can be represented by at least 8 different spelling combinations:

be /biy/   mach*i*ne /məšíyn/
th*e*se /ðiyz/   b*ea*t /biyt/

see /siy/   th*ie*f /θiyf/
c*ei*ling /síylɪŋ/   p*eo*ple /píypəl/

2. On the other hand, *-ea-*, which the student has just learned is often pronounced /iy/ in English, will nevertheless be pronounced /ε/ in such words as *bread* and *read* (past participle) and /ey/ in such words as *break* and *steak*.

R28 Letters may be silent, yet still affect the pronunciation of the vowel:

b*i*t /bɪt/; b*i*te /bayt/
f*i*t /fɪt/; f*igh*t /fayt/

R29 Students may find that some English or international words with which they may be familiar in their own language have a distinctly different pronunciation in English: e.g., sport, football, theater/theatre, film, TV, steak, whisk(e)y, weekend, university, cowboy.

Students will become more conscious of variations of the types described if, instead of merely repeating after the teacher as they read or are corrected, they also construct lists from their reading of different combinations of letters which are pronounced the same, and combinations of letters which have several possible pronunciations.[36]

* Compare notes in class on sound-symbol areas which you yourself have found confusing.

MATERIALS FOR STAGE ONE

If a dialogue-learning approach is being used, an early dialogue the student will read after having practiced it orally may resemble the following:

R30 *The student union*[37]

Bill is talking with Chen and Carlos after class. . . .
(At the cafeteria.) . . .

    BILL . . . Are you both taking the same classes?
CARLOS No. Only biology. I'm studying English and history. Chen is taking engineering courses.
  CHEN You're taking engineering too, aren't you, Bill?
  BILL Yes, I am. It's pretty interesting.
CARLOS What are those people doing?
  BILL They're playing bridge. It's a tradition in the Union. The big table is the "bridge table." Are you living in the dorms?

CARLOS Chen is. I'm not. I'm staying with a family.

BILL That's great! It's a good way to learn English.

CARLOS I'm not learning English. The family is improving their Spanish.

(Construction of suitable dialogues is discussed in detail in Chapter 1.)

Commentary

1. The subject matter is of interest to students.

2. The utterances are authentic.

3. The speech patterns are typical of informal American English. (e.g., tag questions, *pretty* as an intensifier, the exclamation *that's great*).

4. The sentences are short or break into short semantically and structurally replaceable segments (e.g., *Are you both ____ing ...?, You're ——ing, aren't you?, It's a good way to ...*), thus providing opportunities for variation and recombination practice.

5. Provision is made for the study of basic grammar (present tense of *be*: present progressive; two forms of yes-no question: simple inversion and tag; short answers; *be* with nominal and adjectival complements).

6. With additional vocabulary supplied, this dialogue provides a natural stepping stone to the recombinations for reading practice of Stage Two. The forms provided permit interesting recombinations.

7. Sound-symbol correspondences: every vowel and consonant in English is represented in this passage, except /aw/, /oy/, and /ž/. There is ample material for practice of rising and falling intonation patterns combined with phrase junctures, normal and contrastive phrase stress, stress pattern of compounds, and contractions.

When dialogues are not used, the first reading material consists of a graphic representation on the chalkboard, in the textbook, on the overhead projector, or on flashcards of the English sentences being learned orally in the classroom context or in simulated situations. (These are often associated with pictures.)

R31 I'm a teacher. I'm a teacher of English.

Who are you?

I'm Helmut Keller. I'm a student. I'm from Germany.

Where are you from?

I'm from Costa Rica. I'm studying chemistry.

And what's your name?
It's Pablo. I'm Pablo Lorca.

Is your friend from Iran?
No, he's from Iraq. He's studying engineering.

Is Indira studying engineering too?
No, she's studying economics. She's from India.[38]

Stage Two: Familiarization

Students read rearrangements and recombinations of material they have been learning orally. These recombinations may be situational dialogues, conversations that can be acted out in class, or they may take the form of interesting narratives.

The recombinations may be written by the students themselves, thus linking writing practice with reading. All material will be written in informal style. Students may write out such things as directions from the school to their home: these may be passed out to the class and other students asked to identify the address. Students may write down things they are presumed to be doing while other students try to identify the time of day or place associated with these actions. Many other realistic activities can be invented which use the vocabulary and structure the students have learned at this particular stage.

MATERIALS FOR STAGE TWO

R32 When dialogues like R30 have been used in Stage One, a *recombination conversation* like the one below[39] may be used for Stage Two. (The previous occurrence of a similar item in the book from which this passage has been taken is indicated by the following symbols: ID—introductory dialogue; E—explanation; numbers refer to lessons.)

Summary Dialogue

BILL: Where are you going now, Chen? (ID2)
CHEN: I'm playing bridge (ID2) in the Union (ID1) until the next class (ID2).
BILL: It's a good way to improve your English (ID2).
CHEN: I'm not (E1) learning English; I'm learning bridge (ID2). You're going (ID2) to the party (E2) Friday, aren't you (ID2)?
BILL: Of course, I am (E1). That beautiful girl (ID1) in our biology class (ID1) is going with me (ID2).
CHEN: Great (ID2)....

R33 When classroom conversations like R31 are used, recombination readings like the following[40] are appropriate. (A sketch of the family accompanies the text.)

> Miss Vidal comes from Bogotá, Colombia. She's in the United States. Her family is in Bogotá.
>
> Her father's name is Jorge Vidal. He's an engineer. He's forty-four years old. Mrs. Vidal is a housewife. Miss Vidal has a brother. His name is Antonio. He's ten years old. He's a student. Miss Vidal has a sister, too. Her name is Julia. She's five years old. She isn't in school yet.

R34 Sometimes a little whimsy or humor helps. The teacher or students can deliberately create absurd sentences using only words and constructions which have appeared in previous lessons and use these for reading. (The following sentences are based on material typical of a first-year English course.) [41]

> TEACHER Please give me some new sentences with the expressions you already know. If you cannot, I will erase you and put you in the wastebasket.
>
> HENRY All right, I'll try. The desk is in the teacher's pocket. It's ninety-nine years old and it speaks Russian. The teacher is in the tape-recorder. He's studying hamburgers. The chalkboard is eating lunch and the books are talking in the corridor. They're going to the drug-store for the week-end.

It is certain that the student who could read and understand this passage would not be depending on recollection of memorized sentences!

R35 *Recombinations in narrative form*

As a further step away from dependence on what has been learned in conversational form, the following recombination narrative[42] reintroduces words, phrases, and structures previously learned and practiced, but extends the vocabulary range somewhat (all the new words are among the commonest 1,000 words of TWB, six of them among the commonest 500; all but *third* are in the Hill-OUP 1,000 headword vocabulary). New words are starred; new fixed expressions are double starred. A cultural note explains the importance of the Old North Church in Boston. The author has created an entertaining narrative which is nevertheless conversational in tone.

"You Can't Miss It"

My brother* and I wanted* to find a famous* church* in Boston*. We asked a stranger, "How do we get to the Old* North* Church?" "Go three blocks and turn to your left," he said. "You can't miss it." So we walked three blocks and turned to our left, but the church wasn't there. We then asked a second* stranger. He said, "Go three blocks and turn to your left. You can't miss it." But again* we couldn't find the church. Then we asked a third* stranger. "Go three blocks and turn to your left. You can't miss it." This time** we found the church, but we thought: Is everything* in Boston three blocks and a left turn away*? Just then** a stranger walked over* to us and said, "Excuse me, where is the post office? Can you tell me?" "Go three blocks and turn left," my brother said. "You can't miss it."

At Stage Two, students are trained to recognize meaningful segments of thought and read in coherent word groupings. The familiarity of the structure and of most of the lexical items enables students to relate segments of meaning in what they are reading to what has preceded and to keep all of this in their immediate memory while processing what follows. Students are acquiring reading habits basic to fluent direct reading. For this reason reading practice at this stage is best done in class, where the teacher can guide the student in techniques, rather than being set as homework. Questions require answers which force students to recombine known elements in new combinations.

Stage Three: Acquiring reading techniques

Students read simple narrative and conversational material which develops an uncomplicated and entertaining theme. They are introduced to written style and more complicated structure. Vocabulary remains largely in the area of the known with some unfamiliar words whose meaning can be deduced from illustrations, from cognates, or internationally adopted vocabulary, or from the context. (See examples of inferencing in comments on R24.) Reading materials are a step behind what is currently being learned in order to encouraged direct reading in English, a process which becomes exceedingly difficult when too many novelties of vocabulary and structure are encountered at the same time.

A recombination narrative like R35 bridges the gap between Stages Two and Three.

MATERIALS FOR STAGE THREE

R36 This passage is accompanied by a sketch which sets the scene: the school playground, Nip, the gypsy boy, studying his book, the students gathered

around and Carol taunting him. The story from which this extract is taken
is written within a vocabulary of about 800 words, and the words marked
* are explained with English glosses.

"You go and play football"[43]

In the break* Nip took his reading book and went to the corner of the
playground. . . . All the top class came and stood round him. . . .

"How old are you?" asked Tom. Tom had a football under his arm.

"Have you got any brothers and sisters?" asked Carol.

"Do you live in a caravan?" asked Susan.

Nip didn't say anything.

"Why don't you talk?" asked Carol. "Don't you speak English?"

"Of course he does," said Mike.

"He's shy*," said Susan.

"Leave him alone*," said Paul.

"Do you want to play football?" asked Tom.

"No," said Nip.

"All the boys play football in the break," said Tom. "Don't you want to
play football?"

"No," said Nip.

"He wants to read his book," said Paul. "Leave him alone."

"But he can't read," said Carol. "Look at that book. My sister's only six
years old and she can read that book, but he can't."

Some of the class laughed and Errol said angrily, "It's his first day at
school. Nobody can read on their first day at school."

"It's our last year at school, but he's just starting," said Carol.

"Oh, go away and leave him alone," shouted Errol.

"I'm going," said Carol and she walked away slowly. "I'm not allowed
to go near him," she went on. "My Mum doesn't like gypsies. I'm not
allowed to go anywhere near them."

Everybody looked at Nip. He just stood there, holding his book.

"Oh, come on," said Tom. "Let's play football." He kicked the football
across the playground and most of the boys ran after it. Paul and Mike and
Errol stayed with Nip.

"Reading is easy. We'll help you," said Errol.

"We'll read the book to you and point to the words," said Paul.

"You'll soon learn," said Mike.

"No. You go and play football," said Nip, and he walked away from
them.

Commentary

1. The vocabulary and structures of the passage are of the type commonly taught in elementary courses.

2. The language is authentic, contemporary, and suitable for young students. The preponderance of dialogue adds immediacy, and repetition of phrases facilitates direct, fluent reading (as opposed to translating).

3. The extract shows an aspect of the new (English) culture, while at the same time treating the universal theme of the lone alien in a less-than-friendly society.

4. The level of difficulty of the vocabulary is defined, and words beyond that level are glossed.

When fluent reading is considered the primary objective,[44] Stages One and Two are frequently omitted and simple, entertaining narrative and conversational material with much repetition of vocabulary and structures, often profusely illustrated, is used from the beginning. These passages are usually written in such a way that they can be used for dramatic readings or role-playing: in this they resemble the dialogues of Stage One. An example of such material is given below.

R37 *Family Talk*[45]

Mr. and Mrs. Bello and their two children, John and Maria, are eating breakfast. John is fourteen years old. Maria is ten years old. Mr. Bello is reading the newspaper. Mrs. Bello is talking.

"I'm going shopping today," she says. "I'm going to buy some new drapes for the living room."

"Get nice blue ones," says Maria. "I like blue drapes."

"Mother will get what she likes," says John. "Mother doesn't always listen to us."

Mrs. Bello says, "Be quiet, children."

Mr. Bello says, "Children should be seen and not heard."

"Oh no," says John. "Family talk is a good thing here in the U.S.A."

"Well, maybe dinner is a better time for family talk," says Mrs. Bello. "We have more time then."

Commentary

The situation in this extract is culturally neutral—a family at breakfast—but opportunity is taken to depict what are essentially American relations among the members of the family. This is more important than talking about cereals, orange juice, and other more superficial aspects of an American breakfast. The vocabulary is of immediate usefulness and the conversational interchange is natural in tone. The present and present progressive are both demonstrated, and the *going to* form for expressing intentions is contrasted with the present progressive of *to go* and also with the more predictive use of the future tense ("Mother *will get* what she likes".) Above all, the passage is so written that, after it has been read, it can easily be acted out in class and then acted again with spontaneous variations. There are examples of affirmative and negative statements, of active and passive voice, as well as imperatives, so that, even if students are not expected to use all of these forms immediately, they will have already encountered them in discourse when the time comes to give them more concentrated attention.

For students who have passed through Stages One and Two, material for reading at Stage Three will be more demanding than the extract just quoted. In the following passage, R38, there are four new words beyond the 2,000 word level of TWB. Of these, two are in the third thousand (*complained* and *argue*), and two are derivatives of words in the second thousand (*uncomfortable* and *angrily*). The passage is clearly more advanced syntactically. The first paragraph consists of a complex sentence containing two "quasi-passive" constructions, *was . . . known* and *was honoured* (see Quirk et al. (1972), pp. 809–810). The second paragraph has two complex sentences, each containing a *so . . . that . . .* construction expressing result. The third paragraph is a complex sentence containing two nominal clauses (*that she . . .*), and the fourth contains an adjectival clause (*which she . . .*) and participial phrase (*thanking . . .*). Selection of a passage like R38 would normally be linked with the grammatical study of some of these subordinate constructions.

R38 *Florence Nightingale*[46]

Although Florence Nightingale's name was now known to everybody, and she was honoured everywhere for the wonderful work which she was doing in the Crimea, Dr. Hall hated her as much as ever.

. . . He complained that Florence was making the soldiers so comfortable in the hospitals that they did not want to leave them. His idea was to make the hospitals so uncomfortable that the men would be glad to go back to the fighting line.

Then one day Dr. Hall sent for Florence and angrily told her that she was doing more harm than good, and that she must take her nurses back to England.

Florence did not argue with him. Instead, she showed him a letter which she had that day received from Queen Victoria, thanking "Miss Nightingale and her ladies" for all that they were doing.

Dr. Hall had nothing to say.

RECOGNITION OF STRUCTURAL CLUES

For fluent reading, students must be able to detect rapidly meaningful groups of words, even when the lexical content is not clear to them.

Through Stages Three and Four, students will be learning to detect effortlessly the indicators of word classes (parts of speech), the auxiliary and inflectional features of the verb phrase, including the markers of tense, aspect (perfect or non-perfect, progressive or non-progressive), and modality (meanings indicated by the modal auxiliaries); the words which introduce phrases (*in, of, to, before, since* . . .) and clauses (*when, while, because, if, before, since, who, that* . . .) and the particular modifications of meaning they indicate; the adverbs and adverbial expressions which limit the action in time, place, and manner (*now, often, tomorrow* . . . ; *here, there, everywhere* . . . ; *well, a lot, enough, too*——, *very*——, quiet*ly* . . .); and the indicators of interrogation (inversion, use of *do, when? where? who? what? why?* . . .) and negation (*not,* use of *do, never, nothing, no* . . .). Questions will be designed to attract the students' attention to these structural clues.

R39 For rapid comprehension, students should be trained to recognize such features as the *-s/-es* endings on nouns and verbs. These help to mark word classes and hence to indicate the structure of the sentence. They can be confusing, however, with new vocabulary. The student should note that, in the present tense, if the verb has an "s" the subject noun phrase (usually in initial position) will generally not have an "s," and vice-versa, as in the following sentences:

The exam tests the student's knowledge;
The test results were disappointing;
The student works hard;
The hard work results in better marks;
The teacher marks the tests quickly.

R40 Students should be aware of the multiple functions of the word *that*: as a demonstrative determiner and pronoun; as the introducer of an included

sentence after such verbs as *say* and *think* (indirect statement or comple-
mentizer use); and as a relative pronoun:

> Give me that paper.
> Did he say that?
> I don't believe that that was what he said.
> That book is the one that I wanted.

R41 They should be conscious of the two possible positions for the indirect
object after certain verbs (e.g., *give, send, find*), and look for the indicator
to or *for* in learning to determine quickly which is the direct object and
which is the indirect object. If there is no *to* or *for*, then the first of the two
objects is the indirect object.

> I gave the student the books; I gave the books to the student.
> She sent the assistant the student papers; She sent the student papers to
> the assistant. She sent the student his papers.
> He bought the child a present; He bought a present for the child.
> We found them a new flat; We found a new flat for them.

* Discuss other structural clues on which you depend to clarify the meaning
of what you are reading.

7
Reading II:
from dependence to independence

Stage Four: Practice

Students now practice their reading skill with a wider range of language. Reading is of two kinds: *intensive,* where reading is linked with further study of grammar and vocabulary, and *extensive*, where students are on their own, reading for their own purposes or pleasure. In both cases texts are authentic writings by English-speaking authors, but they are carefully selected to be accessible to students at this stage of their development; that is, difficult or complex style or esoteric vocabulary is avoided. As students progress through this practice stage they read material of increasing complexity with a wider and wider range of vocabulary. A recognition vocabulary of about 3,600 words[1] seems a reasonable limitation. This will, of course, be augmented by some specialized vocabulary associated with specific topics, and, in appropriate cases, by cognates and borrowings.

INTENSIVE READING

This provides material for close study of problem areas.

1. *The systems and subsystems of the language*[2]

Students often have difficulty understanding the English system for expressing time relationships and particularly the subsystems for expressing action in the past.

R42 Through reading, the student becomes conscious of the fact that in English what has taken place can be expressed either in *time value* through the use of the *simple past tense* or as an *aspect* (a way of looking at an action or situation), where the verb phrase may combine tense with *perfect, progressive*, or *perfect progressive* forms.[3]

She came to New York in 1939, and has lived there ever since. Although she never studied English in school, and has never learned to speak it well, she has made many friends in the city, particularly among people from her native country. She failed to get a license because of her language, but her friends have helped her get enough work to live on.

Commentary

Came, studied, failed are simple past tense: they refer to events which took place at a definite time in the past and can be dated. *Has lived, has learned, has made, have helped* all refer to actions which were begun in the past but which continue to be carried on or to have relevance in the present.

R43 Compare the variations of tense and aspect in the following:

'Our son will be a great man one day,' said his mother. 'He's made a good start. In one week he's found somewhere to live. He's made good friends. He's started at South Seas School. Every day he went to school in a clean white shirt.'

Jin-Bee smiled. All this had happened in his first week in the city, and many other things which his family did not know.

GERALDINE KAYE, *Jin-Bee Leaves Home*[4]

R44 In a more formal style:

The 1960s has been a decade of liberation. Women have been swept up 1
by that feeling along with blacks, Latins, American Indians, and poor 2
whites. The result for women has been a growth of a new women's move- 3
ment. . . . This new movement has criticized almost every part of American 4
society and has rejected many old assumptions about the nature and role 5
of women. A short time ago the movement was concerned about male 6
chauvinism and psychological oppression; now it is concerned with under- 7
standing the economic and social roots of women's oppression. But the most 8
important change of all has been the loss of fear. . . . 9

MARLENE DIXON, "Why Women's Liberation?"[5]

Commentary

To make students more aware of the distinction between simple past tense and present perfect forms, they may be asked questions like the following:

1. What does the perfect verb form in the first sentence tell you about the date of writing of the selection?

2. What would be the effect of changing *has been, has criticized, has rejected* to simple past tense (lines 3–5)?

3. Why does the author change from present perfect to simple past in *was concerned* (line 6)? Why does she change back to the present perfect in the last sentence (*has been*)?

Focusing the students' attention on the choices of verb forms in well-written passages will make the English way of expressing past action, and specifically the distinctive uses of the simple past (*went*), the present and past perfect (*have gone* and *had gone*), the past progressive (*were going*), and the perfect progressive (*have been going* and *had been going*) appear more rational and meaningful. Many other problems of English usage are also more efficiently studied through the thoughtful analysis of a text than through the study of a rule illustrated by examples detached from the wider context of interacting rules. Nor is translation of sentences into English especially effective when the students' native language does not make a particular distinction in parallel fashion.

* Look for passages of English which show clearly the difference between the simple tenses (present or past) and the progressive aspect (present or past). Work out questions which would bring a student to an understanding of this distinction.

2. *Contrastive problems of meaning*

It is in functioning language that students will begin to assimilate the differences in coverage of semantic space of English words which seem to be equivalent in meaning to certain words from their own language. As examples, consider the meanings covered by the following words in American and British English.

R45 The American word *check* has a range of meanings which are not covered by the word in British English. A table will make clear the correspondences and divergences:[6]

	Meaning	American	British
noun	a position in chess	check	check
	a sudden stopping or restraining of a movement or action	check	check
	a control	check	check
	an examination for errors	check	check

	Meaning	American	British
	a pattern of crossed lines or squares	check	check
	a token given when belongings are deposited	check	check
	✔	check	tick
	(as in banking)	check	cheque
	statement of amount owed (in a restaurant, etc.)	check	bill; check
	inspection (e.g., medical)	check-up	check-up
	counter where one pays and takes one's goods in self-service store/shop	check-out (counter)	check-out* (counter)
	place for leaving coats in restaurants, etc.	check-room	cloak-room
	place for leaving belongings at stations, etc.	check-room	left-luggage office
interjection	yes, o.k.	check	yes, right
verb	stop, restrain, control, examine	check	check
	find out ("I'll check")	check	find out
	deposit (belongings)	check	leave
	correct (student papers)	check	mark
	sign in (to a hotel)	check in	register; check in*
	pay one's bill and leave (a hotel)	check out	pay one's bill; settle up; check out*

* According to the OALDCE, the same terms are used for these meanings in both American and British English. Not all current British dictionaries list phrases with *check* for these meanings, however, and certainly such phrases are not in universal use in Britain.

* Make a list of the various words used in the major language spoken by your students to convey these multiple meanings of *check*. Then examine your list and set down other meanings which these words convey which are not covered in English by *check*.

R46 Many words present difficulties in going from one part of the English-speaking world to another. It is possible to construct a chain of words linked together by different meanings in GA and GB. In the following table the GB word is the subject and the GA word is the predicate complement.

A scone	is	a biscuit;
a biscuit	is	a cracker;
a cracker	is	a popper;
a popper	is	a snapper.

Even this is simplifying things since GB *biscuit* can be either GA *cracker* or *cookie*.

Students who expect to be familiar with more than one variety of English should be aware of differences in the range of meanings of common words as used by Americans, Englishmen, Scotsmen, Irishmen, Welshmen, Australians, or Canadians.

* 1. See what other chains of this type you can construct.
2. Make parallel lists for divergent terms in GA and GB for meals, parts of the car, and articles of clothing.

Students come to appreciate the resources of the English language when they *listen* to the plays, poems, and prose they have studied intensively being acted, recited, or read by American or British actors and sometimes by the writers themselves.

This is the stage for intellectually challenging ideas and the cultivation of aesthetic values. Material for Stage Four should be selected for the literary, informational, or provocative value of its content, not merely as a language vehicle. Questions should go beyond Who? What? When? Where? How (manner)? and yes-no questions to considerations of implications, that is, Why? If . . . then what? and How (explanation)? questions.[7]

EXTENSIVE READING

This gives students the opportunity to use their knowledge of the language for their own purposes. It is an individualized or shared activity as each student prefers. With some help from the teacher in selection as they need it the students read for their own pleasure short stories, plays, short novels, newspapers or magazines specially written for schools, or selected articles and advertisements (particularly those profusely illustrated) from American, British, or other English-language sources. They may read for information about a topic which interests them or prepare a project, a report, or a debate with a friend or a group of friends. They attempt to increase their reading speed. Setting timed goals may help them in this. They learn to tolerate a certain vagueness, reading whole sections at a time in order to establish the general meaning so that they can develop their ability to deduce from semantic and syntactic clues in the context the meaning of unfamiliar words and phrases.[8]

MATERIALS FOR STAGE FOUR

Passages like *Florence Nightingale* (R38) may be read and discussed in class at Stage Three to supplement the steady diet of the intermediate level textbook or used for the *extensive reading* of Stage Four, which should always be at a lower level of difficulty than material for intensive reading.

R47 A book published in 1963 gives the following passage for study at the lower intermediate level. In reprinting the first two (of three) paragraphs of the selection, we have italicized all words, except proper names, not within the first 3,600 words of TWB.

Mr. Pickwick and his friends are waiting in the cold on the outside of the Muggleton coach, which they have just attained, well wrapped up in *great-coats, shawls* and *comforters*. The *portmanteaus* and *carpet-bags* have been *stowed* away, and Mr. Weller and the guard are endeavoring to *insinuate* into the *fore-boot* a huge *cod-fish* several sizes too large for it— which is *snugly* packed up, in a long brown basket, with a layer of straw over the top, and which has been left to the last, in order that he may *repose* in safety on the half-dozen barrels of real native oysters, all the property of Mr. Pickwick.

The interest displayed in Mr. Pickwick's countenance is most *intense*, as Mr. Weller and the guard try to *squeeze* the *cod-fish* into the boot, first head first, and then tail first, and then top upward, and then bottom upward, and then *sideways*, and then *longways*, until the guard *accidentally* hits him in the very middle of the basket, *whereupon* he suddenly disappears into the boot, and with him, the head and shoulders of the guard himself.

CHARLES DICKENS, *The Pickwick Papers*
(London: Chapman and Hall, 1869),
with minor adaptations

Commentary

1. Admittedly this is not the whole of the selection used in this book of readings, but even the addition of the final paragraph, in which Mr. Pickwick buys drinks for Mr. Weller and the guard and they all set off in the coach, fails to enliven the passage or make it interesting to a student at this level. Indeed, is this isolated selection of much interest to anyone who knows nothing else about Mr. Pickwick, Mr. Weller, and their friends?

2. The two paragraphs contain 17 words not in the first 3,600 words of the TWB. These include seven compounds, all of which have at least one familiar element (*great-coats, carpet-bags, fore-boot, cod-fish, sideways, longways, whereupon*), but since the meaning of compounds is not additive, this knowledge of a part does not ensure recognition of the meaning of the whole. We have, then, 17 new words in 184 running words, a rate of one new word in 11. Scherer recommends a rate of one new word in 35.[9] Scherer also recommends that the new words be spaced evenly, that the new vocabulary be useful, and that new words "be surrounded by contextual clues so that it is possible to infer the meaning."[10] The reader should look again at the italicized words in the preceding passage in the light of these recommendations, and should note as well the rare senses in which some of the words are used (*attained, insinuate, boot*).

3. While the content of the selection is simple, the sentences are long and involved, placing a strain on the memory of the student who is making any attempt at direct reading of the extract.[11] (Notice that the two paragraphs are made up of only three sentences.) There are other potentially confusing features, e.g., the switch from the impersonal pronoun (*which*) to the personal (*he*) in referring to the cod-fish in the second sentence of the first paragraph; and the ambiguity of "The interest displayed in Mr. Pickwick's countenance . . ." in the second paragraph.

We may say that this passage was intended for intensive reading and therefore extension of vocabulary and knowledge of structure. Four of the italicized words are hardly likely to be encountered in further reading or communication (*great-coat, portmanteau, carpet-bag, fore-boot*). In the following passage, there are seven words beyond the 3,600 most frequent (using the TWB count, and not including proper names, dates, and numbers). One of these is *adjective,* presumably well-known to students at this stage; another is *unparalleled,* a regular derivative of a word within the 3,600 range; two others are compounds where one (*awe-struck*) or both (*rainbow*) elements would be known at this level. This leaves five new words (*awe-struck, flaunting, gorge, chasm* and *rainbow*) in approximately 135 running words, three of them easily guessed from the context.

The passage is certainly more interesting for Stage Four students than R47, especially as it can easily be accompanied in the text by a spectacular picture.

R48   But the greatest sight of all, unparalleled in the world, the sight everybody wants to see, is the Grand Canyon. The first white men looked into the great gorge in 1540. They were a side party scouting from Coronado's main force, and they were awe-struck. The Grand Canyon may be a wonderful sight, as it was for the Spaniards, or a scientific event, or a religious experience—and it may well be all three. Every visitor, after he has recovered from the shock of his first look into this chasm a mile deep and ten miles across, flaunting every color of the rainbow and making beggars of adjectives, wants to know two things: When did this happen? and What caused it? The answers are simple: It happened twelve million years ago and the Colorado River did it.

                                             EDWIN CORLE, "*Arizona*"[12]

It may be objected that the verb phrases in this passage are mainly in the simple present and simple past, but it is not difficult to find passages with more complex verb phrases and sentences, which are, nevertheless, not made unnecessarily difficult by an overload of infrequent and obscure vocabulary items.

R49   "Mother, can I come into your room?" Laura turned the big glass doorknob.
       "Of course, child. Why, what's the matter? What's given you such a colour?" And Mrs. Sheridan turned round from her dressing-table. She was trying on a new hat.
       "Mother, a man's been killed," began Laura.
       "*Not* in the garden?" interrupted her mother.
       "No, no!"
       "Oh, what a fright you gave me!" Mrs. Sheridan sighed with relief and took off the big hat and held it on her knees.
       "But listen, mother," said Laura. Breathless, half-choking, she told the dreadful story. "Of course, we can't have our party, can we?" she pleaded. "The band and everybody arriving. They'd hear us, mother; they're nearly neighbours!"
       To Laura's astonishment her mother behaved just like Jose; it was harder to bear because she seemed amused. She refused to take Laura seriously.
       "But, my dear child, use your common sense. It's only by accident we've

heard of it. If someone had died there normally—and I can't understand how they keep alive in those poky little holes—we should still be having our party, shouldn't we?"

Laura had to say "yes" to that, but she felt it was all wrong. She sat down on her mother's sofa and pinched the cushion frill.

"Mother, isn't it really terribly heartless of us?" she asked.

"Darling!" Mrs. Sheridan got up and came over to her, carrying the hat. Before Laura could stop her she had popped it on. "My child!" said her mother, "the hat is yours. It's made for you. It's much too young for me. I have never seen you look such a picture. Look at yourself!" And she held up her hand-mirror.

KATHERINE MANSFIELD, "The Garden Party"[13]

Commentary

Of the thirteen words in this selection which are not in the first 3,600 of TWB two are easily guessed compounds (*dressing-table* and *hand-mirror*) and four are regular derivatives of words within the 3,600 range (*breathless, astonishment, normally, heartless*). Another compound (*doorknob*) could easily be guessed, leaving six new words (*poky, sofa, pinch, cushion, frill, popped*) in about 250 running words, or about one in every 40 words. (Admittedly, four of these are in a single sentence, but with an illustration accompanying the selection this would not pose a major problem.) It seems one has to search to find a passage as tediously difficult as R47 in completely unadapted material, unless one deliberately looks for nineteenth-century writing which is heavily descriptive.

＊ Examine some reading passages in textbooks in common use for Stage Four to see how they measure up to the criteria discussed; then find some suitable passages in novels and short stories in the library and share them with your fellow students, before adding them to your personal file.

Stage Five: Expansion

At Stage Five, students can read a wide variety of materials in their original form without becoming discouraged. At most there will have been some judicious editing to eliminate odd paragraphs of excessively complicated structure and rare vocabulary. Once again the material the students are encouraged to read entirely on their own, their extensive reading, will be more readily accessible in language and content than that which is being studied intensively. Reading is now a technique, not an end, and language is a vehicle and a model. Students are expected to be able to discuss not only the content but the implications of what they have been reading.

Material for intensive reading is chosen with a view to developing the student's aesthetic appreciation, imagination, and powers of judgment and discriminative reasoning. Students learn to scan for information, to read with careful attention, and to extract the major ideas and arguments. Attention is paid to matters of style in writing, and, where feasible, students are given some experience in exact translation from English into their native language to make them more conscious of the choices involved in literary writing and the potentialities of their own language, as well as the English language. Reading is still linked with *listening* (to plays, poems, readings, speeches), with *writing* (of reports, summaries, commentaries, and, for self-selected students, even poetry), and with *speaking* (discussion of ideas, themes, and values). Students seek to penetrate the minds and hearts of English-speaking people and compare and contrast their attitudes and aspirations with their own. They continue to read widely on subjects which interest them personally (political, social, scientific, artistic, practical) and prepare presentations in which they share what they have enjoyed with their fellow students.

Teachers need not feel at a loss in providing widely diversified reading for their Stage Five students, since material now being made available by publishers is much more varied than in previous decades.

* Examine advertisements in recent journals and publishers' catalogues to see how many areas of interest you can identify in recently published books of readings.

Students at Stage Five still need help with more difficult aspects of English written style. Many students, for instance, never grasp the essential differences between the common logical connectives such as *however, nevertheless, (and) yet, in any case, besides, furthermore, moreover, consequently, so* or *and so, therefore,* yet words such as these are indispensable for understanding the development of thought and for drawing implications. A situational technique may be used to familiarize students at this level with their meaning.

R 50 A key sentence is selected, such as:

He hasn't paid his debts.

A situation is described in English and the student is asked to link this key sentence with the idea: you lend him money again, in some such way as:
He hasn't paid his debts, *and yet* you lend him money again.

Other possibilities are:

> He hasn't paid his debts. He has no intention of doing so.
> He hasn't paid his debts. He has no intention of doing so, *moreover.*
> He has not paid his debts. *Furthermore,* he has no intention of paying.
> He hasn't paid his debts. I just won't go out with him any more.
> He hasn't paid his debts, *so* I just won't go out with him any more.
> He has not paid his debts; *and therefore* I refuse to go out with him again.
> He hasn't paid his debts. We can't refuse to sell him the extra paint.
> He hasn't paid his debts. *Nevertheless,* we can't refuse to sell him the extra paint.
> He hasn't paid his debts. This isn't the first time.
> He hasn't paid his debts. *Besides,* this isn't the first time.

Important clue words like these are sometimes omitted entirely from the English course, with the result that students continue for years to express themselves in simple sentences, or link sentences only with *and* and *but* and are incapable of recognizing the significance of the logical connectives in modifying the meaning of what they are reading. A careful study should be made of the way an argument is developed in English through a succession of such connectives.

READING WITH WRITING

A class that is reading for information would find practicing these connectives orally very difficult. A written exercise which requires analysis of the logical development and choice among possible connectives may be used instead.

R51 Write out the following passage as a paragraph, selecting from the logical connectives supplied those which will provide the most natural development of thought.

Thank you very much for lending me this book. (Furthermore, so, actually) I'm afraid I didn't understand much of it. (Consequently, on the other hand, however) I read less than half of it! (Thus, besides, nevertheless) it's a subject that interests me. (Therefore, moreover, consequently) it's one that I need to know more about for my work. (In fact, thus, besides) this isn't the first time that I've tried to find out something about it, as you may remember. (Therefore, in fact, and yet) you can see I'm not giving up! (Furthermore, however, thus) I haven't got a lot of time to spend on it. (So, nevertheless, on the other hand) perhaps you'd be good enough to send me that simpler book you mentioned.

MATERIALS FOR STAGE FIVE

Some textbooks propose for intensive reading in a general course at this level material like the following:

R52 *Sonnet XVII*

When I consider how my light is spent
   Ere half my days, in this dark world and wide,
   And that one talent which is death to hide
   Lodged with me useless, though my soul more bent
To serve therewith my Maker, and present
   My true account, lest He returning chide;
   "Doth God exact day-labour, light denied,"
   I fondly ask: but Patience, to prevent
That murmur, soon replies: "God doth not need
   Either man's work, or His own gifts; who best
   Bear His mild yoke, they serve Him best: His state
Is kingly; thousands at his bidding speed,
   And post o'er land and ocean without rest;
   They also serve who only stand and wait."

                   JOHN MILTON

Naturally enough these fourteen lines would require at least fourteen footnotes. Important, and moving, as the poem is, it is not clear how average intermediate-level students could do more than decipher it, whereas they would be able to read easily and with enjoyment many poems of Robert Frost, W. B. Yeats, A. E. Housman, or Walter de la Mare. For a general textbook, then, this poem is unsuitable, whereas it might fascinate Group D, which has chosen to specialize in literary analysis.

A poem which could delight many non-specialized students and make English poetry accessible to them is this one from *The Green Helmet and Other Poems*, by W. B. Yeats.[14]

R53 *Brown Penny*

I whispered, 'I am too young.'
And then, 'I am old enough';
Wherefore I threw a penny
To find out if I might love.

'Go and love, go and love, young man,
If the lady be young and fair.'
Ah, penny, brown penny, brown penny,
I am looped in the loops of her hair.
O love is the crooked thing,
There is nobody wise enough
To find out all that is in it,
For he would be thinking of love
Till the stars had run away,
And the shadows eaten the moon.
Ah, penny, brown penny, brown penny,
One cannot begin it too soon.

This poem, in contrast to R52, is easily understood by all students. Its theme is universal, yet immediate, calling forth an emotional response with little need for explanation.

Many other twentieth-century poems are equally accessible to the general student. As an example, we may take the following poem of Robert Frost.[15]

R54 *Stopping by Woods on a Snowy Evening*

Whose woods these are I think I know.
His house is in the village, though;
He will not see me stopping here
To watch his woods fill up with snow.

My little horse must think it queer
To stop without a farmhouse near
Between the woods and frozen lake
The darkest evening of the year.

He gives his harness bells a shake
To ask if there is some mistake.
The only other sound's the sweep
Of easy wind and downy flake.

The woods are lovely, dark, and deep,
But I have promises to keep,
And miles to go before I sleep,
And miles to go before I sleep.

Again, the theme is universal and appealing to modern students. The poem would be learned by heart with pleasure by many and added to their store of treasured literary memories. In this way poetry becomes a personal experience, not another arduous classroom assignment.

With prose readings similarly, care must be exercised in the selection of materials for Group C. (Group D, as we have noted, is a self-selected group of specialized interests with a declared desire to explore literature.) Some books offer selections like the following, whose language is not inaccessible but whose content would be difficult for the average student of English.

R55 He got off the car. In the country all was dead still. Little stars shone high up; little stars spread far away in the flood-waters, a firmament below. Everywhere the vastness and terror of the immense night which is roused and stirred for a brief while by the day, but which returns, and will remain at last eternal, holding everything in its silence and its living gloom. There was no Time, only Space. Who could say his mother had lived and did not live? She had been in one place, and was in another; that was all. And his soul could not leave her, wherever she was. Now she was gone abroad into the night, and he was with her still. They were together. But yet there was his body, his chest, that leaned against the stile, his hands on the wooden bar. They seemed something. Where was he?—one tiny upright speck of flesh, less than an ear of wheat lost in the field. He could not bear it. On every side the immense dark silence seemed pressing him, so tiny a spark, into extinction, and yet, almost nothing, he could not be extinct. Night, in which everything was lost, went reaching out, beyond stars and sun. Stars and sun, a few bright grains, went spinning round for terror, and holding each other in embrace, there in a darkness that out-passed them all, and left them tiny and daunted. So much, and himself, infinitesimal, at the core a nothingness, and yet not nothing.

D. H. LAWRENCE, Sons and Lovers[16]

A passion for the chronological presentation of literary masterpieces must be curbed at this stage. If students are to become fluent in reading and using contemporary language, they need to read much contemporary or near-contemporary writing. If the oral skills are to be kept at a high level, reading material must be such that the students can discuss its content and implications with ease and confidence. This does not mean that the content must be of little literary or cultural value, as the following extract from Margaret Craven's novel, *I Heard the Owl Call My Name*,[17] demonstrates.

R56 The novel is the story of the last days of a young vicar who has a fatal illness and only a few years to live. For his final post his bishop sends him to a remote Indian parish in British Columbia, where he lives and learns among the Indians and is accepted by them.

But after Christmas, when the snow turned to slush and the rain fell, the children were kept inside and the men played La-hell in the social hall long into the night, Mark felt a strange little wind of dissent which seemed to whisper in the firs, to precede him, to follow him wherever he went.

He spoke of it to old Peter, the carver, who was down with a cold.

"Peter, what is it? What is this unease that is now in the village?" and the old man looked at him long and carefully before answering.

"It is always so when the young come back from the school. My people are proud of them, and resent them. They come from a far country. They speak English all the time, and forget the words of Kwákwala. They are ashamed to dip their food in the oil of the óolachon which we call gleena. They say to their parents, 'Don't do it that way. The white man does it this way.' They do not remember the myths, and the meaning of the totems. They want to choose their own wives and husbands."

He faltered as if what he was going to say was too painful to utter.

"Here in the village my people are at home as the fish in the sea, as the eagle in the sky. When the young leave, the world takes them, and damages them. They no longer listen when the elders speak. They go, and soon the village will go also."

"Kingcome will be one of the last to go, Peter."

"Yes, but in the end it will be deserted, the totems will fall, and the green will cover them. And when I think of it, I am glad I will not be here to see."

Commentary

This story is relevant to the problems of the modern world and would lead to discussion of interest to the students, yet in language it is within the reading scope of Stage Five. Scherer suggests a vocabulary of at least 5,000 words for the last stage before liberated reading.[18] In the passage above, there are six words not within the TWB 5,000-word range, not counting proper names, foreign words, and regular derivatives. Two of these six could easily be guessed from the context (*slush* and *faltered*), leaving in a text of about 300 words only four (*dissent, firs, myths, totems*) that would require explanation for a student at this level.

* Look for suitable poems, stories, essays, scenes from plays, and short novels which you think would appeal to Stage Five students and which are accessible in vocabulary range and complexity of structure. (Keep careful notes of bibliographic details and page references.) Share your discoveries with others in your class and add them to your file for future reference.

Stage Six: *Autonomy*

Students who have reached this stage should be encouraged to develop an independent reading program tailored to their special interests. They should be able to come to the teacher on a personal basis at regular intervals to discuss what they have been reading and share the exhilaration of their discoveries.

Their reading may be in some special area of literature which interests them, or they may be reading widely with the aim of finding out as much as they can about the cultural attitudes or the civilization of the English-speaking peoples. On the other hand, they may have some specialized interest they wish to pursue: a scientific or technical subject; the theories behind modern architecture; urban problems; public health; folklore; advertising techniques; or business methods. An independent reading unit becomes more purposeful if it leads to some form of display: an illustrated presentation to interested English classes or an article for the school magazine or college newspaper. Independent study of this type for advanced students stimulates self-disciplined motivation and is an excellent preparation for autonomous intellectual exploration in later life.

Ordering the reading lesson

The reading lesson is not a quiescent interlude as some teachers seem to think. Because students have learned to associate sound and symbol in their native language, it does not follow that they know how to extract the full meaning from what they see in print. For the teacher the reading lesson or reading assignment has six parts.

1. *Selection* of suitable material at an appropriate level of reading difficulty for this particular group of students; selection of the right amount of material for the time available and for arousing and maintaining interest in the content of the text.

2. *Preparation* by the teacher who checks on: the necessary background information; words which need explaining (and how best to explain them: by visual aid, action, English definition or synonym, or translation); structural complications; obscurity of meaning or allusion; and the most effective way to arouse interest in this particular text.

The teacher who has prepared the material ahead of time can often slip some of the unfamiliar vocabulary into class discussions and exercises in a preceding lesson, or can center an oral lesson around a semantic area germane to the reading text, thus not only introducing useful vocabulary but also preparing students unobtrusively for intelligent guessing when they are face to face with the text. A review of certain grammatical features may refresh the students' memory so that comprehension is not impeded by structural complexity.

3. *Introduction* of the material to the students. This introduction may take the form of the provision of background information or some explanation of cultural differences, either directly—visually or orally—or indirectly, during some other activity when the students may have been given the opportunity to find out information which will be useful for a later reading lesson. Sometimes the introduction will take the form of a provocative discussion on a question which is raised in the reading text, with the students then reading more alertly as they find out how the author has viewed the problem or whether the outcome is as they had anticipated. This approach is particularly valuable at Stage Five when a writer is developing difficult concepts or setting out a complicated discussion of ideas. Stimulating the students' own thinking about the central issue or problem helps them to anticipate the probable meaning of unfamiliar vocabulary and to perceive disguised cognates and borrowed words in the matrix of the development of ideas.

4. *Reading.* Throughout these chapters on reading, and particularly in the discussion of the different stages, many practical suggestions have been given as to ways to approach the actual reading of the passage. These should be exploited on different occasions to ensure that the reading lesson does not fall into a set pattern. Individualized reading assignments also should be designed with variety of activities in mind. The cardinal principle for each approach (except for Group E: *Translation*) is that it should encourage students to keep looking ahead for meaning rather than stopping at each word to seek an exact native-language equivalent.

5. *Discussion.* It is at this point that the teacher is able to gauge and increase the student's overall comprehension of the passage, not by explaining and restating, but by encouraging the student to go back to the passage and look into it more carefully. Suggestions for improving this part of the lesson are developed in the next section.

6. *Application.* Reading is not an isolated activity. In a language class it should lead to something, and thus be integrated with the improvement of all skills. This idea is developed below in the section *Integrating the Language Skills*, p. 258.

* From all the indications scattered throughout this section, draw up three different lesson plans for the reading of R57 below.

Assisting and assessing reading comprehension

The following passage will be used as a basis for demonstration and evaluation of various methods for assisting and assessing the student's comprehension of reading material. In each example, items given are for illustration only and in no case represent a complete set.

If the text in R57 is to be used for Stages 3 or 4, we suggest that it be adapted by substituting for the words marked * the more frequent words given in the right-hand margin (see Commentary below). In the discussions which follow the text we will presume it has been adapted in this way.

R57   Joy and George Adamson have tried to change their pet lioness, Elsa, into a wild animal able to live independently of them in the African jungle. Elsa has left them but returns for brief visits, and they are not sure that she has finally accepted her new life.

Elsa's final test

During the night we were awakened by the most alarming	1
lion growls mixed with the laughing hyenas. We listened,	2
expecting Elsa to come in at any moment, but morning	3
dawned and she did not return. As soon as it became light	4
we went in the direction from which the growls had come,	5
but stopped after a few hundred yards, startled by an	6
unmistakable lion grunt* coming from the river below us. *growl	7
At the same time we saw an antelope and some vervet* *(delete)	8
monkeys racing in flight through the bush. Creeping	9
cautiously* through thick undergrowth down to the river, *carefully	10
we found the fresh pugmarks* of at least two or three *pawmarks	11
lions in the sand; they led across the river. Wading* *Going across	12
through*, we followed the still wet spoor* up the opposite *pawmarks	13
bank when I noticed not fifty yards away, through the	14
dense* bush the shape of a lion. While I strained *thick	15
my eyes to see if it was Elsa, George called to her. She	16
walked away from us. When George repeated his call she	17
only trotted faster along the game path until we saw the	18
black tuft* on the end of her tail switch* for the last time *fur, *move	19
through the bush.	20
We looked at each other. Had she found her destiny*? *fate	21
She must have heard us; by following the lions she had	22
decided her future. Did this mean that our hopes for her	23
return to her natural life had been fulfilled? Had we	24
succeeded in letting her part from us without hurting her?	25
We returned to camp alone, and very sad. Should we	26
leave her now, and so close a very important chapter of our	27
lives? George suggested that we should wait a few more	28
days to make sure that Elsa had been accepted by the pride.	29

I went to my studio by the river and continued to write 30
the story of Elsa, who had been with us until this morning. 31
I was sad to be alone, but tried to make myself happy by 32
imagining that at this very moment Elsa was rubbing her 33
soft skin against another lion's skin and resting with him 34
in the shade, as she had often rested here with me. 35

JOY ADAMSON, *Born Free*[19]

Commentary

All the words in this passage, as adapted, are within the TWB 3,600-word range, with the exception of the specialized vocabulary items *hyena, antelope,* and *pride*; the easily-guessed derivatives and compounds *unmistakable, undergrowth, pawmarks*; and the verbs *trotted* and *fulfilled* (both within the TWB 3,800-word range, and both easily understood from the context).

    1. *Content questions*, that is, Who? What? When? Where? How (manner)? and yes-no questions, are most appropriate at Stage Three.

R58 a. What did the Adamsons expect after they were awakened?
      They expected Elsa to come in at any moment.
    b. Where did the lion pawmarks lead them?
      The lion pawmarks led them across the river and up the bank.
    c. What did Joy do after she returned to camp?
      Joy continued to write the story of Elsa.

Commentary

Questions of this type are too simple for Stages Four and Five. Answers to the questions can be copied directly from the text with a little infusion of words from the question itself. They do not necessarily require comprehension of the text; once students have identified the place in the text where the answer can be found they respond to structural clues—*What . . . expect? expected Elsa . . .* ; *Where? across . . . across the river*; *What did Joy . . . ? Joy continued . . .*

    2. *Implication questions*, that is, Why? If . . . then what? and How (explanation)? questions, should be asked at Stages Four and Five.

R59 a. If Elsa had come to George when he called, what would it have shown?
      It would have shown that she was not ready to leave them and live with the wild lions.

b. Why did it make Joy happy to think of Elsa resting with the lions?

Because Joy knew that Elsa could not stay with them indefinitely (or: Because Joy wanted Elsa to make her life in the wild; or alternatively: Because Joy wanted Elsa to be accepted by the wild lions).

Commentary

Question (a) requires the student to answer from lines 21–25 a question based on lines 16–20. Question (b) is based on lines 32–35 and requires an answer from a whole section of the text (lines 21–29). Some teachers insist that students copy out, or repeat, the relevant part of the question and thus always answer with a complete sentence. If the aim is to evaluate degree of reading comprehension, this is really busy-work at this point and can become laborious for the student, with no particular gain in skill. The student who has not done so should not be penalized. Note that with questions of this type there will be a number of possible answers, depending on the way the student chooses to express the idea.

The problem arises: If one is evaluating reading comprehension, should one require skill in composition, written or oral, at the same time? If students have demonstrated quite clearly that they have understood the passage by giving the right facts in answer to the questions, should they be penalized for writing or phrasing their answers in incorrect English, since this has nothing to do with reading comprehension? At Stage Five one should expect students to be able to express themselves in simple correct English. For some students at Stage Four, and certainly at Stage Three, it may be better to try other methods of eliciting information gained from reading. If the method outlined is used because students are seeking to attain a high level in all skills, a form of dual credit will be adopted: allowing some credit for comprehension and some for the way the answer is formulated.

3. *Multiple-choice questions* are frequently used.
a. At Stage Three, *sentence completions* requiring only discrimination among several short alternative phrases may be used. The choices are usually set out in written form; if they are given orally, they also test listening comprehension and auditory memory.

R60 Choose a completion for each of the following sentences according to the information given in the text you have just read:

The Adamsons stopped near the river

A. to watch the antelopes and monkeys;
B. because they saw a lion coming from the river;

C. because they heard a lion nearby;

D. because they expected Elsa to come back across the river . . .

Commentary

The choices are designed so that the correct answer (C) is quite clear to the student who understood the text. (A), (B), and (D) pick up expressions used in the text which may attract students who did not understand completely what they were reading. (A) could attract a student who did not understand the passage but who sees in lines 8–9: *we saw an antelope and some monkeys.* (B) points to line 7: *lion . . . coming from the river.* (D) seems reasonable to the student who understood the preceding sentence (line 3: *expecting Elsa to come in at any moment*) but is vague about the immediate context of *stopped.* Multiple-choice selections must always be designed so that they reflect some element in the text which may have been misunderstood, but the correct version should never reproduce word for word some sentence in the text. The choices should also be plausible completions—in this case (A), (B), (C), and (D) are all possible reasons why the Adamsons might have stopped. There must be no ambiguity in the choices which could cause an intelligent student to hesitate between possibilities. If students are warned in advance, there can occasionally be more than one correct choice in a set.

R61 Joy _____ that Elsa had been accepted by the pride.

A. knew

B. feared

C. heard

D. hoped

Commentary

With single-word completions, once again, it is important that the correct completion does not parallel a sentence the student can identify in the text without understanding its meaning. Since the purpose of this exercise is to assess comprehension of the passage, it is important that the choices contain words whose meanings the students may be expected to know.

b. At Stages Four and Five, multiple-choice sets will consist of *longer statements* which the student must be able to comprehend as well as the original text.

R62 The Adamsons were sad because

A. Elsa ran away from them when George called her;
B. they wanted Elsa to leave the lions and return to them;
C. an important and happy part of their life had ended;
D. they felt they had hurt Elsa by returning to camp without her.

Commentary

Once again, each of the choices is plausible in the context. (A) draws attention to lines 16–18 (*George called to her . . . she only trotted faster. . . .*), (b) is for students who did not understand what the Adamsons were trying to do but who see *I was sad to be alone* in line 32, (C) is correct, (D) points to lines 24–25 and would attract a student who did not understand that the Adamsons had been afraid of hurting Elsa but believed that they had not.

Variation: In an expository text, one sentence which is important in the comprehension of the development of ideas may be chosen and students asked to select a correct paraphrase for this idea from several alternatives.

DIGRESSION

In "How to Pass Multiple-Choice Tests when you Don't Know the Answers" Hoffman[20] sets out for ambitious but indolent students a few rules based on common faults of multiple-choice tests. Below are seven which are applicable to reading comprehension tests.

1. With five alternatives the correct answer tends to be the third, with four alternatives the second or third.

2. An alternative which is much longer or shorter than the others tends to be the correct answer.

3. With a sentence to complete: if the alternative when added to the stem does not make a grammatical sequence, that alternative is not the correct item. In English, when the stem requires a verb ending in -*ing* a verb in the simple form will not be the correct choice, e.g.: After the separation, Herbert couldn't *get used to*: (A) eating alone (B) walking to work (C) cook for himself (D) having no one to talk to.

4. Look for clues in other questions.

5. If two alternatives are exactly the same except for one word, one of them is usually the correct answer.

6. "None of the above" is usually wrong.

7. Find out before the test if there is a penalty for guessing the wrong answer.

* Apply these rules to some tests you have constructed to see if a wily
student could have "guessed" his way to an A.

4. *True-false-don't know checks.* True-false checks are useful as a
quick assessment of reading comprehension, particularly for extensive-
reading assignments. If students are given two points for a correct answer,
lose a point for an incorrect answer, but do not lose a point for answering
Don't Know, they will be less likely to make wild guesses and the score
will more truly reflect their comprehension of the passage.

R63 Read the following statements and check whether each is T (True) or
F (False) according to the information in the passage you have just read.
If you are not sure circle D (Don't Know).

1. T F D   The Adamsons looked for Elsa because they wanted her to
             come back.
2. T F D   When George called Elsa to him, she disappeared among
             the trees.
3. T F D   The Adamsons knew that a natural life would hurt Elsa.
4. T F D   The Adamsons wanted to be close to Elsa a little longer
             because she was so important to them.

Commentary

As with multiple-choice items, all statements must be plausible in the
context and must be based on possible misunderstanding of specific phrases
in the text or incorrect association of phrases. Care must be taken not to
develop a pattern of correct responses, e.g., TFTFTF, or TFFTTFFTT.
There is no need for an equal number of T's and F's: students are quick to
discover that this is usually the case and will adjust their answers accordingly. Correct statements should not be so phrased that they repeat exactly
the words of the text.

True-False questions provide a good opportunity to test the student's
attention to *structural clues.* For instance, Item 4 in R63 plays on the dual
possibility that the word *close* may be a verb or an adjective. In lines 27–28,
the conjunction *and* is a signal that another verb is to be added and, since
no preposition like *during* or *for* precedes "a very important chapter of our
lives," this group of words is clearly the direct object of the verb *close*, not
a time phrase telling for how long they had been *close* (adjective). When
close is read as an adjective the sentence is patently ungrammatical. Less-
informed or careless readers, however, who are not sensitive to such
structural clues may be misled by *so* preceding *close* (mistaking this for the

common combination of intensifying adverb and adjective). Students who make this kind of mistake will probably not recognize the word "chapter" and therefore fall easily into incorrect assumptions about the semantic relations between *close* and the words "important" and "our lives" in its immediate vicinity.

5. *Questions in English requiring answers in the student's native language.* We have discussed the particular problems of reading comprehension questions requiring written or spoken answers in English. When the teacher knows the native language of the students in a homogeneous language group, it is possible to avoid this problem by asking questions in English to which the students respond in their native language. This makes it impossible for a student to frame a response using words from the question or the text without knowing their meaning. It also requires comprehension of the questions, which are in English, as well as the main text. It usually gives students the opportunity to explain the meaning of the text more fully.

R64 Why did George call to Elsa a second time?

(Answer in the student's first language: He wanted to be sure that she had heard him so that she would know they were nearby. They wanted her to realize that she could return to them if she wished, that they were not rejecting her.)

Commentary

Many students who understood the text perfectly would have trouble saying all this in correct English. This method enables the teacher to dig more deeply into the students' comprehension of what they have read. If this approach is used, questions should not move methodically through the text so that the student can pinpoint the particular sentences in which the answers can probably be found, but should require the student to think about and interpret the content of large sections of the text.

6. *Asking questions in the student's native language to be answered in that language* is not advisable. Such questions often provide weaker students with translations of vocabulary they did not know and clues to the meaning of complex structures. The sequence of the questions also sometimes supplies a kind of résumé of the meaning. *Questions in the native language to be answered in English* would be pointless. Students capable of answering the questions in English would also be capable of understanding the questions in English, and once again the questions in the native language would supply the students with crutch-like clues to the meaning

of many sections of the text which would make it difficult to judge their real knowledge of English.

7. *Anticipatory Questions.* With a difficult text, students may be supplied with questions before they begin to read. These questions are designed to lead the readers to seek for certain information which will make the passage clearer to them. Anticipatory questions are more appropriate for expository and informational passages than for a narrative like R57. However, questions like the following would make the student look carefully at the text.

R65   1. What did the Adamsons want to find out before they left Elsa in the wild?

      2. Why were their feelings mixed after she left them?

8. *Résumé with key words omitted.* After students have read the text and put it away, they may be supplied with a résumé in English of the content, with certain words omitted. They then show by the way they complete the résumé how well they understood the text and how much attention they paid to the vocabulary.

R66 The Adamsons wanted Elsa, their _____, to go back to her _____ state. At night they were _____ by loud _____. But Elsa did not _____ to them. They went to _____ for Elsa, and finally _____ her. But she had _____ to stay in the _____. They planned to _____ in their camp for a few days to be _____ Elsa was accepted by the _____.

9. *Assessing overall comprehension.* Depending on the content of the passage, students may be asked to do such things as:
    a. supply in English a suitable title for a film of the story and subtitles for the main sections into which it could be divided;
    b. make a chart of the relationships of the persons in the story;
    c. sketch (or describe) a suitable stage setting for a dramatization of the scene;
    d. draw a map showing the various areas in which the action took place;
    e. write a brief day-to-day diary of the adventures of the central character;
    f. outline the plot under the headings: presentation of characters, development, climax, dénouement (or unraveling of the complications).

10. *Assessing comprehension of expository reading.* (Exercises of the types below would be suitable for R67.)
    a. Give the passage a suitable title. (In this case no title would be supplied with the text.)

b. For each paragraph, give the main gist in one sentence, then set down the important details related to the central idea, showing clearly their relationships in the development of this idea.

Exercises (a) and (b) would be given and completed in the native language for Group A, who are reading for information, but in English for Groups C and D.

c. Below are four sentences for each paragraph in the text. Select from the four choices in each case the one which best sums up the central idea of that paragraph. (Choices are given in English.)

d. Rearrange the following statements to form a simplified, but consecutive, account of the development of ideas in the passage you have just read. (The student is presented with a jumbled set of paraphrases of statements made in the text. The statements are in English, but are so worded as not to be identifiable by simple matching with the text.)

e. For Group A: In which paragraphs are the following ideas discussed? (Paraphrased summaries of the ideas in the passage are given in English, care being taken to see that they are so expressed that they cannot be matched from the text without being fully understood. To give practice in reading rapidly to extract the main ideas, the student is set a time limit within which to complete the exercise.)

* Below is a reading passage suitable for Stage Four or Stage Five. Develop some questions of the different types which have just been described and discuss in class their effectiveness.

R67 *The Automobile Revolution*[21]

In the year 1906 Woodrow Wilson, who was then president of Princeton University, said, "Nothing has spread socialistic feeling in this country more than the automobile," and added that it offered "a picture of the arrogance of wealth." Less than twenty years later, two women of Muncie, Indiana, both of whom were managing on small incomes, spoke their minds to investigators gathering facts for that admirable study of an American community, *Middletown*. Said one, who was the mother of nine children, "We'd rather do without clothes than give up the car." Said the other, "I'll go without food before I'll see us give up the car." And elsewhere another housewife, in answer to a comment on the fact that her family owned a car but no bathtub, uttered a fitting theme song for the automobile revolution. "Why," said she, "you can't go to town in a bathtub!"

This change in the status of the automobile from a luxury for the few to a necessity for the many—a change which, as we shall see, transformed American communities and daily living habits and ideas throughout the half century—did not come about suddenly. It could not. For it depended upon three things. First, a reliable, manageable, and not too expensive car. Second, good roads. And third, garages and filling stations in great number. And all these three requirements had to come slowly, by degrees, each strengthening the others; a man who had tried to operate a filling station beside a dusty road in 1906 would have speedily gone bankrupt. . . .

F. L. ALLEN, *The Big Change*

Building and maintaining an adequate vocabulary (Stages Four and Five)

Moulton gives foreign-language students three practical recommendations for acquiring vocabulary: "First, never 'look a word up' until you have read the whole context in which it occurs—at least an entire sentence. . . . Second, don't be afraid of making 'intelligent guesses'. . . . Third, make a special list of your 'nuisance words'—the ones you find yourself looking up over and over again. Put them down on paper and memorize them."[22] These recommendations may well be passed on to students as an essential form of personal discipline. Going beyond this, however, the teacher may develop exercises to help students to "increase their word power" in English through focusing on form, focusing on meaning, expanding by association, and recirculating the vocabulary they have acquired.

FOCUSING ON FORM

Often students are not given guidelines for multiplying the vocabulary they already know through recognition of related forms.

Many are not familiar with simple facts about word-formation in English such as those exemplified in R4 and R5.[23] They should become familiar with the changes of meaning resulting from the addition of prefixes and suffixes, from changes in stress, and from compounding; and with differences in syntactic function of identical or similar forms.

R68 In learning to look analytically at new words, students should become familiar with the *common prefixes*. Prefixes most often alter the meaning, rather than the syntactic function, of the word:

untie, uninteresting; presuppose, pre-marital; desegregate, decentralized; reconsider, rerun.

Some prefixes are prepositions or adverbs with which the student may already be familiar:

over-react, over-weight; under-staffed, undergo; extraordinary, extra-sensory; counter-productive, counter-revolutionary.

Students should also learn to recognize a prefix that has changed its shape because of its phonetic environment:

insufficient, illogical, immovable, irrelevant; conform, compatriot, cooperate, collateral.

R69 Students should be taught to recognize the underlying and possibly familiar stems in words marked by *derivational suffixes,* and to understand the grammatical and semantic function of these suffixes.

nouns (derived from nouns; verbs, adjectives): magician, golfer, orphanage; survival, replacement, migration; independence, ugliness, sanity;
verbs (derived from nouns; adjectives): patronize, glorify; activate, gladden;
adjectives (derived from nouns; verbs; adjectives): beautiful, mindless, trendy; readable, moving; sickly, reddish;
adverbs (derived from nouns; verbs; adjectives): homeward, nightly, clockwise; laughingly; invisibly.

R70 Many pairs of words in English are phonologically distinguished solely or chiefly by *stress.* Students whose only interest in English is in being able to read it may treat these pairs as homonyms or single items, like the much larger set of unchanging forms which belong to more than one form-class (*back, walk, cross;* see R72 below). Students who want to be proficient in the spoken language, however, will need to be aware of this phonological distinction. They may be helped in reading by learning that words they have distinguished orally are in fact spelled the same way and are closely related in meaning. They should be made aware of the systematic patterns of stress variation and vowel alternation in such pairs as the following:

noun	*verb*
prójèct	projéct
ínsùlt	insúlt
récord	recórd
cóndùct	condúct

adjective	*verb*
ánimate	ánimàte
séparate	séparàte
móderate	móderàte

R71 New words may also be understood through recognizing *compounds.* Compounding remains a prolific source of new words in English, and the compounding patterns are too numerous and complex to treat exhaustively here or in any but advanced English classes.[24] However, students must learn the distinctive stress pattern of compounds ($'+\,'$),[25] and the most common structural types. They can be further helped in making intelligent guesses in their reading by studying the main kinds of syntactic relations that can exist between elements of a compound.

By far the largest class of compounds in English is composed of nouns, and most of these have a noun as the second element or head-word:

blackbird, paperclip, fanmail, airport.

Some compound nouns have a different structure, however.

take-off, drop-out, die-hard.

R72 Finally, students need to realize that there is a very extensive class of words characterized by their *lack* of formal distinguishing features: the hundreds of *forms in English which function as both verbs and nouns.*

fall, catch, run, show, move.

Exercises

1. Students may be asked to give nouns corresponding to adjectives (*dark: darkness; rare: rarity*); adjectives corresponding to nouns (*mist: misty; space: spacious*); verbs corresponding to nouns (*type: typify; slave: enslave*); nouns corresponding to verbs (*create: creation; teach: teacher*); adverbs corresponding to adjectives (*simple: simply; careful: carefully*); verbs corresponding to adjectives (*bright: brighten; stable: stabilize*); adjectives corresponding to verbs (*produce: productive; wash: washable; assume: unassuming*); phrases corresponding to compounds (*daydreaming: dreaming during the day; homework: work to be done at home*); compounds corresponding to phrases (*someone who drives a cab: a cab-driver; someone who has dropped out of school: a drop-out*).

2. Students may be asked to change the meaning of sentences by the *addition of a prefix* to a word italicized:

I was *happy* when he left; I was *unhappy* when he left.
He still liked his *wife*; He still liked his *ex-wife*.

Or they may complete possible utterances by repeating one of the words with a different suffix:

He didn't *play* well—he wasn't a good (*player*).
Please *introduce* me—I need an (*introduction*).

3. For practice with compound constructions, students may be asked to create sentences where compounds are contrasted with other constructions using the same words (for instance, adjective + noun, noun + noun, noun + verb). Proper stress patterns should be used.

The White House is a white house.
Some grandmothers are grand mothers.
A baby doctor is not a baby doctor.
The earthquake made the earth quake.

FOCUSING ON MEANING

Valuable practice in vocabulary building is provided when students are asked:

1. To supply paraphrases or definitions for words in a text they have just read (They attended a concert: they went to a concert; After his illness, he recovered quickly: he got well quickly; I'm going to telephone you: I'm going to call/ring you up; She had stage-fright: she was afraid of going on the stage).

2. To identify from multiple-choice items the correct paraphrases or definitions for certain words in the text (in R56: damage = [A] *change,* [B] *modernize,* [C] *injure,* [D] *age quickly*).

3. To find words in the text to match paraphrases or definitions supplied (in R56: Find the words in the text which mean [A] *feel offended by,* [B] *do harm to*).

4. *To complete sentences, based on a text,* with certain words on which they will need to focus their attention. These sentences should not reproduce the original text exactly and should usually require the student to reuse the vocabulary in a different form, e.g., in a different person, number, or tense, as in the following from R57:

a. The lion growls awakened and _____ the Adamsons.
b. After _____ the wet pawmarks, they saw the shape of a lion.
c. Back at her studio, Joy _____ Elsa resting with another lion.

5. *Exercises may be unrelated to a known text,* e.g., students discover for themselves, through dictionary search, synonyms and antonyms (*wicked, evil; help, assist; intelligent, stupid; winner, loser*). They may compete to see who can find the largest number of synonyms and antonyms in a given period of time. Learning to enjoy a purposeful search for information in dictionaries and grammars is an important preparation for autonomous progress. (See also W68–75.)

6. Students *complete an unfamiliar text* in a plausible way by supplying for each blank a word carefully selected from multiple-choice alternatives. This type of exercise can be developed with simple texts or more complex

texts, serving as an amusing and challenging exercise right through to the advanced level.

R73 I have a (uncle, sister, brother) who often gets himself into (difficulties, troubles, problem). (Some, the, an) other day he tried to (drive, parking, stopped) his car when (a road, road, the road) was covered (over, with, of) ice. Naturally he (slip, slides, skidded) and came near to (hitting, run into, colliding) another car. Now he (must, refuses, won't) drive any more, (though, even, accept) in good weather.

Commentary

A passage such as this teaches students to pay attention to distinctions of meaning, but it is also an exercise in reading comprehension. Students should write out their completed versions as coherent paragraphs, rather than merely circling choices. In this way they can read their versions through to see that they make sense and then read them aloud to their fellow students. With a little ingenuity, passages can be designed to have several possible final versions, and students can be encouraged to reconstitute the several possibilities. Advanced students may like to prepare such passages for the other students to complete. (Teachers or students who do not feel confident in constructing passages in the language themselves can easily adapt paragraphs from books or magazines.)

✱ .Find in various composition and reading texts other types of exercises which focus on meaning distinctions and discuss their effectiveness.

EXPANDING BY ASSOCIATION

We tend to recall words through meaningful associational bonds, and words tend to appear in texts in collocations, that is, in relation to centers of interest or semantic areas (*exam* is likely to appear in texts in which *school, book, student,* or *teacher* appear; *car, tire, gas/petrol,* and *driver* are very likely to occur together). It is for this reason that learning vocabulary in context is much more valuable than learning isolated words.

Exercises

Many possibilities suggest themselves, and teachers can think of their own, once they understand the necessity for developing chains of associations and for expanding nuclei. Many of these exercises can take the form of games or team competitions which can be directed by the students themselves. Three come immediately to mind.

R74 What action do you associate with the following objects? Follow the pattern:

Bread?   You eat it.

In each case give as many alternatives as you can think of. The team gains points for every alternative its team members can discover.

A book?   You read it.
               You open it.
               You study it.

A job?   You look for it.
               You like it.
               You hate it . . .

R75 As each object is named, give the English word for a person you associate with it. You must answer in three seconds.

paper?   student
chalk?   teacher
letter?   postman
plane?   pilot

Alternatively: As each person, animal, or object is named, give the English word for a place you associate with it. You must answer in three seconds.

car?   street, road, garage
horse?   stable, farm
money?   bank, shop

R76 Intelligence test series can be adapted as follows. This exercise can be used from elementary to advanced levels and, again, students may be encouraged to make up further exercises themselves.

In the following lists underline the word which does not seem to belong with the others in the series:

blue, red, cold, green
stone, flower, tree, grass
hearing, seeing, touch, understanding (This item can be answered in two ways: by form or by semantic area.)

RECIRCULATING VOCABULARY ACQUIRED

Students learn new words with every passage they read. Often they forget them rapidly because they do not encounter them again for a long while.

All kinds of games and exercises can be introduced to enliven the class, while giving students the opportunity to retrieve words they have learned in the past and recirculate them through their conscious minds. In this way the ease with which these words can be retrieved, when required, is increased. The following suggestions will bring to mind other possibilities. They are arranged in approximate order of difficulty.

R77 From the parallel lists of words given select *pairs which have a natural association*:

sea   soldier
bakery   ship
war   bread

Students working in teams may make their own parallel lists to try out on members of the other teams.

R78 Begin with the word *tree* and write down rapidly any ten English words which come to your mind. Write whichever word you think of. Do not try to develop a logical series.

The lists, when completed, may be read aloud for amusement. Series may come out like the following:

tree, flower, smell, perfume/scent, lady, dress, shop, street, police, prison.

tree, bird, nest, egg, breakfast, morning, school, classroom, books, library.

R79 *Semantic areas.* Write down as many words as you can think of which have a natural association with *tree* (or . . .). Points will be given to the team having the largest number of different words.

tree, grass, lawn, garden, flower, trunk, branches, leaves, nest, fruit . . .

Or: Write down all the words you know which have a similar meaning to *house*.

house, home, apartment/flat, cottage, bungalow, mansion, villa, hut, castle, palace . . .

R80 Make as many words as you can from the letters in "That's a tree." No letter may be used more times than it appears in the sentence.

that, a, tree, hat, tar, rate, tat, three, area, threat, heat, at, the, seat, seer, teat, hear, sea, see, sat, set. . . . .

R81 Write down all the idiomatic expressions you can think of which contain the word *head* (or . . .) and make up a sentence to show the use of each.

> head: to be head of, to go to the head of, to go to one's head, hard-headed, headstrong, heady, to head, to get (something) through one's head, thickheaded, heads or tails (in flipping a coin), to head(someone) off, headlong, head man, to head for, a head for (business), head over heels. . . .

R82 List any five words on the chalkboard and ask students to make up a brief story incorporating all five, e.g.: noise, sea, bananas, trousers, book.

R83 Simple crossword puzzles may be constructed by different students and then tried out on their fellow-students. These provide practice in recalling words from their definitions or by association. Students may use definitions they find in monolingual dictionaries, thus giving them a purposeful familiarity with such dictionaries. Some crossword puzzle books for students are available commercially: e.g., a series of four (*A First Crossword Puzzle Book, A Second,* etc.) by L. A. Hill and P. R. Popkin (London: Oxford University Press, 1968 ff.). Crosswords and other language puzzles and games may also be found in W. R. Lee, *Language Teaching Games and Contests* (Oxford University Press, 1974) and in P. Hauptman and J. Upshur *Fun with English* (New York: Collier Macmillan International, 1975).

Scrabble sets geared to the letter frequencies of English can be bought, and these can be both useful and amusing for students to use.

Vocabulary enrichment and retrieval should be woven into the lesson fabric or the learning packet as an important and purposeful activity, not dredged up to fill in time on the day when the teacher and the class are suffering from end-of-the-week fatigue. By encouraging the students to play with words, the teacher can help to increase their interest in words in relation to concepts and in association with other words, and to refine their appreciation for nuances of meaning.

* Think of further ideas for vocabulary expansion and retrieval and develop these into possible classroom or individual activities.

Integrating the language skills at Stages Three to Five
READING AND WRITING

> Students may be asked a series of questions which, when answered in sequence, develop a summary or résumé of the material read. They may write an ending to a story or play of which they have read part, or develop

a different ending from the one in the book. They may write letters which one character in the story might have written to others. Completed compositions may be passed around, with the writer's consent, to be read by other students. Students may create their own stories on similar themes to those they have been reading. They may write dramatizations of some parts of the narrative which will be acted in class or at the English club. Comprehension of extensive reading undertaken on an individualized basis will often be demonstrated in activities of this kind.

After reading a play, students may write the story as it might appear in a theater program, adding short descriptions of the characters. Should opportunity arise to act parts of the play before other classes, the best synopsis will be printed in a program for distribution.

Further suggestions for integrating reading and writing will be found in Chapter 9.

READING AND LISTENING COMPREHENSION

Students may listen to a story, play, poem, or speech by a famous person and then read it, or they may read first and then listen to a worthwhile reading or dramatic presentation of what they have read. The aural element adds vividness and life to the reading unit. Students may take turns listening to tapes of news broadcasts from an English-speaking source (United States, Great Britain, Canada, Australasia), and then write summaries of the news which will be posted for other students to read, thus integrating listening, writing, and reading in a purposeful activity. Before listening to an English play, students may read a synopsis of the action. In this way they are better prepared to comprehend because they have some expectations to help them project meaning.

In some ways the processes of fluent, direct reading for meaning appear to parallel the processes of listening comprehension. We recognize in a quick, impressionistic way semantic elements and syntactic units, interrelating those we have selected and are holding in our memory with what follows, then rapidly revising expectations when these are not supported by the later segments we identify. Practice in direct reading of a text which is readily accessible to the students at their present level of knowledge, while they are simultaneously listening to a taped model reading it in meaningful and expressive segments, can help students develop useful habits of anticipation and syntactic identification in both of these skills. Later they can practice rapid reading of a text to which they have already listened without a script.[26] (For further suggestions, see Chapter 3.)

READING AND SPEAKING

Students should be provided with frequent opportunities to give in English the gist of what they have been reading. They may be encouraged to prepare their own questions to ask of others in the class. When small groups are engaged in similar extensive reading projects they should discuss together what they have discovered. Students reading individually may share what they have been reading with others. Some of the material read will serve as a basis for oral presentations of projects; some will be dramatized in the original form or through extempore role-playing; and some will provide ammunition for discussions and debates. Many other ideas can be gleaned from Chapter 2.

READING AND PURPOSEFUL ACTIVITY

At all levels students should be encouraged to do research reading in an area which interests them in order to find the information necessary to carry out some activity. A few indications are outlined below, but at Stages Three through Five students should be expected to propose their own.

1. Students read advertisements for a particular type of product in magazines in order to prepare a commercial for a class television or radio show.

2. Students find out information about a popular American or British singer in order to introduce a session of records of his or her songs.

3. Students read a play carefully in order to design a stage setting for a class performance or play-reading.

4. Students seek out information on events, people, costumes, or social customs at a particular period in American or British history in order to produce a pageant for some historical anniversary.

5. Students study tourist brochures, guide books, geography, history, and art books in order to give an illustrated lecture or slide commentary on some part of the English-speaking world.

6. Students read through English-language cookbooks in order to prepare some American or British dishes for an English Club festivity or an International Day celebration.

7. Students undertake tasks set out by the teacher or another student in the form of detailed instructions which lead to the collecting or making of something which can later be brought back as proof of the completion of the task.

At Stage Three, the well-known *Scavenger Hunt* can be adapted to the English class. Students work in pairs to find and bring to the class next day a series of strange objects which are described in English on instruction cards. They win points for their team for each object they find.

R84 One list might be: a flashlight without batteries, two hard-boiled eggs, an American stamp, a bottle opener, a foreign coin, an advertisement for a furnished room, yesterday's meteorological chart, a snail shell, a copy of *Hamlet*, a plastic coathanger.

While students are looking for these things they read and reread the list so that the words become impressed on their minds. Then, when showing the objects in class, they must state what each one is and how they came to acquire it.

Improving reading speed

The reading speed of different students varies considerably in their native language. The teacher must, therefore, expect considerable variation in the reading of the foreign language. To become fluent readers students must acquire the skill of reading whole word groups and whole sentences in English and of holding material in their memory over larger and larger sections as they move on with the developing thought.

1. At Stages Two and Three an overhead projector can be used to encourage continuity of reading. The text is moved slowly upward on the roll, so that the slower readers are encouraged to keep their eyes moving forward while the faster readers are not impeded, as would be the case if only one line were shown at a time. This is the process frequently used in films or on television where there is a long introduction to, or explanation of, the story. This procedure will be associated with silent reading for information, rather than reading aloud, since the aim is to help individual students improve their reading rate.

2. At Stages Three and Four, students may be timed in reading a certain number of pages to a pre-established comprehension criterion level. Mere pace without adequate comprehension is pointless. Since this is an individual endeavor, students should be encouraged to improve their own rate rather than compete with others in number of pages read.

3. As an encouragement to practice *scanning*, which is a very useful reading skill, students may be given questions to which they are to find as many answers as possible in a given time.

4. Students will increase their reading speed in a natural way if they have set themselves the clearly defined goal of reading in a stated period of time a certain amount of material selected by themselves because of the interest of the subject matter.

8
Writing and written exercises I: the nuts and bolts

The Soviet psychologist Vygotsky draws our attention to the fact that all the higher functions of human consciousness, that is, those which involve more than mere physical skill, are characterized by *awareness, abstraction,* and *control.*[1] For example, learning to pronounce the allophones of /t/ by a process of successive approximations in imitation of a model may be relatively easy. Learning to say /t/ in response to various graphic combinations in a script and in a variety of graphic contexts is already more complicated. It demands the recognition of abstract representations and their conversion from a visual to a phonic form, before the skill acquired in the simpler act can come into operation in the new situation. In short, it requires awareness of the relevance of the graphic symbol, recognition of what it stands for in the phonic medium, as well as control of the production of the sound. It also requires awareness of what other graphic symbols stand for, since the phonetic realization of the phoneme normally represented by the letter *t* will be [tʰ] if that letter comes initially in a stressed syllable (e.g., *tall*), but it will be [t] after *s* (e.g., *stop*). Abstract processes such as those described above are in operation when one writes the letter *t* in response to the sounds [tʰ] or [t].

That a graphic representation of sound combinations is an abstraction with an arbitrary relationship to that which it represents is frequently overlooked. Convention alone makes the relationship between sound and written symbol predictable. The abstract quality of a written communication is intensified by:

1. its *complete detachment from expressive features,* such as facial or body movement, pitch and tone of voice, hesitations or speed of delivery, and emotional indicators such as heightened facial color or variation in breathing;

2. its *lack of material context:* surroundings, feedback from inter-locutors, relevant movement (hence the attraction of the comic book for modern readers);

3. its *displacement in time:* a written communication may be read as soon as it is written (like a note slipped to a companion) or months, years, or centuries later. It is interesting that we often do not understand a note we ourselves wrote when we find it years later.

The operation of writing, unlike speaking, must be performed as it were in a void, in response to a personal internal stimulus. Consequently, the writer must compensate for the absence of external contextual elements by the deliberate inclusion and elaboration of explanatory details which the speaker would omit.

For reasons such as these, Vygotsky suggests that the comparative difficulty for the child in acquiring facility in speech and in writing approxi-mates that of learning arithmetic and algebra. All children learn to speak and express themselves effectively in speech at about the same age, even though some by personality and temperament may be more articulate than others. On the other hand, many people never learn to express them-selves freely in writing. Even with careful instruction, there is a con-siderable lag between the achievement of an expressive level in speech in one's native language and a similar level of expressiveness in writing—a gap which, for many, widens as their education or life experience pro-gresses. Certainly, many learn quite quickly to "write things down," if these are not too complicated, but this is the least demanding aspect of writing. Many who know how to "write things down" in their native language avoid expressing themselves in writing almost completely, even in personal letters. To write so that one is really communicating a message, isolated in place and time, is an art that requires consciously directed effort and deliberate choice in language. The old saying, "If you can say it, you can write it," is simplistic in its concept of the communicative aspect of writing. On the other hand, "He talks like a book" emphasizes the elaborations and com-prehensive explanations of written messages which are quite unnecessary in face-to-face communication.

WRITING AND OTHER LANGUAGE ACTIVITIES

We must not be surprised, then, that a high level of written expression is so difficult to attain in a foreign language. It cannot be achieved by chance,

as a kind of by-product of other language activities, although it draws on
what has been learned in these areas. Good writing implies a knowledge of
the conventions of the written code (the "good manners" of the medium);
to be effective, it needs the precision and nuances which derive from a
thorough understanding of the syntactic and lexical choices the language
offers; to be interesting, it requires the ability to vary structures and
patterns for rhetorical effect. So good writing will not develop merely
from practice exercises in grammar and vocabulary choice. Experience in
speaking freely seems to facilitate early writing, which often parallels what
one would say. For the development of a writing style, however, much
acquaintance with the practical output of native writers in all kinds of
expressive styles is essential. Familiarity with the great variety of expression
to which the language lends itself gives the neophyte writer an intuitive feel
for an authentic turn of phrase that can be acquired in no other way.

Included in this chapter are activities which associate writing with
experiences in listening, speaking, and reading. (Further suggestions are to
be found in Chapters 3 and 7.)

WHAT ARE WE TEACHING WHEN WE TEACH "WRITING"?

As with oral communication, we can classify writing activities as either
skill-getting or *skill-using* (see model C1), with the same need for
bridging activities that resemble the desired communicative activity to
facilitate transfer from one to the other. *Interaction through the written
message* is the goal: what is written should be a purposeful communication,
on the practical or imaginative level, expressed in such a way that it is
comprehensible to another person. Otherwise, we are dealing with hermetic or esoteric writing of purely personal value which can be set down in
any idiosyncratic code.

Skill-getting, for oral or written communication, is based on knowledge
of the way the language operates (*cognition*). Many grammatical rules
are the same for speech and writing (e.g., the agreement of subject and
verb in certain conventional ways: *we try* /wiy tray/; *he tries* /hiy trayz/;
the use of *do* in the formation of negatives and questions with most simple
verb forms, except those of *be* and *have*[2]). Other rules vary according to
the degree of formality of the spoken or written communication (e.g.,
formal writing: "Indeed it is difficult to avoid regarding the senator's
statement as patently ridiculous"; informal speech: "That's a laugh, that
is!").[3] Note that a personal letter may retain many of the features of informal chat, whereas a scholarly lecture given on a formal occasion adheres
in the main to the same rules as a written paper or scientific report. In an
orally oriented course, early writing will consist of the writing down of what
one would say, moving further away from oral forms as knowledge of the
rules of written language advances.

Learning the rules and conventions of written language is reinforced by writing out examples and applying the rules in new contexts, thus developing *awareness of the abstraction and control of its graphic manifestation.* For written language, this activity parallels the oral-practice exercises which help students develop flexibility in structuring their oral expression. Writing things out helps with the organization of material to be held in memory and clarifies rules at points of uncertainty. It gives concrete expression to abstract notions. All of this is, however, merely preliminary activity which is pointless unless it is serving some clearly understood purpose of meaningful communication.

Considerable disappointment and frustration will be avoided if the nature and purpose of any particular writing task are clearly understood by student and teacher alike. In this chapter and the next, we will discuss writing under four heads. These do not represent sequential stages but, rather, constantly interwoven activities. They are:

I. *Writing down:* learning the conventions of the code.

II. *Writing in the language:* learning the potential of the code (we shall include here grammatical exercises and the study of samples of written language to develop awareness of its characteristics).

III. *Production:* practicing the construction of fluent expressive sentences and paragraphs.

IV. *Expressive writing or composition:* using the code for purposeful communication.

Finally, *translation* will be discussed at some length as a separate activity.

I. Writing down

Activities of this type, although apparently simple, contribute to awareness. Students either copy or reproduce without the copy in front of them. To do this accurately, they must focus their attention on the conventions of writing: spelling; capitalization; punctuation; paragraphing; ambiguous forms (e.g., *'s* can represent the possessive ending, *is, has,* or even *does* as in *What's he do?*); number conventions (W6); abbreviations (*etc., i.e., e.g., p.m.*), and so on.

This activity prepares for eventual expressive writing. It is, however, useful in itself. Language users need to be able to interpret and copy down printed schedules, timetables, records, details of projects, charts, formulas, prices, recipes, new words and phrases they wish to remember. They should be capable of writing down accurately and comprehensibly oral arrangements and instructions for themselves and others. As students studying in the language they may need to copy accurately diagrams, details of experiments, quotations from literary works.

WRITING A DIFFERENT SCRIPT

For students who are learning to use a different script, the first writing task will be the acquiring of an acceptable system of writing English with either cursive or printed lettering, or both. The many manuals prepared for teaching the English writing system to the native speaker may be useful here, but these must be used critically. They may insist on superfluous refinements in letter formation and yet, quite understandably, not give sufficient emphasis to problems which beginning students of English face in reading and writing in the Roman alphabet for the first time: learning to begin at the top left-hand corner of the page; moving from left to right; using a bottom line as a reference point for letters; connecting letters within words according to certain conventions of lines and spacing.

A useful technique for learning a new alphabet is tracing, beginning with individual letters, often enlarged and framed to display proper alignment, and then going on to words and short sentences. Students should learn to make the strokes of each letter in an efficient pattern of sequence and direction, that is, they should note in what order the parts are made and in what direction the pen is moving for each part.

When independent (non-tracing) writing is attempted, the teacher must be sure that it preserves the distinctive features—distinctive to "English eyes"—of the letters and connective lines. An *o* connected to the following letter by a line coming from the bottom of the *o* rather than the top may interfere with the reader's perception of the message, regardless of how perfectly formed the *o* itself is.

Once students have had some experience tracing English script, (or some other type of training in forming the letters for those students who are too sophisticated to trace), they may practice copying words and sentences. Ordinarily, we think of copying as the trivial task of writing down something we see before us in print, or in printed or cursive script— something on a chalkboard or in a letter, for instance. For students beginning another language written in a familiar alphabet, learning to write down what they see may require learning many new conventions (see p. 271), but for students learning a new writing system at the same time the task is much greater and far from trivial. Before they can be expected to focus their attention on conventions of spelling and punctuation, they must develop the even more rudimentary ability to produce on their paper an *acceptable* version of the letters they see before them, that is, a version which may differ in some respects from what they have before them, but which will be readily recognized by a native English reader. (Compare, for example, the cursive and printed forms of *a, e, f, g, s,* and the variations in recognizable forms of these from careful to careless writing.) Learning a new script for a new language must be recognized as a special task where early formation of efficient motor habits is desirable and monitored practice is warranted.

Writing in a new script will normally be integrated with other learning activities in the language class. Teachers may wish to formulate simpler versions of the exercises described in *Copying,* below, which link writing with reading; and in *Reproduction,* activities 7 and 8, which link writing with speaking (see p. 269). Before the activity described in *Copying* 1, for example, students might be given the sentences appropriate to the figures in handwritten, rather than printed form, and be asked first to trace, then to copy them. Later, they would learn to read them in printed form. Similarly, for *Reproduction* 7, emphasis will be on the writing from dictation of regular, non-problem words first, until facility has been acquired with the new script. (See also *A Different Script* in Chapter 6, p. 196.)

COPYING

1. (E) Students are given dittoed sheets with simple *outline* illustrations, or stick figures, suggesting the lines of a dialogue or parts of a narrative they have been studying. They transcribe from the text sentences which are appropriate to each sketch.

2. (E) Each student copies a line of dialogue and passes it to a neighbor, who copies out an appropriate response. This operates like a *chain* dialogue (C25), with students selecting utterances and appropriate responses from any material they have studied.

3. (E) Students copy the initial part of an utterance and pass it on to their neighbors for a *completion*, or students choose and copy completions for parts of utterances supplied on a dittoed sheet, trying to make as many different sentences as they can with each opening phrase.

4. (E) Students make new sentences by copying segments from *substitution tables*. This activity familiarizes the students with the logical segmentation of sentences into subject, verb, object, and adverbial extensions.

W1 (E) Make six different sentences by selecting one segment from each column in the following table:

Jack	meets	Helen	in front of the restaurant
The doctor	finds	the little boy	behind the house
The girl	notices	the cat	in the street
The teacher	sees	the policeman	near the school

Note: If pronoun subjects of the third person singular are used along with others, it is advisable to keep subject and verb in the one column to accustom elementary-level students to the correct combination of pronoun subject and verb ending:

W2 (E)

We keep	the pencils	on the desk
He puts	the books	on the table
They notice	the papers	in the drawer

Developing sentences from a substitution table becomes a more thoughtful process when only some subject items can be appropriately used with some of the verb items, some of the objects, and so on. Moody[4] gives the following example of such a substitution table:

W3 (E)

					did not have a car.
		sea			could not afford an air ticket
		train			could not go there by train
He	traveled by	air	because	she	knew the ships were all full
She		car		they	
They		lorry		he	wanted to get there quickly
		bus			did not want to pay too much money

New tables of this type can be developed as a writing exercise by groups of students for use by other students, thus moving into the second activity: writing in the language.

5. (E) Students copy from the chalkboard a simple poem or the words of a song they have been learning orally. A familiar poem like Housman's "When I was one-and-twenty," with its segments of interpolated speech, can be a useful copying exercise. Students might also enjoy copying the words of a favorite song such as "Clementine." The syntactic inversion of some of the phrases ("Light she was . . .", "Drove she ducklings . . .") should not worry the students unduly, since poetry and verse are often unusual in any language.

* Find for your personal file some suitable short poems for elementary classes. Share these with other members of the class and discuss their appropriateness.

REPRODUCTION

Copying activities 1, 2, and 3 may also be reproduction exercises, with students writing the utterances, or completing them, from memory.

6. (E) *Scrambled sentences* are sometimes used as a stimulus to the reproduction of a dialogue or narrative. This technique forces students to think of the meaning of what they are reproducing. Credit should be given for ingenuity in working out novel but possible recombinations.

7. (E) Students write down from *dictation* utterances they have learned or recombinations of familiar segments, or they may concentrate on the spelling of more difficult words in *spot dictation* (see R26).

(E and I) The spot dictation may focus on subjects and verbs (agreement, reduced and irregular forms) or on personal or relative pronouns.

8. (I and A) *Dictation of unfamiliar material* as an exercise in auditory recognition and accurate reproduction has been a standard classroom technique for centuries. The passage to be dictated should normally have some thematic relationship to something already read or discussed. It can often provide supplementary material worth keeping on some subject of cultural interest. The standard procedure is described below. There are also several possible variations which are useful language-learning aids.

a. *Standard procedure.* The material is read in its entirety at a normal, but unhurried, pace. It is then dictated in meaningful, undistorted segments, each segment being read twice. After students have looked over what they have written, corrected obvious mistakes, and tentatively filled in gaps according to semantic or grammatical expectations, the passage is read again at a normal pace to enable students to check on doubtful segments. After opportunity for a final check, students correct their own versions from a model. If one student has written the dictation at one side of the chalkboard, or for projection on the overhead projector, the correction process is facilitated: students suggest corrections and the teacher is able to comment on errors probably committed by other students as well or answer questions about problem segments. Each dictation should be regarded as an opportunity for learning, not as a test. For this reason, immediate correction is desirable, before students have forgotten which segments they found difficult and why they solved the problems as they did. Since it is difficult for students to detect all the errors in their work, they should exchange papers for a final check by a classmate.

b. *Variations.*

i. (E) *Students are encouraged to repeat the segment* to themselves before writing it. This forces them to make identification decisions before they begin writing and strengthens their memory of what they have heard.

ii. (E and I) If interpreting the aural signal and writing the message down accurately is a valuable exercise, there is no reason why students should be limited to an arbitrary number of repetitions of the segments.

The dictation may be taped and *students encouraged to keep playing the passage over* until they have been able to take down the complete message.

iii. (E and I) Students are asked to *hold longer and longer segments in their immediate memory* before beginning to write. In this way they are not working with echoic memory, but are forced to process the segments, that is, interpret them and situate them syntactically in the structure of the sentence, before reproducing them. Dictation then becomes more challenging and more meaningful.

iv. (I) *The speed of the dictation is gradually increased* as students become more adept at making the various morphological adjustments, particularly those which are not apparent in the spoken signal.

v. (I and A) *The repetition of segments is eliminated* and students are expected to listen carefully, retain the segment they have heard only once, and write it down without expecting further help. This forces students to concentrate on the message and the semantic and syntactic expectations it arouses.

vi. (A) Finally, students should be able to *take down a dictated letter or report*, with their own set of abbreviations, and write it out, or type it up correctly, as they might be expected to do in a business situation. This activity can be practiced individually with tapes.

FOCUSING ON SPELLING AND PUNCTUATION

1. (E and I) This goes beyond the initial stages. The teacher can focus the students' attention on spelling conventions by asking them to work out for themselves, from reading passages or dialogues they have studied, *probable rules of spelling* like the following:

W4 /s/ may be spelled *c* before *e, i,* or *y: certain, receive; city, recipe; bicycle, cylinder.*

/k/ may be spelled *c* before *a, o,* and *u: cat, came; come, college; cut, current.*

/k/ is usually spelled *ck* finally in monosyllables: *back, lock.* It may also be spelled *qu* as in *liquor,* or *que* as in *antique.*

This is a suitable small group activity. It can be undertaken whenever particular spelling problems emerge in dictation or writing practice.

2. (E and I) *The uses of the apostrophe* pose persistent problems for students. To become acquainted with current practice they may be given the research project of finding out from printed texts how apostrophes are used. Through personal observation they will easily discover facts like the following:

W5 1. The apostrophe is used to represent the omitted letter or letters in contracted forms. The commonest contractions are those of *not* and forms of *be* and *have: is not = isn't; he is* or *he has = he's; it is* or *it has = it's; they have = they've.*

2. The apostrophe is used in writing possessive forms. The general rule is that an apostrophe is placed after a word (either singular or plural) before the *s* of the possessive: *John's book, the cat's whiskers, the children's teacher.* Where the possessive *s* is not added, as in plural forms ending with *s*, the apostrophe comes at the end: *the boys' room, the Hendersons' house.*[5] The apostrophe is not used in the possessive forms of pronouns, *his, hers, its, ours, yours, theirs: The book is his, not hers; They followed the river to its source.*

When students have discovered regular patterns in the use of the apostrophe, they find it easier to remember. (I and A) This project may be continued to cover more intricate rules for the use of the apostrophe, e.g., in expressions of time and measure.

Note: Correct use of the apostrophe should not be so emphasized that it becomes an important element in the grading or evaluation of writing in the beginning stages. Native speakers of English show considerable confusion as well as variation in the use of the apostrophe in possessive forms when they are writing. (Advanced students should be encouraged to bring in examples of the misuse of the apostrophe in print, e.g., Europe Faces It's Driest Summer; The James' Arrive in Chicago.) Emphasis should be placed where it belongs—on fluent, idiomatic writing comprehensible to a native speaker, not on incidental graphic features.

LEARNING NUMBER CONVENTIONS

Misunderstandings can result from the use of native-language numerical conventions in English writing.

W6 (E)   Students should be familiar with such devices as the indicators for decimals and for thousands, e.g., 11.5 (eleven and five-tenths, usually read as "eleven point five"); 3,365,820 (three million, three hundred and sixty-five thousand, eight hundred and twenty); abbreviations like 6 ft. 3 in.; 25 mi.; 360 km.; no. 9; 1st, 2nd, 3rd, 4th; 4 hp; 60 mph; and with ways of writing times (10:45 a.m., 17.30) and dates (11/30/76 or 30.11.76, the latter being used in Great Britain and becoming more widely used in the United States). It is also useful for students to learn the handwritten forms for English numbers where these differ from those to which they have been accustomed in their own writing system.

These special features can be practiced in projects such as *describing a trip from Denver, Colorado, to San Francisco, California,* in which the student studies timetables, route maps, and area maps and gives full details of times of departure and arrival, distances traveled, and heights of surrounding mountains. Prices of rooms and meals in the United States can be found in such publications as the Mobil Guides (available at bookshops) or by writing to hotel or motel chains for their information brochures.

PROOFREADING

It is a commonly held opinion that students should not be shown incorrect English because they will learn the errors in the text and these misapprehensions will be difficult to eradicate. This assumption does not seem to have been scientifically tested. It is clear that young teachers who are not native speakers improve in their control of the syntax and spelling of English as they teach it, yet they see a great deal of incorrect English in the process. The difference, in the latter case, is that these young teachers are looking for errors and check facts in grammars or dictionaries whenever they are uncertain about correctness of usage or form in the exercises and compositions they are marking. This attitude of alertness to erroneous forms, and pleasure in finding the facts when in doubt, needs to be developed in students so that they will take an interest in proofreading their own work before submitting it for checking or grading by the teacher. It can be cultivated by an occasional problem-solving competition along the following lines.

W7 (E and I)   *Preparing the final text*

1. The teacher takes a text of a level comprehensible to the student and types it out, double- or triple-spaced, with a certain number of spelling errors of the type the students themselves tend to make (e.g., *there* for *their, comming, recieve*), some faults in capitalization (*thursday, You*), a few typing slips which do not change pronunciation (*seperate, owt, raceing*) and some other typing slips which constitute morphological or syntactic inaccuracies in written language (e.g., *a important book, their gone, he want his dinner*).

2. The students work in pairs or small groups to prepare a perfect text for the final typing. Each group has a different text, a pencil of a distinctive color, and a group symbol which they put beside each correction they make. Students may check in dictionaries, grammars, or their textbooks.

3. Points will be awarded for every correction made and deducted not only for errors not detected but also for miscorrections.

4. After a time, corrected texts are passed on to the next group for rechecking. Groups gain further points for discovering miscorrections and undetected errors in the texts from other groups, but they lose points for

wrongly challenging another group's corrections, (In this second round, it is essential that groups remember to put their group symbol beside their corrections and recorrections.)

5. Final results in points for each group will usually have to be deferred till the next day, to allow the teacher time to sort out the different corrections and challenges. The perfected texts, with corrections still visible, are then retyped on dittoes by those students who are learning business skills. The final text is then used for some class or individualized activity.

6. When the next composition is due, students are given some class time to proofread each other's work and write suggested improvements in colored pencil.

* The rules for the spelling of the principal parts of certain regular verbs[6] (e.g., *change, plan, omit, visit, carry*) are frequently not made clear to students, yet they can provide a considerable shortcut to the mastery of this troublesome feature. It is also reassuring for students to see that these rules give further evidence of the underlying regularities of English spelling.

Make notes for your teaching file of these regularities, with lists of some of the commonest verbs in each of the categories. Work out an interesting activity students could undertake to discover many of these regularities for themselves (e.g., *hope: hoped, hop: hopped; omit: omitted, visit: visited; cry: cried, deny: denied, carry: carried*).

II. Writing in the language

Writing down words from an English dictionary inserted into native-language patterns in native-language word order is not "writing in the language."

W 8 From old age, Japanese wives have done almost of the things with their both hands.

Commentary

This extract from a Japanese student's composition is clearly not English. Rather, it is Japanese structure dressed in English lexicon—a form of fractured English which may, or may not, be comprehensible to native speakers of English, depending on their patience and imagination or their knowledge of the native language of the writer. Our students will want to go beyond this stage. Unless they can eventually write so that their meaning is immediately comprehensible to an English-speaking reader, they are wasting a great deal of precious time on this demanding activity.

To acquire an adequate foundation for autonomous writing, students study the potential for diversity of meaning of the English syntactic system. They seek to understand how it works (*cognition* in model C1) and essay the expression of a variety of meanings in written exercises (thus learning *production* through the *construction* of fluent, idiomatic sentences). This controlled micro-practice, like limbering-up exercises, is useful for developing the linguistic flexibility needed to communicate specific meanings.

PRESENTING THE GRAMMAR: COGNITION AND ABSTRACTION

Students must not only understand the grammatical concepts they encounter, but also appreciate how each, like a link in a coat of chain mail, interrelates with all the others in one fabric—the English language system. They may practice a concept in isolation, e.g., the simple past tense, *they finished*, becoming familiar with its form and primary function. No concept, however, is fully assimilated until it can be used, or its specific meaning recognized, in a matrix of other grammatical concepts (e.g., *they finished last night* as contrasted with *they were finishing when the bell rang*). Students must be able to select, with conscious differentiation of meaning, what they need from this matrix (e.g., whether *they finished, they were finishing, they have finished, they had finished* or *they were about to finish* is the most appropriate).

It is this need for our students to comprehend grammatical concepts in relation to, or in contrast with, other grammatical concepts which guides us in selecting among the *various ways of presenting the grammar*.

1. The teacher, or more usually the textbook writer, decides, for example, that the students should now learn the past progressive (or negation or the relative pronoun). This decision is an arbitrary one and the next lesson is designed accordingly. The forms of the past progressive are set out in a paradigm and the way it is used explained and demonstrated in some example sentences. Students are then asked to write out the past progressive forms of some verbs and to use them in written (or oral) exercises or translation sentences.

This is the standard *deductive approach*.[7] It highlights aspects of the grammar extracted from the matrix. The new forms being learned then need to be incorporated into reading or oral activities, where their relationships with other aspects of the grammar may be observed; otherwise, the students will tend to think of them as separate "rules" rather than elements in an interacting system. This deductive approach is incorporated, in a non-arbitrary fashion, as part of 3 below.

2. Students may encounter a new aspect of the grammar in a matrix of language and become curious about its function. This is the initial stage of *inductive learning*.

a. Students may hear a form which is unfamiliar to them as they are listening to oral English. They may look puzzled or ask about it. In response, the teacher explains that this is a way of expressing past action and discusses its use. Opportunity is then provided for the students to hear other examples of the use of this past tense form in further oral work.

b. The past progressive may be encountered in reading material. Its function may be inferred from the context and then discussed in relation to other expressions of time relations. The forms and use of the past progressive are then practiced orally in other contexts or in written exercises.

3. Students may need an expression of past time for something they wish to say or write. They ask for the forms they need. The teacher tells them briefly how to create past time forms (e.g., simple past and past progressive) from known verbs and explains the difference between expressions for a single past event and a past action in progress which is related to another past event. The teacher then encourages the students to use other examples of these past time forms in what they are trying to say or write. This is a *deductive approach in response to a felt need*.

Each of these approaches has its use for specific age-groups or for particular aspects of the language. The deductive approach is most useful for mature, well-motivated students with some knowledge of the language who are anxious to understand the more complicated aspects of the grammatical system; students who have already learned one foreign language and are interested in the way this language deals with certain grammatical relationships; and adult students in intensive courses who have reasons for wishing to understand as quickly as possible how the language works. The inductive approach is very appropriate for young language learners who have not yet developed fully their ability to think in abstractions[8] and who enjoy learning through active application; students who can take time to assimilate the language through use; and those studying the language in an environment where they hear it all around them. Most classroom teachers use a mixture of inductive and deductive approaches according to the type of student with whom they are dealing and the degree of complication of the problem being presented.

What about grammatical terminology?

Grammatical terminology has long been the bugbear of teachers of a new language. Even switching from traditional terms to those used by any of the several competing systems of contemporary grammatical study does not seem to solve the problem. Students learn new terms and a schematic apparatus readily enough without coming to grips with the concepts they represent.

Ultimately, teachers of English must take the responsibility themselves for teaching the student as much, or as little, abstract grammar with its associated terminology as seems to be needed by each particular group. Teachers must feel free to adapt or invent terminology which they find helps their students grasp the concepts and use the language effectively. Choice of grammatical terms may depend in part on the relationship between English and the students' native language, and on the transferable (and sometimes cognate) terms with which students may already be familiar. The teacher has to assess whether using terms corresponding to those used in the study of the native language will help the students' understanding of English structure, or will hinder it by leading to expectations of more similarities than actually exist. It may often be more useful in the early stages to talk about the simple form, the *s*-form, and the *ing*-form of a verb, and their behavior with other words, rather than about the first, second, third person, singular and plural, present tense forms; the infinitive with and without *to*; the present participle and the gerund. Focusing on formal surface features does not mean that students will not have to grasp, ultimately, the underlying grammatical relations to which the more sophisticated syntactic terms refer. Students must understand that *I like coffee* and *He used to ski* are normal English sentences, but *He like coffee* and *He's used to ski* are not. Individual teachers need to determine which terms are most effective in displaying the structure of the language for a given level. They should experiment with their own non-traditional ways of talking about grammar and continue with those that work.

How do written exercises for learning grammatical concepts differ from oral practice?

1. Oral exercises provide the opportunity for many more examples of the rule to be practiced, immediately corrected, and repracticed in a given time.

2. When exercises are practiced orally, the observant teacher can judge more accurately when to skip some exercises which performance indicates are not needed, and when to add further exercises to ensure assimilation of the rule.

3. Oral exercises can be used to prepare students for written exercises by allowing opportunity for questions and comment on obvious areas of misunderstanding and a rapid repracticing of the point at issue.

4. Written exercises provide useful reinforcement of what has been practiced orally; they help to build in concepts through the abstract process of thinking out the written forms.

5. Written exercises have an individual diagnostic function, revealing what sections of the work have not been thoroughly assimilated by a particular student and where their application in wider contexts is not fully understood. It is in written exercises that one focuses the student's attention on specific problems, rather than in expressive writing where the student is attempting to do a number of things at the same time.

6. Because they allow time for editing and re-editing, written exercises are less likely than oral exercises to reflect slips due to inattention or

momentary distraction, and are often better indicators of genuine mis-understanding of the functioning of the system.

7. Certain aspects of the language need to be practiced in writing be-cause they are more fully expressed in the written code, e.g., function words which are unstressed and reduced in speech: the *have* which is pronounced /əv/ in *should have gone;* the *to* which is pronounced /ə/ in *want to see;* the *her* which is pronounced /ə/ in GB *met her last night;* and troublesome homophones like: *there, their, they're; its, it's; to, too, two.*

8. It is easier for students to submit in writing several possible versions, in which they can show how one rule parallels, interacts with, or contrasts with other rules.

9. Written exercises allow time for consulting references (dictionaries, grammars, or the textbook) and can, therefore, take on problem-solving characteristics.

10. Written exercises allow students with physical or emotional aural difficulties, or with slow response reactions, to demonstrate what they know through a medium in which they feel more relaxed.

COGNITIVE EXERCISES

Whether the grammar has been presented deductively or inductively, a time comes when the students need to try for themselves whether they can use the various parts of it in novel contexts to express specific meanings. Through cognitive exercises they explore its possibilities and become more conscious of the constraints it imposes. They also clarify for themselves their individual areas of vagueness and miscomprehension.

Several very commonly used types of exercises may be termed cognitive, in the sense that they require of the student an abstract comprehension of the workings of the grammatical system. It is not surprising, therefore, that in form some of them resemble various well-known tests for estimating intelligence and ability to undertake abstract learning tasks. Success in these types of exercises does not necessarily mean that students will be able to think of the appropriate rules at the appropriate moment when they are composing sentences themselves. It is, however, a step on the way, since this basic knowledge is indispensable for effective language use. Students must, however, clearly understand that such exercises mark only a begin-ning—a foundation on which to build the all-important structure of personal meaning.

Under this heading we will consider multiple-choice exercises, fill-in-the-blank and completion exercises, the cloze procedure, and exercises in living language for the inductive exploration of particular problems of grammar. Conversions, restatements, expansions, and combinations will be considered under *Production*.

Some of these types of exercises are also dealt with in Chapter 4 and occasional reference will be made to the discussion in that section. Most of these exercises are also commonly used as *tests*.

Multiple-choice exercises

A *typical multiple-choice grammar exercise* will look like the following:

W 9 (E or I)   Circle in the margin the letter corresponding to the correct form to complete the following sentences when

A = is   C = does
B = has   D = no extra word

1. She _____ eating breakfast.	A	B	C	D
2. What _____ that word mean?	A	B	C	D
3. _____ he driven that car before?	A	B	C	D
4. What _____ your father do?	A	B	C	D
5. Peter _____ never seen snow.	A	B	C	D
6. Who _____ always knows the answer?	A	B	C	D
7. Why _____ that dog following us?	A	B	C	D
8. _____ Jenny usually eat lunch at school?	A	B	C	D

Commentary

1. This exercise forces students to think over carefully the various rules for the use of the auxiliary in the simple present, present progressive, and present perfect of verb forms in statements, yes-no questions, and question-word questions. They must understand the whole sentence and the implications of other parts to be able to select successfully.

2. The number of choices is too great for a student to succeed through guessing, except by a fluke. The fluke probability is also reduced by the fact that the students think they know at least some of the items and so are not depending on pure guesswork for the complete exercise.

3. If a separate computer answer-sheet is used, the exercise may be machine-scored as a test. The answer format of W9 can be rapidly checked with an easily constructed punched-stencil key (with holes punched to mark the positions of the correct answers).

4. The W9 format provides a useful mechanism for students in individualized programs to check their mastery of certain concepts and their readiness to move on.

5. It is easy to construct from a basic model several equivalent versions of an exercise of this type by changing the lexical items, and thus the

semantic context, while retaining the grammatical context. The following three items are equivalent in grammatical difficulty and test the same rule:

W10 a. When _____ the bus coming?
b. Why _____ they crying?
c. What _____ your mother making?

From the point of view of knowledge of the rule, the following items are also equivalent.

d. How _____ you feeling today?
e. More important, how _____ the presidential campaign affecting the day-to-day functioning of the executive branch?

Note, however, that (e) contains expressions and vocabulary of a level of difficulty above the level of the grammatical item sought. The introductory *More important* is advanced level, or at least intermediate; *presidential campaign* and *executive branch* are culturally linked phrases which would disconcert an elementary-level student—the only one who would normally be working through exercises in the use of these auxiliaries.

6. It is essential in this type of exercise or test that each of the items be as unambiguous as possible. Students should not have to hesitate over possible interpretations while they try to decide what the instructor had in mind.

W11 a. _____ John heard about it?
b. Has John heard about it?
c. Had John heard about it?
d. John heard about it?

Items (b), (c) and (d) are possible English questions in the appropriate context. (d = Did John hear about it? and usually suggests some surprise on the part of the person asking the question.) Clearly the constructor of item (a) had the particular problem of the auxiliary in mind and, therefore, expected (b) or (c). Instructions should make it clear whether leaving a blank unfilled is one of the options. Providing more context can also reduce the number of choices, as in W12, where both *has* and *had*, but not an unfilled blank, are possible. An unfilled blank in W12 (a) would yield a sentence representing only the most informal style of English.

W12 a. _____ John heard about it yet?
b. What _____ John heard about it?

This multiple-choice format can be used for a number of areas of grammar, including the choice of *tenses* and *aspects*:

W13 (I) Read the following sentences carefully. Circle in the margin the letter corresponding to the tense or to the tense and aspect of the verb that you would use to complete the sentence when

A = simple past
B = past progressive
C = present perfect
D = past perfect

1. That's the best film I _____ this year.　　　　　A　B　C　D
   (see)
2. They _____ in Europe six months when I first　A　B　C　D
   (live)
   met them.
3. If she _____ the situation, she would　　　　　A　B　C　D
   (understand)
   explain it to us.
4. While we _____ for the bus, we heard a loud　A　B　C　D
   (wait)
   bang.
5. The cake would have been better if it _____　　A　B　C　D
   (be)
   in the oven longer.
6. He asked me how I was every time I _____　　A　B　C　D
   (see)
   him.
7. They arrived just as I _____ supper.　　　　　A　B　C　D
   (get)
8. He discovered that he _____ his wallet.　　　　A　B　C　D
   (lose)

Commentary

1. This is clearly a review exercise since it requires comparative knowledge of the use of the simple past, the present and past perfect, and the past progressive verb forms, including the choice of the appropriate form for the *if*-clauses of conditional sentences.

2. The exercise tests knowledge of the functioning of the language

system, not ability to produce the forms required. As it is constructed, it is useful as an objectively corrected test of cognitive assimilation of the rules. When using W3 as an exercise, students would, of course, also fill in the appropriate forms of the verbs in the blanks.

3. In constructing items to test ability to select correct verb forms, one must give sufficient indicators of time relationships to make the appropriate choice clear. In most of the above examples, the verb forms required in the blanks are syntactically constrained by other tenses in associated clauses (as in 3: *If she understood the situation, she would explain it to us*); temporally constrained by a superordinate verb (as in 6: *He asked me how I was every time I saw him*); or clearly indicated by adverbial time expressions (as in 2: *They had lived in Europe six months when I first met them*).

4. Other factors which have been kept in mind in constructing the items are:

a. that the sentences should be of a type that the students might encounter or wish to use;

b. that the vocabulary and general construction of each sentence should be of a level that the students can easily comprehend, so that they are not distracted from the real task of deciding on tense and aspect.

The same format can be used for practice in *distinguishing among expressions* whose precise usage is often confusing.

W14 (1) Circle in the margin the letter corresponding to the most appropriate completion for the following sentences when

A = back   D = out
B = along   E = off
C = through F = up

1. I liked the first volume, but I can't get _____ the second.   A B C D E F

2. Be sure to get _____ the bus at the second stop.   A B C D E F

3. Although we were cousins, we didn't get _____.   A B C D E F

4. If you lend him money, you'll never get it _____.   A B C D E F

5. Was she rude? Yes, she told me to get   A B C D E F

Commentary

In this example, the number of items is not equal to the number of choices. This is one way to avoid selection by pure elimination procedures. Another way is to write the items so that some of the choices are appropriate for more than one item.

The novice multiple-choice item constructor should not be misled by the final product into underestimating the difficulty of constructing unambiguous, useful test items in this format. The first step is to make a careful list of exactly which items it is desirable to include. After the test has been constructed and carefully scanned for ambiguities, inappropriate vocabulary, unintentional comprehension difficulty or obscurity, stilted expressions, unlikely meanings (e.g., _____ *she ever worn clothes?*), and a regular pattern order of correct choices (e.g., ABCABC),[9] it should be passed on to another person to be read and checked for these weaknesses. Even experienced test constructors are sometimes temporarily blinded by the knowledge of their intentions.

A similar format may be used for testing the students' understanding of the *meanings of words*.

W15 (E or I)   Circle in the margin the letter corresponding to the phrase which correctly completes the sentence:

1. The mother of your father or mother is your   A   B   C   D

    A. stepmother
    B. grandmother
    C. godmother
    D. mother-in-law

2. The son of your brother or sister is your   A   B   C   D

    A. nephew
    B. cousin
    C. niece
    D. godson

3. The sister of your father or mother is your   A   B   C   D

    A. great-aunt
    B. uncle
    C. stepsister
    D. aunt

Commentary

1. Kinship systems differ widely from culture to culture. It is interesting and useful for a student to learn the principal terms and the kinds of distinctions they make. In English, but not in all languages, the same set of terms is used for the relations of both one's mother and one's father; sex is distinguished in the terms *uncle* and *aunt, niece* and *nephew*, but not in *cousin*.

2. These items would not be given to students out of the blue. The exercise is obviously based on material in the students' textbook.

3. This type of exercise can be fun to make up and groups of students may be asked to construct exercises for other groups of students. Another format, which is not suitable for a test because of the fifty-fifty chances it provides, but which is very amusing to construct and to answer, is as follows:

W16 (E or I)   Some of the following statements are sensible and some are ridiculous. Circle in the margin

   A: if the sentence is sensible,
   B: if the sentence is ridiculous.

   1. A magazine is a newspaper-shop.   A   B
   2. A cold is a drink with ice in it.   A   B
   3. A bus-stop is a bus that often stops.   A   B
   4. A laboratory is a place for research.   A   B
   5. A library is a bookshop.   A   B
   6. A picnic is a meal one eats outdoors.   A   B

The multiple-choice format can be used also to test appreciation of *appropriate rejoinders, responses, or comments* as in the following:

W17 (E)   Circle in the margin the letter corresponding to the most appropriate response to the following questions:

   1. Can you change a dollar? (GA)   A   B   C   D
       A. That's quite enough.
       B. I think so.
       C. Fine, thank you.
       D. I heard it's four francs fifty. . . .

Alternatively, the student may be asked to select the appropriate response in a particular situation.

W18 (E)   Circle in the margin the letter corresponding to the appropriate response in the situation described.

1. In a food shop, you meet Mr. Johnson, who is the   A B   C   D
principal of the school where you are a student. You
say to the principal:

   A. Hi, Mr. Johnson. How's everything?
   B. You have to eat too, eh?
   C. Hullo, Mr. Johnson. How are you?
   D. Well, Mr. J. Fancy seeing you here!

* Construct a multiple-choice test for the forms of the personal pronouns or for tag questions (e.g., He left, *didn't he?*). Try the test out on other members of the class. Discuss the strengths and weaknesses of the various tests constructed by the class members.

Fill-in-the-blank exercises

Some weaknesses of this format have already been discussed in Chapter 4, particularly the type of construction which makes these exercises mechanical busywork. To earn a place as a cognitive exercise, the fill-in-the-blank activity must demand of the student *understanding of the complete sentence and careful thought*. W13 meets this criterion as a fill-in-the-blank exercise when each verb has to be written in with the correct form for the tense or the tense and aspect selected. The purpose of W13 can also be achieved in the format of W19.

W19 (E or I)   Read the following sentences carefully and write in the blank the most appropriate past-time form of the verb in the margin.

buy	1. Last week my father _____ my mother a new car.
leave	2. I told him that she _____ the shop already.
wait	3. Joan _____ for me when I arrived.
understand	4. She spoke very fast, but I _____ everything.
be	5. I think you _____ in this place long enough.
eat	6. By the time they were ten years old they _____ at Maxim's dozens of times.

Commentary

1. In this exercise, the students must first look carefully at all indicators of time relationships in each sentence. Then, having selected an appropriate verb form, they must make decisions about this particular verb and its

auxiliary, if any, asking themselves such questions as: Is the verb regular or irregular? Is an auxiliary required? Which one? Which person and number?

2. If items are written in, the exercise cannot be mechanically scored.

3. Each item should be allotted at least two points so that credit may be given to students who choose the correct verb form, even if they make some mistake in the spelling of the words.

4. Students may be asked to write out the whole sentence. This depends on whether W19 is used as a practice exercise in writing or as part of a test with a large number of items to be covered in a restricted amount of time. If students do write out the whole item, points should not be deducted for slips in copying other parts of the sentence when the fill-in item is correct. If the copying is careless throughout, a penalty of two or three points may be deducted from the total for this specific fault.

5. Note that constructions requiring the separation of a verb form consisting of two words (questions based on inversion, most negatives, and phrases with such adverbs as *just*) have to be avoided in a format like W19, unless the student is given the option of leaving a blank unfilled. These constructions would normally require that the verb form be divided by the subject (*Was* Joan *waiting* . . . ?), by the negative word (. . . *had* never *left* . . .), the adverb (. . . *had* just *eaten* . . .), or some combination of these (*Haven't* you *been* . . . ?). If more than one blank were given in a sentence, the problem would then arise as to whether to deduct a point from the student who had written the correct verb form but failed to put the words in the correct blanks, that is, in the correct position in the sentence. Depending on the level of the student, one would expect the words to be correctly placed as a matter of course, or one would allot an additional point to these items to allow for the two decisions the student had to make.

At the intermediate and advanced levels fill-in-the-blank exercises can become very demanding as in a *mixed, overall structure test* with no guides to the blanks:

W20 (I and A)   Complete the following sentences appropriately as indicated by the clues in the sentences.

1. I knew he _____ arrive the next day.
2. He insisted _____ finishing the test even though the bell had rung.
3. We'd better go, _____n't we?
4. They used to steal money _____ the cash register.

5. I don't understand _____ you mean.
6. She's interested _____ mathematics.
7. That was the question _____ bothered me.
8. We're _____ to having dinner rather late in the evenings.

The fill-in-the-blank format is also useful for *testing irregular verb forms in context*.

W21 (I and A)   Write in the margin the correct form of the verb on the left, as indicated by the clues in the sentences.

1. speak	He had often _____ to her about his father.	1. _____
2. ride	They _____ steadily for five days before they reached the mountains.	2. _____
3. wear	We threw things away long before they were _____ out.	3. _____
4. sing	She had a lovely voice and often _____ for us.	4. _____

Commentary

1. In a complete exercise more items would be given for each verb.

2. The format with blank in the right-hand margin provides for rapid correction of the test, since all the answers are in one column. As a class exercise, it would be preferable for students to write in the blanks within the sentences so that they could read over the complete sentence as they checked the appropriateness of their choice of verb form.

3. A set of such exercises, with alternative versions, covering all the common irregular verbs is useful in an individualized program. Students can then check regularly their control of this troublesome area.

The fill-in-the-blank exercise may take the form of a *connected passage* of prose. This is a common way of giving practice in, or testing, choice among past-time forms of verbs.

W22 (A)   Write out the following passage, putting each verb into the form for the expression of past time which best fits the context: simple past, past progressive, or past perfect; active or passive voice. Be sure to put the adverbial expressions (in parentheses) in the right place with respect to the verb form.

The great Muscari, the wild and courageous young Italian poet, _____
                                                                    (walk)
into his favourite restaurant, beside the blue waters of the Mediterranean.

Servants, dressed in white, _____ the tables for an early lunch. The
(prepare)

restaurant _____ by little orange and lemon trees, and Muscari
(surround)

_____ at these with satisfaction.
(look)

Muscari never _____ without his sword, with which he _____
(travel) (win)

many brilliant fights, or without his mandolin, with which he actually

_____ to Miss Ethel Harrogate, the young daughter of an English
(play)

banker on holiday. Like a boy, he _____ both fame and danger, and
(desire)

especially if he _____ some beautiful woman.
(help)

The banker and his lovely daughter _____ at the hotel attached to
(stay)

Muscari's restaurant; that was why it was his favourite restaurant. He

_____ round the room and _____ at once that the English guests
(glance) (see)

not yet _____ down from their rooms. The restaurant was still
(come)

empty. But from a seat which almost _____ by one of the small
(hide)

orange trees, a man _____ up and _____ towards him. He
(get) (come)

_____ clothes quite different from the poet's.
(wear)

Adapted from G. K. CHESTERTON,
"The Paradise of Thieves"[10]

Clearly, this format is also useful for other areas of grammar, e.g., the recurrent problem of which preposition to use after different expressions when they are followed by the *-ing* form of a verb. This is a more natural way to practice this feature than by writing out lists of expressions classified according to the preposition that follows.

W23 (I or A)   Complete the following passage by inserting the preposition *by, in, of, on,* or *to* as required by the context.

Although we were used _____ bargaining, we got tired _____ arguing with street-vendors all the time. Even when we were not interested _____ buying anything, they would insist _____ following us. Sometimes we would succeed _____ getting rid of them only _____ going back to the hotel.

Uses for fill-in-the-blank exercises are limited only by the imagination of the instructor, as witness the following miscellany:

W24 (E or I)   With stimulus given in the student's native language. (We will use French as an example.)

(qu'est-ce que)   1. _____ does that sign mean?
(qui)   2. I asked her _____ told her the story.
(qui)   3. They found the car _____ had been stolen.

Commentary

This kind of exercise would be possible only where there were close correspondences between the structures of the two languages. In actual fact indications in the native language are quite unnecessary for any of these items. In item 2, for instance, the indirect question and the phrase *tell the story* with no subject expressed require the interrogative pronoun *who*. To make the meaning more obvious to the student more context could be supplied in some cases, e.g., for (1): *I'm curious. _____ does that sign mean?*

W25 (E or I)   With English paraphrase as stimulus.

Betty _____ (to) go home early to help her mother.
(Betty is under an obligation to go home early to help her mother.)

Commentary

Presumably *has to* or *must* is sought. With this type of exercise care must be taken to see that the paraphrase is not in less familiar language than the item sought. Here *obligation* might lead a student to use the expression *is obliged to*. This would form a possible sentence for which credit should be given.

W26 (I)   With grammatical indications given.

Danny and Davy_____ all afternoon.
                    (swim, past perfect progressive)

Commentary

This would be a more cognitive type of exercise if a suitable context were given for the item rather than the precise verb-form reference (see W13, W19, and W20). In this example, only the form for the verb and the student's familiarity with grammatical terminology are being tested, not the use. Both form and use would be tested in:

> Danny and Davy _____ all afternoon when the owners of the pool
>   (swim)
> arrived.

W27 (E or I)   With information given in associated sentences to show what is required.

1. Lucy is a good cellist. Mabel doesn't play very well.
   Lucy is a _____ cellist than Mabel.
2. Fred is six feet tall. Bill is six feet tall, too.
   Bill is _____ tall _____ Fred.

The cloze procedure

If we combine the idea of W20 with the sequential format of W22, we arrive at the cloze procedure. Strictly speaking, the cloze procedure, as developed for native speakers, was a test of reading comprehension. It consisted of giving the student a passage to complete in which every *n*th word was deleted. In one passage it could be every fifth word, in another every tenth word, or whatever the examiner chose. This will immediately recall the discussion in Chapter 3 of Cherry's uncertainties of a spoken message and Schlesinger's semantic-syntactic decoding. In a cloze test, native speakers project expectations about the development of the message. Since second- or foreign-language learners have also to think carefully about grammatical detail, in a cloze test or exercise for these students the blanks need not be kept rigidly to a set pattern. The cloze procedure provides an interesting and thought-provoking exercise, which trains the students to look carefully at all structural clues and to range around within a semantic field for related concepts. It is good preparation for careful reading and a useful overall written test.

W28 (E)   Sylvia and Nancy decided to _____ a walk. They _____ wanted _____ swim, but the sea was _____ cold. So they _____ on the big rocks by the _____. Suddenly they _____ to a large pool of _____ made _____ the tide. They took _____ their shoes and _____ their feet in the water. _____ was lovely and _____. . . .

Commentary

1. Any completion which makes sense in the context and fits into the grammatical structure is acceptable. Passages can be constructed which are more ambiguous than W28, thus allowing more scope for student ingenuity. (See also W47).

2. (I and A) After a reading passage has been studied intensively, the students may do a cloze test on it to see how much of the vocabulary and grammatical structure they have retained.

3. W28 is a segment demonstrating a technique for an exercise. In a full-length cloze test, the first sentence (and often the last) of the extract are left intact and the deletion of words is performed objectively, according to the predetermined system.

* Prepare a cloze test from one of the passages in Chapters 6 or 7.

* Look at fill-in-the-blank exercises in various textbooks and suggest ways to make them more intellectually stimulating.

Beyond the elementary level

Inductive learning need not be limited to a few early lessons of patterned oral practice of the type discussed in Chapter 4. At the intermediate and advanced levels, the students' curiosity can be channeled into discovering for themselves quite complicated sets of rules which they tend to remember better because they themselves have worked them out.

The Rosetta procedure[11]

(I or A) The rules for indirect statement (or reported speech) and indirect question can be discovered inductively from manifestations in written script.

The students express curiosity about differences they have observed between directly and indirectly quoted speech and hazard guesses as to the rules governing these divergencies. The teacher then gives them the following sets of sentences to study and asks that they develop from them coherent rules which will explain the differences in the forms (in W29, the differences between 1. and 2.).

W29   1. My wife and I got up as usual when the alarm rang yesterday morning. "It seems very dark," my wife said. "Yes, but it's cloudy," I pointed out. "What do you want for breakfast?" my wife asked me. "Toast and coffee will be enough," I said, and added, "I think I'll take the car, because it's so late." I finished breakfast, left the house, but saw no one in the street. "Where is everybody?" I wondered. Finally I saw a milkman. "What time is it?" I asked him anxiously. "It's five-thirty," he told me, and then inquired, "What's the trouble?" "I got up two hours early," I explained sadly. As he walked off I heard him mutter, "Some people have an easy life." When I got inside I found my wife in bed asleep. I said to myself, "Some people certainly do."

2. My wife and I got up as usual when the alarm rang yesterday morning. My wife said that it seemed very dark. I agreed, but pointed out that it was cloudy. My wife asked me what I wanted for breakfast. I said toast and coffee would be enough, and added that I thought I'd take the car, because it was so late. I finished breakfast, left the house, but saw no one in the street. I wondered where everybody was. Finally I saw a milkman and asked him anxiously what time it was. He told me it was five-thirty, and then inquired what the trouble was. I explained sadly that I had got up two hours early. As he walked off I heard him mutter that some people had an easy life. When I got inside I found my wife in bed asleep. I said to myself that some people certainly did.

Learning from living language

Even at the advanced level, students may find the subtleties of the use of the auxiliary *would* difficult to grasp.[12] Students will have been familiar with some of the uses of *will* and *would* from the elementary level: *will* in expression of future time (*They will be here tomorrow*) and "weak volition" (*I'll find it*); both *will* and *would* in polite requests (*Will you turn it off now, please? Would you help him with that?*); *would like* as a softened form of *want* in polite requests and invitations (*I'd like two, please; Would you like to come with us?*) By the intermediate level, students have learned or are learning *would rather* (= *prefer*); and *would* as the past tense of *will* in direct speech and expressions of future-in-the-past, and in conditional constructions, both open and hypothetical: *She says she will help me; She said she would help me. He'll tell them tomorrow; He would tell them tomorrow. If I find one, I'll give it to you; If I found one, I'd give it to you; If I'd found one, I'd have given it to you.*

Other meanings of *would* are less easy to grasp. For these, the teacher may give advanced students extracts of living language in which the context clarifies the meaning or nuance supplied in part by *would*. Through an exercise of this type, the students focus on the variable semantic contribution of this auxiliary and the formal indications (lexical or phonological) of its role.

W30 (A) Examine the following extracts carefully, and identify the meaning of *would* in each case: Is it related to the uses of *would* in indirect speech, future-in-the-past, or conditional sentences that you have studied? If not, what other meaning does it convey?

1. Between herself and all the places there was a space like an enormous canyon she could not hope to bridge or cross. The plans for the movies or the Marines were only child's plans that would never work, and she was careful when she answered.   (Carson McCullers)

2. ". . . I don't want to be cut in pieces by this thing. I've had enough. I'm too old to suffer." "Why should you suffer, my darling? I love you." "So you imagine, but you would soon be unfaithful. And you would tell me lies. I would look into your eyes and I would know that you were lying and I would be in hell."   (Iris Murdoch)

3. Thus, for example, there are languages that realize the concepts of time exclusively in adverbial systems, while others do this partly in the verb and partly in the adverb. A learner of such a language would have first to realize that the verb is marked for tense and aspect and then to discover which verbal forms related to which time notion.

                                                                    (S. Pit Corder)

4. They thought it was finished, but she would show them. The wedding had not included her, but she would still go into the world.

                                                                    (Carson McCullers)

5. His Mother, as She dried her eyes,
   Said, "Well—it gives me no surprise,
   He would not do as he was told!"   (Hilaire Belloc)

6. "Do you mean to say you pushed that cart all the way from Notting Hill through all that traffic?"

   "It's downhill," said Tallis.

   "That's just the sort of thing you would do to upset people and put them in the wrong. It's not funny."   (Iris Murdoch)

7. "I could not give the telegram to Mr. Barrymore himself. I gave it to Mrs. Barrymore. She promised to hand it over to Mr. Barrymore at once."

   "Did you see Mr. Barrymore?" I asked.

   "No, sir, I tell you he was upstairs."

   "If you didn't see him, how did you know he was upstairs?"

   "Well, surely his own wife would know where he was," said the postmaster, angrily.   (Arthur Conan Doyle, from an adapted text)

8. "Many things don't work in here," he said. "One day a man brought in a Lee-Metford, and that wouldn't work."   (E.M. Forster)

9. As a rule, when the story was over, they would sit for a moment and then suddenly get busy doing something in a hurry. . . .

(Carson McCullers)

10. An old farmer was driving his wife to the market with his horse and cart. With his wife in the back of the cart, he started off along a bumpy road, which went beside a little river. On the way, he heard a splash, but paid no attention. When the farmer got to town, an acquaintance asked him where his wife was. The farmer looked back at the empty cart, thought for a moment, and replied, "That'd be yon splash."

(Old anecdote)

Commentary

1. These examples provide enough material to alert students to the complications of meaning of *would*, to stimulate their curiosity to identify its meanings in what they are reading, and to help them to use it in a more versatile fashion.

2. Several meanings of *would* can be extracted from the examples in W30.

a. In 1 and 2, verb phrases with *would* are used in a hypothetical framework, with the hypothetical condition projected into the future, but only implied: "plans that would never work" *if she tried them*; "you would soon be unfaithful" *if we entered into this affair*.

b. A hypothetical situation is similarly presupposed in 3, but here there is no distinct future projection. The condition implied in the extract is *if someone were studying such a language*.

c. The meaning of *would* in 4 is strong determination, further marked by emphatic stress on *she* in the first sentence, and on *still* in the second. Here *would* is the past tense of *will*.

d. In 5 and 6, strong determination is part of the force of *would*, but in these extracts *would* has emphatic stress, and suggests in addition that the behavior is characteristic or typical, that it is to be expected. (The impoliteness sometimes implied by the answer *I wouldn't know* comes from this sense of expectation in the word *would*. *I wouldn't know* may mean much more than just *I don't know* or *I'm not in a position to know*: uttered in an impatient way it can mean *I'm not the sort of person who might be expected to know that; therefore you are silly or foolish to ask me*.)

e. The use of *would know* in 7 also conveys the meaning that the speaker considers it *characteristic* or *to be expected* that the wife knows; he does not say: *Well, his own wife knows where he is*.

f. The meaning of *wouldn't work* in 8 is close to *didn't work*, but there is something more—it contains the implication: *in spite of my efforts*. Here again *would* is the past tense of *will*. The phrases *it won't start, it wouldn't go* (*run, move, rise,* etc.) suggest *(Something) refuses* or *refused to (respond appropriately to someone's efforts)*. Stemming from this is the additional nuance of personification. Saying *The sun wouldn't shine* or *The bread won't rise* endows the subjects with an underlying will, hence with a kind of life of their own. (This "personifying" use of *will* or *would* is of a kind with the folk use of the feminine personal pronoun *she*, rather than *it*, for machines, engines, and ships: *There she goes! Give'er the gun! Fill'er up! She's the western combination, she's the Wabash Cannonball.*)

g. The verb phrase *would sit* in 9 indicates customary activity in the past. *As a rule* gives an important clue to this meaning. *Will* is also occasionally used in this sense for present time (*He'll just sit all day rocking*), but the simple present (*He just sits all day . . .*) is perhaps more frequent.

h. The *(woul)d be* of 10 indicates probability, or surmise on the basis of logical necessity. In contemporary English, it would be more customary to use *must have been* in this (hardly likely) situation: "That is what the splash *must have been.*" (Notice that the farmer is concerned with explaining the *splash.*) One still hears such related expressions, in response to a knock on the door, for example, as *That will be (X), That would be (X),* as well as *That must be (X).*

(I and A) The difference between the future with *will* and the *going-to* future continues to be a problem for successive groups of English-language students. The distinction between the meanings of promise or determination or conditionality expressed by *will* and the idea of present intention or cause implied by *be going to* is not a familiar one to most students. Consider the following example.

W31 We will just walk up to people and know them right away. We will be walking down a dark road and see a lighted house and knock on the door and strangers will rush to meet us and say: Come in! Come in! We will know decorated aviators and New York people and movie-stars. We will have thousands of friends. . . . We will belong to so many clubs that we can't even keep track of them all. We will be members of the whole world.

From CARSON MC CULLERS, *The Member of the Wedding*[13]

Commentary

This short passage shows the meaning of the *will* future in a way that a deductive explanation alone cannot. The repeated *we will* expresses the force of the speaker's determination and her emotional involvement with the future she is foreseeing and promising herself. It also heightens the inherent irony: her projections are quite without foundation in her present situation; we know (and she too no doubt knows) that the events she is predicting so feverishly will never happen.

Only through living language can we really assimilate differences like these which are fundamental to the effective use and understanding of English. (See also R42–44.)

Teachers who wish to retain and improve upon the level of their English will seek opportunities to visit English-speaking countries. Meanwhile, they will read widely and constantly in English for pleasure. Material of the type used in W30 and W31 can be collected by teachers from their own reading of newspapers, magazines, plays, novels, or books of general information.

* Find other material of this type to clarify the uses of the tenses and aspects in contemporary written English. Remember that there must be sufficient context in each item to establish the particular meaning conveyed by the use of one verb form rather than another.

Deductive learning also has its place at the advanced level. Because of the subtlety of the distinctions and the paucity of comparable examples in any one text, it would be very time-consuming, for instance, to try to work out inductively the rules for the use of the subjunctive or putative *should* in indirect statements of request in English:[14] *We ask that visitors sign their names; They insisted that he go/should go with them; I recommend that she be allowed to drop the course,* or *I recommend that she should be allowed to drop the course.* There are, in the first place, only a few verbs that take this construction, and even with these verbs the occurrence of the pattern is restricted mainly to formal writing and "officialese" as in *He recommended that parliament be dissolved; I hereby order that the prisoner be released.* Furthermore, many of the verbs that take the subjunctive or putative *should* may also be followed by other constructions: *We ask visitors to sign their names; They insisted on his going with them; He recommended the dissolution of parliament,* the choice of construction in these cases being to a large extent unpredictable from the point of view of the learner.

For these reasons, the use of the subjunctive or putative *should* in indirect requests would normally be explained deductively. Students may be given a list of verbs which enter into these constructions (such lists are found in most advanced textbooks), with the commonest verbs indicated in some way, e.g., *ask, insist, demand, recommend.* In addition, the students' attention may be drawn to passages of living language in current reading which illustrate the various ways of expressing indirect request: with a *that* clause containing the subjunctive or *should* (*She ordered that the trees be/should be removed*), with an infinitive construction (*She ordered them to remove the trees*), or with a derived noun (*She ordered the removal of the trees*). Students should also be encouraged to notice the difference in the tone and in the amount of information conveyed by the choice made among the various alternatives.

✱ Begin a collection of suitable extracts for the advanced level demonstrating interesting uses of *negation forms* and share them with other members of the class.

GRAMMAR AND WRITING SKILL

However grammatical concepts are introduced and demonstrated, it is essential that the students' activity be directed as soon as possible to the *concept in use*. Understanding the operation of the grammar, observing its functioning, or practicing the effective use of it in exercises will not ensure that the student can use it efficiently in writing.

Experiments in the writing of English by native speakers have shown specifically that the formal study of grammar and of grammatical terminology does not improve skill in writing.[15] Native speakers who can control the grammar of their language in speech and have been taught in elementary and secondary school how it operates still write ungrammatical and incomplete sentences. Formal grammar is an abstract study. After language learners have been shown how the various parts of the language system operate, they seem to benefit more from discussion of the types of errors they are making in their writing in relation to what they were trying to say, with opportunity provided to correct their errors in context, than from a second (third, fourth, fifth?) exposition of the workings of the English pronoun system.[16] In this way they focus on the details they partly know or do not know, rather than having their attention dispersed over a wider area of abstract concepts.

9
Writing and written exercises II: flexibility and expression

III. Production: flexibility measures

Cognitive exercises of the types described, despite their usefulness in clarifying grammatical concepts, do not require students to construct their own sentences to express their personal meaning, nor to develop their ideas in logical and coherent paragraphs within a larger discourse. "Knowing about" is not "knowing how." *Practice is needed in actual sequential writing.* Having learned about the various parts of the machine, and parts of parts, and how these synchronize in action, the student needs to set the machine in motion with the different parts active in weaving the intricate pattern of meaning. Here guidance is helpful in learning which parts will operate together to form new patterns. Student aptitudes vary widely in writing. Some need considerable help in developing a smooth and effective operation; others seem intuitively to take off and create interesting patterns of their own. The teacher needs to distinguish these types early and *individualize writing activities* so that all students benefit to the maximum, according to their preferred styles of activity.

Although writing within a framework and expressive writing will now be discussed in sequence, it must be emphasized that opportunities for expressive writing should be provided as soon as possible. Even elementary-level students should have opportunities to experiment with the potential for expression of their rudimentary knowledge of the language. Students should not, however, be left to sink or swim in such a difficult area. Most students need some guided practice in using new combinations and explor-

297

ing possibilities of expression, if they are to go beyond simple, uncomplicated sentences. When they wish to express more sophisticated ideas in the
new medium, they need resources other than Fractured English, which is
often a mish-mash of half-learned English filled out with literal translations
from the native language.

Expressive writing experiments with all the possibilities of syntax and
lexicon. If there is to be transfer from guided practice in using this potential, then the practice itself must be recognizably purposeful and applicable.

This section will concentrate on measures for developing flexibility in the
construction of sentences and paragraphs within the shelter of a framework.

CONVERSIONS AND RESTATEMENTS

The problems of single-sentence conversions have been discussed at length
in Chapter 4. Since they are to be found in any textbook, examples of all
the different kinds will not be given here. Some will be examined in detail
to show ways in which they can be made to serve the ultimate purpose of
developing ability to write clearly, comprehensibly, and expressively.

Conversions are cognitive exercises in that they require the student to
think through the rules and select the ones applicable to the particular case
under consideration. Two of the commonest types are the following.

W32 (E)   Rewrite the following sentences replacing the singular nouns with
plurals and making all necessary changes.

1. The man goes to the field to give hay to a hungry sheep. (Expected
   conversion: The men go to the fields to give hay to hungry sheep.)

W33 (E)   Answer the following questions in the affirmative replacing the
italicized words with pronouns.

1. Does *your husband* like *the green tie*?
   (Expected conversion: Yes, he likes it.)
2. Do you know *Jane*?
   (Expected conversion: Yes, I know her.)

Students may learn to complete exercises like W32 and W33 accurately,
without there being any necessary transfer of what has been learned to
expressive writing. Some items of this type may be useful for familiarizing
students with the mechanics of these operations, but, as soon as the
students seem to have grasped the idea, they should be given a more
interesting and imaginative task like W34, which requires of them the same
types of operations in a simulated, possible situation. (After completing the
writing, they may act out the short scene they have created.)

W 34 (E or I)

1. You've just bought a camera, but unfortunately your first pictures are all dark. You go back to the shop to ask the shopkeeper to exchange it for another one. The shopkeeper doesn't believe you bought the camera in his shop and an argument develops. Write down the discussion you have with him.

This subject should elicit sentences like the following:

CUSTOMER	Excuse me. I bought this camera here last week, but it doesn't work. Look at this picture. It's all dark.
SHOPKEEPER	You didn't buy that camera here, I'm sure. I don't sell that kind. I can't do anything for you. You'll have to take it back to the shop where you bought it.
CUSTOMER	But I bought it from your wife. She recommended it because she uses one like it herself. Anyway, here is the sales slip. . . .

2. You've just bought two films, but unfortunately they're the wrong size. You have a similar experience: the shopkeeper tells you he didn't sell you the films because he doesn't keep that size. Write down the discussion between you.

Possible discussion:

CUSTOMER	Excuse me. I bought these films here on Saturday, but they're the wrong size. Will you change them, please.
SHOPKEEPER	You didn't buy those films here. I don't sell films like that. I'm afraid I can't do anything about it. You'll have to take them back to the shop where you bought them. . . .

* Take from a textbook an exercise for converting conditional clauses from one tense to another (e.g., *If I see you, I'll take your picture* for conversion into *If I saw you, I'd take your picture* or *If I'd seen you, I'd have taken your picture*), then work out a more imaginative exercise which would elicit these types of conversions in a creative framework.

A conversion becomes a *restatement* when it retains the general form of the original, but the changes made are more than mere switches from singular to plural, from nouns to pronouns, from statement to question, or from affirmative to negative. W35 below is a conversion and W36 is a

restatement using the same basic material. (For Steinbeck's original statements, see W36.)

W 35 (1)   Steinbeck says that the poor immigrants arriving in the United States
wanted a better life for their children.

No longer, he says, would the children be like their parents and live as
they did. They would be better, they would live better, they would know
more, they would dress more richly, and if possible they would change from
their father's trade to a profession.

Write out these hopes as direct instructions in the future tense from the
father to his children, beginning: "You will no longer be like your
parents."

W 36 (1)   Steinbeck writes of the deep desire of poor immigrants arriving in the
United States for a better life for their children.

"No longer," he says, "was it even acceptable that the child should be
like his parents and live as they did; he must be better, live better, know
more, dress more richly, and if possible change from his father's trade to a
profession. . . ."[1]

You are an immigrant from Calabria in Italy. Write a letter to your old
mother at home telling her your aspirations for Sergio and Maria in their
new homeland.

The restatement comes closer to *composition* or *expressive writing,*
when W36 is followed by W37.

W 37 (1)   You have read Steinbeck's account of the aspirations of poor immigrants to New York. How would you describe the hopes of the "home-
steaders" who moved west to establish farms in the interior of the United
States in the nineteenth century?

SENTENCE MODIFICATION

Flexibility in writing means being able to make a sentence say what you
want it to say and to say it vividly, humorously, poignantly, obliquely, or
succinctly.

W 38 The simple notion: *I want to go with you* can be expressed with all kinds
of nuances:

I'm coming too!
Of course, I'll come with you.

I'll most certainly accompany you.
It'll be a pleasure to go with you.
Please don't go without me!

Or the notion *I can't go with you*:

I would naturally love to go with you, but unfortunately . . .
It isn't that I don't want to go with you, but . . .
Don't wait for *me*!
Sorry!

PRACTICE IN TYPES OF SENTENCES

Students should learn early to try to express similar ideas in different forms
from various points of view. One amusing way to do this is to take a
particular situation and ask the students to express the reactions of a
number of people to it.

W39 (E or I)   A young doctor hurries out of a hospital and quickly crosses a
narrow street which is filled with rush-hour traffic. This rash action pro-
vokes comments from all kinds of people. What do you think the following
people said? (Follow the indications given.)

The doctor's wife (exclamation, order, question)
Policeman (question)
A child to her mother (question, observation)
A bus driver (question, observation)
A pedestrian to the policeman (question, observation)
A young man on a motorcycle (exclamation)
An old lady to the child (order, question)
A shopkeeper from the door of his shop (observation)

Since what is written is intended to be read, students may copy down
the comments they have proposed for W39 as one side of a dialogue,
exchange papers with other students, and complete the dialogues for
acting out.
One side of the dialogue might read:

W40 The doctor's wife: Derek! Derek! Do come back! Do you want to kill
yourself?

. . . .

Policeman: Who's that idiot rushing across the road between the lights?

. . . .

Child to her mother: Can we cross now? That man did.

. . . .

Bus driver: Did you see that nut? He's crazy!

. . . .

Pedestrian to policeman: Can't I cross now? The traffic's not moving.

. . . .

Combinations

If students are to write well they must be shaken out of the shelter of the simple sentence and the compound sentence with *and* and *but*. One way of eliciting complex sentences from students has been the combination exercise.

W 41 (E)   Combine the following pairs of sentences into one by using relative pronouns.

1. I went to visit the Indian artist.
   He painted the Taj Mahal.
   (Expected combination: I went to visit the Indian artist who painted the Taj Mahal.)

2. My aunt made the soup.
   I ate the soup.
   (Expected combination: I ate the soup [that] my aunt made.)

or (E) Combine the following sets of sentences into one sentence without using *and* or *but*.

3. Do you see that policeman?
   He is stopping the cars.
   He is letting the old lady cross the road.
   (Expected combination: Do you see that policeman stopping the cars to let the old lady cross the road?)

   Too many of these become busywork exercises. After a few examples, the students know what is expected of them and their energies are taken up with "completing the set."
   A more interesting approach which challenges the student's ingenuity is as follows.

W 42 (E)   Students are asked to think of simple sentences—any simple sentences. These are written on the chalkboard in the order in which they are supplied. Students are then given time, singly, in pairs, or in groups, to combine these sentences in any way they like to make a sensible paragraph.

No simple sentences may be used and only one *and* and one *but* for joining clauses are permissible in each paragraph. Adverbs, adjectives, and a few phrases may be added to improve the narrative.

Below is an example of how the procedure might work.

Sentences provided by students:

The man leaves the house.
The baker sells bread.
A cat chases a mouse.
The dog barks.
The mother scolds her little boy.
The little boy drops his toys.
Santa Claus kisses the children.

Possible paragraph:

The baker sells bread during the day, but at night he puts on a red suit and a white beard and leaves the house to play Santa Claus at the shopping center. He kisses the little children before he gives them toys. Suddenly a dog barks because it sees a black cat chasing a tiny mouse. As a little boy is rushing over to see the cat he drops his toys. His mother who is very upset scolds her little boy in front of Santa Claus.

Contractions

Writing in English can be made more concise and succinct if certain clauses are reduced to phrases (*before he began the lecture—before beginning the lecture; because they made mistakes—because of their mistakes*) and some phrases reduced to single words (*the man who drives the cab—the cab driver; the person who committed the crime—the criminal*). Instead of giving students a series of disconnected sentences to contract in specific ways, the teacher may provide a complete passage and ask students to use their ingenuity to reduce its length by at least a third without omitting any of the information it contains.

Expansions

Students should have many opportunities to expand simple statements by using all the variations they have been learning—to flex their writing muscles as it were. Most textbooks provide a number of expansion exercises, but these are usually very dull affairs. Sometimes a list of adjectives is set down beside a series of simple sentences and students are asked to expand the sentences by inserting adjectives from the list. In other cases, the student is given a series of adverbs or adverbial phrases and asked to expand a set of simple sentences by inserting these at the appropriate places. Students may complete these exercises dutifully, but it is doubtful whether they thereby improve their ability to write in the language, since they contribute nothing of their own invention to the task. Most of the cognitive learning involved in these tasks can be accomplished as effectively or at least more briskly in the types of oral exercises described in Chapter 4.

Even if staid exercises like those described above appear in an imposed textbook, teachers should be prepared to think up more imaginative ways of presenting the same material. Writing assignments should be interesting, amusing, or useful—never boring or trivial.

Below are some suggestions for creative approaches to the same problems.

Expanding with adjectives. Students can be handed a passage like C58 and asked to describe the scene in San Francisco the morning after the snowfall as it appeared to different people.

W 43 (I)   San Francisco has had its biggest snowfall in 89 years. It came as a great surprise. The drought had been so bad that ranchers had had to sell off their cattle before they were ready and farmers had lost three hundred million dollars in crops. San Francisco Roman Catholics had been asked yesterday to pray for rain. This morning it was snowing hard and a couple of feet of snow covered the Sierra Nevada mountains where the ski resorts had been paralyzed for most of the season. Now it is beginning to rain.

Clearly this heavy snowfall is a blessing to some and a nasty inconvenience to others. As a reporter for a San Francisco newspaper, you are trying to give a rounded picture of different people's reactions to the snow. Write a report for your paper describing in their own words how the scene looked to a farmer, a cab driver, a ski instructor, and a Roman Catholic priest whom you interviewed. Use as many adjectives and adjectival constructions as you can to make your report vivid for your readers.

Expanding with adverbs.

W 44 (I)   Your neighbor's wife sings loudly when she's taking a shower in the mornings, but unfortunately not everyone appreciates her singing. Describe how the following people react to this phenomenon. (Take "she sings" as your basic sentence frame and show the differences in viewpoint by your use of adverbs and adverbial expressions indicating where, when, how, and why.)

    1. The lady's husband talks to her boss about it.
    2. Her son tells a school friend about it.

    3. You talk about it to your hairdresser.
    4. The cleaning woman tells a neighbor.
    5. The mailman talks to his wife.

Possible answer 5: That lady at 115 Chestnut Street sings so loudly when she's taking a shower that I can hear her quite distinctly from the front of the house. She sings flat too!

Expanding frames. Sometimes students are asked to expand what have been called *dehydrated sentences.*

W 45 (E or I) Write out the following outline in complete sentences in the past tense, supplying any words missing and making all necessary changes. Capital letters indicate new sentences and proper names. Insert appropriate punctuation marks.

    / summer vacation / be / here / last / Eva / mother / wake / up early / morning / that she / be not / late / She / know / she / hurry / because /train / be / leave / at seven / sharp / Just / Eva / put / her coat / she / hear / horn outside / There / be / cab / mother / call / Be / you ready

W 46 Unraveled, the passage reads as follows:

    The summer vacation was here at last. Eva's mother woke her up early that morning so that she wouldn't be late. She knew she should hurry because the train would be leaving at seven o'clock sharp. Just as Eva was putting on her coat she heard a horn outside. "There's the cab," her mother called. "Are you ready?"

This format can be useful for testing ability to introduce grammatical features at required points in the sentence, although the same kinds of demands are made by the cloze procedure within a framework which is much closer to normal language. (Cf. W28.)

W 47 _____ summer vacation _____ here _____ last. Eva _____ mother _____ her up early _____ morning so _____ she _____ not be late. She knew she _____ hurry because _____ train _____ be leaving at seven _____ sharp. Just _____ Eva was _____ on her coat she _____ a horn outside. "_____ the cab," _____ mother _____. "_____ you ready?"

Commentary

A few more grammatical features are supplied for the student in W47 than in W45 and there are several places which allow for more than one possibility, but these are not necessarily undesirable features. In W45, students may become confused by the number of decisions they have to make. W47 does not have the distortions of English which are imposed by the W45 format.

Because of their artificiality, dehydrated sentences can become something of a chore, and therefore counter-productive. A note of reality is added if the dehydrated frame is presented in the form of *news headlines* or *telegrams* for expansion.

Fortunately, there is available in the real world a type of script which resembles the dehydrated sentence but which gives students authentic contact with many aspects of life in English-speaking countries, namely, the *classified advertisements* (*ads*) in the daily newspapers. One copy of any leading big-city newspaper published in English (the Sunday *New York Times* or the *Daily Telegraph*, for instance) will supply the teacher with several thousand items from which to draw, dealing with everything from positions vacant, apartments to let, cars and animals for sale, lost property, or vacation opportunities. The less abbreviated classified advertisements supply useful clues for the interpretation of the more abbreviated.

W 48 (I)   Write out in full the following advertisements from the *Boston Globe*[2] for apartments for rent. Study their location on a map, then write a letter in English to a friend telling him or her about the advantages of the various apartments and why you decided to rent one rather than the others.

1. CAMBRIDGE, 5 min. fr. Harvard Sq., lux. & moderate studios, 1, 2 & 3-bdrm apts., ht & hw, air cond., dishwasher & disposal, some bal. & frpls., furn. or unfurn., pkg avail. $190 & up. 547-1250.

2. BRIGHTON, 1/2 mo. rent free, new mod. lge. 2 bdrm apts., a/c, terr., walk to stores & buses, 1 min. to Storrow Dr. and Mass. Pike, close to Harv. Bus. Schl., MIT, BU. Avail. now to Sept 1, $290–$315 inclu. utils. & pkg. No dogs. Owner 232-8659, 787-4936.

3. ARLINGTON HEIGHTS, mod. 1st flr., 2 bdrms, dinrm, WW. livrm., c.t. bath, d&d, kit. w. refrig., parking, lease, sec. dep. req., avail. 9/1, $275 unhtd. Owner, 646-3652.

At the advanced level, such ads can be used as the basis for a practical writing project. Students can learn a great deal from the advertisements for positions vacant.

W 49 1. RN—Sat. & Sun. Excell. wkend position, 16 bed pre/post op. unit for mentally retarded, pediatric thru geriatric. EXCELLENT SALARY. Conv.

to Route 128, Waltham. Free pkg. Call 891-2817. E. Kennedy Shriver Ctr. An equal oppty. employer M/F.

2. Sales Engineer—Expanding 25 yr. old leading instrument manufacturer is rounding out select 25 persons national sales force with high paying, growth potential openings for Technical Sales, representative in New England states and New York City areas. Need successful professionals who can interact w. management as well as product users on individ. and gp. levels. Need Technical Associates degree or equiv. in exp. plus familiarity with instruments. Min. 2 yrs sales exp. and ability to travel. Fixed territory selling of Transistor testers to estab. distributors. Excel. income, weekly draw against commissions, expense account plus bonus and company benefits includ. profit sharing. Send resume to H30, Globe office.

3. Teachers. Cert. reqd, New Eng., Libr, Math, Sci, LD, Eng, Mus, Phys, Rdg, Health, Girls PE, Chem, Spec Ed, Hear. Speech Ther, Sch Psych, Art, Agri, Span/Eng, Guid, Fr/Span, Exp'd Elem, Bus Ed. Many vocational—others. Teachers Agency, (603) 772-3962.[3]

From a number of such advertisements, students can make lists of the kinds of qualities and qualifications which appear to be important to employers in different occupations. (They can also learn a great deal about American and British business approaches and advertising techniques.) They may then list in English the qualifications they feel they possess, select an appropriate advertisement, and write an application for the position advertised.

THE IDEA FRAME

Dehydrated sentences and cloze tests control the structures the students will use. Some experienced teachers feel that progress toward expressive writing is more rapid if content rather than structure is controlled.[4] The students, relieved of the complete responsibility for the development of the content, can concentrate their energies on vigorous writing and can experiment with various possibilities for expressing an idea. (In this sense, the advertisements of W48 and W49 can be considered idea frames.)

1. The idea frame may be related to current reading. For instance, the reading passage, R36, may be taken as a basis for writing activities. Here we have a new student who is not like his classmates and has not had the same opportunities for education that they have had. The following idea frames can be developed from the passage.

W 50 (1)   A questionnaire is developed in such a way that, when it is answered consecutively, it produces a coherent paragraph:

1. What did Nip do during the break?
2. Who came over to ask him questions?
3. What kinds of questions did they ask him?
4. How did Nip respond?
5. What did they want him to do?
6. Why did Carol make fun of him?
7. How did the students react to Carol's remarks?
8. Did they persuade Nip to join them?

A set of questions like this provides the students with a developing situation and some essential vocabulary. It should not, however, be the final stage. The students should then be asked to write creatively, thus reusing language material they have just acquired in new ways to express their own ideas.

W 51 (1)   In this story we see Nip from the outside. Tell in Nip's own words how he felt and what he thought during this incident.

2. Stevick's microtexts can provide useful idea frames (see Chapter 2, p. 53). After a text has been discussed orally, students may be asked to describe a similar situation in which they found themselves, the implications for their particular situation of the arguments in the text, the reasons why they could not agree with the writer of the text, and so on.

3. The land of make-believe. The students as a group invent an imaginary setting as a background for some of their writing activities.

W 52 (E, I, or A)   The students *invent a country*, give it a name (*Wallamalla*), design its map, describe its history, its economy, its living conditions, and its problems with its neighbors. (If the class in working in small groups, each group has its own country and displays its map prominently on its section of the bulletin board.) From time to time, they write about events which affect the *Republic of Wallamalla.*

—Wallamalla has plans to set up a new university outside of the capital city. Explain why Wallamalla needs another university. Describe in detail the proposal for the new university and the reactions of the students of the old University of Wallamalla to the establishment of a rival institution.
—The Republic of Wallamalla is in danger! The Kingdom of Birovia has just declared war and invaded our eastern provinces! Write down the

news bulletins broadcast by Radio Wallamalla during the first three days of this emergency.

W53 (E or I)   The students *invent a family* and keep a copy of all the data: number of children and their names, ages, and interests, cousins, aunts, and uncles, where they live, what they do for a living and what they enjoy doing in their leisure, their friends, neighbors, and pets, some of their well-remembered joys and misfortunes, and their hopes and plans for the future. They occasionally tackle problems like the following:

> Aunt Lucinda who lives in a little town in the south has just announced that she intends to marry her neighbor, a retired gentleman of 82. She is 79. Write down for posterity the letters relating to this affair (letters from her niece, from her godson, from her fiancé, the replies she wrote, etc.).

W54 (E)   For the elementary level, a *treasure island* is a fruitful notion. The students themselves will provide plenty of ideas for bringing it into existence and for projects associated with it. If the class is divided into groups, each group may use the same island but have its own theories on where and how the treasure is hidden.[5]

INTEGRATED LANGUAGE ACTIVITIES WITHIN AN IDEA FRAME

Writing with visual

1. (E or I)   *Objects*. Students are shown some object and asked to write a *concise description* which would distinguish it from all other objects, e.g., a pencil, a book, an eraser, or a window. The descriptions are read out in class and other students try to show how the descriptions could apply to different objects. The written description is then further refined to meet these objections.

Variation. (E) An adaptation of *Kim's Game*. Students are shown briefly a tray of jumbled objects. Each student may look at the tray for one minute. Students then list as many objects as they can remember with a short descriptive comment, e.g., *a white handkerchief with blue flowers*. Students read out their lists with descriptions and discuss the objects they forgot.

2. (E or I)   *Persons*. Students write descriptions of no more than two sentences in length of persons in the class, in school, in the news, on television, or pictured in the textbook. No names are given. The descriptions written by one group are circulated to other groups who try to guess who has been described.

3. (E or I) *Pictures.* Students bring to class pictures selected from magazines or newspapers. Photographs of unexpected situations are useful. These are distributed at random. Students write anecdotes, descriptions, or explanations about the pictures which are then read to the class. Students may correct their versions as they read them, while other students suggest improvements. The students then rewrite their versions for grading. Students select by vote the most interesting compositions which will be posted, with the picture, on the bulletin board or reproduced in the class newspaper.

4. (E or I) *Cartoons.* Students working in pairs are given cartoon strips without balloons or captions. The students write the captions for their series of sketches, developing the story line. For this, they use *written forms* of English. They then exchange cartoons and write balloon dialogue for the characters in each other's stories (using *spoken forms* of English). Pairs work together in perfecting their cartoons which are later displayed on the bulletin board for the amusement of the rest of the class. (Note: single-picture cartoons are more difficult since they require witty comments. These may be used at the advanced level.)

5. (I or A) *Films.* Short silent films and documentary sound films may be used to stimulate written composition. For second-language learners, television serials are useful and students may be given homework assignments related to these.

Writing with speaking and listening

Many activities are listed in C67, under Writing. To these may be added the following:

1. (E or I) The composition is given orally and discussed with other students before being written in its final form. (See *Oral Reports* in Chapter 1.)

2. (E or I) After students have acted out dialogues they have studied, they write, singly or in groups, original dialogues which recombine the material in new situations. They then act their dialogues for the rest of the class.

3. (E or I) Students are given a partial dialogue, that is, with the utterances of one participant but not the other. They make up the other half of the dialogue so that it fits in with the half supplied. (See also *Situation Tapes* in Chapter 1.) They then act out their different versions. (Originality and whimsicality are encouraged.)

4. (E or I) Activities 1, 2, and 3 in the section *Writing with Visual,* p. 309, may be performed orally.

5. (E or I) *Gossip.* This is an old party game which makes an amusing writing exercise for groups of eight or less. The eight questions below are typed on a sheet with plenty of space, not only for the written answer but also to allow the paper to be turned back to hide what has been written.

Student A answers the first question, turns back the sheet to hide the answer, and passes the sheet to Student B, who does likewise with the second question. The paper is passed on for all eight questions. Each student in the group begins a sheet, so that up to eight sheets can be circulating at once. When the last questions have been answered, the papers are unfolded and the incongruous results are read to the group.

Questions:

1. Who?
2. Met whom?
3. Where?
4. What did he say?
5. What did she reply?
6. What did they do?
7. What was the result?
8. What moral can you draw from this incident?

6. (I or A) *Rigmarole.* This is also played in groups. Each person is given a sheet of paper on which is written the opening sentence of a story. The recipients read what is written and add a sentence of their own. The papers are then circulated around the group, with each student adding a sentence to each story. The last student in each case writes a concluding sentence and gives the story a title. The completed stories are then read aloud to the group. The results are frequently hilarious.

7. (I or A) *What's your opinion?* Students bring in information on current controversial issues which they present to the class. After class discussion of the data and the problem, students write out their own opinions on the issue, with any supporting information they have been able to find. They then present this viewpoint orally to the class, or to a small group, as a basis for further discussion. In a second-language situation, this preparation is then put to use by inviting to the class proponents of both sides of the issue to participate in an open discussion with the now well-informed students.

8. (E) Students listen to a story on tape or as told to them by the teacher or an advanced student. They then write the story out in their own words, adding embellishments in keeping with the theme as they wish.

9. (I or A) Students take a story they have been reading, rewrite it in simple English, then tell the story to an elementary class.

10. (I or A) Students interview in English visiting speakers of English, or local residents who speak English, about their special interests and then write up the interview for the class newspaper or the bulletin board. If the school newspaper can be persuaded to print the interview in English, this will arouse the curiosity of other students about language study. (If no native speakers are available, a fellow teacher of English agrees to be interviewed in English on some hobby or special interest.) In a

second-language situation, this type of activity is assigned frequently to encourage the students to use their increasing command of English for useful purposes in personal contact with members of the English-speaking community.

11. (E or I)   Students are given a skeleton outline with blanks of a lecture, discussion, interview, story, or play they are to hear on tape. (At the elementary level, the outline may be like C57; at the intermediate level it will omit segments of vital information.) After listening, students either complete the outline or use it as a guide in writing up their own account of what they heard.

12. (I or A)   Students listen to interviews with or speeches by political leaders, national figures, artists, or writers. They make notes on what they have heard; they complete their notes in group discussion with other listeners; finally, they use the material they have noted in a research project.

13. (I or A)   Students complete a written research project on a leading personality from an English-speaking country. After this has been presented to the class and discussed, the students listen to a speech by, or interview with, this personality.

14. (I or A)   Students watch an English-language documentary film and use the information in it for a written research project.

15. (E)   *Writing with listening at the beginning stage:* Postovsky[6] reports an experiment in which adult students of Russian performed written drills from spoken input, without speaking themselves, for one month of intensive study (six hours per day with additional homework). They heard only native speakers. After one month, they were superior in morphology and also in pronunciation to the regular audiolingual group. This approach is not necessarily transferable to other age groups and other situations, but it has interesting implications.

Writing with reading

Some suggestions have already been given in the section *Integrating the Language Skills* in Chapter 7. To be able to write well, students need to read widely, thus familiarizing themselves with the way recognized writers write in English. They must, through much experience with written texts, develop their ability to assimilate information directly in English and to think in English so that their writing acquires the rhythms and associations of the English-language writer.

1. (E or I)   Students rework the linguistic material of a story by rewriting it from the viewpoint of a different character, or from the changed perspective of one of the characters when writing in retrospect. R56 may be rewritten as a discussion between the vicar and one of the young Eskimoes returning to the village for Christmas after a year away at school. Other reading passages may provide a format through which the

students can treat an analogous situation, e.g., R67 could provide ideas for a parallel discussion of the place of television in the American family.

2. (I or A)   After careful reading of a text, students sum up its main thrust by giving it a title. They then identify the *main topics* and trace *the development of thought* through each paragraph. The processes associated with C52, C53, and C54 may be applied at this point. The students set down the main ideas in a logical sequence in simple active declarative sentences. This skeleton outline is then put away. Another day, the students take the outline and write a text of their own from it. They then compare their text with the original to see what they can learn linguistically from the comparison.

3. (I or A)   The appropriate use of *logical connectives* is a problem in writing a new language, yet it is essential to the coherent development of ideas. This subject is discussed in Chapter 7, R50 and R51. The procedure in R51 can be applied to full paragraphs and to a reasoned argument of several paragraphs in length.

4. (I or A)   An excellent intellectual and linguistic exercise is the *résumé* or *summary*: the gathering together of the main ideas of the text in succinct form. This is a useful art in this busy age. To do this well, students have to understand the text fully and rethink it in concentrated terms which they express in English. Applied to sophisticated texts, this is certainly an advanced-level activity, but it can be practiced with less complicated texts at the intermediate level. An even more demanding activity is the *précis* which requires that the passage be expressed in other words at about one-third of its original length.

5. (I or A)   Writing can be associated with *rapid reading*. Students need to learn to skim through informational material to draw from it the specific facts they require for some definite project. For this, they are given a set of questions beforehand and a specified period of time to find and write down the information from a long article or a chapter of a book.

(E)   This approach can be used also with narrative material for *extensive reading* as soon as students begin to read longer passages for pleasure. It can also serve as a familiarization process before the students study sections of the material in detail.

6. (I or A)   Where students are encouraged to read English-language articles and books of their own choice from an extensive reading library, they should also be expected to write short *reactions* of a paragraph or two to what they have read. These brief communications should not be stereotyped book reports or summaries of the content, but quite personal, reflecting the concern of the student with some aspect of the material: information gained from it, or imaginative ideas derived from the reading. The most interesting of these may, with the writer's permission, be posted on the bulletin board to encourage or discourage other students from

choosing the same reading material. (This moves beyond the frame to expressive writing.)

7. (I)   The cloze procedure can be used for introductory courses in *literature* for redeveloping sensitivity to the author's choice of a particular word in preference to other semantic alternatives. As Benamou has explained, this process involves both structure and divergence from that structure. Structure is present when the context of the whole text makes it possible to fill in a missing element with little effort. Understanding the total organization is the main concern. Divergence occurs when the gap is filled by an unexpected element of the author's choosing. And it is this divergence between what the reader expects and what the author says which provides a measure of the style.[7]

8. (A)   Further sensitivity to literary style can be encouraged at the advanced level by attempts at writing short passages in imitation of the style and approach of particular authors.

9. Further suggestions will be found later in this chapter in *Normal Purposes of Writing,* 3 and 4.

Writing with reading, speaking and listening

(I or A)   Second-language learners listen for several weeks to a *television serial* or a *situation comedy series,* discussing the characters and their problems in class after each episode. They are then asked to write a probable continuation for next week's episode of the serial (or a new situation development for the comedy series), either as a narrative script or in dialogue form. They are expected to respect the relationships, personalities, and present situation of the characters. Copies of these episodes are circulated for reading among the members of the class, who discuss the accuracy of representation and probability of the episode in the light of what they know from the original series. The most interesting and amusing episodes are then acted out in class by groups of students. As a continuation, groups of students invent their own soap operas, with personalities of their own choosing, and write regular instalments which they act out in class.

PRACTICE IN STYLES OF WRITING (A)

Arapoff has suggested a format within which students may practice various styles of writing. Taking the content of a simple dialogue, students are encouraged to rewrite it in the form of direct address, narration, paraphrase, summary, factual analysis, assertion, in essay form, as argumentative analysis, with evaluation of the argument, as a critical review which objectively examines the validity of the evidence, and as a term paper. This interesting approach should be studied in the original article, "Writing: A Thinking Process."[8]

Shortening Arapoff's sequence somewhat, the teacher would proceed as follows.

1. Students would be given a short *dialogue* like W55 as foundational content.

W55   BILL   Hi, Mary.
      MARY   Hi.
      BILL   Where are you going?
      MARY   To the beach. Why don't you come along?
      BILL   I think it's going to rain. Look at those clouds.
      MARY   It *can't* rain again today! It's rained every day this week.

2. Next students rewrite W55 as *direct address* in a narrative framework.

W56   "Hi, Mary," said Bill.
      "Hi," the girl answered.
      "Where are you going?" he asked.
      "To the beach," Mary replied. "Why don't you come along?"
      "I think it's going to rain." Bill pointed. "Look at those clouds."
      "It can't rain again today!" his friend exclaimed. "It's rained every day this week."

3. Students then write a paraphrase of W55 in *narrative form*.

W57   Bill greeted Mary.
      Mary greeted Bill.
      He asked her where she was going.
      She said that she was going to the beach. She asked Bill to go along.
      He answered that he thought it was going to rain. He told Mary to look at the clouds.
      Mary said that it couldn't rain again that day. It had rained every day that week.

4. This is followed by a *summary* written very concisely in one or two sentences.

W58   When Mary asked Bill to go to the beach with her, he said that he thought it was going to rain, and told her to look at the clouds. However, she said that it couldn't rain again that day since it had rained every day that week.

5. Next, the main argument of the passage is set out in the form of an *assertion*.

W 59 Bill and Mary had opposite ideas about the weather: he was a pessimist and she was an optimist.

6. Finally, this analysis leads to a short *essay* on optimists and pessimists.

W 60 Write a short essay on the subject: The Pessimist versus the Optimist.

7. The further steps proposed by Arapoff—*argumentative analysis, evaluation of the arguments, critical review* of the essay, and *term paper*—would require a careful study of styles of writing. The complete project would be a very interesting undertaking for the student of English who must learn at some stage to write various kinds of essays, seminar and term papers, and even critical reviews for undergraduate and graduate courses in the English medium and also for English majors or concentrators in a foreign-language setting.

IV. Expressive writing or composition

If we wish students to write English spontaneously, we must give them opportunities to acquire confidence in their ability to write. We must, however, expect shavings on the floor in the process. Learning to write is not a natural development like learning to speak. As Arapoff has observed: "Everyone who is a native speaker is not necessarily a 'native writer'."[9]

Our students will have varying degrees of interest in writing as a form of self-expression, even in their native language. If they are to submit willingly to the discipline of learning to write well in English, they will need to see some *purpose in the writing activity*. In this way writing is differently motivated from speaking, which is an activity in which most people readily and frequently engage every day of their lives. In speaking, students without much to contribute can often adroitly involve others and support them enough, with their attention and interest, to free themselves of the necessity to participate fully. (This support function is a normal form of communicative involvement which the student of a new language should also learn to fulfill acceptably.) Faced with a blank page, however, the unimaginative student does not have this alternative.

Personality plays an important role in writing, as it does in speaking. Some feel inhibited as soon as they take pen in hand, although they might have expressed themselves orally without inhibitions. These students need a clearly defined topic, often an opening sentence, or even a framework, to get them started. Just as some are terse in speech, others are incapable of being expansive in writing—they do not waste words and elaborate the obvious. These students find it hard to write a full paragraph, or a complete composition, on something as irrelevant to their preoccupations as "What I did last weekend" or "A day on a farm." We must not forget that there are also some students who are most reluctant to expose their real thoughts on paper, sometimes because, in their experience, teachers have never really cared what they thought. In speech they can be vague, whereas in written English this is rarely acceptable, except in poetry. For them, also, writing as a class exercise is unappealing.

In the second-language situation, these problems may be compounded by the fact that some students, in an adult basic education or bilingual class particularly, have had little or no experience with writing in their first language. Teachers should ascertain facts like these about their students' backgrounds and begin practice in writing at the most obviously useful level, related specifically to the immediate needs of the students. They should draw explicitly on what the students know most about and link writing closely to some purposeful project until the students gain confidence in expressing themselves in the graphic mode.

For these reasons among others, we cannot expect all of our students to achieve a high standard of expressive writing in our language class. For many, we will be satisfied if they are able to write what they want or need to say with clarity and precision.

There are students, of course, who enjoy writing, and these will want to write from the beginning. Many of them will have already acquired a style of writing in their first language which has been praised and encouraged. Such students often feel frustrated when they find they cannot express themselves in the new language at the same level of sophistication as they do in the old. In their efforts to do so, they often load their writing with poorly disguised translations of their native-language expression. The enthusiasm of these students must be encouraged, while they are guided to see that writing well in another language means thinking in the forms of that other language. This does not mean just the adoption of its semantic distinctions and syntactic structures, but also its approach to logic and the development of an idea. Even in writing style, there are culturally acquired differences.[10] A student whose native culture encourages allusive and indirect rhetorical development finds it hard to be explicit, just as one who has learned to express ideas by building logical step on logical step finds it difficult to indulge in what seem to be digressions from the line of thought. Even students who are natural writers need guidance in adapting to the rhetorical style of a new language.

WHAT WRITING MAY BE CALLED "EXPRESSIVE"?

"Expressive" writing does not necessarily mean imaginative or poetic writing. Not all students have the gift of imagination. Writing is expressive if it says what the student wants it to say in the situation. If writing is to be a natural, self-directed activity, the student must have the choice between writing for practical purposes or creating a work of imagination. Even where guidance is offered—that is, where students are given a structure and facts on which to base their writing—they should always have the privilege of ignoring what is offered if they can write from their own inner inspiration.

What is needed is writing for the *normal purposes of writing,* not just as a self-contained language exercise. In a diversified English language program,[11] students have the opportunity to concentrate on the use of English for specific purposes: the reading of contemporary informational materials, concentrated aural-oral development, the study of literature, translation or simultaneous interpretation, the learning of special skills through English (e.g., sports, photography, music, or art), or the acquiring of certain subject matters taught in English (e.g., American or British history and political institutions, biology, chemistry, or whatever other discipline concerns them). Clearly, then, what is "expressive" in such cases depends on the student's own goals.

Except in specialized or bilingual programs, where students learn to write in the language in order to study in the same classes as English speakers, writing should not be a distinctive activity. It should, rather, be a natural ingredient in ongoing activities. Since one writes better in a language on a subject which one has experienced in that language, students more inclined to the practical should have experiences learning in English about practical things, while imaginative topics will spring naturally out of experiences (whether graphic, aural, or visual) with literature of the imagination and other artistic manifestations of the creative mind.

NORMAL PURPOSES OF WRITING

These will be organized in six categories under two main headings: *Practical* (everyday living, social contact, getting and giving information, study purposes) and *Creative* (entertainment, self-expression).

Practical use

1. *Everyday living.*

a. *Forms and applications.* Students learn to fill in customs declarations, passport applications, entry permits, identity information, and applications for positions. In a second-language situation, this becomes a very important area and learners of English can render a real service, while improving their own command of the language, by seeking out monolingual speakers of their native language who are immigrants, transient workers, or temporary residents in order to help them to fill in social security, medical, or welfare claims and credit applications, and complete income tax returns.

b. *Arrangements and records.* Students should know how to write notes and notices setting out arrangements for travel, meetings, lectures, concerts, dances, weekend excursions, or competitions. They should be able to write up short accounts of activities for English-language club records or for the class or school newspaper.

c. *Orders and complaints.* Students should know how to order goods and services, and how to protest errors in shipping or billing, shoddy quality of goods, or neglect of services. They should be able to write for hotel rooms, information on study abroad, or subscriptions to newspapers and magazines. They should know the correct formulas for commercial and official correspondence of various kinds. These can all be given a realistic twist by basing them on information in newspapers and tourist pamphlets. Students may write, for instance, to the Chamber of Commerce, Tourist Information Center, or the university or public library in the town in which they are interested and request information for friends and relatives, if not for themselves, or for use with a research project.

2. *Social contact.* Students should learn the correct formulas for congratulations and various greetings, and ways of notifying others of family events or changes of circumstances. They should be encouraged to use this knowledge by sending such greetings and announcements to friends and correspondents or displaying them on the bulletin board.

Students should be encouraged to write to correspondents in English-speaking countries. In the foreign-language situation, classes should be twinned with English-speaking classes of a similar level in English-speaking countries, so that they may exchange projects giving personal, local, and national information, illustrating youth trends and customs, and describing ways of spending leisure time, and so on.

3. *Getting and giving information.* Students gather information for projects, collate it, and report it to others in written form. They prepare comments in writing on controversial articles in newspapers and magazines for later presentation as oral reports or for circulation in the class as a basis for discussion. They may take articles reporting the same event from two English-language newspapers (or discussing the same topic from two magazines), and write résumés of the content for discussion in class. They may prepare items of international, national, local, or school news for wall, class, or school newspapers. They may take turns in preparing weekly bulletins of news from English-language newspapers, or newscasts, for their own class and for distribution to more junior classes. They distribute similarly reviews of English-language films which are being shown at school or in the local area.

4. *Study purposes.* Students who intend to make English a major study need practice in taking notes of lectures and of reading material. They should know how educated native speakers of English develop a line of thought. They need to be able to write good abstracts, reports, essays, literary analyses, and term papers.

Creative expression

5. *Entertainment*. Students write skits, one-act plays, or scripts for their own radio and television programs (which may be taped or shown on closed-circuit television for the entertainment of other classes). They write out program notes for a fashion parade, or captions for a display of students' baby pictures or unidentified photographs of famous people. They write parodies of well-known advertisements or radio and television commercials. They prepare puzzles and mystery stories for other members of the class to solve.

6. *Self-expression*. Students write stories, poems, nonsense rhymes, nursery rhymes, biological sketches, and autobiographical narratives. They keep personal records of their thoughts and experiences as resources from which to draw material for creative writing. (A good starting-point for the inexperienced, or those lacking in confidence, is the writing of a story, poem, or autobiographical incident in the style of an author they have just been reading.)

WRITING AS A CRAFT

Even with motivation to express oneself in written form, coherent, readable material does not necessarily flow from the pen. Nor is such writing merely a matter of composing carefully constructed grammatical sentences. Lucid writing is only possible when writers have clarified their own thinking on the subject and know how they wish to present their viewpoint or develop their argument. The ideas may be obscure, even esoteric or hermetic, but the writers themselves know that this is what they want to say and their readers try to penetrate their thought. Muddled thinking, however, leaves readers confused and frustrated.

Arapoff calls the process basic to writing "purposeful selection and organization of experience."[12] If one of the objectives of the English course is ability to write well and expressively in English, then the teacher must guide the students in developing their skills in analyzing their thoughts, shaping them into central and subordinate ideas, and developing lines of thought which carry their readers to the heart of the matter. The English teacher cannot presume that the students already know these things from some other course.

How can we interest students in the process of reflecting on what they really want to say and organizing it before starting to write? This initial stage becomes more attractive as a group experience. The students in the group pool their ideas, break off to gather more information if necessary, discuss various ways of organizing their ideas into a central line of thought, with major topics and subordinate ideas related to these major topics. They decide on a title to express the central theme, a way of introducing the material so that the reader's attention is caught, and the type of conclusion to which they will direct the development of thought. The actual writing is then done in small groups (or individually, if there are students who prefer to work alone). The draft elaboration of the theme is then discussed by the group; the choice of words is refined, and the syntactic structure is tightened up, with transitional elements supplied where these are still lacking. Finally the rhythm and flow of the writing receive special attention, as the completed text is read aloud. The group texts are then dittoed for presentation to and discussion by the class as a whole.

This type of group elaboration of a composition ensures some proofreading for inaccuracies of spelling and grammar. Valette[13] suggests that the group approach be used also to establish criteria for correcting and assessing the texts prepared by the groups. The students are asked to rank the compositions before them in order of preference. They then "describe which qualities they think characterize a good composition. The class might come up with categories such as: organization, good opening sentence, appropriate use of vocabulary, original imagery, etc." The class then looks over each composition and rates it on a scale decided on by themselves and weighted according to group decision. After the class has perfected its scale in relation to the actual compositions it is considering, this rating scale is adopted by the teacher for grading tests of writing. Valette's procedure has two advantages: the students consider the system fair since they participated in its design and modification, they also understand by what criteria their writing will be graded, and they have guidelines for improving their work in the future.

Some teachers will object that this system cannot ensure that all errors in the text are corrected. This is true. The question arises: for expressive writing should all inaccuracies and errors be corrected in every composition? Most of us have ourselves experienced the discouragement of staring in horror at a veritable forest of red marks and comments on a piece of writing over which we had toiled in the belief that we were achieving something worthwhile. The place for fastidious correction is at the stage of cognition and production exercises. If students are making serious errors persistently, more practice exercises should be provided at the point of difficulty. When students are writing to express their ideas, corrections should focus on incomprehensibility, inapt word choice, and errors in grammatical form or syntactic structure which mislead the reader. The most serious mistakes must be those which native readers can tolerate the least, rather than those kinds of inaccuracies which native writers themselves commit. Students can be trained to proofread their work for blemishes, as suggested in the previous chapter, but penalizing students for sheer inaccuracy of surface detail at the expressive stage encourages the production of dull, unimaginative, simple sentences, with students taking refuge in the forms they have thoroughly mastered over a long period of study.

With expressive writing, students should learn to check their completed drafts for things other than punctuation and spelling errors. They should be looking at the way their thought falls naturally into paragraphs and their use of logical connectives and other transitional devices which show the development of thought and cement internal relationships. They should seek ways to eliminate repetitions, tighten the structure through judicious use of complex and compound sentences, and highlight ideas through nuances of word choices and their combinations.

The ever-present danger of students resorting to thinly disguised native-language structure and lexicon when seeking to express their meaning in English cannot, of course, be ignored. Students should be sensitized to this problem, which is most likely to arise when the ideas they are trying to express are complex. They should be encouraged to break down a complex idea into a series of simple active affirmative declarative sentences in English which represent the facets of its meaning, and then to rebuild these into complex or compound sentences which respond to the rules of combination and modification in English as they know them. Francis Bacon said: "Reading maketh a full man, conference a ready man, and writing an exact man."[14] It is when we try to express our meaning in writing that we discover where our ideas are fuzzy or incomplete. Trying to set down the elements of our meaning in simple form pinpoints areas of confusion and uncertainty and forces us to ask ourselves what we are really trying to say. Then, and then only, can we seek the best way to express our ideas in another language.

It cannot be emphasized too strongly that students learn to write well in English by doing all the planning and drafting of their compositions, and discussion of appropriate content, *in English*. The teacher must help the students from the beginning to acquire confidence in writing directly in the new language. Where students have done their initial planning and early writing in their native language and have then translated what they wanted to say into English, the writing is usually stilted, lacking the feeling for the language and the natural flow and rhythm toward which the student should be aiming. If the flexibility measures recommended earlier in this chapter are adopted, students will have experience, even at the elementary level, in trying to express their own ideas and imaginings in English. Where the writing program is associated with oral language activities of the creative type described in Chapter 2, students begin to think in English and to compose English sentences spontaneously without nervousness or inhibition.

Correcting and evaluating expressive writing

A number of systems for grading expressive writing have been proposed, each of which has merits for particular situations or students with specific aims.

The following guidelines have emerged from the experience of many teachers.

1. One learns to write sequential prose by writing sequential prose. Practice exercises are merely muscle-flexing. What one does correctly in structured practice, one does not necessarily observe when trying to express one's own meaning.

2. It is better to draw the attention of students to a few important faults in their writing at a time and to encourage them to improve these, rather than to confuse them with a multiplicity of detail which they cannot possibly assimilate immediately.

3. The persistent errors of a number of students lead to group discussions and practice. At the intermediate and advanced levels these errors provide a logical framework for a review of grammar based on existential frequency of commission.

4. Students should be encouraged to keep checklists of their own weaknesses, since these, as with errors in spoken language, will vary from individual to individual.

5. Time should be taken in class for students to check their work before submitting it for grading. Editing is a normal part of native-language writing and should be equally normal for second- or foreign-language writing. Research has shown that students "can reduce their grammatical and mechanical errors—including spelling and capitalization—more than half by learning how to correct errors before submitting their papers."[15]

6. Similarly, class time should be given to the perusing and immediate correction of scripts in which the errors have been marked, so that students may ask questions and receive explanations as they need them.

7. An active correction process is more effective than the passive reading by the student of corrections written in by the instructor.

8. Several active correction processes have been proposed:

a. Errors are merely underlined. Students, alone or in groups, decide in what way their writing was inadequate and make changes.

b. Errors are underlined and marked with a symbol which acts as a guide to the kind of error made (e.g., T = tense, WO = word order, V = lexical choice etc.).

c. Errors are underlined and given numbers which refer to sections of a brief review of grammar rules to which all students have access.

d. Errors are underlined, with no comments or symbols, but no grade is assigned until the student resubmits a corrected script.

e. Errors are not indicated specifically, but a check mark is placed in the margin opposite the line where the error occurs. Students must identify the actual errors themselves.

f. Knapp[16] adopts a positive, rather than a negative, approach to grading expressive writing. He establishes a Composition Check-List of items to which students should pay attention in writing compositions. While correcting, he assigns red pluses for all items successfully handled. Students try, from composition to composition, to increase the number of pluses on their individual checklists. Lack of pluses arouses student concern so that they seek help in overcoming specific weaknesses. (Careless mistakes are merely underlined.)

9. Writing more felicitous expressions in on the script can be time-wasting for the teacher, unless few such suggestions are made and these are discussed with the students who are encouraged to use the suggested expressions in later writing.

Scoring systems

The subjective nature of grades assigned to written expression has long been criticized. Where one teacher is involved and the students know what that teacher expects, the unreliability of the scoring and ranking is reduced. In allotting a grade, an experienced teacher is considering the interplay of a number of factors. If the number of scripts is not too great, and the teacher is not too tired or harassed, the grading will normally be reasonably consistent.

Inexperienced teachers would, however, do well to consider what qualities they are looking for and to assign grades according to some weighted system until they acquire more confidence. Where more than one corrector is involved with the ranking of one group or of parallel groups, agreement should be reached on the weighting they are assigning to different factors.

The following weighted checklist is proposed for discussion:

W 61   *Weighted assessment scheme for expressive writing in a second or foreign language*

1. Organization of content (focus, coherence, clarity, originality)

                                                                      20 per cent

2. Structure
   a. sentence structure (appropriateness, variety, word order)
   b. morphology (accurate use of paradigms, verb and noun endings, forms of pronouns, etc.)
   c. use of verbs (forms, tenses, sequence of tenses, agreements, etc.)

                                                                     40 per cent

3. Variety and appropriateness of lexical choices   20 per cent
4. Idiomatic flavor (feeling for the language, fluency)   20 per cent

Commentary

1. At the advanced level, there will also be consideration of content in addition to organization of content. Further variation of this checklist will

be developed where students have reached the stage of writing in English essays on literary, cultural, or other informational subjects.

2. Students should be aware of the criteria adopted for the asessment of their writing.

Research in native-language writing[17] has shown that for assessment of achievement two compositions on different subjects written on two separate occasions produce a more reliable evaluation than one composition. It has been found that the performance of good writers varies more than that of poor writers. The fairest procedure is to assess the student according to the grade of the more successful of the two compositions. Apart from the common factor of day-to-day variability in inspiration and energy, the finding seems intuitively transferable to the assessment of writing in a new language, in that a particular student may find one composition topic unduly cramping from the point of view of content or vocabulary area.

Translation

Translation is both a skill and an art, of considerable practical and esthetic value in the modern world, as it has been down the ages. It provides access for millions to the scientific and technical knowledge, the great thoughts, the artistic achievements, and the societal needs and values of the speakers of many tongues.

In the teaching of languages, it has been at different periods either an accepted or a controversial element, depending on prevailing objectives and teaching preferences. It was a keystone of the learning and testing process in the grammar-translation approach. Direct-method theorists de-emphasized it as a learning device, excluding it from early instruction as much as possible, while admitting it as an art at advanced stages. Audio-lingual textbooks in the foreign-language situation often printed native-language translations opposite the early dialogues, or on the reverse of the page, and included translation drills for practice. Translation of continuous passages from the native language into the language being learned was, however, considered an advanced exercise in this approach also.

Unfortunately, much of the discussion of the place of translation in language learning has been at cross-purposes, since the kind of translation and its function in the learning process have not been specified. The following aspects of translation need to be differentiated in such discussion.

1. Translation may be from the language being learned into the native language or from the native language into the new language.

2. Translation may be *oral* or *written*.

3. Translation may be used as a *learning* or a *testing* device or it may be practiced for its intrinsic value as a *practical skill* or a *discriminating art*.

4. Translation may be *simultaneous*, as in oral interpretation which draws on the interpreter's internalized knowledge of both languages, or carefully *edited* and re-edited after consultation of dictionaries and grammars, as in literary or technical translation.

5. *Oral translation* from the second or foreign language to the native language may be a classroom technique by which the teacher rapidly clarifies the meaning of an unfamiliar word or phrase in listening or reading exercises. It may be the way the student is required to demonstrate aural or reading comprehension. It may also, at the advanced level, be a sophisticated activity like oral interpretation. (Since most professional oral interpreters translate only from their second or third language into their native, or dominant, language, this would also be the direction of any classroom practice of this demanding process.) Oral translation from the native language to the language being learned may be used for practice or testing of the application of grammatical rules.

6. *Written translation* of samples of English into the native language may be a device to test comprehension of factual detail. On the other hand, written translation into English may be used to test application of the rules of grammar, as in the translation of sample sentences or the translation of passages in the native language that have been carefully designed to elicit structures, vocabulary, and idiomatic expressions similar to those in some English text recently studied (*translation in imitation of a text*). Either type of translation may be an advanced activity to test ability to transfer meaning comprehensively and elegantly from one language code to the other.

In view of these many ways in which the term "translation" is used, it is difficult to take a position for or against its use in the English-language class. Rather, one should consider the possible contributions to language learning of each of these activities at various levels and in relation to the objectives of the course.

The main objection to translation as a teaching device has been that it interposes an intermediate process between the concept and the way it is expressed in the foreign language, thus hindering the development of the ability to think directly in the new language. It may be argued that even when students are taught by direct methods, they often mentally interpose this intermediate translation process themselves in the early stages. Such mental translation usually disappears as a superfluous step when students become familiar with the language through continual exposure to it. Teachers will need to decide for themselves which position they will take in this controversy, whether to eschew all translation or use it judiciously for certain purposes. Here we will discuss such judicious use and also opportunities to engage in translation as an activity in its own right at the advanced level.

TRANSLATION AS A TEACHING/LEARNING DEVICE

Translation from the second or foreign language to the native language

This process is useful for clarifying the meaning of certain abstract concepts, some function words and logical connectives, and some idiomatic
expressions which context alone does not illuminate. Such translation, if
used too frequently, can become a crutch, reducing the amount of effort
given to inferencing[18]—a process which is of considerable importance in
autonomous language use. Some teachers like to make quick oral checks of
comprehension of reading and listening materials by asking for native-
language equivalents of certain segments of the messages. In moderation,
and in association with other checks of comprehension conducted in the
target language itself, this procedure can pinpoint and eliminate some areas
of vagueness for the student.

In the early stages, some judicious translation of common expressions
can familiarize students with different levels of language. Such expressions
will normally be presented through situations in which they would be used.
Even then, however, it is not always perfectly obvious to the student that
different relationships are expressed by the choice, for instance, of *Good
morning, Peter. How are you?* rather than *Hi, Pete. How's it going?*

Translation from the native to the second or foreign language

1. *Translation of isolated sentences.* This process as a practice exercise
has been brought into disrepute by its excesses. Sentences of improbable
or infrequent occurrence, constructed so that they positively bristle with
problems, have made language learning an ordeal for many students, without doing more than convincing them of their inadequacies. Such sentences
may still be found in many contemporary textbooks.

The process can be useful, however, when a set of short sentences which
focus on a particular grammatical feature is used as a stimulus for eliciting
formulations in English, as in the following examples.

W 62 For practicing the form and order of pronoun objects.

The student is given a set of short sentences in the native language, along
the lines of the following.

Say the following in English:
1. (I give him the book.)
2. (He gives her the book.)
3. (He gives it to Jane.)
4. (She gives me the book.)
5. (She gives it to me.)
6. (He gives it to her.)

Commentary

W62 is a familiarization exercise. Conducted orally, it may be a chaining activity, with students proposing short sentences for each other to translate. It may appropriately be accompanied by action. See also *Oral translation drills*, p. 146.

2. *Translation in Imitation of a Text*. This is a specially constructed exercise which is useful for identifying student problems in grammatical and vocabulary usage in written English. The instructor extracts from a passage of English, which has been read and studied, useful features the student should be able to use. A native-language text which requires the use of these features is then prepared for translation into English. The students translate the passage without consulting the original on which it is based, and then examine the original to see where they can improve or correct their translations. Group discussion is useful at this stage.

W 63 *Translation in Imitation of a Text* based on R67

Translate into English.

(A paraphrased version of R67 will be given to the students in their native language along the lines of the following.)

When he was president of Princeton University, Woodrow Wilson declared that the automobile had spread socialistic feeling in the United States because it demonstrated the arrogance of wealth. Only twenty years later, two women who were living on small incomes told investigators that they would do without food and clothes rather than give up their cars. . . .

TRANSLATION AS A SPECIALIZED STUDY[19]

Once we go beyond the transposition into English of sentences and sequences of sentences that either parallel what the students have already encountered or test what they are learning at the time, we approach translation as a demanding, often frustrating, study in its own right. Genuine translation involves the exploration of the potential of two languages. It not only involves the students in serious consideration of the expressive possibilities of the new language, but also extends their appreciation of the semantic extensions and limitations of their first language and the implications for meaning of its syntactic options. It is, then, an appropriate undertaking in an advanced course, or even at the intermediate level when a particular group of students is especially interested in attaining competence in it. It may be offered as an advanced option in an individualized or small-group program, or as a specialized course among diversified options.

Translation must be distinguished from the extracting of information from a text. Much information can be gleaned without exact translation, although readers may resort to translation at times to clarify important details. (See *Reading for Information* in Chapter 6, p. 189).

Translation and meaning

The teacher will want to sensitize students interested in translation to the many facets of meaning with which they will have to deal. This provides an excellent context for familiarizing them with basic concepts of linguistics.

Translation involves careful analysis of the meaning of the source text. Students consider various aspects of the meaning they have extracted and rethink it in terms of the target language so that as little is added and as little is lost as possible. They learn a great deal as they discover that it is not always possible to attain exact equivalence and as they evaluate possible versions to see which most fully captures all the implications of the original. They will find that they need to look beyond single words, segments of sentences, or even complete sentences to whole stretches of discourse as they make their decisions. Much can be thrashed out in group working sessions as they ask themselves some searching questions[20] about the text they wish to translate.

1. What type of writing does the passage represent: descriptive, narrative, conversational, expository, argumentative, polemical, or some other? What are the features of this style in the target language?

2. What is the overall meaning of this passage in its context in a larger discourse? Is it a serious development of ideas or is it satirical? Is it deliberately vague? Is the original inaccurate or fallacious? Is it carelessly put together? (Any of these characteristics, and many others, must be faithfully reproduced.)

3. Is the tone of the passage assured, hesitant, dogmatic, humorous, solemn, neutral, or something else?

4. Is the passage boring, repetitive, exciting, laconic, provocative, mysterious . . . ?

5. Is the general structure such that it can be reproduced in the translation or would an equivalent in the target language require different sentence division or repositioning of segments, for emphasis or for other reasons?

6. How can the time relationships in the source text be most clearly expressed in the target language? (This is not always a question of which tenses to select.)

7. For which lexical items is the semantic content different from seemingly equivalent lexical items in the target language? Should additional lexical items be introduced to carry the meaning which would otherwise be lost or can this extra meaning be carried by grammatical morphemes or by implications from syntactic choices.

W 64 He ate in the dark or by the light through the stove door left ajar. There was still no lamp, no candle. The fixer set a small splinter aside to mark the lost day *and crawled onto his mattress.*[21]

Commentary

The very expressive segment which we have italicized indicates how quite simple expressions may be very difficult to translate succinctly into another language. He "crawled onto his mattress" in English contains the ideas not only of movement, direction, and weariness, but also the almost animal level of life to which the fixer had been reduced. Not all languages can convey all of these nuances of meaning in one short culminating segment. Some can express the ideas of movement, direction, and weariness, without the feeling of hopelessness of the original. Others can convey the weariness and hopelessness without the movement and direction. The translator may have to decide which element of meaning to sacrifice at this point (or to include elsewhere) in order to avoid a clumsy anticlimactic ending to the sentence. (Try translating this group of words into the language you know best.)

    8. Do superficially equivalent expressions in the original and in the proposed translation have different denotative (referential) meaning or connotative (emotive) meaning? "False friends"[22] fall into these categories.)
    9. Are there sociolinguistic or emotional levels of language or specialized fields of knowledge implicit in the text which will need careful attention in the translation?
    10. Are there culturally related items in the source text which will need to be rethought in relation to the cultural concepts of the speakers of the target language or should literal translations be used for these to preserve in the translation the foreign flavor of the original?
    11. Are there figurative, rhetorical, or specifically literary aspects of the language of the original which require careful transposition?
    12. Are there any idiosyncratic features of the author's style observable in this passage? Are there any mechanisms in the target language which would convey the same impression?

    Clearly such a task is formidable for a language learner. If students are not to be discouraged, they will need to be given much practice with translation graded in difficulty, with particular passages selected because they allow the student to focus on specific problems. Students will also derive considerable benefit from the pooling of ideas in group preparation of a final translation, and from discussion of the efficacy of published translations of passages they themselves have attempted to translate.

* Compare the following translations with the original texts (W65: German into English; W66: Spanish into English; W67: French into English).

In each case, do you think the translator has captured the level of language and tone of the original and reproduced the full meaning?

W 65 Compare the English translation with the original German from *Haus ohne Hüter* by Heinrich Böll.[23]

A. Diese Schonung genoß Will sein Leben lang. "Ein bißchen schwach, ein bißchen nervös"—und Nachtschweiß, das wurde für ihn zu einer Rente, die seine Familie ihm auszuzahlen hatte. Martin und Brielach gewöhnten sich eine Zeitlang daran, morgens ihre Stirnen zu betasten, sich auf dem Schulweg das Ergebnis mitzuteilen, und sie stellten fest, daß auch ihre Stirnen manchmal etwas feucht waren. Besonders Brielach schwitzte nachts häufig und heftig, aber Brielach war von der Stunde seiner Geburt an nicht einen Tag lang geschont worden.

B. Will had enjoyed being coddled all his life. The night sweats had provided him with a permanent allowance from his family. For a while Martin and Brielach used to feel their foreheads on their way to school to persuade themselves that theirs, too, were sometimes quite damp. Brielach in fact often perspired heavily in the night, but no one had ever coddled *him*.

W 66 Compare the English translation with the original Spanish passage from *Requiem por un Campesino Español* by Ramón J. Sender.[24]

A. Mosén Millán se decía: es pronto. Además, los campesinos no han acabado las faenas de la trilla. Pero la familia del difunto no podía faltar. Seguían sonando las campanas que en los funerales eran lentas, espaciadas y graves. Mosén Millán alargaba las piernas. Las puntas de sus zapatos asomaban debajo del alba y encima de la estera de esparto. El alba estaba deshilándose por el remate. Los zapatos tenían el cuero rajado por el lugar donde se doblaban al andar, y el cura pensó: tendré que enviarlos a componer. El zapatero era nuevo en la aldea. El anterior no iba a misa, pero trabajaba para el cura con el mayor esmero, y le cobraba menos. Aquel zapatero y Paco el del Molino habían sido muy amigos.

B. Mosén Millán said to himself: "It's too soon. Besides, the peasants haven't finished their threshing yet." But the dead man's family would have to come. Those slow, ponderous and solemn funeral bells were still tolling. Mosén Millán stretched his legs and the tips of his shoes appeared from below his alb and rested on the rush mat. The alb was ravelling at its hem, his shoes were cracked where they bent in walking. "I'll have to send them to be repaired," thought the priest. The cobbler was newly arrived in the village. The former one had not attended Mass, but he had worked for the priest with the greatest care and had charged him less. That cobbler and Pr͞   ᴅ been fast friends.

W67 Compare the English translation with the original French from *Le Petit Prince* by A. de Saint-Exupéry.[25]

A. J'ai donc dû choisir un autre métier et j'ai appris à piloter des avions. J'ai volé un peu partout dans le monde. Et la géographie, c'est exact, m'a beaucoup servi. Je savais reconnaître, du premier coup d'oeil, la Chine de l'Arizona. C'est très utile, si l'on s'est égaré pendant la nuit.

J'ai ainsi eu, au cours de ma vie, des tas de contacts avec des tas de gens sérieux.

B. So then I chose another profession, and learned to pilot airplanes. I have flown a little over all parts of the world; and it is true that geography has been very useful to me. At a glance I can distinguish China from Arizona. If one gets lost in the night, such knowledge is valuable.

In the course of this life I have had a great many encounters with a great many people concerned with matters of consequence . . .

❋ *Discuss the decisions made by the translators* of the passages in W68: French into English; W69: German into English; W70: Spanish into English. *Do you consider these decisions necessary and effective?*

W68 Discuss the decisions made by the translator of this passage from Camus' *L'Etranger*.[26]

A. J'étais assez loin de lui, à une dizaine de mètres. Je devinais son regard par instants, entre ses paupières mi-closes. Mais, le plus souvent, son image dansait devant mes yeux, dans l'air enflammé. Le bruit des vagues était encore plus paresseux, plus étale qu'à midi. C'était le même soleil, la même lumière sur le même sable qui se prolongeait ici.

B. I was some distance off, at least ten yards, and most of the time I saw him as a blurred dark form wobbling in the heat haze. Sometimes, however, I had glimpses of his eyes glowing between the half-closed lids. The sound of the waves was even lazier, feebler, than at noon. But the light hadn't changed; it was pounding as fiercely as ever on the long stretch of sand that ended at the rock.

W 69 Discuss the decisions made by the translator of this passage from Thomas Mann's *Zauberberg*.[27]

A. Dergleichen erfuhr auch Hans Castorp. Er hatte nicht beabsichtigt, diese Reise sonderlich wichtig zu nehmen, sich innerlich auf sie einzulassen. Seine Meinung vielmehr war gewesen, sie rasch abzutun, weil sie abgetan werden mußte, ganz als derselbe zurückzukehren, als der er abgefahren war, und sein Leben genau dort wieder aufzunehmen, wo er es für einen Augenblick hatte liegenlassen müssen. Noch gestern war er völlig in dem gewohnten Gedankenkreise befangen gewesen, hatte sich mit dem jüngst Zurückliegenden, seinem Examen, und dem unmittelbar Bevorstehenden, seinem Eintritt in die Praxis bei Tunder & Wilms (Schiffswerft, Maschinenfabrik une Kesselschmiede) beschäftigt, und über die nächsten drei Wochen mit soviel Ungeduld hinweggeblickt, als seine Gemütsart nur immer zuließ. Jetzt aber war ihm doch, also ob die Umstände seine volle Aufmerksamkeit erforderten und als ob es nicht angehe, sie auf die leichte Achsel zu nehmen.

B. Such was the experience of young Hans Castorp. He had not meant to take the journey seriously or to commit himself deeply to it; but to get it over quickly, since it had to be made, to return as he had gone, and to take up his life at the point where, for the moment, he had had to lay it down. Only yesterday he had been encompassed in the wonted circle of his thoughts, and entirely taken up by two matters: the examination he had just passed, and his approaching entrance into the firm of Tunder and Wilms, shipbuilders, smelters and machinists. With as much impatience as lay in his temperament to feel, he had discounted the next three weeks; but now it began to seem as though present circumstances required his entire attention, that it would not be at all the thing to take them too lightly.

W 70 Discuss the decisions made by the translator of this passage from *Un millón de muertos* by José María Gironella.[28]

A. Una hora después, todos los milicianos que participaron en la gran operación se habían retirado a sus casas y casi todos dormían. Dormía incluso el catedrático Morales, a quien de repente entraba una gran fatiga. Dormía también Cosme Vila, el cual había abierto la puerta de la alcoba descalzo y de puntillas para no despertar al pequeño. Su mujer le preguntó, en la oscuridad: "¿Qué hora es?" Cosme Vila contestó, desnudándose: "Las cuatro y media."

A las cinco empezó la gran operación del dolor. Mientras hubo estrellas en el cielo y camiones repletos de milicianos recorrieron la ciudad, ningún familiar de ningún detenido, ni siquiera de los que fueron arrancados de sus hogares aquella misma noche, se atrevió a salir. Había corrido la voz de lo que iba a suceder; pero tener miedo no era excusa válida para enfrentarse con las patrullas. Así que, a lo largo de la noche, el alma murió a cada chirriar de neumático y los ojos se clavaron en las rendijas de las persianas.

B. An hour later, all the militiamen who had taken part in the big roundup had gone home and most of them were asleep. Professor Morales was sleeping, too, suddenly overtaken by immense weariness. Shortly after opening the bedroom door on tiptoe in his bare feet so as not to awaken the child, Cosme Vila too had sunk into sleep. His wife had spoken out of the darkness, asking, "What time is it?" and Cosme Vila had replied as he was undressing, "Four-thirty."

The exodus of the bereft began at five. As long as there were still stars in the sky and trucks filled with militiamen roaming the streets of the city, no relative of any detained man, not even of those dragged from their homes that very night, would dare to go out. News of what had been about to happen had spread rapidly, but to be afraid was no valid excuse for confronting the patrols. Accordingly, throughout the night, the soul fainted at every slither of tires and the eyes remained riveted on the slats of the venetian blinds.

Translation from English into the native language

As with other aspects of the language course, translation can begin with *useful things which are near at hand.*

1. Students translate English *labels, slogans,* and *advertisements,* trying to produce native-language versions which ring true to the commercial style to which they are accustomed. This activity can lead to interesting discussions of differences of approach to the consumer.

2. Students translate *instructions* for the use of products for relatives or for local merchants (car salesmen or dealers in cameras, stereo equipment, or radios, for instance), or *cooking recipes* for themselves or friends. Where necessary, they use specialized dictionaries to help them. Students can learn a great deal by studying amusing translations into English and working back to the original languages of the translators to see what misconceptions misled them. (Travel brochures and instruction booklets accompanying imported appliances and products are fruitful sources for oddly expressed translations.)

3. Students translate interesting sections of *letters from correspondents* to publish in the school newspaper or share with others in the geography or social studies class.

4. Students translate *historical documents*, such as the *Declaration of Independence* or the *United Nations Charter,* for use in their history class; selections from important *political speeches* or *communiqués* (taken from newspapers or news magazines) for a political science or international relations class; *scientific articles* for the science class; words of *songs* for the school choir.

5. Some students become interested in attempting the translation of passages in all kinds of styles and moods; others try to develop real proficiency in scientific or technical translation in specialized fields.

6. Some students, deeply interested in language and in literature, might work together (or individually) to produce a *poem* in their native language which is a translation of a poem in English. (A translation of a poem in poetic form is a new creation.) This would be submitted for publication in the school magazine or a community newspaper.

* Begin a file with bibliographic details of bilingual dictionaries available for specialized fields for speakers of the languages spoken by your students.

* *Titles of books* and advertising *slogans* are difficult to translate because in their abbreviated form they must have rhythmic appeal and an attractive sonority, while calling up appropriate associations in the language in which they are to be used. (These associations are often familiar from literature, proverbs, or common sayings, and so must be parallelel, rather than translated.) Try translating into another language:

a. Milk is a natural!
b. It figures. It's Pant-her! (advertisement for women's pants)
c. *Gone with the Wind*
d. The song title "Blowing in the Wind"

Techniques for translation from English into the native language. Early attempts at translating from English into the native language often result in gibberish, particularly when students have not yet learned how to use a bilingual dictionary efficiently. Even intelligent students often fracture their native language in an extraordinary way when they are concentrating on "translating" rather than transposing concepts into a comprehensible equivalent in their own language.

W73 illustrates the involuntary amnesia with regard to the language one has spoken from birth which many students seem to develop in this situation.

W71 An English-speaking student asked to translate French passage A may produce the type of English in B.

A. C'est l'année suivante que j'ai eu l'idée de matérialiser mon pays imaginaire. J'ai acheté d'énormes cahiers . . . et je me suis mis à découper dans des prospectus d'agences de voyage des paysages, des villes, des ports que j'ai collés sur les pages de ces cahiers. Je les ai reliés ensuite . . . de manière à former un ensemble. . . .

B. Student translation: It is the following year that I had the idea of materializing my imaginary country. I bought enormous exercise books and put myself to discovering in the prospectuses of agencies of voyages the countries, the villages, the ports that I collected on the pages of these exercise books. I relied on them then . . . and managed to put one together.

Commentary

1. Many students have felt frustrated when this type of translation was rejected. They knew what most of the passage was about and could have answered a comprehension test fairly adequately. This student does not understand what a translation should be like.

2. Many of the weaknesses of this type of response can be corrected by asking students to read their translations aloud. As they read, they become conscious of the odd quality of what they have written in their native language and often correct it as they proceed. Group discussion helps to refine the final version.

3. Group discussion before individual writing of the translation is also helpful in impressing on the student that the passage has a sensible, sequential meaning. Part of the translation may be written on the chalkboard or the overhead projector as the group works it over. The students then complete the translation individually, comparing their versions with each other to decide on the best possible translation.

4. Before considering their translations final, students should ask themselves the following six questions:

a. Have I respected contrasts between the structure of English and that of my own language?

b. Have I fallen for any *false friends?* (See p. 192.)

c. Have I used my common sense with time relations?

d. Have I used all the clues in the passage to help me translate unfamiliar words?

e. Have I used the appropriate style and level of language?

f. Does the final translation really sound as though it had originally been written in this language?

Translation into English

We can place translation from the native language into the foreign or second language in perspective, as a student activity, by asking ourselves the question which has become one of the central preoccupations of this book: To what normal uses can such an activity be put? For translation into the native language, we were able to find many uses. For translation into English, the first one which springs to mind for an elementary- or intermediate-level student in a non-English-speaking country is the translating of school brochures, local area information booklets, or articles from school magazines or newspapers for inclusion in a twinned schools exchange project, or for sending to an English-speaking correspondent who does not know the native language of the student. An advanced-level student may have opportunities to translate letters or instructions for a commercial firm which is exporting local products. This is usually the work of a professional translator, however. In a school situation, this activity will usually be much less useful than practice in translating from English into the native language. In writing letters or preparing reports, students should be encouraged to write directly in English, not to translate into English scripts they have composed in their native language.

On the other hand, in a second-language situation, students may be able to perform a real service for members of their native-language community by translating into English for them letters of application or complaint, requests for information or for reimbursement, or reports of community activities for local newspapers. In each of these cases, the tone of the English translation and the use of correct formulas for particular situations are of great importance, demanding considerable skill on the part of the translator. Students can learn a great deal that will be of use to them in later life by working on such projects with the help of the teacher.

The production of an acceptable translation into English is for most students a means, not an end—a means for developing sensitivity to the meanings expressed in a stretch of discourse in one's own language and to the different linguistic mechanisms used by the two languages to convey these meanings. Students learn to translate ideas, not words. This type of exercise is, therefore, an analytic activity. Through a comparative examination of the syntactic and semantic systems of English and the native language and the cultural contexts in which they operate, students attempt to expand their own potential for expression in the English language.

Techniques for translation from the native language into English. 1. If students are to gain the benefits from a comparative study of two language systems, teachers must avoid the types of passages one finds in some textbooks which distort the native language to make it more like English in order to make the translation process "easier" for the student.

2. Since this is an intellectual exercise—an active, conscious process of attacking linguistic problems—it is a suitable project for group discussion and preparation before individual drafts are prepared by each student.

3. Students will begin by analyzing certain basic stylistic factors which

will affect the whole translation, e.g., Is the passage informal and conversational in tone so that I should use non-literary, or at any rate non-formal, expressions and vocabulary items, as well as short sentences, rather than long sentences with several embedded clauses?

4. Students will learn to use monolingual and bilingual dictionaries and grammars efficiently to verify the appropriateness of their proposed translations.

5. Students will learn to check their own work for basic inaccuracies in writing (mistakes in agreement, in spelling, apostrophes, punctuation, capitalization, or paragraph indentation, wrong tense forms). This mechanical task should be the student's own responsibility. (Students may keep checklists of the types of mistakes to which they are prone.) Students may help each other by double-checking each other's work.

6. Group correction and discussion of the translations proposed by the students in relation to the model translation presented by the teacher is more effective than returning individually corrected scripts, since it focuses the students' attention on one thing at a time and gives them several opinions to consider.

7. Translation into English should be a *study of translation techniques.* Several variants may be tried.

a. Students may compare their translations with a professional translation of the same passage, discussing the merits and insufficiencies of the two versions.

b. Students may be given a translation of the passage which was made by a student in another class. They then discuss proposed corrections and improvements to this translation before attempting their own version.

c. Students may discuss the qualities of the translations of the same passage by two professional translators.

d. Students in one group may translate an English passage into the native language, then pass their translation to another group to translate it into English. Subsequent discussion of the original English passage, the translation, and the re-translation will illuminate many of the problems of conveying every aspect of meaning in a translation and the variety of ways in which a sentence may be interpreted.

EXPLORING THE DICTIONARY

We profess that one of our aims in teaching another language is to open up to our students the world of language itself. Part of this world is the wonder of words—their multiplicity, their variety, their elasticity, their chameleon-like quality of changing and merging in different environments. We know that different languages view reality from different perspectives and that many of these cultural differences are reflected in words and in their nuances of meaning. Yet frequently we keep our language learners impoverished in this area, depriving them of the opportunity to explore another world of words.

For this, the dictionary can be an invaluable friend. Instead of steering our students away from it, we should teach them to use it effectively. We should provide interesting opportunities for them to familiarize themselves with various kinds of dictionaries as aids in their pursuit of personal fluency in speech and writing.

Of course, the dictionary can mislead the neophyte. Until the student has learned how to consult a dictionary, there will be the inevitable crop of "This watch does not walk well" and "I have my stomach today." We must provide the kinds of experiences that will make these aberrations a passing phase.

Quite early, and certainly by the intermediate level, our students should have learned that there are three kinds of dictionaries available to them: the standard monolingual kind to which they are accustomed in their native language, the monolingual English-language learner's dictionary, and the bilingual (which they will certainly find at home or in the local bookshop if they do not find it in the classroom). Each of these should be accessible to them and they should learn to use them purposefully and discriminatingly.[29]

1. *The standard monolingual dictionary.* Among the most recent and widely used of the dictionaries in this class are, in the United States: *The American Heritage Dictionary of the English Language* (the same, except for the title, as *The Heritage Illustrated Dictionary of the English Language: International Edition*); *The Funk and Wagnalls Standard College Dictionary, The Random House College Dictionary, Webster's New Collegiate Dictionary,* and *Webster's New World Dictionary of the American Language*; in Great Britain: *The Shorter Oxford English Dictionary, The Concise Oxford Dictionary of Current English,* and *The Pocket Oxford Dictionary of Current English.*[30]

In the following discussion we will refer to *The American Heritage Dictionary* (AHD) for illustrative purposes.

a. It will be easy to interest students in the AHD by encouraging them to browse through its pages and note the array of photographs, sketches, and diagrams in its margins. (The clues to finding the answers in W68–69 will, of course, not appear in the students' quizzes.)

W72 (I)   1. What kind of activity would you call *slapstick*? (The answer is to be found in the photograph accompanying the entry *slapstick.*)

2. What American states are now in the land acquired by the *Louisiana Purchase*? (Answer in the map accompanying the entry *Louisiana Purchase.*)

3. Portraits of national leaders often appear on the *currency* of different

countries. On what U.S. coin is there a portrait of President Kennedy? (The coin is pictured on the page headed *Currency*.)

b. This initial interest can be quickened by a few competitive general knowledge quizzes which lead students to explore the *encyclopedic information* in the dictionary, showing them that it is not difficult to extract this kind of information, even though it is in English.

W73 (I or A)   1. Is the *spider* an insect? (Answer under entries *spider* and *insect*.)

2. Where does the name *America* come from? (Answer under entry *America*.)

3. Why do we talk about *Greenwich* mean time? (Answer under *Greenwich time*.)

Commentary

Obviously questions like the above could lead to further, more detailed questions, but this questionnaire is not intended as a test. Since its purpose is to arouse interest in searching for information in the dictionary, the questions should provide an interesting experience in themselves. For intermediate and advanced students the questions may very well be written in English, so long as the general appearance of the quiz is not so forbidding as to be self-defeating.

Very soon, groups of students, or individuals, should be enthusiastic enough to make up their own questions to try out on each other.

c. Next, we introduce the student to entries concerned with *language usage*.

W74 (I or A)   1. What are some of the meanings of the adjective *funny*? What level of usage does the dictionary assign to the expression, "A fun group of people?" Does the expression mean "A funny group of people"?

2. What is the difference between: a. *concave* and *convex*; b. *uninterested* and *disinterested*? What are the judgments of the Usage Panel on the use of the words in b. as synonyms?

3. You are familiar with the following words as nouns. What is their meaning as verbs? *chicken (out)*, *cow*, *crow*, *dog*, *duck*, *monkey (around/about)*, *parrot*, *wolf*.

d. From this point on, it should be possible to incorporate the consultation of a standard English dictionary or a learner's English dictionary (see 2., below) into as many activities as possible and to direct students to it to find out many things for themselves.

e. At the advanced level, we may interest students in *etymologies*.

W75 (A)   1. What is the meaning of the following words and what do they have in common? *bowdlerize, boycott, chauvinism, sandwich.*

2. The following words link us with ancient civilizations. Explain their origins in relation to their meaning: *hermetic, erotic, martial, algebra, vandal.*

f. *Word formation* is a fascinating study, already discussed in R4 5 and R68–71. Advanced students should pursue this area further for its intrinsic interest.

W76 (A)   Suffixes often change the part of speech or grammatical function of the words to which they are attached, e.g., the verb *read* plus the suffix *-er* makes the noun *reader*. Although most *prefixes* do not change the part of speech of the word, a few do.

What is the meaning of the following verbs? a. *befriend, belittle*; b. *derail, defrost*; c. *disbar, disillusion*; d. *embody, empower*; d. *endanger, enthrone.*

2. *The learner's dictionary* (monolingual English). Yorkey lists eight such dictionaries. (seven British and one American)[31] and considers that they "serve at various levels of instruction as a useful transition to a regular English dictionary."[32] The learner's dictionaries are of course smaller than the standard dictionaries (those in Yorkey's list ranging from about 3,000 to 50,000 entries, compared with the 150,000 or so entries of most of the standard desk dictionaries); they may restrict themselves to a small defining vocabulary (usually about 1,500 words); and they often contain informational appendices not found in dictionaries for native speakers.

The following examples suggest ways in which the *Oxford Advanced Learner's Dictionary of Current English* (OALDCE) may be used.

W77 (E or I)   One student has written that an English class contains Chineses, Italians, Japaneses, Swedes, and Swisses. How many of these forms are correct? (Students find the answer in Appendix 6: Geographical Names. Note 3 gives the rule for forming the plural when the word for the person is derived from the name of the country.)

W78 (E or I)   1. How is the word *tune* pronounced? /tyuwn/ or /tuwn/? (Students look up the entry *tune.*)

2. What is peculiar in the relationship between spelling and pronunciation in the following words: *who, write, know, gnaw, psychology, mnemonic, pneumonia, thyme?* (Students look at the pronunciation guides supplied for these words.)

W 79 To what part of the OALDCE would you, as a teacher, refer a student who writes the following sentences: 1. *That night a strange thing was dreamed by her; 2. *The teacher explained them the problem? (The Introduction to the Dictionary contains a section, *Verb Patterns,* which gives information on the syntactical patterns into which verbs enter. Each pattern in this section is assigned a number. Every verb entry in the body of the dictionary is given the appropriate pattern number (or numbers) as a guide to the correct usage of that verb. The writer of sentence 1 would be referred to VP6B, the pattern for verbs which have a direct object but which cannot be made passive, and the writer of sentence 2 to VP14, the class of verbs which take a direct object and a following prepositional phrase which is like an indirect object in meaning, but which cannot be placed, without its preposition, before the direct object.)

3. *The bilingual dictionary.* It is this dictionary which all students have tucked away in their desks, usually in a very abbreviated paperback edition, and to which they refer to produce the howlers with which every teacher is familiar.

a. We should help our students by recommending a dependable, reasonably-priced bilingual dictionary which will be used consistently during their studies, so that they will know how to use it when they are on their own.

b. With classes of homogeneous native-language background, a larger, more comprehensive bilingual dictionary will be made available for reference in the classroom and in the library, alongside the monolingual dictionaries like those discussed.

c. Students will be given practice exercises in dictionary search so that they become familiar with the various features —pronunciation guides; abbreviations for parts of speech; levels of language and usage (nonstandard, slang, archaic, or obsolete); relationships with other words (i.e., the rubric under which to find derivatives); grammatical indicators; and the sample sentences demonstrating general use and inclusion in specifically idiomatic expressions.

d. Finally, and most importantly, students will be trained to check meaning in both parts of the dictionary. The newcomer to English who depends on only one half of the bilingual dictionary to form sentences like "I was late because I was embarrassed by my baggages" needs to learn to check meanings and usage in the English to native-language section before using unfamiliar words.

EXPLORING THE GRAMMAR

Students at the advanced level who wish to write well must learn to find answers to their own questions about written English. At this stage they should be given practice in formulating the questions they want answered in such a way that they can find the information they need in an English grammar book. For this, they need to know the basic grammatical terms in English, as used in the particular grammar book to which they have access, so that they can make efficient use of the index.

A student who wishes to know whether to write "She has been waiting to see you since six o'clock this morning" or "She was waiting to see you since six o'clock this morning" will need to know that this is a question of the use of the *present perfect progressive* as opposed to the *past progressive* and that the answer will be found under *Tenses: present perfect progressive* or *Tenses: past progressive*, or simply under the name of the tense, in most grammars. (In some, the student will need to look under *Aspect.*[33])

Learning terms of this type is unexciting, but it can be made more appealing by giving the students interesting problems to solve through personal search in the grammar book. When they feel at home with the book, they will enjoy finding answers to their own questions by themselves, instead of asking other people.

Questions like the following may be proposed. For purposes of demonstration, we will show how this information might be obtained by consulting A. S. Hornby, *Guide to Patterns and Usage in English.*[34] The technique is transferable to any well-indexed grammar book. (The indications for finding the answers would not be given to the students.)

W 80 (A)

1. Should I write a. *She still is waiting*, or b. *She is still waiting?*

(Answer: The student looks for *Adverbials* and finds Adverbials in Mid-Position. In the Index of Words, *still* is listed as a separate item.)

2. I sometimes read a. *None of my friends was there*, and sometimes b. *None of my friends were there*. Which should I use?

(Answer: *None (det.)* is listed, that is, *none* as a determiner. This problem is discussed there.)

3. I often hear *I don't know who you mean*. Is this acceptable in written English?

(Answer: The student will find the answer under *Interrogative Adjectives and Pronouns.*)

Students can be asked to propose their own problems, which will be worked into a *search questionnaire*.

Suggested assignments and projects

Communicating (chapters 1–3)

1. Write a situational dialogue suitable for the second month of elementary instruction. Write a critique of the first draft of your dialogue, then rewrite it if necessary. From your final dialogue write a spiral series and a situation tape. (You may find that what you have written needs considerable adaptation for the situation tape. You should try the script for the tape out on several people to see if it is workable.) If you have the facilities available, record your tape in the form in which it would be used by students.

2. Choose a grammatical feature. Write a grammar-demonstration dialogue to display the various facets of this feature. Construct a unit showing how you would exploit this feature in guided oral practice, in student-directed practice, and then in some communication activity. (Consult also chapter 4.)

3. Design a module for small-group activity which explores some facet of the everyday culture of Britain, the U.S.A., Australia, Canada, or some other English-speaking country. Include normal communicative activities and some culminating display for sharing the material with the whole class.

4. Take a unit or lesson from a direct-method textbook and examine the types of activities proposed. Design a learning packet for individualized instruction for a unit for small-group work using this material. (Remember

that individualized instruction does not mean independent study. This distinction is important if communication skills are to be developed.)

5. Design in detail for the intermediate level an aural-oral communication course based entirely on normal uses of language. Your course should supply ample opportunity for developing facility in listening to all kinds of English and for expressing oneself in different situations and styles of language. (Think of ways of stimulating genuinely self-directed activity by the students. Do not make the course dependent on expensive equipment and aids to which the average English-language or bilingual teacher would not normally have easy access.)

6. Take two textbooks designed specifically for conversation courses. Analyze and comment on the types of communicative activities they promote, using the following heads as an outline.

Situations. For what situations is practice provided? Are these adequate? useful? culturally illuminating? Could the material be adapted easily to other situations?

Normal uses of language. How do the types of activities proposed relate to the normal communicative categories of chapter 2? What other categories can you establish from this examination?

Strategies of communication. What techniques for expressing personal meaning within a limited knowledge of the language do these texts encourage? What other strategies do learners of English need to practice? How could these be incorporated into these texts?

7. Design two listening comprehension tests—one multiple-choice and the other based on normal language activities. Discuss for each of the tests the problems involved in assessment of the degree of listening skill and in administration in a practical teaching situation.

8. Design in detail a course for developing facility in listening along with facility in reading. State the level at which the course would be offered and give your reasons for offering it at that level. (See also chapters 6 and 7.)

Oral practice for the learning of grammar (chapter 4)

9. Take six Type A exercises from current textbooks and show how each could be developed as a Type B exercise.

10. Take a unit for grammatical practice from a current textbook, classify the types of exercises proposed, and design further exercises of the

types described in chapter 4 which are not already included but which you would consider suitable for practicing this area of grammar.

11. Draft a series of oral exercises for teaching the use of question words in English. Draw freely from the various types described in chapter 4, passing from teacher demonstration to student-directed application to autonomous student production.

12. Examine critically the oral exercises for the learning of grammar on a set of tapes accompanying a current textbook. What are their best features and their weaknesses? Propose types of exercises that would, in your opinion, make them more interesting and more useful for developing ability to use the language in interaction.

Teaching the sound system (chapter 5)

13. Make a tape of your own reading of one of the evaluation passages S39–40. Choose the four most striking weaknesses in your production (see S38) and work out articulatory descriptions, empirical recommendations, and remedial exercises which would help students to correct these same faults.

14. Work out some multiple-choice items to test aural discrimination of /ʊ/uw/; /č/š/; /s/θ/; GB /o/ɔ/; GA /ə/a/; *I like/I'd like* when they occur in context in normal word groups.

15. Make some tapes of your students conversing in English. From an analysis of these tapes, list in descending order of frequency the ten features of English pronunciation (including stress, intonation, and juncture) for which you consider they need the most remedial practice. Compare your list with those of other students or teachers and discuss the differences.

Reading (chapters 6 and 7)

16. Take a survey of interests in reading material in the class you are teaching (or in which you are practice teaching). Find suitable materials in English to meet these interests at different stages of reading development. List these (with complete bibliographic information) and explain the reasons for your selection.

17. a. Take a reading passage or story your students have found difficult to read and another they enjoyed but did not consider particularly difficult.

b. Compare the two texts according to: level of difficulty of vocabulary, structural complexity, interest of content, familiarity or unfamiliarity of content, and any other criteria you consider relevant.

c. Ask your students to write down why they found one passage difficult and the other accessible.

d. Compare (b) and (c) and give what seems to you the most reasonable explanation of the students' reactions to the two texts.

18. Undertake a survey of English-language newspapers and magazines available in your area (from the U.S.A., Britain, Canada, Australia, or other English-speaking areas). Examine various aspects of their content and rate them appropriate or inappropriate in content and language for Stages 4, 5, and 6.

19. The physical aspects of a reading text are important factors in readability. Examine a number of books for reading development in English from the point of view of:

a. varieties of type (italics, boldface, etc.) and length of line;

b. layout (spacing, headings and subheadings, breaks in the text);

c. convenience and placing of supplementary helps (glosses, notes, etc.);

d. usefulness and attractiveness of illustrative material;

e. general appearance of the body of the text;

f. attractiveness and durability of the cover;

g. any other physical features which have attracted your attention.

20. Find two textbooks which include the same reading selection. Compare the way the material has been presented and exploited in each (adaptation, if any, of the original text, layout, glosses and supplementary helps, types of questions and exercises, interest and usefulness of these for a particular stage of reading development, integration of reading with other skills).

21. Examine some American or British children's books and comic books from the point of view of vocabulary level, grammatical complexity, and content. Classify them as possibilities for supplementary reading at specific stages of reading development.

Writing (chapters 8 and 9)

2. On separate occasions within the same week, give your students three tests of one grammatical feature (e.g., form and use of predicate possessive pronouns—*mine, yours,* etc.): a multiple-choice test, a cloze test, and a set of stimulus sentences to translate into English. Make graphs of the number of errors made by the students on each test. Repeat the

tests in a different order for another feature and examine these results as well. Give an analysis of what this informal experiment has revealed about the relative difficulty and discriminatory power of the three tests, and the most persistent problems for the students who are learning these features.

23. Examine a textbook for elementary English-language instruction. What part does writing play in this book? Are the writing activities integrated with the other skills? Are they imaginative and interesting for students of the age to which the book is directed? Are they purposeful? What suggestions can you make to improve their effectiveness?

24. Examine a manual for advanced English composition for students whose first language is not English. Do the types of activities provided leave scope for personal initiative? Are they directed toward normal purposes of writing? What aspects of writing have been ignored? What suggestions would you make for a revised edition of the manual?

25. Examine a book (A) written for instruction in the writing of the native language (English or some other language). Compare it with a book (B) intended to improve foreign- or second-language writing. What ideas can be gleaned from the study of A for the improvement of B, or vice versa?

Appendix A

Phonemic symbols used in the transcription of English in this book (PGTESFL)

VOWELS

AMERICAN (GA)

/iy/	as in	beet	/uw/	as in	boot
/ɪ/		bit	/ʊ/		book
/ey/		bait	/ow/		boat
/ɛ/		bet	/ɔ/		saw
/æ/		bat	/ay/		bite
/ə/		but	/aw/		bout
/a/		father, got	/oy/		boy

BRITISH (GB)

/iy/	beet	/ʊ/	book
/ɪ/	bit	/ow/	boat
/ey/	bait	/ɔ/	saw
/ɛ/	bet	/o/	got
/æ/	bat	/ay/	bite
/ɜ/	bird	/aw/	bout
/ə/	ago	/oy/	boy
/ʌ/	but	/ɪə/	here
/a/	father, hard	/ɛə/	hair
/uw/	boot	/ʊə/	sure

CONSONANTS

/p/	pack	/v/	very
/t/	toe	/ð/	then
/k/	kind	/z/	zoo
/č/	chin	/ž/	measure
/b/	big	/m/	make
/d/	day	/n/	nice
/g/	go	/ŋ/	sing
/ǰ/	joy	/r/	rain
/f/	face	/l/	let
/θ/	thin	/w/	well
/s/	sit	/y/	you
/š/	she	/h/	hot

STRESSES

Word stresses
    primary: bútter   tertiary: oútfīt   weak: mátter

Phrase stresses
    primary: at sêven o'clóck
    secondary: at sêven o͞'clóck
    tertiary: nòt a p͞ínk ône
    weak: nòt a͞ pínk ône
    contrastive: a ré̋d ône, nòt a pínk ône

Pitch levels: 1, 2, 3, 4[†]
    ²Gòod ³mórning¹ #
    ²Did yôu sày ⁴fɪ̋fty⁴ ||

[†] = extra high pitch which often accompanies contrastive stress; it does not occur in the text of this book.

Junctures
    Phrase: final fall # :   ²He's jûst ³léft¹ #
                 final rise || :   ²Àre they ³hére³ ||
                 utterance medial (sustained) | :   ²Yés² | ²I ³thínk ²sò² ||
    Internal: open (indicated by space) :   pine tree
                 closed (indicated by no space) : pantry

Phonetic symbols used in transcriptions in this book

[tʰ], [kʰ]   aspirated stops
[ƀ]   voiced bilabial fricative
[l]   unvelarized (clear or bright) non-fricative lateral continuant consonant

[ɫ]   velarized non-fricative lateral continuant consonant
[ɫ̩]   syllabic [ɫ]
[l̆]   lateral flap
[ř]   retroflex flap

Other phonetic symbols used have approximately the value assigned by the International Phonetic Alphabet. This is widely reproduced and may be found, for example, in *The Principles of the International Phonetic Association* (London: The International Phonetic Association, 1949).

Appendix B
Table of Transcribing Alphabets

REFERENCES:

Column headings refer to the following books:

AMERICAN

Lado-Fries: English Language Institute Staff, Robert Lado and Charles C. Fries. *An Intensive Course in English. English Pronunciation: Exercises in Sound Segments, Intonation, and Rhythm* (Ann Arbor, Mich.: The University of Michigan Press, 1958).

Trager-Henderson: Trager, E. C., and Henderson, S. C. *Pronunciation Drills for Learners of English: The P.D.'s* (Washington: The American University Language Center, 1957).

Croft-Davis: Croft, K., and Davis, A. L. *A Practical Course in English for Foreign Students* (Washington: American University Language Center, 1957).

Prator-Robinett: Prator, C. H., and Robinett, B. W. *Manual of American English Pronunciation*. 3d ed. (New York: Holt, Rinehart and Winston, 1972).

Bowen: Bowen, J. D. *Patterns of English Pronunciation* (Rowley, Mass.: Newbury House, 1975).

AHD: *American Heritage Dictionary* (New York: American Heritage Publishing Co. and Houghton Mifflin, 1969).

IPA Kenyon: Kenyon, J. S. *American Pronunciation*, 10th ed. (Ann Arbor, Mich.: George Wahr, 1962).

BRITISH

Gimson-Trim: Gimson, A. C. *An Introduction to the Pronunciation of English*, 2d ed. (London: Edward Arnold, 1970), and Trim, J. *English Pronun-*

ciation Illustrated. 2d ed. (Cambridge, Eng.: Cambridge University Press, 1975).

CPD: Lewis, J. W. *A Concise Pronouncing Dictionary of British and American English* (London: Oxford University Press, 1972).

OALDCE: Hornby, A. S. *Oxford Advanced Learner's Dictionary of Current English*. 3d ed. (London: Oxford University Press, 1974).

POD: *Pocket Oxford Dictionary* (London: Oxford University Press, 1969).

IPA Jones: Jones, D. *The Pronunciation of English* (Cambridge, Eng.: Cambridge University Press, 1950).

Table of transcribing alphabets

key word		AMERICAN								BRITISH			
	PGTESFL	Lado-Fries	Trager-Henderson	Croft-Davis	Prator-Robinett	Bowen	AHD	IPA: Kenyon	*PGTESFL*	Gimson-Trim	CPD-OALDCE	POD*	IPA: Jones
CONSONANTS													
pen	p	p	p	p	p	p	p	p	p	p	p	p	p
bad	b	b	b	b	b	b	b	b	b	b	b	b	b
tea	t	t	t	t	t	t	t	t	t	t	t	t	t
did	d	d	d	d	d	d	d	d	d	d	d	d	d
cat	k	k	k	k	k	k	k	k	k	k	k	k	k
get	g	g	g	g	g	g	g	g	g	g,g	g	g	g
chin	č	č	č	č	tš	ch	ch	tʃ	č	tʃ	tʃ	ch	tʃ
June	ǰ	ǰ	j	ǧ	dž	j	j	dʒ	ǰ	dʒ	dʒ	j	dʒ
fall	f	f	f	f	f	f	f	f	f	f	f	f	f
very	v	v	v	v	v	v	v	v	v	v	v	v	v
thin	θ	θ	θ	θ	θ	th	th	θ	θ	θ	θ	th	θ
then	ð	ð	ð	ð	ð	dh	*th*	ð	ð	ð	ð	dh	ð
so	s	s	s	s	s	s	s	s	s	s	s	s	s
zoo	z	z	z	z	z	z	z	z	z	z	z	z	z
she	š	š	š	š	š	sh	sh	ʃ	š	ʃ	ʃ	sh	ʃ
usual	ž	ž	ž	ž	ž	zh	zh	ʒ	ž	ʒ	ʒ	zh	ʒ
man	m	m	m	m	m	m	m	m	m	m	m	m	m
no	n	n	n	n	n	n	n	n	n	n	n	n	n
sing	ŋ	ŋ	ŋ	ŋ	ŋ	ng	ng	ŋ	ŋ	ŋ	ŋ	ng	ŋ
leg	l	l	l	l	l	l	l	l	l	l	l	l	l
red	r	r	r	r	r	r	r	r	r	r	r	r	r
yes	y	y	y	y	y	y	y	j	y	j	j	y	j
wet	w	w	w	w	w	w	w	w	w	w	w	w	w
how	h	h	h	h	h	h	h	h	h	h	h	h	h

key word	PGTESFL	Lado-Fries	Trager-Henderson	Croft-Davis	Prator-Robinett	Bowen	AHD	IPA: Kenyon	PGTESFL	Gimson-Trim	CPD-OALDCE	POD*	IPA: Jones
	AMERICAN								BRITISH				
VOWELS AND DIPHTHONGS													
see	iy	i	iy	iy	iy	iy	ē	i	iy	iː	i	ē	iː
sit	I	I	i	i	I	I	ĭ	I	I	I	I	ĭ	i
say	ey	e	ey	ey	ey	ey	ā	e	ey	eɪ	eɪ	ā	ei
set	ε	ε	e	e	ε	ε	ĕ	ε	ε	e	e	ĕ	ε
sat	æ	æ	æ eh	æ	æ	æ	ǎ	æ	æ	æ	æ	ǎ	a
bird	ər	ər	əhr ər	ər	ər	ər	ûr	ɝ	3†	3ː†	3(r)	ēr	əː
over	ər	ər	ər	ər	ər	ər	ər	ɚ	ə†	ə†	ə†	‡	ə
ago	ə	ə	ə	ə	ə	ə	ə	ə	ə†	ə†	ə†	‡	ə
but	ə	ə	ə	ə	ə	ə	ŭ	ʌ	ʌ	ʌ	ʌ	ŭ	ʌ
father	a	a	ah	a	a	ɑ	ä	ɑ	a	ɑː	ɑ	ah	ɑː
not	a	a	ɑ,ɔ	a	a	ɑ	ŏ	ɑ,ɒ	o	ɒ	o	ŏ	ɔ
boot	uw	u	Uw	uw	uw	uw	o͞o	u	uw	uː	u	o͞o	uː
book	ʊ	U	U	u	U	U	o͝o	U	ʊ	ʊ	ʊ	o͝o	u
boat	ow	o	ow	ow	ow	ow	ō	o	ow	əʊ	əʊ	ō	ou
saw	ɔ	ɔ	ɔh	ɔ	ɔ	ɔ	ô	ɔ	ɔ	ɔː	ɔ	aw	ɔː
by	ay	aɪ	ɑy	ay	ay	ay	ī	aɪ	ay	aɪ	ɑɪ	ī	ai
now	aw	aU	ɑw	aw	aw	aw	ou	aU	aw	aʊ	aʊ	ow	au
boy	oy	ɔɪ	oy	ɔy	ɔy	oy	oi	ɔɪ	oy	ɔɪ	ɔɪ	oi	ɔi
hear	Ir	Ir	ihr	ir	Iər	Ir	îr	Ir	Iə†	Iə†	Iə(r)	ēr	iə
hair	εr	εr	ehr	er	εər	εr	âr	εr	εə†	εə†	eə(r)	ār	εə
sure	ʊr	Ur	Uhr	ur	Ur	Ur	o͝or	Ur	ʊə†	ʊə†	ʊə(r)	oor	uə

* These are the symbols used in the "Phonetic Scheme," p. xiii (POD). Pp. xiv–xv give additional rules for "Pronunciation without Respelling."

† May be followed by /r/ before another vowel.

‡ Represented by vowels (±r) without diacritics, except ah, aw, ow, oi, oor, owr.

Notes

Abbreviations used in notes and bibliography

ADFL   *Bulletin of the Association of Departments of Foreign Languages* (MLA, New York)

AHD   *American Heritage Dictionary* (New York: American Heritage Publishing Co. and Houghton-Mifflin, 1969)

BSV   Basic Sight Vocabulary, from E.W. Dolch, *Teaching Primary Reading* (Champaign, Ill.: The Garrard Press, 1960)

CPD   J. Windsor Lewis, *A Concise Pronouncing Dictionary of British and American English* (London: Oxford University Press, 1972)

ELT   *English Language Teaching* (London)

ETF   *English Teaching Forum* (USIA)

FLA   *Foreign Language Annals* (American Council on the Teaching of Foreign Languages or ACTFL)

GA   General American

GB   General British

GSL   Michael West, *A General Service List of English Words*. Rev. ed. (London: Longmans, Green, 1953)

IJAL   *International Journal of American Linguistics*

IPE   A.C. Gimson, *An Introduction to the Pronunciation of English* 2d ed. (London: Edward Arnold, 1970)

IRAL   *International Review of Applied Linguistics*

KEV   English Language Services, *The Key to English Vocabulary* (New York: Collier-Macmillan, 1965)

MLJ   *Modern Language Journal* (National Federation of Modern Language Teachers' Associations)

NEC   Reports of the Working Committees of the Northeast Conference on the Teaching of Foreign Languages

LL   *Language Learning* (University of Michigan, Ann Arbor)

LTLA   *Language Teaching and Linguistics: Abstracts* (Cambridge, Eng.: Cambridge University Press)

OALDCE A.S. Hornby, *Oxford Advanced Learner's Dictionary of Current English* (London: Oxford University Press, 1974)

ODCIE A.P. Cowie and R. Mackin, *Oxford Dictionary of Current Idiomatic English* (London: Oxford University Press, 1975 ff.)

POD   *Pocket Oxford Dictionary of Current English* (London: Oxford University Press, 1969)

TQ   *TESOL Quarterly* (Teachers of English to Speakers of Other Languages)

TWB   E. Thorndike and I. Lorge, *The Teacher's Word Book of 30,000 Words* (New York: Teachers College, Columbia University, 1944)

1 Communicating

1. The terms "skill-getting" and "skill-using" have been borrowed from Don H. Parker, "When Should I Individualize Instruction?" in Virgil M. Howes, ed., *Individualization of Instruction: A Teaching Strategy* (New York: Macmillan, 1970), p. 176.

2. The rationale for interaction activities of this type is set out in "Talking Off the Tops of Their Heads" in Wilga M. Rivers, *Speaking in Many Tongues,* expanded 2d ed (Rowley, Mass.: Newbury House, 1976), pp. 21–35.

1. STRUCTURED INTERACTION

1. How this can be done is discussed fully in W.M. Rivers, "From Linguistic Competence to Communicative Competence" in *TQ* 7 (1973), pp. 25–34. Reprinted in Rivers (1976a), pp. 36–48.

2. From *Informal Speech*, Edward D. Carterette and Margaret Hubbard Jones (Berkeley: University of California Press, 1974), p. 384.

3. Ibid., p. 385, gives the transcription of the passage. The transcriptional notation used in their discussion is equivalent although not identical to that used in this book.

4. There is currently a great interest in developing rules for the placement of both word and phrase stress. See Chapter 14, "Focus, Theme, and Emphasis," in R. Quirk, S. Greenbaum, G. Leech, and J. Svartvik, *A Grammar of Contemporary English* (London and New York: Longman Group and Seminar Press, 1972), and W. B. Dickerson, "Predicting Word Stress: Generative Rules in an ESL Context," *TESL Studies* (University of Illinois) 1 (1975), pp. 38–52.

5. One might think of saying *information* instead of *material* here, but to native speakers information is not necessarily lost. In a situational context, they do not need the full form of the auxiliary in C4. But the full form may be crucial to the learner's understanding. If we take the concept from information theory that information is the reduction of uncertainty we see that, at the beginning, foreign-language learners have the wrong set of expectancies; they are looking in the signal for cues they may not get, and do not recognize available cues which for the native speaker would be uncertainty-reducing. For the *Uncertainties of a Spoken Message*, see Chapter 3, p. 64.

6. All comments in parentheses in the description of the five styles are based on M. Joos, *The Five Clocks* (New York: Harcourt, Brace and World, 1961).

7. New York: E. P. Dutton, 1974, pp. 48–49.

8. For a further brief discussion of styles in spoken English and examples of dialogues in several styles, see "Styles of Language" in M. N. Bruder, *MMC: Developing Communicative Competence in English as a Second Language* (Pittsburgh, Pa.: University Center for International Studies, University of Pittsburgh, 1974), pp. 165–66.

9. John R. Searle, *Speech Acts: An Essay in the Philosophy of Language* (Cambridge, Eng.: Cambridge University Press, 1969), p. 16.

10. Ibid., p. 16.

11. For a thorough discussion of this subject see W. M. Rivers, "Individualized Instruction and Cooperative Learning: Some Theoretical Considerations," in Rivers (1976a), pp. 236–55.

12. "Semantics plays a central role in syntax," George Lakoff in "On Generative Semantics," in D. D. Steinberg and L. A. Jakobovits, eds., *Semantics* (Cambridge, Eng.: Cambridge University Press, 1971), p. 232, Footnote *a*.

13. Discussed more fully in W. M. Rivers, *Teaching Foreign-Language Skills* (Chicago: The University of Chicago Press, 1968), pp. 78–80.

14. C. Gattegno, *Teaching Foreign Languages in Schools: The Silent Way* (Reading, U.K.: Educational Explorers Ltd., 1963). The Silent Way is described in more detail in *ADFL* 5 (1973–74): C. Dominice, "The Silent Way: A Student Looks at Teaching" (pp. 23–24), and C. Perrault, "The Silent Way: An Experienced User Speaks" (pp. 25–26).

15. Ibid., p. 39.

16. Ibid., p. 21.

17. Ibid., p. 38.

18. Ibid., p. 40.

19. Ibid., p. 24.

20. The Gouin series is described in detail, with class procedure, in R. Titone, *Teaching Foreign Languages. A Historical Sketch* (Washington, D.C.: Georgetown University Press, 1968), pp. 33–37. A similar approach to the beginning stages was taken by M. D. Berlitz, the founder of the Berlitz schools.

21. From François Gouin, *The Art of Teaching and Studying Languages*, trans. H. Swan and V. Bétis, (London: George Philip and Son; New York: Charles Scribner's Sons, 1892), p. 131. This has a contemporary ring. The Berkeley linguist, Wallace Chafe, considers the verb to be central in semantics. In *Meaning and the Structure of Language* (Chicago: The University of Chicago Press, 1970) he suggests as "a general principle that semantic influence radiates from a verb" (p. 190) and in his work he considers the verb central and the noun peripheral (p. 96).

22. Gouin (1892), p. 162.

23. Ibid., p. 174. Example C11 is Gouin's original example written in 1890. Note the following: "towards" in line 1 is the usual form in General British English (GB), whereas "toward" is normal in General American English (GA); "I draw near to the door," as a precise movement in the series, would probably be replaced in modern GA and GB by the less formal "I come close to the door."

24. See J. J. Asher, "The Learning Strategy of the Total Physical Response: A Review," *MLJ* 50 (1966), pp. 79–84. Asher claims that the association of action and sound results in longer retention, at least for listening comprehension.

25. Developed by the Institute of Modern Languages in Washington, D.C., and described in John Schumann, "Communication Techniques," *TQ* 6 (1972), pp. 143–46.

26. E. B. de Sauzé's approach is described in *The Cleveland Plan for the Teaching of Modern Languages with Special Reference to French* (Philadelphia: The John C. Winston Company, 1929). Ralph Hester, ed., in *Teaching a Living Language* (New York: Harper and Row, 1970), p. x, claims that the verbal-active method, a "rationalist direct method," derives from de Sauzé. Yvone Lenard dedicated her verbal-active textbook, *Parole et Pensée* (New York: Harper and Row, 1965) to Emile B. de Sauzé, a "maître de l'enseignement."

27. Y. Lenard, "Methods and Materials, Techniques and the Teacher" in Hester, ed. (1970), p. 37.

28. Karl C. Diller, "Linguistic Theories of Language Acquisition," in Hester, ed. (1970), pp. 16–17, 18; and also K. C. Diller, *Generative Grammar, Structural Linguistics, and Language Teaching* (Rowley, Mass.: Newbury House, 1971), pp. 25, 27.

29. Lenard in Hester, ed. (1970), p. 36.

30. Ibid., p. 50.

31. Ibid., p. 55.

32. Adapted from Y. Lenard, *Parole et Pensée. Introduction au français d'aujourd'hui.* Deuxième Edition (New York: Harper and Row, 1971), p. 341.

33. L. G. Kelly in *25 Centuries of Language Teaching* (Rowley, Mass.: Newbury House, 1969) traces the use of the dialogue in foreign-language teach-

ing back to the *colloquium* of the Middle Ages (p. 120). Dialogues are also used in G. Lozanov's Suggestopedia, which is described in J. Bancroft, "Foreign Language Teaching in Bulgaria," *Canadian Modern Language Review* 28(1972):9–13.

34. 13-1 DIALOG in William E. Rutherford, *Modern English*, 2d ed., Vol. 1 (New York: Harcourt Brace Jovanovich, 1975), p. 259.

35. There seems to be a misconception among some foreign-language teachers that only learning grammar rules and working deductively and analytically can be called "cognitive." Actually from the point of view of cognitive psychology any process which requires students to think, to extract meaning from any symbolic behavior (action, strange utterance, pictorial representation), to work out generalizations from examples or instances (induction), is a cognitive operation. See W. M. Rivers, "The Foreign-Language Teacher and Cognitive Psychology," in Rivers (1976a), pp. 109–130, and Rivers (1977).

36. Earl W. Stevick of the Foreign Service Institute, Washington, D.C., originated the "microwave cycle" which he described in "UHF and Microwaves in Transmitting Language Skills" in E. W. Najam and Carleton T. Hodge, eds., *Language Learning: The Individual and the Process, IJAL* 32, 1, Part 2 (1966), Publication 40 of the Indiana University Research Center in Anthropology, Folklore, and Linguistics, pp. 84–94. In *Adapting and Writing Language Lessons* (Washington, D.C.: Foreign Service Institute, 1971), pp. 310–15, Stevick explains that he developed this device from the question-answer technique of Thomas Cummings in *How to Learn a Foreign Language* (privately published, 1916), and that *he now prefers the term Cummings device*. The device has been used with good results in Peace Corps and Foreign Service Institute materials in a variety of languages. Chapter 6 and Appendices P, Q, and R of Stevick (1971) give detailed examples of the device in languages as diverse as English, French, Lao, Bini, Kikuyu, and Ponapean.

37. Stevick (1971), p. 311.

38. Ibid., pp. 312–13.

39. Stevick (1966), p. 92.

40. Stevick (1971), p. 314.

41. Ibid., p. 37.

42. Lenard in Hester (1970), p. 50, says "There should be (an oral composition) for every lesson, to be followed the next day by a written one. The oral composition becomes, in fact, the most important exercise of the verbal-active method in building the elements of which fluency is composed: the ability to speak at length, aloud, clearly and confidently, in front of other people, and to use the words and structures that you know freely and correctly in order to say what you mean."

43. Ibid.

44. Ibid., p. 56.

45. Francis A. Cartier reports that a team of programmers under his direction at the Defense Language Institute English Language Branch has developed a series of situational conversations on tape along these lines for individual learning and practice. These tapes seek to elicit certain structures. It was found that students experienced a definite feeling of rapport with the speakers and would work through the tapes several times to try to improve their efforts.

2. AUTONOMOUS INTERACTION

1. Rivers (1968), p. 201. An approach to language learning which begins with student innovation is *Community Language Learning*, which is rooted in Charles Curran's ideas, most fully developed in *Counseling-Learning in Second Languages* (Apple River, Ill.: Apple River Press, 1976). For a description of CLL, see E. W. Stevick, *Memory, Meaning and Method: Some Psychological Perspectives on Language Learning* (Rowley, Mass.: Newbury House, 1976), pp. 125–33.

2. Emma M. Birkmaier, "The Meaning of Creativity in Foreign Language Training," *MLJ* 55 (1971), p. 350.

3. Abraham H. Maslow, *Motivation and Personality,* 2d ed. (New York: Harper and Row, 1970), Chapter 4: "A Theory of Human Motivation" sets out this hierarchy. Its importance in communication in the foreign-language classroom is discussed in Earl W. Stevick, "Before Linguistics and Beneath Method" in Kurt Jankowsky, ed., *Language and International Studies,* Georgetown University Round Table on Languages and Linguistics 1973 (Washington, D.C.: Georgetown University Press, 1973), pp. 99–106.

4. C. B. Paulston examines the notion of communicative competence as the social rules of language use in "Linguistic and Communicative Competence," *TQ* 8 (1974), pp. 347–62.

5. C. B. Paulston and H. R. Selekman, "Interaction Activities in the Foreign Language Classroom, or How to Grow a Tulip-Rose," *FLA* 9 (1976), pp. 248–54.

6. Selekman, in Paulston and Selekman (1976), p. 253, tells of the shock and disappointment experienced by one of his students in Pittsburgh when he discovered that the ostensibly monolingual Hebrew speaker to whom he thought he was speaking on the telephone spoke perfect English.

7. Described fully in Paulston and Selekman (1976), pp. 252–53.

8. Alexander Lipson, "Some New Strategies for Teaching Oral Skills," in Robert C. Lugton, ed., *Toward a Cognitive Approach to Second Language Acquisition* (Philadelphia: Center for Curriculum Development, 1971), pp. 231–44.

9. Paulston and Selekman (1976), p. 254.

10. Lipson (1971), p. 240.

11. Stevick (1971), pp. 365–90.

12. There are interesting lists of English words borrowed from other languages in P. Strevens, *British and American English* (London: Collier-Macmillan, 1972), Chapter 3. See also R13 and fn Chap. 6.3.

13. We have adopted this term from the work of the Committee for Out-of-School Education and Cultural Development of the Council for Cultural Cooperation (CCC) of the Council of Europe. See *Systems Development in Adult Language Learning* (Strasbourg: CCC, Council of Europe, 1973), pp. 67–68. The contributing experts to this publication were J.L.M. Trim, R. Richterich, J. A. van Ek, and D. A. Wilkins.

14. A. Howatt, "The Background to Course Design," in J. P. B. Allen and S. Pit Corder, eds., *Techniques in Applied Linguistics. The Edinburgh Course in Applied Linguistics,* Vol. 3 (London: Oxford University Press, 1974), p. 7.

15. CCC (1973), p. 63. The authors state that their classification is intended as "a working hypothesis designed to clear the ground for future research." Those particularly interested in the teaching of languages to adults should consult the survey article, "Languages for Adult Learners," by J. L. M. Trim, in *LTLA* 9, No. 2 (April, 1976), pp. 73–92, which concludes with an extensive Classified Bibliography on Adult Language Learning.

16. For the breakdown of some 44 occupational categories, see CCC (1973), p. 68.

17. CC (1973), p. 68.

18. F. François, "Contexte et Situation," *Linguistique. Guide alphabétique* (Paris: Denoël, 1969), p. 65. Quoted in CCC (1973), p. 68.

19. Paraphrased from J. Lyons, *Introduction to Theoretical Linguistics.* (Cambridge, Eng.: Cambridge University Press, 1969), p. 413, as quoted in CCC (1973), p. 68.

20. CCC (1973), p. 68.

21. The very detailed description of how this approach was used at the Administrative College of Papua New Guinea may help others to develop similar courses. See S. Copland, "A Communicative Skills Course for Administrators in Papua New Guinea," *ELT* 30(1976):245–53.

22. Passage transcribed word for word from a tape of authentic conversation recorded from a Boston radio station on February 6, 1976. Ordinary citizens call the disk jockey by phone and the listener hears both sides of the subsequent discussion.

23. Stevick (1973), p. 100.

24. Ibid.

25. See "Individualized Instruction and Cooperative Learning—Some Theoretical Considerations," in Rivers (1976a), pp. 236–55.

3.　LISTENING

1. P. T. Rankin, "Listening Ability: its Importance, Measurement, and Development," *Chicago Schools Journal* 12, pp. 177–9, quoted in D. Spearritt, *Listening Comprehension—A Factorial Analysis* (Melbourne: Australian Council for Educational Research, 1962), p. 2.

2. Spearritt (1962), pp. 92–93. Spearritt adds "There is some evidence that performance on listening comprehension tests is related to performance on inductive reasoning, verbal comprehension and certain types of memory tests." The view that there is a distinctive listening comprehension factor has been queried by T. G. Sticht in "Learning by Listening", in J. B. Carroll and R. O. Freedle, eds., *Language Comprehension and the Acquisition of Knowledge* (Washington, D.C.: V. H. Winston & Sons, 1972), p. 294.

3. R. E. Troike, "Receptive Competence, Productive Competence, and Performance," in J. E. Alatis, ed., *Linguistics and the Teaching of Standard English to Speakers of Other Languages or Dialects.* Report of the Twentieth Annual Round Table Meeting on Linguistics and Language Studies (Washington, D.C.: Georgetown University Press Monograph No. 22, 1970), pp. 63–73.

4. See T. Bever, "The Cognitive Basis for Linguistic Structures" in J. R. Hayes, ed., *Cognition and the Development of Language* (New York: John

Wiley and Sons, 1970), and "Linguistic and Psychological Factors in Speech Perception and Their Implications for Teaching Materials" in Rivers (1976a), pp. 131–44.

5. These two levels, the recognition and selection levels, are discussed fully in relation to listening comprehension in Rivers (1968), pp. 142–43.

6. N. Chomsky in *Aspects of the Theory of Syntax* (Cambridge, Mass.: The MIT Press, 1965), p. 9, says that "a generative grammar is not a model for a speaker or a hearer. It attempts to characterize in the most neutral possible terms the knowledge of the language that provides the basis for actual use of language by a speaker-hearer."

7. For some perceptual strategies, see Bever in Hayes, ed. (1970), pp. 287–312.

8. Colin Cherry, *On Human Communication* (New York: John Wiley and Sons, 1957), p. 277.

9. Ibid., p. 277.

10. From a tape recorded by WMR in January, 1976, during a visit to Australia. This speaker was explaining the situation in an articulate, conversational way, despite the "disorderly" appearance of C36. As we listen, we do not notice every sound segment that is uttered because we are anticipating the message. It is, therefore, quite difficult to take down in this fashion every detail of what was actually uttered. One has to listen again and again to some segments of the tape to overcome one's deeply ingrained habits of discounting the unessential in what one is hearing.

11. For a detailed discussion of hearing as a stochastic process, that is, based on expectations, see Charles F. Hockett, "Grammar for the Hearer," in R. Jakobson, ed., *Structure of Language and its Mathematical Aspects* (American Mathematical Society, 1961), pp. 220–36.

12. The seminal book in this area was E. T. Hall, *The Silent Language* (New York: Doubleday, 1959). See also R. L. Birdwhistell, *Kinesics and Context: Essays on Body Motion Communication* (Philadelphia: University of Pennsylvania Press, 1970) which has an extensive bibliography, and, by the same author, "Some Body Motion Elements Accompanying Spoken American English," in L. Thayer, ed., *Communication: Concepts and Perspectives* (London: Macmillan and Washington, D.C.: Spartan Books, 1967), pp. 53–76.

13. Walter Cronkite on the CBS News from New York, February 5th, 1976.

14. Walter Cronkite on the CBS News, February 4th, 1976.

15. A detailed description of these stages is given in Rivers (1976a) pp. 131–44. See also U. Neisser, *Cognitive Psychology* (New York: Appleton-Century-Crofts, 1967), Chapter 7: Speech Perception.

16. Asher (1966), pp. 79–80.

17. Ibid., pp. 80–82.

18. G. A. Miller's term in "The Magical Number Seven, Plus or Minus Two: Some Limits on our Capacity for Processing Information," *Psychological Review* 63 (1956), pp. 81–96.

19. The pros and cons of the backward buildup technique are discussed in detail in Rivers (1968), pp. 171–72.

20. The April Fools' Day custom as learned by WMR as a child was as

follows: up until noon, one played practical jokes on one's friends trying to trick them so that they became April Fools; after twelve o'clock, practical jokes were out and pintails (as in C49) were in.

21. A detailed discussion of the stress and intonation patterns of American English may be found in J. D. Bowen, *Patterns of English Pronunciation* (Rowley, Mass.: Newbury House, 1975), and for British English in A. C. Gimson, *An Introduction to the Pronunciation of English* (IPE), 2d ed. (London: Edward Arnold, 1970), and for a fuller treatment Roger Kingdon, *The Groundwork of English Stress* and *The Groundwork of English Intonation* (London: Longman, 1958).

22. Processes involved in fluent reading are compared with processes of listening in Rivers (1976a), pp. 142–43.

23. From H. Golden, *So What Else is New?* (New York: Fawcett World Library, 1967), pp. 41–42 (with some adaptations by WMR).

24. The information in this paragraph and the quotation are from "Research in Listening Comprehension", by Andrew Wilkinson, *Educational Research* 12 (1970), pp. 140–141.

25. Golden (1967), p. 26.

26. Bever in Hayes, ed. (1970), p. 291.

27. This is basic to the controversy between the Transformational-Generative grammarians who support the Standard Theory and the Generative Semanticists. Chomsky has stated that "there must be, represented in the mind, a fixed system of generative principles that characterize and associate deep and surface structures in some definite way—a grammar, in other words, that is used in some fashion as discourse is produced or interpreted" (*Language and Mind*, 1st ed. 1968, p. 16). According to G. Lakoff, "the theory of generative semantics claims that the linguistic elements used in grammar have an independent natural basis in the human conceptual system . . . Generative Semantics takes grammar as being based on the independently given natural logical categories, . . . and on natural logical classes . . ." (from "The Arbitrary Basis of Transformational Grammar" in *Language* 48 (1972), pp 77–78).

28. These are basic to Fillmore's Case Grammar: Fillmore adds other functions such as instrument and experiencer.

29. Bever in Hayes, ed. (1970), pp. 286–99. The strategies are described as follows: Strategy A, p. 290; Strategy B, p. 204; Strategy C, p. 296; Strategy D, p. 298.

30. In transformational-generative grammar each clause is considered a sentence and assigned the symbol S.

31. I. M. Schlesinger, *Sentence Structure and the Reading Process* (The Hague: Mouton, 1968), pp. 122–41.

32. John Chancellor on the NBC Nightly News from New York, February 5th, 1976 (slightly shortened). Original text in C58.

33. This chart is a completely revised and expanded version of the one in Rivers (1968), pp. 151–54.

34. Short-term retention, as used in this chart, is not synonymous with short-term memory. Echoic memory is useful for only a few seconds, during which the listener still has recourse to the raw data. Active verbal memory (immediate memory or short-term memory) can hold from five to nine cog-

nitive chunks created by the listener (e.g., short phrases or groups of digits). This material is then recoded for storage in long-term memory. The expression short-term retention, as used in this chart, is a pragmatic one, referring to the short interval that elapses before what the student has heard is put to some active use. Students are not expected to hold the material in their memory for use at a later stage, as they are for the long-term retention of Stage D. For a detailed discussion of theoretical work on memory, see B. S. Melvin and W. M. Rivers, "In One Ear and Out the Other: Implications of Memory Studies for Language Learning," in J. Fanselow and R. Crymes, eds., *On TESOL '76* (Washington, D.C.: TESOL, 1976).

35. Cloze tests are discussed in Chapters 8 and 9. For a full discussion of cloze tests, with bibliography, see J. W. Oller, Jr., "Cloze Tests of Second Language Proficiency and What They Measure," *LL* 23 (1973), pp. 105–118. See also R. M. Valette, *Modern Language Testing*, 2d ed. (New York: Harcourt Brace Jovanovich, 1977), pp. 212–15.

36. A similar techique is described and discussed by S. Belasco in "C'est la Guerre? or Can Cognition and Verbal Behavior Co-exist in Second-Language Learning," in R. C. Lugton, ed. (1971), pp. 223–24. In Belasco's approach, the student is provided from the beginning with a text with visual hints to deviations from the standard style of language. Here, at the advanced level, we suggest a purely listening and writing task.

4. ORAL PRACTICE FOR THE LEARNING OF GRAMMAR

1. G. Roger and S. Wormald, *England Calling,* III: *Fact and Fancy* (Paris: Librairie Hatier, 1936), p. 193, translated by WMR.

2. See Quirk et al. (1972), p. 189.

3. Ibid., p. 190.

4. R. and M. Carpentier-Fialip, *Grammaire de l'anglais vivant*, éd. rev. (Paris: Classiques Hachette, 1935), p. 148.

5. Ibid., p. 10.

6. Ibid., p. 148.

7. M. Kuhan, *Les Auteurs anglais du programme*. Brevet Supérieur 1914–1917. 2ᵉ éd. (Paris: Librairie Ch. Delagrave, 1913), p. 142.

8. Roger and Wormald (1936), p. 25.

9. Kuhn (1913), p. 142.

10. GA and GB have different preferred usage with *have* in the interrogative and negative. *Have* with *do-* periphrasis is used in GA in these cases. While this form is becoming current in GB also, it is not generally used when *have* expresses possession or personal characteristics. For example, *you have a carpet* has the following conversions in GA: *Do you have a carpet? You don't have a carpet. Don't you have a carpet?* and in GB: *Have you (got) a carpet? You haven't (got) a carpet. Haven't you (got) a carpet?* (*Have got* is common in these cases in GB informal style.) Compare GA: *Does she have red hair?* with GB: *Has she got red hair?* When the sense of *have* is that of habitual, general practice, the preferred form in GB is *Do you have*, as in *Do you have milk in your tea?* (as the usual thing). For further information, see Hornby (1975), pp. 7–9, and Quirk et al. (1971), pp. 80 and 388.

11. The use of substitution tables has been traced back to Erasmus in the sixteenth century. See L. Kelly (1969), p. 101. Harold Palmer gives examples of substitution tables and advocates their use in *The Scientific Study and Teaching of Languages* (London: Harrap, 1917).

12. The term *possessive adjective* is used in A. S. Hornby, *Guide to Patterns and Usage in English*, 2d ed. (London: Oxford University Press, 1975), p. 121. For attributive possessive pronouns used as determiners (*my, her,* etc.) and predicative possessive pronouns (*mine, hers,* etc.), see Quirk et al. (1972), p. 213.

13. An interesting analysis of drills into mechanical, meaningful, and communication categories is made in C. B. Paulston, "The Sequencing of Structural Pattern Drills," *TQ* 5 (1971), pp. 197–208. This analysis is further developed in C. B. Paulston and M. N. Bruder, *From Substitution to Substance: A Handbook of Structural Pattern Drills* (Rowley, Mass.: Newbury House, 1975), and in C. B. Paulston and M. N. Bruder, *Teaching English as a Second Language: Techniques and Procedures* (Cambridge, Mass.: Winthrop Publishers, 1976). The subject is also discussed in "Talking off the Tops of Their Heads" in Rivers (1976a), pp. 21–35.

14. T. G. Bever, "Language and Perception," in G. A. Miller, ed., *Communication, Language, and Meaning: Psychological Perspectives* (New York: Basic Books, 1973), pp. 155–57.

15. The underlying structural relations in sentences like 5 and 6 are discussed in N. Chomsky, *Language and Mind,* enlarg. ed. (New York: Harcourt Brace Jovanovich, 1972), pp. 36–37.

16. Ellipsis is not haphazard. For a full discussion of usage in this area, see Quirk et al. (1973), pp. 536–50. Ellipsis of this type is not substandard speech but a common characteristic of familiar speech. (See C5).

17. The concept of Type A and Type B exercises is developed more fully in W. M. Rivers, "From Linguistic Competence to Communicative Competence," *TQ* 7 (1973), pp. 25–34. Reprinted in Rivers (1976a), pp. 36–48.

18. For a useful discussion of the complexities of placing adverbs in an English sentence, see Hornby (1975), pp. 165–81, and Quirk et al. (1973), pp. 426–520.

19. A useful list of American English rejoinders and exclamations is given in J. M. Dobson, *Effective Techniques for English Conversation Groups* (Rowley, Mass.: Newbury House, 1974), pp. 125–30. Teachers are reminded that many expressive rejoinders slip in and out of fashion, while others remain standard features of English speech. They should keep informed in this area.

5.   TEACHING THE SOUND SYSTEM

1. It is presumed that most trainee teachers and practicing teachers have at some time studied the English sound system (either American or British or both). This very sketchy introduction to the terminology used by structural phonologists (and, later in the chapter, generative phonologists) is included for the benefit of the occasional student to whom it is new. A thorough discussion of teaching techniques which may be derived from structuralist and transformational-generative linguistic theory may be found in R. L. Politzer, *Linguistics*

and Applied Linguistics: Aims and Methods (Philadelphia: Center for Curriculum Development, 1972).

2. Clifford H. Prator, Jr., and Betty Wallace Robinett, *Manual of American English Pronunciation*, 3d ed. (New York: Holt, Rinehart and Winston, Inc., 1972), p. xiv. Italics in the original.

3. See, for example, the University of Chicago Press (Chicago, Ill.) *Contrastive Structure Series,* Charles A. Ferguson, Gen. ed.: W. G. Moulton, *The Sounds of English and German,* 1972; F. B. Agard and R. J. Di Pietro, *The Sounds of English and Italian,* 1965; R. P. Stockwell and J. D. Bowen, *The Sounds of English and Spanish,* 1965. Two useful bibliographies of contrastive studies are: *A Bibliography of Contrastive Linguistics,* John H. Hammer and Frank A. Rice, eds. (Washington, D.C.: Center for Applied Linguistics, 1965); and Dorothy A. Pedtke, Bernarda Erwin, and Anna Maria Malkoc, eds., *Reference List of Materials for English as a Second Language* (Washington, D.C.: Center for Applied Linguistics, 1969), "Contrastive Studies," pp. 111–18.

4. For contrastive analysis, see: Robert J. Di Pietro, *Language Structures in Contrast* (Rowley, Mass.: Newbury House, 1971); G. Nickel, ed., *Papers in Contrastive Linguistics* (Cambridge, Eng.: Cambridge University Press, 1971); and James E. Alatis, ed., *Contrastive Linguistics and its Pedagogical Implications,* Georgetown University Round Table on Linguistics and Language Studies (Washington, D.C.: Georgetown University Press 1968); S. Pit Corder, *Introducing Applied Linguistics* (Harmondsworth, Eng.: Penguin Books, 1973), Chap. 10: "Selection 2: Contrastive Linguistic Studies," pp. 224–55. For a presentation of English sounds in the form of contrasting pairs and a list of languages whose speakers might be expected to experience difficulty with each pair, see Don L. F. Nilsen and Alleen Pace Nilsen, *Pronunciation Contrasts in English* (New York: Simon and Schuster, Inc., 1971).

5. See Ronald Wardhaugh, "The Contrastive Analysis Hypothesis," in *New Frontiers in Second Language Learning,* John H. Schumann and Nancy Stenson, eds. (Rowley, Mass.: Newbury House, 1974), pp. 11–19. This book is a collection of essays on error analysis and interlanguage, whose thesis we might summarize as follows: *Differences* between two languages, even assuming they could be clearly identified by the techniques of contrastive analysis, do not adequately predict the *difficulties* of the new-language learner.

6. That some differences in sound systems pose greater problems than others has long been recognized. Stockwell and Bowen (1965) tried to set up a hierarchy of difficulty for English speakers learning Spanish. Their theoretical framework is of interest. In their discussion of the teaching of pronunciation, they show that not all errors are equally important. More recent studies in error analysis emphasize this aspect. Schumann and Stenson, eds. (1974) point out that some errors are simply "performance errors" due to "memory lapses, fatigue, confusion, or strong emotion" (p. 5). Other errors may result from teaching materials or procedures used, and should, of course, concern teachers and text-book writers. A third class of errors is significant for what it can tell us about how languages are learned, that is, errors which reveal the *strategies* the student is using in acquiring the new code, e.g., transfer from the native language, transfer from other languages with which the student may be familiar, generalization, and overgeneralization. See L. Dušková, "On Sources of Errors

in Foreign Language Learning," *IRAL* 7 (1969), pp. 11–36; J. C. Richards, "Error Analysis and Second Language Strategies," in Schumann and Stenson, eds. (1974), pp. 32–53; and Corder (1973), Chap. 11: "Selection 3: The Study of Learners' Language: Error Analysis," pp. 256–94. For a discussion of the notion of *interlanguage:* "a separate linguistic system based on the observable output which results from a learner's attempted production of a TL [target language] norm," see L. Selinker, "Interlanguage," in Schumann and Stenson, eds. (1974), pp. 114–36. A very useful assessment of this area, with bibliography, is given by S. N. Sridhar, "Contrastive Analysis, Error Analysis, and Interlanguage: Three Phases of One Goal?" *Studies in Language Learning* (Urbana, Ill.: Unit for Foreign Language Study and Research), Vol. 1, No. 1 (1975), pp. 60–94.

7. For further information on this subject, see S. A. Schane, *Generative Phonology* (Englewood Cliffs, N.J.: Prentice-Hall, 1973). Much more difficult, but fundamental as the starting point for most work in generative phonology as applied to English, is Noam Chomsky and Morris Halle, *The Sound Pattern of English* (New York: Harper and Row, 1968).

8. W. B. Dickerson, "Generative Theory in TESL Practice," *MLJ* 61 (1977), p. 187.

9. Ibid., p. 182. For further treatment of this approach, see W. B. Dickerson, "The Wh Question of Pronunciation: An Answer from Spelling and Generative Phonology," *TQ* 9(1975):299–309.

10. See also R. Quirk, *The Use of English* (London: Longmans, Green and Co., Ltd., 1963), pp. 79–96: "What is Standard English?" and A. H. Marckwardt, "American and British English," in H. B. Allen and R. N. Campbell, eds., *Teaching English as a Second Language: A Book of Readings*, 2d ed. (New York: McGraw-Hill, 1972), pp. 234–42.

11. For recent books and articles which discuss what kind of English to teach and how to deal with language variation see J. D. Bowen, "Linguistic Variation as a Problem in Second-Language Teaching" in Allen and Campbell, eds. (1972), pp. 242–50; Prator and Robinett (1972), pp. x–xi; W. B. Dickerson, "Phonological Variability in Pronunciation Instruction: A Principled Approach," *TQ* 10(1976):177–91; Corder (1973), Chap. 9 (Selection 1: Comparison of Varieties), pp. 201–23.

12. These are the varieties represented in OALDCE and identified as follows: "In its own country each of them is the variety of English most associated with national broadcasting and least restricted in its geographical distribution" (p. xii). They can be regarded as standard according to Quirk's criterion: in its own country each one is "that kind of English which draws least attention to itself over the widest area and through the widest range of usage," R. Quirk (1963), p. 95. For General American, see Prator and Robinett (1972) and J. D. Bowen (1975). For General British, see A. C. Gimson's IPE (1970) and J. Windsor Lewis, *A Guide to English Pronunciation* (Oslo: Universitetsforlaget, 1969).

13. This is not an exhaustive treatment of the differences. See also J. Windsor Lewis, "American and British Accents of English," *ELT* XXV (1971):239–48; Strevens, (1972), pp. 67–81 (Strevens's "Transcription of General American Pronunciation," p. 71, unaccountably omits two sounds: /æ/ and /ɔ/). There

are also brief discussions of some of the differences in the introductory sections of Hornby's OALDCE and J. Windsor Lewis, *A Concise Pronouncing Dictionary of British and American English* (CPD) (London: Oxford University Press, 1972).

14. Marckwardt in Allen and Campbell, eds. (1972), p. 237.

15. Bowen (1975), p. 39.

16. Gimson (1970), p. 206.

17. In current phonemic representations of the GB vowel system (Gimson in IPE, Lewis in CPD, Hornby in OALDCE), the vowels of *meet* and *boot* are represented not as diphthongs but as simple vowels or long vowels: Gimson has /i:/, /u:/, /ɑ:/, /ɔ:/, and /ɜ:/; the second elements of the diphthongs are /ɪ/ and /ʊ/ (the vowels of *bit* and *put*) rather than /y/ and /w/; the first element of the diphthong of *boy* is /ɔ/; and that of the diphthong of *boat* is /ə/, reflecting the phonetic shape of the principal allophone [əʊ] (a much more central first element than GA /ow/). Lewis lists /ɜ/ and /ʌ/ as additional mid central vowels in his chart of GA, but these are treated as /ər/ and /ə/, respectively, in the analysis used here. For a fuller treatment of these points, see the paragraphs on *r* on pp. 158–59, and the discussions in Bowen (1975), pp. 52–57, and Prator and Robinett (1972), p. 5, n. 2, and pp. 96–98.

18. This chart was suggested by Nicholas Temperley. For clearly presented articulatory information on GA and GB, see items under footnote 12.

19. Sometimes a student will succeed in making the correct sound in a somewhat different way, but most students will need the teacher's help and will profit from precise instructions.

20. Bowen (1975), p. 53.

21. Robert L. Politzer and Frieda N. Politzer, *Teaching English as a Second Language* (Lexington, Mass.: Xerox, 1972), p. 102.

22. Prator and Robinett (1972), p. 96.

23. Bowen (1975), p. 52.

24. Prator and Robinett (1972), p. 96.

25. Prator and Robinett (1972), pp. 96–97. Italics in the original.

26. Bowen (1975), p. 52.

27. Prator and Robinett (1972), pp. 97–98.

28. Lonna Dickerson, "English Consonants: Pronunciation Difficulties of Japanese, Korean, and Spanish Speakers," (Urbana, Ill.: unpublished paper, 1970), p. 18.

29. Examples in this sentence from Bowen (1975), p. 138.

30. Information supplied by Milton M. Azevedo, University of California at Berkeley.

31. L. Dickerson (1970), p. 15.

32. Bowen (1975) contextualizes minimal pairs (*This is a wood/good stove,* p. 72) and uses visual aids, gestures, actions to convey the differences in meaning. See also J. D. Bowen, "Contextualizing Pronunciation Practice in the ESOL Classroom," *TQ* 6(1972), pp. 83–94.

33. For GA, consult Bowen (1975), chapters 7, 8, and 9; Prator and Robinett (1972), Chapters 3, 4, 5, and 6. For GB, consult Gimson (1970), chapters 10 and 11.

34. Some varieties of British English use the "short a" for *dance* while

retaining the "broad a" for some other forms in this group (notably some Australian and some provincial English varieties).

35. For the history of this alternation, see Albert Marckwardt, *American English* (New York: Oxford University Press, 1958), pp. 69–71.

36. Sound-spelling correspondences in English are treated in several recent books and articles. A comprehensive presentation of the subject is given in Axel Wijk, *Rules for the Pronunciation of the English Language* (London: Oxford University Press, 1966). Peter MacCarthy, *English Pronunciation* (Cambridge, Eng.: W. Heffer & Sons, 1950) gives forms in both phonemic and orthographic transcription, and has a particularly useful Index of English Spellings, pp. 170–72. See also Richard L. Venezky, *The Structure of English Orthography* (The Hague: Mouton, 1970); and Prator and Robinett (1972), Lesson 15, "Long and Short Vowels," (pp. 159–69), and Lesson 16, "Spelling and Vowel Sounds," (pp. 170–81). R. & F. Politzer (1972), gives lists of correspondences, orthographic———→phonemic symbol and phonemic———→orthographic symbol (pp. 105–20). The relation between vowel alternation and spelling is treated in Robert L. Oswalt, "English Orthography as a Morphophonemic System: Stressed Vowels," *Linguistics* 102(1973): 5–40.

37. The checklist given below may be compared with the Accent Inventory (with Diagnostic Passage and Check List of Errors) which was published to accompany Prator and Robinett (1972).

II *The written word*

6. READING I: PURPOSES AND PROCEDURES

1. More research is needed to determine which basic grammatical relations in English are essential in enabling a person to read English with comprehension.

2. J. McGlathery describes such a course in "A New Program of Substitute and Supplementary German Language Courses" in W. M. Rivers, L. H. Allen, et al., eds., *Changing Patterns in Foreign Language Programs* (Rowley, Mass.: Newbury House, 1972), pp. 248–53.

3. Examples in R13 are adapted from O. Jespersen, *Growth and Structure of the English Language*, 9th ed., (Garden City, N.Y.: Doubleday, 1955), Chapter VII: "Various Sources," pp. 157–60. This chapter treats borrowings into English from other than the Scandinavian, French, and Latin languages.

4. Jean Praninskas attacked this problem by examining the frequency of lexical items on every tenth page of ten textbooks used by the freshman class at the American University in Beirut for the study of mathematics, chemistry, biology, physics, psychology, sociology, history, and English language and literature. From a corpus of 272,473 token items she established the *American University Word List* (London: Longmans, 1972).

5. For an explanation of *cooperative learning*, see W. M. Rivers, "Individualized Instruction and Cooperative Learning: Some Theoretical Considerations," in Rivers (1976a), pp. 250–52.

6. See R. Mead and A. D. Lilley, "The Use of Visual Materials in Teaching English to Economics Students," *ELT* 29(1975), p. 152.

7. J. D. Corbluth, "English?—or 'Special English'?" *ELT* 29(1975), p. 280.

8. Ibid., p. 281.

9. Ibid., p. 285. For a discussion of this subject, see R. J. Cowan, "Lexical and Syntactic Research for the Design of EFL Reading Materials," *TQ* 8(1974):389–99.

10. Some students are able to reach this stage more rapidly through the experience of living for a time in an English-speaking community—unfortunately, many do not have this opportunity.

11. Extracted from S. Costinett, *Orientation in American English: Reader 3* (Silver Spring, Md.: Institute of Modern Languages, Inc., 1970), p. 3. Our citations from the *Orientation in American English* Series in a chapter on reading should not obscure the fact that the main thrust of this series, with its use of the techniques of Situational Reinforcement® (SR®), is the development of skill in natural, meaningful oral communication. The development of reading and writing skills reinforces the material spoken and heard in class everyday.

12. E. L. Thorndike and I. Lorge, *The Teacher's Word Book of 30,000 Words* (TWB) (New York: Bureau of Publications, Teachers College, Columbia University, 1944). A more recent American count is H. Kučera and W. N. Francis, *Computational Analysis of Present-Day American English* (Providence, R.I.: Brown University Press, 1967).

13. M. West, *A General Service List of English Words*, rev. and enlarged ed. (GSL) (London: Longmans, Green, 1953).

14. Preface, and Introduction, p. ix. The method of establishing the frequency lists is more fully described in the Introduction and Part III, "Explanaatory Notes, Descriptions, and References to Descriptions, of the Four Word Counts," pp. 249–55.

15. Thorndike and Lorge, (1944), p. ix.

16. *The Interim Report on Vocabulary Selection* (London: P. S. King, 1936). Laurence Faucett, Michael West, Harold Palmer, and E. L. Thorndike worked on this project.

17. West (1953), p. xi. The semantic counts of Thorndike and Lorge were based on a sample of 5,000,000 words; the various meanings of a word were established on the basis of the meanings differentiated in the *Oxford English Dictionary*. See West (1953), p. xi.

18. West (1953), p. viii.

19. E. W. Dolch, *Teaching Primary Reading*, 3d ed. (Champaign, Ill.: The Garrard Press), 1960; p. 255.

20. Dolch (1960), p. 241.

21. Ibid., p. 253.

22. Ibid., p. 254.

23. Ibid., p. 254.

24. For further discussion of this approach to reading, see F. Smith, *Understanding Reading* (New York: Holt, Rinehart and Winston, 1971), and F. Smith, ed., *Psycholinguistics and Reading* (New York: Holt, Rinehart and Winston, 1973). For a detailed discussion of various approaches to reading, see J. R. Cowan, "General Linguistics and the Teaching of Reading," in *Studies in Language Learning* (Urbana, Ill.: Unit for Foreign Language Study and Research), Vol. 1, No. 1 (1975), pp. 20–59.

25. English Language Services, *The Key to English Vocabulary* (New York: Collier-Macmillan, 1965), p. vi.

26. These are not commercial publications but are used by OUP authors. These indexes are based not only on GSL and TWB, but also on A. S. Hornby's *Guide to Patterns and Usage in English* (London: OUP, 1954), and L. S. Hill, *Prepositions and Adverbial Particles* (London: Oxford University Press, 1968).

27. The books of the *Ladder Series* are published by Popular Library, Inc. They are available in East Asia, Southeast Asia, Africa, the Near East, and Latin America. They may be ordered from Feffer & Simons, Inc., 31 Union Square, New York, N.Y. 10003, USA.

28. John R. and Janet Shaw, *The New Horizon Ladder Dictionary of the English Language* (New York: A Signet Book, New American Library, 1970).

29. *The Key to English Vocabulary* (London: Collier-Macmillan, 1965), prepared for the Collier-Macmillan English Program by the Materials Development Staff of English Language Services, Inc., under the direction of E. T. Cornelius, Jr., and W. D. Sheeler; the Vocabulary volume is by Earle W. Brockman.

30. *The Key to English Vocabulary*, p. vii.

31. Pfeffer uses the term *utility* vocabulary, see W. M. Rivers and K. M. & V. Dell'Orto, *A Practical Guide to the Teaching of German* (Oxford University Press, 1975), p. 181; Gougenheim and others use the phrase *vocabulaire disponible—personal* or *available* vocabulary, see W. M. Rivers, *A Practical Guide to the Teaching of French* (Oxford University Press, 1975), p. 184.

32. H. A. Keniston, *A Standard List of Spanish Words and Idioms* (Lexington, Ky.: D. C. Heath, 1949), p. vi. Keniston's work is discussed in W. M. Rivers, M. M. Azevedo, et al., *A Practical Guide to the Teaching of Spanish* (Oxford University Press, 1976), pp. 182–83. The reader should note that word lists may be established with the intent of assisting the reader to extract meaning from a text written by others or with the intent of supplying a basic vocabulary for expressing one's own meaning in speech or writing. In the latter case, *cover* becomes an important concept. In devising *Basic English* in the 1920's, C. K. Ogden was seeking to identify "the smallest number of English words with a general enough covering power among them to let a man say almost anything—to say it well enough for his general day-to-day purposes in all the range of his interests however wide," I. A. Richards and C. Gibson, *Techniques in Language Control* (Rowley, Mass.: Newbury House, 1974), p. 27: the section quoted is in Basic English. Richards and Gibson give the Basic English Word List of 850 head-words (pp. 28–29). See also C. K. Ogden, *Basic English: International Second Language* (New York: Harcourt, Brace & World, 1968). J. C. Richards points out that word lists developed from corpora of written materials often omit familiar concrete nouns which native speakers have available to them from their day-to-day experience with the language. In his article, "Word Lists: Problems and Prospects," *RELC Journal* 5, 2 (Dec., 1974):69–84, J. C. Richards gives a list of 300 concrete nouns which were felt by Canadian college students to be the most familiar. He suggests that these be used to supplement basic word lists.

33. S. Frazer, *The Crocodile Dies Twice*, Oxford Progressive Readers, Grade 2 (Singapore: Oxford University Press, 1971). The readers of Grade 2 have a vocabulary restricted to 2900 head words from the Oxford University Press Hill Lists.

34. N. Brooks, *Language and Language Learning: Theory and Practice*, (New York: Harcourt, Brace & World, 1964), pp. 120–25.

35. This concept is explained more fully in "Linguistic and Psychological Factors in Speech Perception with their Implications for Teaching Materials," in Rivers (1976a), pp. 131–44.

36. There are many treatments of sound-symbol correspondences in English. See references cited in note 5.36 (p. 369).

37. Bruder (1974), p. 33.

38. Since an introductory reading passage like this is based on the realities of a particular class, the passage may be constructed by the students themselves who invent questions and statements using material they have learned.

39. Bruder (1974), p. 50.

40. E. J. Hall and S. Costinett, *Orientation in American English*, Text 1 (Silver Spring, Md.: Institute of Modern Languages, Inc., 1974), p. 38. See note 6.11.

41. The idea for this kind of exercise comes from M. Benamou and E. Ionesco, *Mise en train* (London: Collier-Macmillan, 1969).

42. Adapted from W. E. Rutherford, *Modern English*, 2d ed., Vol. 1 (New York: Harcourt Brace Jovanovich, 1975), Unit 2, Reading, pp. 27–28.

43. G. Kaye, *Nowhere to Go*, edited by J. and A. Tedman (London: Oxford University Press, 1971), Chap. 3, pp. 12–14.

44. As in the reading method described in Rivers (1968), pp. 22–24.

45. G. Alesi and D. Pantell, *Family Life in the USA: An Easy Reader* (New York: Regents Publishing Co., 1962), Chap. 1, pp. 1–2.

46. L. Du Garde Peach, *Florence Nightingale* (Loughborough, Eng.: Willis and Hepworth, 1959), p. 40.

7. READING II: FROM DEPENDENCE TO INDEPENDENCE

1. This is equivalent to a count of 23 or above in TWB. The use of TWB in our discussions does not imply that it is the best word-frequency count for use in the preparation and evaluation of materials for any given level. See discussion under *Word Counts and Frequency Lists* in Chapter 6, p. 204.

2. The matter of systems and subsystems of language is discussed in "Contrastive Linguistics in Textbook and Classroom," in Rivers (1976a), pp. 64–72.

3. *Tense* and *aspect* are discussed in Quirk et al. (1972), pp. 84–97. Tenses and the various combinations of tense with perfect and progressive verb forms are discussed in most English grammar books, but not always with the labels used here. Rutherford (1975) does not use the term *aspect*, but rather refers to all combinations as *tenses*; he also uses the term *continuous* for what is referred to here as *progressive* (pp. 87, 92–93, 100, 206).

4. G. Kaye, *Jin-Bee Leaves Home,* J. and A. Tedman, eds. (London: Oxford University Press, 1968), p. 51.

5. From Rutherford's adaptation, in Rutherford (1975), p. 202. Copyright 1969 by Ramparts Magazine, Inc. Reprinted by permission.

6. For an extended treatment of differences between American and British vocabulary, see Norman Moss, *What's the Difference: A British/American Dictionary* (New York: Harper and Row, 1973).

7. We are distinguishing here between (1) How (manner or agent)? questions like: *How did she open the door? She opened the door with a key* (directly quoted from the text), and (2) How (explanation)? questions like: *How did she know that her friend wasn't home? Because all the windows were shut and her friend always left them open* (drawn from several parts of the text).

8. Exercises for increasing reading speed and for developing ability to read in various ways (to get the central idea, to gain full understanding, to get specific information in scanning) are found in D. Harris, *Reading Improvement Exercises for Students of English as a Second Language* (Englewood Cliffs, N. J.: Prentice-Hall, 1966).

9. G. A. C. Scherer, "Programming Second Language Reading," in G. Mathieu, ed., *Advances in the Teaching of Modern Languages,* Vol. 2 (London: Pergamon, 1966), p. 113.

10. Ibid., pp. 114–15.

11. Ibid., p. 120.

12. From "Arizona" by J. A. Corle, *Holiday* 2 (Dec., 1947), pp. 26 ff. This excerpt appears in G. E. Bigelow and D. P. Harris, *The United States of America: Readings in English as a Second Language* (New York: Holt, Rinehart and Winston, 1960), pp. 91–92.

13. From *The Garden Party and Other Stories* (New York: Alfred A. Knopf, 1922), pp. 72–74.

14. In *The Collected Poems of W. B. Yeats* (New York: Macmillan, 1933), pp. 111–12. Copyright 1912 by Macmillan Publishing Co., Inc. Renewed 1940 by Bertha Georgie Yeats.

15. In *The Poetry of Robert Frost*, Edward Connery Lathem, ed., pp. 224–25. Copyright 1923, © 1969 by Holt, Rinehart and Winston. Copyright 1951 by Robert Frost.

16. D. H. Lawrence, *Sons and Lovers* (London: William Heineman, 1956), pp. 419–20. Copyright 1913 by Thomas B. Seltzer, Inc. All rights reserved. Used by permission of Laurence Pollinger Ltd. (agent) and the Estate of the late Mrs. Frieda Lawrence, and the Viking Press.

17. From Margaret Craven, *I Heard the Owl Call My Name* (New York: Doubleday, 1973), pp. 66–67.

18. Scherer (1966), p. 123.

19. From Joy Adamson, *Born Free* (New York: Pantheon Books, 1960), pp. 195–96.

20. Stuart Hoffman, quoted in *Glamour*, August, 1972, p. 39.

21. F. L. Allen, *The Big Change* (New York: Harper, 1972). Reprinted in Bigelow and Harris (1960), pp. 200–201. The vocabulary in R67 has been adapted in some instances by MST.

22. W. G. Moulton, *A Linguistic Guide to Language Learning* (New York: M.L.A., 1966), p. 18.

23. For a treatment of word-formation in English, see Politzer and Politzer (1972), Chap. V, "Teaching Morphology" ("Word Formation," pp. 129–40).

24. Compounds are treated exhaustively in R. B. Lees, *The Grammar of English Nominalizations* (The Hague: Mouton and Co., 1963).

25. Constructions with other stress patterns are sometimes regarded as compounds: *flýing sáucer, chôcolate púdding, hârd-héarted.* The pattern ʹ+ˋ is probably the commonest, however, and the one that is meant by the phrase "compound stress pattern."

26. For further discussion along these lines see "Linguistic and Psychological Factors in Speech Perception . . ." in Rivers (1976a), pp. 131–44.

8.   WRITING AND WRITTEN EXERCISES: THE NUTS AND BOLTS

1. L. S. Vygotsky, *Thought and Language,* trans. E. Hanfmann and G. Vakar (Cambridge, Mass.: The MIT Press, 1962), p. 97.

2. The rules for the formation of negatives and questions with the main verb *have* are more complicated and are not the same for British and American usage. See Quirk et al. (1972), p. 80 (3.18, Note) for a treatment of these rules.

3. Differences between spoken and written language have been discussed in Chapter 1 (C2–6). The subject should be studied in depth in syntax classes for future teachers.

4. The table in W3 is taken from K. W. Moody, "Controlled Composition Frames," *ELT* 19 (1965), p. 150. It is reproduced along with other even more elaborate tables from Moody and N. Arapoff in C. B. Paulston, "Teaching Writing in the ESOL Classroom: Techniques of Controlled Composition," *TQ* 6 (1972), pp. 43–44, where they are called "correlative substitution exercises."

5. There is considerable variation in the use of the apostrophe in the formation of possessives with words ending in *s*, both plural and singular. Many people will. write *Charles' book* and *the James' house*, and pronounce these possessive forms "as they are written," i.e., as a single syllable; others will write them *Charles's* and *Jameses'* and pronounce two syllables; others will write them as one syllable but pronounce them as two. For a treatment of some of the uses of the apostrophe, see J. Praninskas, *Rapid Review of English Grammar*, 2d ed., (Englewood Cliffs, N. J.: Prentice-Hall, 1975), pp. 12, 96.

6. For a statement of these rules, see Praninskas (1975), p. 110, or Quirk et al. (1972), pp. 107–109.

7. Deduction and induction are discussed at the beginning of Chapter 4.

8. According to Piaget's theory of cognitive development, it is not until somewhere between twelve and fifteen years that average children reach the stage of "formal operations," where they are able to use freely verbal, symbolic forms of reasoning. See J. S. Bruner, R. R. Olver, et al., *Studies in Cognitive Growth* (New York: John Wiley, 1966).

9. It is difficult to randomize deliberately the positions of the correct answers in a pattern of A's, B's, and C's. One way of ensuring that one is not subconsciously arranging them in some way is to allot numbers to the letters and

then arrange the correct choices according to a set of telephone numbers selected at random from the telephone book. E.g., A = 1; B = 2; C = 3; D = 4; E = 5; F = 6; the phone numbers are 352–1808; 463–7496; 359–1990; the pattern of correct answers for twelve questions will be C E B A D F C D F C E A. The first part of this randomization has been applied to W14.

10. Adapted from the story as it appears in O. Henry and Others, *The Gifts and Other Stories,* Oxford Progressive English Readers, D. H. Howe, gen. ed. (Hong Kong: Oxford University Press, 1974), p. 38.

11. The whimsicality of the extrapolation in this title is admitted. It was by comparison with the same inscription in demotic and classical Greek that Champollion was able to decipher the hieroglyphics on the Rosetta Stone.

12. For an outline of some of the meanings of *will* and *would,* see Quirk et al. (1972), p. 86, §3.28; pp. 89–90, §§3.32, 3.35; pp. 100–101, §3.47.

13. Carson McCullers, *The Member of the Wedding* (Boston: Houghton Mifflin, 1946), p. 142.

14. These constructions are discussed in Quirk et al., Chap. 12, 12.47, [B3] Finite clause objects, pp. 832–34. A list of verbs that "take putative *should* and subjunctive verb" is given in (c), p. 833. Quirk notes that the subjunctive type "seems to be restricted to AmE in cases where BrE favours other means of expression, such as putative *should* . . ." (p. 833).

15. R. Braddock, R. Lloyd-Jones, and L. Schoer, *Research in Written Composition* (Champaign, Ill: National Council of Teachers of English, 1963), p. 83.

16. This was the finding also for native English writers in the Buxton Study, reported in Braddock et al. (1963), pp. 58–70.

9. WRITING AND WRITTEN EXERCISES II: FLEXIBILITY AND EXPRESSION

1. John Steinbeck, *America and the Americans* (New York: Bantam Books, 1968), p. 113. Original publication, New York: The Viking Press, 1966. W35 is an adaptation of this material.

2. *Boston Sunday Globe,* July 25, 1976. Phone numbers have been changed.

3. Ibid.

4. M. Bracy, "Controlled Writing vs. Free Composition," *TQ* 5 (1971), p. 244.

5. For further suggestions along these lines, see K. Sandburg's "writing laboratories," quoted in Paulston (1972), pp. 57–58.

6. V. Postovsky, "Effects of Delay in Oral Practice at the Beginning of Second Language Learning," unpublished Ph.D. dissertation, University of California at Berkeley, 1970; reported by S. Ervin-Tripp, "Structure and Process in Language Acquisition," in J. E. Alatis, ed., *Bilingualism and Language Contact: Anthropological, Linguistic, Psychological, and Sociological Aspects,* Monograph No. 23 (Washington, D.C.: Georgetown University Press, 1970), p. 340. Students were not prevented from murmuring things over to themselves, but were not required to repeat or produce anything orally as part of the instruction during the first month.

7. Paraphrase of M. Benamou, *Pour une nouvelle pédagogie du texte littéraire.* (Paris: Hachette/Larousse, 1971), pp. 12–13.

8. N. Arapoff, "Writing: a Thinking Process," *TQ* 1 (1967), pp. 33–39. Reprinted in H. B. Allen and R. N. Campbell, eds. (1972), pp. 199–207.

9. N. Arapoff, "Discover and Transform: A Method of Teaching Writing to Foreign Students," in *TQ* 3 (1969), p. 298.

10. This subject is discussed in an interesting article by R. B. Kaplan, "Cultural Thought Patterns in Inter-Cultural Education," *LL* 16 (1966), pp. 1–20, reprinted in K. Croft, ed., *Readings on English as a Second Language* (Cambridge, Mass.: Winthrop, 1972).

11. A number of possibilities for diversification is described in W. M. Rivers, L. H. Allen, et al. (1972).

12. Arapoff (1967) in Allen and Campbell, eds. (1972), p. 200.

13. R. M. Valette in "Developing and Evaluating Communication Skills in the Classroom," *TQ* 7 (1973), pp. 417–18.

14. Francis Bacon, *Of Studies* (1598).

15. R. L. Lyman, "A Co-operative Experiment in Junior High School Composition" (1931), quoted in Braddock et al. (1963), p. 35.

16. D. Knapp, "A Focused, Efficient Method to Relate Composition Correction to Teaching Aims," in Allen and Campbell, eds. (1972), pp. 213–21.

17. See "The Writer Variable" in Braddock et al. (1963), pp. 6–7, where the research of G. L. Kincaid and C. C. Anderson is reported.

18. For more information on inferencing, see Aaron S. Carton, "Inferencing: A Process in Using and Learning Language," in P. Pimsleur and T. Quinn, eds., *The Psychology of Second Language Learning* (Cambridge, Eng.: Cambridge University Press, 1971), pp. 45–58.

19. Teachers interested in translation should be familiar with books like E. A. Nida, *Toward a Science of Translating*, (Leiden: E. J. Brill, 1964), J. C. Catford, *A Linguistic Theory of Translation* (London: Oxford University Press, 1965), and V. Proetz, *The Astonishment of Words* (Austin and London: University of Texas Press, 1971). See also W. M. Rivers, "Contrastive Linguistics in Textbook and Classroom" in Rivers (1976a), pp. 64–72.

20. Note that, since these questions apply to both types of translation, the expression "source text" refers to the text in the language in which it was originally written and the "target language" is the one into which the passage is being translated.

21. From B. Malamud, *The Fixer* (New York: Farrar, Straus and Giroux, 1966), p. 215.

22. "False friends" are discussed in *Reading for Information* in Chapter 6, p. 192.

23. A is from H. Böll, *Haus ohne Hüter* (Cologne and Berlin: Kiepenheuer und Witsch, 1954), pp. 16–17, and B is from the translation of this book *Tomorrow and Yesterday* (New York: Criterion Books, 1957), p. 9. This material, and that acknowledged in Note 27, were assembled by K. M. Dell'Orto and V. Dell'Orto for the *Practical Guide to the Teaching of German* (New York and London: Oxford University Press, 1975).

24. Both A and B are from the bilingual *Requiem por un Campesino Español—Requiem for a Spanish Peasant* (New York: Las Americas Publishing Company, 1960), pp. 6–7. The English translation is by Elinor Randall. The material acknowledged here and in Note 28 was assembled by M.M. Azevedo

for the *Practical Guide to the Teaching of Spanish* (New York and London: Oxford University Press, 1976).

25. A is from A. de St. Exupéry *Le Petit Prince* (New York: Reynal and Hitchcock, 1943), p. 8, and B is from A. de St. Exupéry, *The Little Prince,* translated from the French by Katherine Woods (New York: Harcourt, Brace, and World, 1943), p. 8. The material acknowledged in this note and in Note 26 was assembled by W. M. Rivers for the *Practical Guide to the Teaching of French* (New York and London: Oxford University Press, 1975).

26. A is from A. Camus, *L'Etranger* (Paris: Gallimard, 1942), p. 86, and B is from A. Camus, *The Stranger,* translated from the French by Stuart Gilbert (New York: Alfred A. Knopf and Random House, 1946), p. 74.

27. A is from T. Mann, *Der Zauberberg* (Frankfurt am Main: Fischer, 1960), pp. 12–13, and B is from T. Mann, *The Magic Mountain,* translated from the German by H. T. Lowe-Porter (New York: Knopf, 1968), p. 4.

28. Passage A is from José María Gironella's *Un Millón de Muertos* (Barcelona: Editorial Planeta, 1961) and Passage B is from the English translation of the same book entitled *One Million Dead,* translated by Joan MacLean (New York: Doubleday and Co., 1963), first and second paragraphs of Chapter 1.

29. A useful comparison and evaluation of five American dictionaries and the study aids available with them, as well as a brief survey of monolingual English learner's dictionaries, can be found in R. Yorkey, "Which Dictionary is 'Best'? A Survey of the Latest Desk Dictionaries," *ETF* 12 (1974), pp. 16–33. Yorkey found that a study of the English dictionary was an "exciting eye-opener" when students in a university course used a variety of these recommended desk dictionaries (p. 17).

30. Dates are not given for these dictionaries because reprintings and new editions are frequent. The publishers are as follows: *The American Heritage Dictionary of the English Language* and *The Heritage Illustrated Dictionary of the English Language: International Edition* (New York: American Heritage Publishing Co. and Houghton Mifflin Co.); *The Funk and Wagnalls Standard College Dictionary* (New York: Funk and Wagnalls Publishing Co.); *The Random House College Dictionary* (New York: Random House); *Webster's New Collegiate Dictionary* (Springfield, Mass.: G. & C. Merriam Co.); *Webster's New World Dictionary of the American Language* (Cleveland and New York: World Publishing Co.); *The Shorter Oxford English Dictionary, The Concise Oxford Dictionary of Current English,* and *The Pocket Oxford Dictionary of Current English* (London: Oxford University Press).

31. Yorkey (1974), pp. 22–23.

32. Ibid., p. 16.

33. This applies to Quirk et al. (1972).

34. 2d ed. (London: Oxford University Press, 1975).

General Bibliography

Articles quoted in Notes are not listed in the Bibliography

Alatis, J. E., ed. 1968. *Contrastive Linguistics and its Pedagogical Implications.* Georgetown University Round Table on Languages and Linguistics. Washington, D.C.: Georgetown University Press.

————, ed. 1969. *Linguistics and the Teaching of Standard English to Speakers of Other Languages or Dialects.* Georgetown University Round Table on Languages and Linguistics. Washington, D.C.: Georgetown University Press.

————, ed. 1970. *Bilingualism and Language Contact: Anthropological, Linguistic, Psychological, and Sociological Aspects.* Georgetown University Round Table on Languages and Linguistics. Washington, D.C.: Georgetown University Press.

Allen, E. D., and Valette, R. M. 1977. *Classroom Techniques: Foreign Languages and English as a Second Language.* New York: Harcourt Brace Jovanovich.

Allen, H. B., and Campbell, R.N., eds. 1972. *Teaching English as a Second Language: A Book of Readings.* 2d ed. New York: McGraw-Hill.

Altman, H. B., ed. 1972. *Individualizing the Foreign Language Classroom: Perspectives for Teachers.* Rowley, Mass.: Newbury House.

————, and Politzer, R. L., eds. 1971. *Individualizing Foreign Language Instruction.* Rowley, Mass.: Newbury House.

Bennett, W. A. 1968. *Aspects of Language and Language Teaching.* Cambridge, Eng.: Cambridge University Press.

Billows, F. L. 1961. *The Techniques of Language Teaching.* London: Longmans Green.

Birkmaier, E. M., ed. 1968. *Foreign Language Education: An Overview*. Britannica Review of Foreign Language Education, Vol. 1. Chicago: Encyclopaedia Britannica.

Bowen, J. D. 1975. *Patterns of English Pronunciation*. Rowley, Mass.: Newbury House. (For GA.)

Braddock, R., Lloyd-Jones, R., and Schoer, L. 1963. *Research in Written Composition*. Champaign, Ill.: National Council of Teachers of English.

Brooks, N. 1964. *Language and Language Learning. Theory and Practice*. 2d ed. New York: Harcourt, Brace & World.

Bruder, M. N. 1974. *MMC: Developing Communicative Competence in English as a Second Language*. Pittsburgh, Pa.: The University Center for International Studies.

Burt, M. K., and Dulay, H. C., eds. 1975. *On TESOL '75: New Directions in Second Language Learning, Teaching and Bilingual Education*. Washington, D.C.: TESOL.

———, and Finocchiaro, M., eds. 1977. *Viewpoints on English as a Second Language. In Honor of James E. Alatis*. New York: Regents Publishing Co.

Burt, M. K., and Kiparsky, C. 1972. *The Gooficon: A Repair Manual for English*. Rowley, Mass.: Newbury House.

Catalogue of Selected Materials for English as a Foreign Language. 1975. Washington, D.C.: Information Center Service, U.S.I.A.

Catford, J. C. 1965. *A Linguistic Theory of Translation*. London: Oxford University Press.

Centre for Information on Language Teaching and Research. 1974. *Teaching Languages to Adults for Special Purposes*. London: CILT.

Chastain, K. 1976. *Developing Second-Language Skills: Theory to Practice*. 2d ed. Chicago: Rand McNally.

Cohen, A. D. 1975. *A Sociolinguistic Approach to Bilingual Education*. Rowley, Mass.: Newbury House.

Council for Cultural Co-operation. 1973. *Systems Development in Adult Language Learning*. Strasbourg: Council of Europe.

Croft, K. 1972. *Readings on English as a Second Language*. Cambridge, Mass.: Winthrop.

Crymes, R., and Norris, W. E., eds. 1974. *On TESOL 74*. Washington, D.C.: TESOL.

Delattre, P. 1965. *Comparing the Phonetic Features of English, French, German and Spanish*. London: Harrap.

Diller, Karl C. 1971. *Generative Grammar, Structural Linguistics, and Language Teaching*. Rowley, Mass.: Newbury House.

Di Pietro, R. J. 1971. *Language Structures in Contrast*. Rowley, Mass.: Newbury House.

Dobson, J. M. 1974. *Effective Techniques for English Conversation Groups*. Rowley, Mass.: Newbury House.

Fanselow, J. F., and Crymes, R. H., eds. 1976. *On TESOL '76*. Washington, D.C.: TESOL.

Finocchiaro, M. 1974. *English as a Second Language: From Theory to Practice*. New York: Regents Publishing Co.

————, and Bonomo, M. 1973. *The Foreign Language Learner: A Guide for Teachers.* New York: Regents Publishing Co.

Fishman, J. A. 1976. *Bilingual Education. An International Sociological Perspective.* Rowley, Mass.: Newbury House.

Fraser, H., and O'Donnell, W. R., eds. 1969. *Applied Linguistics and the Teaching of English.* New York: Humanities Press; London: Longmans Green.

Fries, C. C. 1945. *Teaching and Learning English as a Foreign Language.* Ann Arbor, Mich.: The University of Michigan Press.

Gattegno, C. 1972. *Teaching Foreign Languages in Schools: The Silent Way.* 2d ed. New York: Educational Solutions.

Gauntlett, J. O. 1961. *Teaching English as a Foreign Language.* London: Macmillan.

Geffert, H., Harper, R. J., Sarmiento, S., and Schember, D. 1975. *The Current Status of U.S. Bilingual Education Legislation.* Arlington, Va.: Center for Applied Linguistics.

George, H. V. 1972. *Common Errors in Language Learning: Insights from English.* Rowley, Mass.: Newbury House.

Gimson, A. C. 1970. *An Introduction to the Pronunciation of English.* 2d ed. London: Edward Arnold. (For GB.)

Gouin, F. 1892. *The Art of Teaching and Studying Languages.* Trans. H. Swan and V. Bétis. London: George Philip and Son; New York: Charles Scribner's Sons.

Grittner, F. M. 1977. *Teaching Foreign Languages.* 2d ed. New York: Harper & Row.

————, and Laleike, F. H. 1973. *Individualized Foreign Language Instruction.* Skokie, Ill.: National Textbook Company.

Halliday, M. A. K., McIntosh, A., and Strevens, P. 1964. *The Linguistic Sciences and Language Teaching.* London: Longmans.

Harris, D. P. 1969. *Testing English as a Second Language.* New York: McGraw-Hill.

Hauptman, P., and Upshur, J. 1975. *Fun with English.* New York: Collier-Macmillan International.

Hesse, M. G., ed. 1975. *Approaches to Teaching Foreign Languages.* Amsterdam: North-Holland Publishing Co.

Hester, R., ed. 1970. *Teaching a Living Language.* New York: Harper and Row.

Higgins, J. J. 1969. *A Guide to Language Laboratory Material Writing.* Oslo: Universitetsforlaget.

Hill, L. A., and Popkin, P. R. 1968. *A First Crossword Puzzle Book.* London: Oxford University Press. *Second* (1969), *Third* (1970), *Fourth* (1971).

Hines, M. 1973. *Skits in English as a Second Language.* New York: Regents Publishing Co.

Howes, V. M., ed. 1970. *Individualization of Instruction: A Teaching Strategy.* New York: Macmillan.

Jakobovits, L. A. 1970. *Foreign Language Learning. A Psycholinguistic Analysis of the Issues.* Rowley, Mass.: Newbury House.

————, and Gordon, B. 1974. *The Context of Foreign Language Teaching.* Rowley, Mass.: Newbury House.

Jankowsky, K., ed. 1973. *Language and International Studies.* Georgetown University Round Table on Languages and Linguistics. Washington, D.C.: Georgetown University Press.

Jarvis, G. A., ed. 1974a. *Responding to New Realities.* ACTFL Review of Foreign Language Education, Vol. 5. Skokie, Ill.: National Textbook Company.

————, ed. 1974b. *The Challenge of Communication.* ACTFL Review of Foreign Language Education, Vol. 6. Skokie, Ill.: National Textbook Company.

————, ed. 1975. *Perspective: A New Freedom.* ACTFL Review of Foreign Language Education, Vol. 7. Skokie, Ill.: National Textbook Company.

————, ed. 1976. *An Integrative Approach to Foreign Language Teaching: Choosing among the Options.* ACTFL Foreign Language Education Series, Vol. 8, Skokie, Ill.: National Textbook Company.

Jesperson, O. 1905. *Growth and Structure of the English Language.* London: Macmillan.

————. 1904. *How to Teach a Foreign Language.* London: George Allen & Unwin Ltd. Reissued, 1961.

Jones, R. L., and Spolsky, B. 1975. *Testing Language Proficiency.* Arlington, Va.: Center for Applied Linguistics.

Kelly, L. G. 1969. *25 Centuries of Language Teaching.* Rowley, Mass.: Newbury House.

Kenyon, J. S., and Knott, T. A. 1944. *A Pronouncing Dictionary of American English.* Springfield, Mass.: Merriam Co.

Kloss, H. 1977. *The American Bilingual Tradition.* Rowley, Mass.: Newbury House.

Kučera, H., and Francis, W. N. 1967. *Computational Analysis of Present-Day American English.* Providence, R.I.: Brown University Press.

Lambert, W. E., and Tucker, R. 1972. *The Bilingual Education of Children.* Rowley, Mass.: Newbury House.

Lange, D. L., ed. 1970. *Individualization of Instruction.* Britannica Review of Foreign Language Education, Vol. 2. Chicago: Encyclopaedia Britannica.

————, ed. 1971. *Pluralism in Foreign Language Education.* Britannica Review of Foreign Language Education, Vol. 3. Chicago: Encyclopaedia Britannica.

————, and James, C. J., eds. 1972. *Foreign Language Education: A Reappraisal.* ACTFL Review of Foreign Language Education, Vol. 4. Skokie, Ill.: National Textbook Company.

Lee, W. R. 1974. *Language Teaching Games and Contests.* London: Oxford University Press.

Leech, G. N. 1971. *Meaning and the English Verb.* London: Longman.

———— and Svartvik, J. 1975. *A Communicative Grammar of English.* London: Longman.

Logan, G. E. 1973. *Individualized Foreign Language Learning: An Organic Process.* Rowley, Mass.: Newbury House.

Love, F. W., and Honig, L. J. 1973. *Options and Perspectives: A Sourcebook of Innovative Foreign Language Programs in Action, K-12.* New York: Modern Language Association.

Lugton, R. C., ed. 1971. *Toward a Cognitive Approach to Second Language Acquisition.* Philadelphia: Center for Curriculum Development.

MacCarthy, P. 1950. *English Pronunciation.* 4th ed. Cambridge, Eng.: Heffer and Sons. (For GB.)

Mackey, W. F. 1967. *Language Teaching Analysis.* Bloomington, Ind.: Indiana University Press.

Marckwardt, A. M. 1958. *American English.* New York: Oxford University Press.

Mathews, M. M., ed. 1966. *Americanisms: A Dictionary of Selected Americanisms on Historical Principles.* Chicago: The University of Chicago Press.

Melvin, B. S., and Rivers, W. M. 1976. "In One Ear and Out the Other: Implications of Memory Studies for Language Learning," in J. Fanselow and R. Crymes, eds. (1976), pp. 155–64.

Moskowitz, G. 1970. *The Foreign Language Teacher Interacts.* Rev. ed. Minneapolis: Association for Productive Teaching.

Moss, N. 1973. *What's the Difference: A British/American Dictionary.* New York: Harper and Row.

Moulton, W. G. 1966. *A Linguistic Guide to Language Learning.* New York: Modern Language Association.

Newton, A. C., ed. 1975. *The Art of TESOL*, Pts. 1 & 2. *ETF* 13, Nos. 1–4 (Special Issue).

Nickel, G., ed. 1971. *Papers in Contrastive Linguistics.* Cambridge, Eng.: Cambridge University Press.

————, ed. 1976. *Proceedings of the Fourth International Congress of Applied Linguistics*, Vols. 1–3. Stuttgart: Hochschul Verlag.

Nida, E. A. 1964. *Toward a Science of Translating.* Leiden: E. J. Brill.

Nilsen, D. L. F., and Nilsen, A. P. 1971. *Pronunciation Contrasts in English.* New York: Simon and Schuster. (For GA.)

Northeast Conference (1959): F. D. Eddy, ed. *The Language Learner.* Containing: Modern Foreign Language Learning: Assumptions and Implications; A Six-Year Sequence; Elementary and Junior High School Curricula; Definition of Language Competences through Testing.

Northeast Conference (1960): G. R. Bishop, ed. *Culture in Language Learning.* Containing: An Anthropological Concept of Culture; Language as Culture; Teaching of Western European Cultures; Teaching of Classical Cultures; Teaching of Slavic Cultures.

Northeast Conference (1961): S. L. Flaxman, ed. *Modern Language Teaching in School and College.* Containing: The Training of Teachers for Secondary Schools; The Preparation of College and University Teachers; The Transition to the Classroom; Coordination between Classroom and Laboratory.

Northeast Conference (1962): W. F. Bottiglia, ed. *Current Issues in Language Teaching.* Containing: Linguistics and Language Teaching; Programmed Learning; A Survey of FLES Practices; Televised Teaching.

Northeast Conference (1963): W. F. Bottiglia, ed. *Language Learning: The Intermediate Phase.* Containing: The Continuum: Listening and Speaking; Reading for Meaning; Writing as Expression.

Northeast Conference (1964): G. F. Jones, ed. *Foreign Language Teaching: Ideals and Practices.* Containing: Foreign Languages in the Elementary School; Foreign Languages in the Secondary School; Foreign Languages in Colleges and Universities.

Northeast Conference (1965): G. R. Bishop, ed. *Foreign Language Teaching: Challenges to the Profession.* Containing: The Case for Latin; Study Abroad; The Challenge of Bilingualism; From School to College.

Northeast Conference (1966): R. G. Mead, Jr., ed. *Language Teaching: Broader Contexts.* Containing: Research and Language Learning; Content and Crossroads. Wider Uses for Foreign Languages; The Coordination of Foreign-Language Teaching.

Northeast Conference (1967): T. E. Bird, ed. *Foreign Languages: Reading, Literature, and Requirements.* Containing: The Teaching of Reading; The Times and Places for Literature; Trends in FL Requirements and Placement.

Northeast Conference (1968): T. E. Bird, ed. *Foreign Language Learning: Research and Development.* Containing: Innovative FL Programs; The Classroom Revisited; Liberated Expression.

Northeast Conference (1969): M. F. Edgerton, Jr., ed. *Sight and Sound: The Sensible and Sensitive Use of Audio-Visual Aids.* Containing: Non-Projected Visuals; Sound Recordings; Slides and Filmstrips; The Overhead Projector; Motion Pictures; Television; Let Us Build Bridges.

Northeast Conference (1970): J. Tursi, ed. *Foreign Languages and the 'New' Student.* Containing: A Relevant Curriculum: An Instrument for Polling Student Opinion; Motivation in FL Learning; FL's for All Children?

Northeast Conference (1971): J. W. Dodge, ed. *Leadership for Continuing Development.* Containing: Professional Responsibilities; In-service Involvement in the Process of Change; Innovative Trends in FL Teaching; Literature for Advanced FL Students.

Northeast Conference (1972): J. W. Dodge, ed. *Other Words, Other Worlds: Language-in-Culture.* Containing: On Teaching Another Language as Part of Another Culture; Sociocultural Aspects of FL Study; Ancient Greek & Roman Culture; France; Quebec: French Canada; An Approach to Courses in German Culture; Italy & the Italians; Japan: Spirit & Essence; The Soviet Union; Spain; Spanish America: A Study in Diversity.

Northeast Conference (1973): J. W. Dodge, ed. *Sensitivity in the Foreign-Language Classroom.* Containing: Interaction in the FL Class; Teaching Spanish to the Native Spanish Speaker; Individualization of Instruction.

Northeast Conference (1974): W. C. Born, ed. *Toward Student-Centered Foreign-Language Programs.* Containing: The Teacher in the Student-Centered FL Program; Implementing Student-Centered FL Programs; FL's and the Community.

Northeast Conference (1975). W. C. Born, ed. *Goals Clarification: Curriculum Teaching, Evaluation.*

Northeast Conference (1976). W. C. Born, ed. *Language and Culture: Heritage and Horizons.*

Northeast Conference (1977). W. C. Born, ed. *Language: Acquisition, Application, Appreciation.*

Oller, J., Jr., and Richards, J. 1973. *Focus on the Learner.* Rowley, Mass.: Newbury House.

Palmer, H. 1917. *The Scientific Study and Teaching of Languages.* London: Harrap.

Palmer, L., and Spolsky, B., eds. 1975. *Papers on Language Testing 1967–1974.* Washington, D.C.: TESOL.

Paulston, C. B., and Bruder, M. N. 1976. *Teaching English as a Second Language: Techniques and Procedures.* Cambridge, Mass.: Winthrop.

————, and Bruder, M. N. 1976. *From Substitution to Substance: Techniques and Procedures.* Cambridge, Mass.: Winthrop.

Perren, G. E., and Trim, J. L. M., eds. 1971. *Applications of Linguistics.* Cambridge, Eng.: Cambridge University Press.

Politzer, R. L. 1972. *Linguistics and Applied Linguistics: Aims and Methods.* Philadelphia: Center for Curriculum Development.

————, and Politzer, F. N. 1972. *Teaching English as a Second Language.* Lexington, Mass.: Xerox.

Praninskas, J. 1972. *American University Word List.* London: Longmans.

Prator, C. H., Jr., and Robinett, B. W. 1972. *Manual of American English Pronunciation.* 3d ed. New York: Holt, Rinehart & Winston.

Quirk, R. 1963. *The Use of English.* London: Longmans, Green.

————, Greenbaum, S., Leech, G., and Svartvik, J. 1972. *A Grammar of Contemporary English.* London: Longman; New York: Seminar Press.

Richards, I. A., and Gibson, C. 1974. *Techniques in Language Control.* Rowley, Mass: Newbury House.

Rivers, W. M. 1964. *The Psychologist and the Foreign-Language Teacher.* Chicago: The University of Chicago Press.

————. 1968. *Teaching Foreign-Language Skills.* Chicago: The University of Chicago Press.

————. 1976a. *Speaking in Many Tongues.* Expanded 2d ed. Rowley, Mass.: Newbury House.

————. 1976b. "The Natural and the Normal in Language Learning," in H. D. Brown, ed., *Papers in Second Language Acquisition. LL* Spec. Issue 4: 1–8.

————. 1977. "Language and Cognition: Directions and Implications," in M. Gerli and R. Brod, eds. *Language and American Life.* Washington, D.C.: Georgetown University School of Languages and Linguistics and MLA.

————, Allen, L. H., et al., eds. 1972. *Changing Patterns in Foreign Language Programs.* Rowley, Mass.: Newbury House.

————, and Melvin, B. S. 1977a. "Memory and Memorization in Comprehension and Production: Contributions of IP Theory." *Canadian Modern Language Review* 33 (1977): 497–502.

————, and Melvin, B. S. 1977b. "If Only I could Remember it all! Facts and Fiction about Memory in Language Learning," in M. Burt, H. Dulay, and M. Finocchiaro, eds. (1977), pp. 162–71.

————, and Temperley, M. S. 1977. "Building and Maintaining An Adequate Vocabulary." *ETF* 15 (1977): 2–7.

Sauzé, E. B. de. 1920. *The Cleveland Plan for the Teaching of Modern Languages with Special Reference to French.* Philadelphia: The John C. Winston Company.

Saville, M. R., and Troike, R. C. 1973. *A Handbook of Bilingual Education.* Rev. ed. Washington, D.C.: TESOL.

Saville-Troike, M. R. 1976. *Foundations for Teaching English as a Second Language: Theory and Method for Multicultural Education.* Englewood Cliffs, N.J.: Prentice Hall.

Scherer, G. A. C. 1966. "Programming Second Language Reading." In Mathieu, G., ed. *Advances in the Teaching of Modern Languages.* Vol. 2. London: Pergamon, pp. 108–29.

Seelye, H. N. 1974. *Teaching Culture: Strategies for Foreign Language Educators.* Skokie, Ill.: National Textbook Company.

Selinker, L., Trimble, L., and Vroman, R. 1972. *Working Papers in English for Science and Technology.* Seattle, Wash.: College of Engineering at the University of Washington.

Spolsky, B., ed. 1972. *The Language Education of Minority Children.* Rowley, Mass.: Newbury House.

————, and Cooper, R., eds. 1977. *Frontiers of Bilingual Education.* Rowley, Mass.: Newbury House.

Stack, E. M. 1966. *The Language Laboratory and Modern Language Teaching.* Rev. ed. New York: Oxford University Press.

Steiner, F. 1975. *Performing with Objectives.* Rowley, Mass.: Newbury House.

Stevick, E. W. 1966. "UHF and Microwaves in Transmitting Language Skills." In Najam, E. W., and Hodge, C. T., eds., *Language Learning: The Individual and the Process. IJAL* 32, 1, Part 2. Publication 40 of the Indiana University Research Center in Anthropology, Folklore, and Linguistics.

————. 1971. *Adapting and Writing Language Lessons.* Washington, D.C.: Foreign Service Institute.

————. 1976. *Memory, Meaning and Method: Some Psychological Perspectives on Language Learning.* Rowley, Mass.: Newbury House.

Strevens, P. 1972. *British and American English.* London: Collier-Macmillan.

————. 1977. *New Orientations in the Teaching of English.* London: Oxford University Press.

Sweet, H. 1899. *The Practical Study of Languages.* London: Dent. Reprinted 1964. London: Oxford University Press.

Thonis, E. W. 1970. *Teaching Reading to Non-English Speakers.* New York and London: Collier-Macmillan.

Thorndike, E. L., and Lorge, I. 1944. *The Teacher's Word Book of 30,000 Words.* New York: Bureau of Publications, Teachers College, Columbia University.

Titone, R., 1968. *Teaching Foreign Languages. An Historical Sketch.* Washington, D.C.: Georgetown University Press.

Trim, J. 1975. *English Pronunciation Illustrated.* 2d ed. Cambridge, Eng.: Cambridge University Press. (For GB.)

Troike, R. C., and Modiano, N. 1975. *The Proceedings of the First Inter-American Conference on Bilingual Education.* Arlington, Va.: Center for Applied Linguistics.

Valette, R. M. 1977. *Modern Language Testing.* 2d ed. New York: Harcourt Brace Jovanovich.

—————, and Disick, R. S. 1972. *Modern Language Performance Objectives and Individualization. A Handbook.* New York: Harcourt Brace Jovanovich.

Van Ek, J. A. 1975. *The Threshold Level.* With an appendix by L. G. Alexander. Strasbourg: Council for Cultural Cooperation of the Council of Europe.

Wardhaugh, R. 1969. *Reading: A Linguistic Perspective.* New York: Harcourt, Brace & World.

—————. 1974. *Topics in Applied Linguistics.* Rowley, Mass.: Newbury House.

West, M. 1941. *Learning to Read a Foreign Language and Other Essays on Language-teaching.* London: Longmans.

—————. 1953. *A General Service List of English Words.* Rev. and enlarg. ed. London: Longmans, Green.

Wijk, Axel. 1966. *Rules for the Pronunciation of the English Language.* London: Oxford University Press. (For GB.)

Wilkins, D. A. 1972. *Linguistics in Language Teaching.* Cambridge, Mass.: The MIT Press.

—————. 1976. *Notional Syllabuses.* London: Oxford University Press.

Supplemental bibliography

SOME INTRODUCTORY READINGS IN LINGUISTICS
AND PSYCHOLOGY OF LANGUAGE LEARNING

Aaronson, D., and Rieber, R. W. 1975. *Developmental Psycholinguistics and Communication Disorders.* New York: New York Academy of Sciences.

Akmajian, A., and Heny, F. 1975. *An Introduction to the Principles of Transformational Syntax.* Cambridge, Mass.: The MIT Press.

Allen, J. P. B., and Corder, S. P., eds. 1973. *Readings for Applied Linguistics. The Edinburgh Course in Applied Linguistics.* Vol. 1. London: Oxford University Press.

———, 1974. *Techniques in Applied Linguistics. The Edinburgh Course in Applied Linguistics.* Vol. 3. London: Oxford University Press.

———, 1975. *Papers in Applied Linguistics. The Edinburgh Course in Applied Linguistics.* Vol. 2. London: Oxford University Press.

———, and Davies, A., eds. 1977. *Testing and Experimental Methods. The Edinburgh Course in Applied Linguistics.* Vol. 4. London: Oxford University Press.

Bernstein, B. 1971. *Class, Codes and Control.* Vol. 1: *Theoretical Studies towards a Sociology of Language.* London: Routledge and Kegan Paul.

———, 1973. *Class Codes and Control.* Vol. 2: *Applied Studies towards a Sociology of Language.* London: Routledge and Kegan Paul.

Bickerton, D. 1975. *Dynamics of a Creole System.* Cambridge, Eng.: Cambridge University Press.

Bolinger, D. 1975. *Aspects of Language.* 2d ed. New York: Harcourt Brace Jovanovich.

Brown, H. D., ed. 1976. *Papers in Second Language Acquisition.* Spec. Issue 4, Ann Arbor, Mich.: *Language Learning.*

Bruner, J. S., Olver, R. R., et al. 1966. *Studies in Cognitive Growth.* New York: John Wiley & Sons.

Carroll, J. B., ed. 1956. *Language, Thought, and Reality. Selected Writings of Benjamin Lee Whorf.* Cambridge, Mass.: The MIT Press.

———, and Freedle, R. O., eds. 1972. *Language Comprehension and the*

Acquisition of Knowledge. Washington, D.C.: V. H. Winston & Sons.

Chafe, W. 1970. *Meaning and the Structure of Language*. Chicago: The University of Chicago Press.

Cherry, C. 1957. *On Human Communication*. New York: John Wiley & Sons.

Chomsky, N. 1957. *Syntactic Structures*. The Hague: Mouton.

———. 1965. *Aspects of the Theory of Syntax*. Cambridge, Mass.: The MIT Press.

———. 1972. *Language and Mind*. Enlarged Edition. New York: Harcourt Brace Jovanovich. Original edition 1968.

———. 1972. *Studies on Semantics in Generative Grammar*. The Hague: Mouton.

——— and Halle, M. 1968. *The Sound Pattern of English*. New York: Harper and Row.

Clyne, M. G. 1972. *Perspectives on Language Contact*. Melbourne, Australia: Hawthorn Press.

Cole, P., and Morgan, J. L., eds. 1975. *Syntax and Semantics*, Vol. 3: *Speech Acts*.

Corder, S. P. 1973. *Introducing Applied Linguistics*. Harmondsworth, Middlesex, Eng.: Penguin Books.

Curran, C. A. 1976. *Counseling-Learning in Second Languages*. Apple River, Ill.: Apple River Press.

Dingwall, D. O. 1971. *A Survey of Linguistic Science*. College Park, Md.: Linguistics Dept., University of Maryland.

Elgin, S. H. 1973. *What is Linguistics?* Englewood Cliffs, N.J.: Prentice-Hall.

Ervin-Tripp, S. M. 1973. *Language Acquisition and Communicative Choice*. Selected and Introduced by A. S. Dil. Stanford: Stanford University Press.

Ferguson, C. A., and Slobin, D. I., eds. 1973. *Studies of Child Language Development*. New York: Holt, Rinehart & Winston.

Fishman, J. A. 1971. *Sociolinguistics: A Brief Introduction*. Rowley, Mass.: Newbury House.

Fodor, J. A., Bever, T. G., and Garrett, M. F. 1974. *The Psychology of Language: An Introduction to Psycholinguistics and Generative Grammar*. New York: McGraw-Hill.

Fromkin, V., and Rodman, R. 1974. *Introduction to Language*. New York: Holt, Rinehart & Winston.

Gardner, R. C., and Lambert, W. E. 1972. *Attitudes and Motivation in Second-Language Learning*. Rowley, Mass.: Newbury House.

Gibson, E., and Levin, H. 1975. *The Psychology of Reading*. Cambridge, Mass.: The MIT Press.

Giglioli, P. P., ed. 1972. *Language and Social Context*. Harmondsworth, Middlesex, Eng.: Penguin Books.

Glucksberg, S., and Danks, J. H. 1975. *Experimental Psycholinguistics: an Introduction*. Hillsdale, N. J.: Lawrence Erlbaum Associates.

Gumperz, J. J., and Hymes, D., eds. 1972. *Directions in Sociolinguistics. The Ethnography of Communication*. New York: Holt, Rinehart, and Winston.

Greenberg, J. H. 1971. *Language, Culture, and Communication.* Stanford: Stanford University Press.

Halliday, M. A. K. 1973. *Explorations in the Functions of Language.* London: Edward Arnold.

Hatch, E., ed. 1977. *Second Language Acquisition. A Book of Readings.* Rowley, Mass.: Newbury House.

Hayes, J. R., ed. 1970. *Cognition and the Development of Language.* New York: John Wiley and Sons.

Hörmann, H. 1971. *Psycholinguistics: An Introduction to Research and Theory.* Trans. H. H. Stern. New York, Heidelberg, Berlin: Springer Verlag.

Huey, E. B. 1968. *The Psychology and Pedagogy of Reading.* Cambridge, Mass.: The MIT Press. Original publication: Macmillan, 1908.

Hymes, D., ed. 1971. *Pidginization and Creolization of Languages.* Cambridge, Eng.: Cambridge University Press.

Joos, M. 1961. *The Five Clocks.* New York: Harcourt, Brace & World.

Labov, W. 1972. *Sociolinguistic Patterns.* Philadelphia: University of Pennsylvania Press.

Lakoff, G. 1972. "The Arbitrary Basis of Transformational Grammar." *Language* 48:76–87.

Lakoff, R. 1975. *Language and Woman's Place.* New York: Harper Colophon.

Lambert, W. E. 1972. *Language, Psychology and Culture.* Selected and introduced by A. S. Dil. Stanford: Stanford University Press.

Langacker, R. W. 1973. *Language and its Structure: Some Fundamental Linguistic Concepts.* Rev. ed. New York: Harcourt Brace Jovanovich.

Lees, R. B. 1963. *The Grammar of English Nominalizations.* The Hague: Mouton.

Lehmann, W. P. 1976. *Descriptive Linguistics: An Introduction.* 2d ed. New York: Random House.

Lewis, E. G. 1974. *Linguistics and Second Language Pedagogy: A Theoretical Study.* The Hague: Mouton.

Lyons, J. 1968. *Introduction to Theoretical Linguistics.* Cambridge, Eng.: Cambridge University Press.

Mackey, W. F., and Andersson, T., eds. 1977. *Bilingualism in Early Childhood.* Rowley, Mass.: Newbury House.

Maslow, A. H. 1970. *Motivation and Personality.* 2d ed. New York: Harper and Row.

Miller, G. A. 1967. *The Psychology of Communication. Seven Essays.* New York: Basic Books. Published 1969 as *Psychology and Communication.* London: Pelican.

———, ed. 1973. *Communication, Language, and Meaning. Psychological Perspectives.* New York: Basic Books.

———, and Johnson-Laird, P. N. 1976. *Language and Perception.* Cambridge, Mass.: Harvard University Press.

Moore, T. E. 1973. *Cognitive Development and the Acquisition of Language.* New York and London: Academic Press.

Neisser, U. 1967. *Cognitive Psychology.* New York: Appleton-Century-Crofts.

Nilsen, D. L. F. and A. P. 1975. *Semantic Theory: A Linguistic Perspective.* Rowley, Mass.: Newbury House.

Pearson, B. L. 1977. *Introduction to Linguistic Concepts*. New York: Alfred A. Knopf.

Pimsleur, P., and Quinn, T., eds. 1971. *The Psychology of Second Language Learning*. Cambridge, Eng.: Cambridge University Press.

Platt, J. T. and H. K. 1975. *The Social Significance of Speech*. Amsterdam: North Holland and New York: American Elsevier.

Richards, J. C., ed. 1974. *Error Analysis: Perspectives and Second Language Acquisition*. London: Longman.

Ritchie, W., ed. 1977. *Principles of Second Language Learning and Teaching*. New York: Academic Press.

Sapir, E. 1949. *Culture, Language and Personality*. Selected essays edited by D. G. Mandelbaum. Berkeley and Los Angeles: University of California Press.

Schane, S. A. 1973. *Generative Phonology*. Englewood Cliffs, N.J.: Prentice-Hall.

Schlesinger, I. M. 1968. *Sentence Structure and the Reading Process*. The Hague: Mouton.

Schumann, J. H., and Stenson, N., eds. 1974. *New Frontiers in Second Language Learning*. Rowley, Mass.: Newbury House.

Searle, J. R. 1969. *Speech Acts: An Essay in the Philosophy of Language*. Cambridge, Eng.: Cambridge University Press.

Shuy, R. W., and Fasold, R. W., eds. 1973. *Language Attitudes: Current Trends and Prospects*. Washington, D.C.: Georgetown University Press.

Sinclair, J. M., and Coulthard, R. M. 1975. *Towards an Analysis of Discourse. The English used by Teachers and Pupils*. London: Oxford University Press.

Slobin, D. I. 1971. *Psycholinguistics*. Glenview, Ill.: Scott, Foresman.

Smith, Frank. 1971. *Understanding Reading*. New York: Holt, Rinehart, & Winston.

———, ed. 1973. *Psycholinguistics and Reading*. New York: Holt, Rinehart & Winston.

Steinberg, D., and Jakobovits, L., eds. 1971. *Semantics: An Interdisciplinary Reader in Philosophy, Linguistics and Psychology*. Cambridge, Eng.: Cambridge University Press.

Thorne, B., and Henley, N., eds. 1975. *Language and Sex: Difference and Dominance*. Rowley, Mass.: Newbury House.

Turner, P. R., ed. 1973. *Bilingualism in the Southwest*. Tucson: The University of Arizona Press.

Valdman, A., and Walz, J. 1975. *A Selected Bibliography on Language Learners' Systems and Error Analysis*. Arlington, Va.: Center for Applied Linguistics.

Vygotsky, L. A. 1962. *Thought and Language*. Trans. E. Hanfmann and G. Vakar. Cambridge, Mass.: The MIT Press.

Wardhaugh, R. 1976. *The Contexts of Language*. Rowley, Mass.: Newbury House.

———, and Brown, H. D., eds. 1976. *A Survey of Applied Linguistics*. Ann Arbor, Mich.: The University of Michigan Press.

Williams, F., ed. 1970. *Language and Poverty. Perspectives on a Theme*. Chicago: Markham.

Index